D0760939

Monetary Union in Crisis

Also by Bernard H. Moss

THE SINGLE EUROPEAN CURRENCY IN NATIONAL PERSPECTIVE
(co-edited with Jonathan Michie)

Monetary Union in Crisis

The European Union as a Neo-liberal Construction

Edited by

Bernard H. Moss

First published in 2005 by
PALGRAVE MACMILLAN
Houndmills, Basingstoke, Hampshire RG21 6XS and
175 Fifth Avenue, New York, N.Y. 10010
Companies and representatives throughout the world.

PALGRAVE MACMILLAN is the global academic imprint of the Palgrave Macmillan division of St. Martin's Press, LLC and of Palgrave Macmillan Ltd. Macmillan® is a registered trademark in the United States, United Kingdom and other countries. Palgrave is a registered trademark in the European Union and other countries.

ISBN 0–333–96317–2

This book is printed on paper suitable for recycling and made from fully managed and sustained forest sources.

A catalogue record for this book is available from the British Library.

Library of Congress Cataloging-in-Publication Data

Monetary union in crisis: the European Union as a neo-liberal construction / edited by Bernard H. Moss.
p. cm.
Includes bibliographical references and index.
ISBN 0–333–96317–2 (cloth)
1. Monetary unions – European Union countries. 2. Monetary policy – European Union countries. 3. Currency crises – European Union countries. 4. Free enterprise – Social aspects – European Union countries. 5. European Union countries – Economic policy. 6. European Union countries – Economic integration. I. Moss, Bernard H.

HG3942.M665 2005
332.4'94—dc22 2004053036

10 9 8 7 6 5 4 3 2 1
14 13 12 11 10 09 08 07 06 05

Printed and bound in Great Britain by
Antony Rowe Ltd, Chippenham and Eastbourne.

Dedicated to Neysa Post Moss (1942–2003)

The myth of supranational Europe was the way to escape unbearable reality by taking refuge in imaginary worlds.

Maurice Duverger, 1955

Contents

List of Contributors ix

Preface and Acknowledgments xi

1 Introduction: The EU as a Neo-liberal Construction 1
Bernard H. Moss

Part I History of the European Community 27

2 The Neo-liberal Constitution: EC Law and History 29
Bernard H. Moss

3 Raisons d'être: The Failure of Constructive Integration 51
Bernard H. Moss

4 Theories of Integration: American Political Paradigms 74
Bernard H. Moss

5 National Labor Regimes: The EC in Class Context 92
Bernard H. Moss

6 Socialist Challenge: Class Politics in France 121
Bernard H. Moss

7 From ERM to EMU: EC Monetarism and Its Discontents 145
Bernard H. Moss

Part II The Failure of the European Community Quantified: Monetarist Fetters 171

8 Has European Economic Integration Failed? 173
Gerald Friedman

Part III Monetarist Turn in Member-States: Neo-liberal, Social-Democratic, and Communist 197

9 "Ordo-Liberalism" Trumps Keynesianism: Economic Policy in the Federal Republic of Germany and the EU 199
Christopher S. Allen

10 The Political Economy of the UK, 1979–2002 222
Jonathan Michie

11 The "Monetarist" Turn in Belgium and the Netherlands 233
Erik Jones

12 Italy's Long Road to Austerity and the Paradoxes of Communism 249
Tobias Abse

13 Globalization, the Rise of Neo-liberalism, and the Demise of the Swedish Model: An Analysis of Class Struggle 266
Andreas Bieler

Bibliography 281

Index 316

List of Contributors

Tobias Abse is Lecturer in Modern European History at Goldsmiths College, University of London. He is the author of *Sovversivi e fascisti a Livorno: Lotta politica e sociale (1918–22)* (1991) and many articles on twentieth-century Italy, especially on Communism and the Left.

Christopher Allen is Associate Professsor in the Department of International Affairs at the University of Georgia. He is editor of *Transformation of the German Political Party System* (2001) and co-author of *European Politics in Transition*, 4th edn. (2002). He is currently examining democratic representation in parliamentary and presidential systems.

Andreas Bieler is Lecturer in the School of Politics at the University of Nottingham. He is author of *Globalisation and Enlargement of the European Union* (2000), and co-editor of *Non-State Actors and Authority in the Global System* (2000) and *Social Forces in the Making of the New Europe* (2001). His current research is on the role of trade unions in defining the future of the EU.

Gerald Friedman is Associate Professor of Economics at the University of Massachusetts at Amherst. He is the author of *Statemaking and Labor Movements: The United States and France, 1870–1914* (1998) and has written on European and American economic history, labor economics, and trade unionism. He is currently exploring the reasons for the decline of institutional economics.

Erik Jones is Resident Associate Professor of European Studies at the Johns Hopkins Bologna Center. He is author of *The Politics of Monetary Union* (2002), and "Economic Adjustment and Political Transformation in Small States" (forthcoming). His research centers on problems of economic governance in Belgium, the Netherlands and the European Union.

Jonathan Michie has held the Sainsbury Chair of Management at Birkbeck College, University of London, since 1997. He had previously worked at the Judge Institute of Management at Cambridge University and for the European Commission on economic issues. He has edited *Reader's Guide to the Social Sciences* (2001), and many volumes on economic management and employment issues.

Bernard H. Moss is a professor of modern European history who has taught at the New School for Social Research in New York City, the University of Southern California in Los Angeles, Auckland University in New Zealand, and King's College of the University of London. The author of *The Origins of the French Labor Movement 1830–1914: The Socialism of*

Skilled Workers (1976), he has written extensively on French and comparative labor and socialism. With an LLB in European Law from the LSE he has extended his interests to the EU as co-editor of *The Single European Currency in National Perspective: A Community in Crisis?* (1998) and is editor of the present volume.

Preface and Acknowledgments

This book contains a re-interpretation of the European Community or Union (EC or EU) as a neo-liberal construction that functioned on behalf of employers and the owners of capital to ensure market competition, sound money, and profitability against the collective inflationary force of wage earners and unions supported by the interventionist democratic nation state. In the 1990s neo-liberalism became the *pensée unique*, the only acceptable doctrine for capitalist elites and policy makers in European countries and institutions (*Le Monde diplomatique*, January 1995) just as its disastrous economic and social consequences in slow growth, mass unemployment, and insecurity came under challenge, most dramatically in France, by working people from below.

Neo-liberalism dictated reduced public and social spending and relative wages, tight money with low inflation, free trade, and the commercialization and privatization of public concerns and services. As the prominent French sociologist Pierre Bourdieu put it, it was a program for destroying those social or public collective structures that restrained or regulated market forces for the sake of the majority and that ultimately depended upon the democratic nation state, the modern repository of universal values and the public realm (*id.*, December 1998). We show how the EC was built so as to undermine the interventionist capacity of the democratic state.

Neo-liberalism was distinguished from classical nineteenth century liberalism in so far as it was a reaction to wage-led inflation and the union-backed welfare state and thus required state action to accomplish, to tighten the money supply, restrain public and social spending, deregulate and free up markets and curb union power while maintaining a modicum of social protection for legitimation purposes. In the form of ordo-liberalism it structured the new capitalist West German state that the US constructed from the ashes of Nazi destruction. As the natural "organic" philosophy of finance capital, it had always influenced national treasuries and central banks before becoming the *pensée unique* for employers, governments, centrist parties and the EC in the 1980s.

Because West Germans disposed of accomodationist unions and an export-oriented societal consensus, they were able to stop inflation and the growth of the welfare state in the early 1970s by means of strict monetary policy whereas countries that allowed unhampered class struggle like Britain, France, and Italy had to confront and defeat militant union power through the discipline of monetary union, budget cuts, deregulation and privatization. The hidden aim of monetary union, the Exchange Rate Mechanism (ERM), after 1981, and EMU (Economic and Monetary Union), which established the single currency, was to increase profitability by diminishing state spending, inducing unemployment and reducing the wage share of new wealth created. Pro-business forces in all member-states used the supranational market framework and ideals of the EC and the discipline of ERM and EMU as external constraints against higher public spending and wages and benefits demanded by the working majority.

This history elaborates, theorizes, models, and substantiates the critique originally made by the European Left, by the Communists and many Socialists, of the Common Market as an instrument of wage compression, of capitalist discipline and control. The social and theoretical standpoint is that of labor and an open multilayered model of political class struggle, similar to that underpinning the classic E.P. Thompsons's *The Making of the English Working Class* (Moss, 1993, 2004) and work associated in the 1970s with the *Review of Radical Political Economics*.

This book was written alongside the growing recognition in the 1990s of the failure of free market neo-liberalism and free trading globalization to produce promised economic and physical security, social equality and a decent life for all and the dawning awareness, first manifested in the large French no vote against the Maastricht treaty in 1992, that the EC was not a solution but a main cause of the problem. Treated in the literature as an expression of, or defence against, globalization, the EC and monetary union were actually one of its progenitors, one of its trailblazing instruments. Constructed around competitive market principles backed by West Germany, supranational EC law, and employers and capitalists, particularly large exporters and multinationals, the EC could only develop in a neo-liberal direction.

The EC and monetary union were invoked by pro-business domestic forces as an external constraint on labor to solve a crisis of wage-led inflation and profitability. They helped halt the expansion of wages, benefits, and public services in the long boom and put downward pressures on them in the enduring crisis of investment and productivity that followed. But the job insecurity and welfare and public service cuts engendered by EU-backed liberalization created the backlash of a new working class extended to include public service, professional and managerial personnel and the young against the external constraint of the EU and monetary union. Contrary to predictions of the end of communism and the working class, EU-induced neo-liberalism enlarged the size of the working class touched by job insecurity, tight money and budget cuts to include middle-class wage-earners previously immune to the economic slowdown. The resistance and protests of this enlarged wage-earning class to the downward pressure exercized by the EU and EMU on wages, benefits, and services, which were most pronounced in France, lay behind the renationalization of the EU that occurred after Maastricht in 1992 and the introduction of the Euro in 1999. Deepening national divisions over the pursuit of neo-liberal macroeconomic policy resulted in the crisis of the stability pact that broke out in 2003 adding to the constitutional one. One of the singularities of the book I co-edited with Jonathan Michie on monetary union published in 1998, *The Single Currency in National Perspective*, was to have foreseen this crisis.

This history makes a more radical, probably contentious, claim that the ultra-liberal character of the EC and its crisis were inscribed in the historical origins and juridical framework of the 1957 Treaty of Rome. The EC may have consolidated capitalist control but it was bound to fail as a supranational state because of mass popular and governmental resistance to its free market utopia, derived from the moral ideas of Adam Smith and latterly Friedrich Hayek, of a single competitive market and hard currency freed from the public or social restraints that depend upon the power of the democratic nation state.

This is a revisionist history that challenges much received wisdom not only about the political and class neutrality of the EC, but also about the so-called state, managed or mixed economies and the welfare and interventionist state, which supposedly underlay post-1945 growth and prosperity. It questions the static application of economic theory, neo-classical, Keynesian or Marxist, to history as well as legitimating social myths about the welfare state, Christian Democracy, the efficacy of social partnership between unions and management, and the inevitable "end of history," that of communism and the working class.

The introductory first chapter offers a summary of the argument and narrative of the EC as a neo-liberal construction, particularly the monetarist turn after 1981. Chapter 2 elucidates the economic, political, ideological, and geo-political diplomatic origins of the 1957 Rome Treaty and its neo-liberal principles, provisions, and logic. As interpreted and enforced by the Commission and European Court of Justice, the treaty set up a new supranational market order with levers that could be pulled by pro-business domestic forces to move and keep national politics oriented in a neo-liberal direction. The critical evaluation of the EC's social, regional, environmental, and technological interventionism in Chapter 3 serves to correct the misconception that the EC represented a social democratic "third way" between free market capitalism and socialism. It shows how its various social laws and technological projects – with the limited exceptions of equal pay for equal work for women, environmental protection and regional aid for Spain – if not actually designed to foster competition were undermined by its market principles and policies.

Chapter 4 is a critique of the paradigms used by academic specialists to understand the EU. Both the founding social democratic paradigm of neo-functionalism utilized by Ernst Haas and his students and the liberal intergovernmental one of Andrew Moravcsik, which resulted from reflections on the single market program, were based upon the Progressive American model of interest group pluralism. Questionable when applied to American history, this model had little to say about European societies and polities. Europe was always an "American" dream in both material and ideological terms. Based more on myths about globalization, technological imperatives, and the inevitable decline of the nations-state than on the social democratic model, current justifications or rationalizations of the EU are also here contested.

The central fifth chapter places the origins and development of the EC in the context of long economic waves, labor mobilization and divergent macro-economic (macro) and industrial relations (IR) regimes pulled in opposite directions by France and Germany. The labor mobilization engendered by the long boom, channelled by diverse macro and IR regimes, produced a strike–wage–welfare–price spiral and wage-led profit squeeze in the 1970s. This squeeze and resulting investment slow-down could have been resolved by further nationalization or socialization of the economy as proposed by some Socialists and Communists. Only the profitability crisis was temporarily resolved by the monetarist turn to restrain money supply, wages, benefits, and public spending, which depressed the economy and caused mass unemployment and job insecurity. The illusions of endless growth and prosperity generated by the long boom in the middle classes precluded the socialist solution and forced the manual working class to bear the brunt of the economic crisis in the 1970s before it enveloped the entire wage-earning class in the 1990s.

The neo-liberal EC project could only go so far as its indispensable but resistant member-state France would allow. Following the course of the economic cycle and class politics in France Chapter 6 questions the myth of a recalcitrant state capitalist regime. Official French resistance to EC neo-liberalism based primarily upon the strength of working-class Communism was more that of an ideological and institutional overhang than of interventionist substance. When push came to shove French social democrats capitulated to EC and German-led neo-liberalism. The prime minister Guy Mollet surrendered French social demands to the Germans in the Rome treaty of 1957 just as François Mitterrand, faced with internal opposition from Catholic-oriented Euroenthusiasts like Jacques Delors, abandoned his socialism in 1983 leading the way in the EC to the single market and currency. By enmeshing social democrats in an internationalist European project, the EC prevented the formation, contemplated seriously by Mitterrand in 1983, of a protectionist regime that could defend workers against deflationary global market forces as happened to some degree in the 1930s.

The final chapter on EC history traces the origins of EMU and the Euro from the Rome treaty through the neo-liberal realignment of states around the ERM. The German government and pro-business forces in each country used the framework and principles of the EC to construct a monetary union as a dike to stop and roll back working-class gains. But the immediate initiative for EMU came from the failed socialist Mitterrand, anxious to leave a

European monument to his glory regardless of French traditions and social consequences. Like the Rome treaty Maastricht represented the capitulation of French interventionism to German neo-liberalism. The convergence criteria of Maastricht and their enforcement under the 1996 Stability and Growth Pact aggravated the crisis of investment, productivity, and employment in Europe producing a backlash against neo-liberalism and a crisis of confidence and representation in national governments, employers, mainstream parties, and the EU.

Beyond my own work on French labor and the left, the contemporary press and official documents, this history is mainly derived from a critical reading of existing scholarship. One important book in particular, Moravcsik's *The Choice for Europe*, provided a template both for sources and for the questions asked and alternative answers given. There is no artificial scholastic effort here to present a balanced picture of the arguments in the literature or a comprehensive record of the data, but rather to endeavor to select those facts in combination with others that fit the puzzle and offer the best explanation of the driving forces behind the EU. The bibliography ranges over many aspects of the EC and member-states since 1945, but is by no means exhaustive. My findings and conclusions are validated less by a comprehensive collection of data than by the general patterns and trends discovered on the basis of preliminary hypotheses and assumptions. My statistical data are neither continuous nor original, but selected to demonstrate general trends and patterns. Data and secondary conclusions may be open to challenge but I expect, especially in view of the deepening macro and IR divisions among member-states and fiscal and constitutional crisis, that the overall explanation of the EU as a neo-liberal construction will stand.

The history of the EC and monetary union in the context of economic cycles, labor mobilization, and national political economies in Part I is reinforced in Part II by an econometrically based study of member-state performance by Gerald Friedman and complemented in part three by a series of chapters on member-states. Friedman's chapter confirms the relative economic failure of European integration. Contrary to conventional expectations Friedman finds that the free trading advantage of lower costs, scale economies and comparative advantage in the EC were minimal and outweighed by the costs of monetary union, which prevented governments from conducting counter-cyclical, especially expansionary fiscal and monetary policies. French growth was sharply reduced when it abandoned the more flexible expansive macro policy practiced in the US and aligned itself at high interest and exchange rates with the German Deutsche Mark in monetary union.

The national chapters deal with the central theme of the monetarist turn but in contrasting ways: Christopher Allen on Germany, Erik Jones on the Low Countries, Tobias Abse on Italy, Andreas Bieler on Sweden and Jonathan Michie on Britain. I am grateful to these authors for having cooperated with this project, participated in the preparatory seminar, responded to editorial suggestions and completed this work, also to Miguel Martinez Lucio of Leeds University, Dorothy Heisenberg of Johns Hopkins University, Martin Marcussen and Niels Christiansen of Copenhagen University and Gérard Duménil and Dominique Lévy of CEPREMAP in Paris, who made contributions.

The reader deserves an explanation of how an American historian brought up in the conformist 1950s has come to write a history of the EC that challenges so much conventional wisdom. I owe it first to my father, Morris Moss, who, a poor scholarship student from Rochester New York, loved to recount to me stories of Cornell University in the early Depression and who always wondered what had happened to the critical economists he had known then. I also owe it to the Amalgamated, the trade union cooperative housing project in which I grew up, which made me curious about alternative pasts and futures, and to the professor of European history at Cornell, Edward Fox, whose grand narrative about the rise of the bourgeoisie, the nation state and Western democracy inspired me to become a certain kind of historian.

A historian of the French left and labor, I expanded my interests to the EU with an LLM in European Law at the LSE where I had the fortune to meet two specialists, the historian Alan Milward and law teacher Francis Snyder, with a skeptical turn of mind. I learned much about critical economics collaborating on a first book about monetary union with Jonathan Michie, Professor of Management at the Birkbeck College of the University of London. I received valuable moral support from George Ross of Brandeis University, director of the Harvard Center for European Union Studies, Wolfgang Streeck of the Max Planck Institute in Frankfurt, Ezra Suleiman of Princeton University, Leo Panitch of York University in Canada, Werner Bonefeld of York University in the UK, Erik Jones of the Bologna Center of Johns Hopkins University, Gary Marks of the European Union Center at the University of North Carolina, Sue Murphy of St Georges Medical School of the University of London and Serge Halimi of *Le Monde diplomatique*.

I greatly benefited from the work done by the University Association for Contemporary European Studies (UACES) in the UK, which helped finance a conference on the single currency in national perspective at King's College in October 1996, and together with the Centre for European Governance directed by Erik Jones, a preparatory seminar for this book at Nottingham University in May 2002. I would also like to thank my students in European Studies at both Aston University in Birmingham and King's College in London for lending a sympathetic ear to my heterodox teaching on the EU.

Special mention must go to my friend and comrade Jim Mortimer, General-Secretary of the British Labour Party during the 1985 miners' strike, who imparted the wisdom of his many fruitful years in the labor movement, and to Steve Jefferys, Director of the Institute for Research on Working Lives at London Metropolitan University, who co-chairs my seminar on French Labour, the Left and Political Economy, which kept me focused on both France and the labor movement during research for this book. Gerald Friedman of the University of Massachusetts at Amherst, a master of both econometric and labor history, served as virtual co-editor, advising on matters of economic thought and commenting on several drafts.

I would also like to thank Steve Jefferys, Jonathan Michie, Dorothy Heisenberg, Sue Murphy, Herrick Chapman of New York University, John Grahl of London Metropolitan University, John Kelly of the London School of Economics, Catherine Hoskyns of the University of Coventry, and Councillor John Mills of the Labour Group of the London Borough of Camden for commenting on portions of the manuscript.

Finally, this book is dedicated to my wife Neysa Post Moss, who helped nurture me and this book through many difficult years and who sadly died before she could see the fruits of her love and care. I am also grateful to my son David for his technical computer support and for putting up with a demanding but loving father all these years.

Bernard H. Moss

1

Introduction: The EU as a Neo-liberal Construction

Bernard H. Moss

The European Economic Community (EC) or Union (EU) into which it was incorporated in 1992 has always enjoyed favorable academic press. Of literally thousands of scholarly books and countless articles devoted to the subject, nearly all were apologetic in tone or substance, barely any critical of the long-term project of achieving an "ever closer union" of European nation states.[1] The reigning narrative was that of the weakening of the nation state under the impact of trade interdependence or financial globalization and the salutary growth of supranational power. From the inception the single market and currency were viewed by the Commission and others as the crowning step in the subordination of the nation state to a supranational authority that would take on its elemental functions and capture the loyalty of its citizens. While business and liberal economists identified with the project of market liberalization, social democrats, notably the first academic specialists, saw it taking on the functions of the emerging welfare state just as later ones would justify it as a check to US-led global market forces. Only in the 1990s came serious recognition of its roots in national politics and its own neo-liberal agenda.[2]

Along the way the EC was surrounded with myths and haloes that made it immune to critical scholarly analysis. Its sanctity came first from its presumed role as preserver of the peace in Europe, especially between the age-old rivals of France and Germany, and even more importantly as a bulwark against Communism. Second, it was thought necessary for growth and prosperity to create a larger competitive market with the lower factor costs, comparative advantages and economies of scale that had made America so productive. Those who felt uncomfortable with its market principles were assuaged by timid interventionist ventures into social, environmental, regional, and high tech policy, spreading minimal standards to poorer members and notionally shielding Europe from the worst effects of globalization.

It was treated as a unique hybrid flower cut off from its roots in national politics and economies, a sui-generis system with its own predestination, laws of motion and procedures, which required its own euphemisms to describe – spillover, soft law, epistemic communities, the open method of coordination, and so on. One EU textbook (Hix, 1999) presented a self-contained political system without making more than passing reference to the inter-governmental European Council (Council), which gave overall direction, or to national governments, which controlled the legislative Council of Ministers (council). Nearly all EC measures were taken at face value as measures of true European integration and supranational authority, including soft-law whose application remained open to continual negotiation and non-binding open coordination, without investigating their impact on the ground except among policy-making elites. Just as the constitutional convention of 2003 (Stuart, 2003), specialists tended to see EC expansion as an end in itself.[3]

Every constitutional innovation was greeted as a unifying step, including the complex legislative procedure of codecision, involving a shuttling back and forth between Commission, council and the European Parliament (EP); the so-called Lisbon process after 2000, which promised to achieve the contradictory goals of high tech competitiveness, deregulation and social cohesion but which in the opinion of even the Commission had manifestly failed by 2004 (*International Herald Tribune*, January 22, 2004); and the muddled pastiche of the draft constitution of 2003, which masked creeping EU competence behind a façade of treaty consolidation (Chapter 2). The Eurogroup of currency members, initiated by France as a Euro-Keynesian antidote to the deflationary stability pact of 1996, was hailed as a supranational economic government when it merely served to initiate punitive action against countries that breached the budget deficit limit (cf. Puetter, 2003).

Too many scholars became invested in the EC as a livelihood and cause to the detriment of European studies, the study of national societies and polities, and public understanding of other member-states. EC studies became a growth industry and achieved quasi-disciplinary status in American and British universities with the help of subsidies, grants, the European University Institute in Florence and the nomination of Jean Monnet professors paid by the Commission.[4] The American political scientists, known as neo-functionalists, who founded the field, hypothesized a self-propelling mechanism of integration known as spillover in which national interest groups, notably trade unions, would transfer their loyalty to self-aggrandizing EC institutions to better achieve their regulatory objectives when the basic treaty aim was actually deregulation. The theory floundered when General de Gaulle, playing real national politics, vetoed further supranational integration, when workers revolted against the wage restraint required by integration after 1968, and currency flows in the 1970s appeared to give globalization greater importance than regional integration (Chapter 4).

With the creation of the single market and currency in the 1990s specialists abandoned social democratic and neo-functionalist rationales (cf. Tranholm-Mikkelsen, 1991) for more realistic market-oriented teleologies such as trade interdependence, financial globalization and high tech development (Moravcsik, 1998a; Sandholtz and Sweet, 1998; Gillingham, 2003). The national backlash against the Maastricht treaty of 1992, which innovated in both supranational and inter-governmental directions, introduced a note of caution into predictions of nation state demise. Renouncing teleology, scholars treated the EU as a directionless system of multilevel governance (e.g. Marks, 1993; Caporaso, 1998; Moravcsik, 1998b) as though the temporary equilibrium of intergovernmental and supranational forces could last forever. Disillusioned socialists, liberals and postmodernists could vaunt with equal fervor the end of univocal national identity, power, and responsibility in favor of a more pluralistic decentered mode of governance (e.g. Weiler, 1999; Schmitter, 2000; cf. Callinicos, 1989).

The very proliferation of EC literature and courses convinced students that it was the wave of the globalized or regionalized future. In actuality scholars exaggerated the degree of globalization, misconstruing it to mean the end of the nation state (cf. Todd, 1998). The American high tech boom and bust in the 1990s saw a slowing down and decline of intra-EU trade and investment relative to GNP, which had been stagnant in manufacturing for the founding states since the 1970s.[5] The nationalization of social, cultural, and political life – the end of localisms, abstract universalisms and empire – begun in the nineteenth century and deepened by the growth of the welfare state continued with nationalist resurgence in the former Soviet bloc, China, Africa, the Middle East and elsewhere, US military unilateralism, the popular revolt against globalization, and the re-assertion of national rights in the EU after Maastricht. The growth of the democratic welfare state presented the paradox of a particularist structure that incorporated the universal values of the public realm. Modern states do more for their citizens and impinge on peoples' lives more intimately than ever before, particularly in providing public services and redistributing the national income (Moss, 2000).

Principles of subsidiarity with its presumption of national prerogative, of state's rights and exemptions, and the possibility of elective ad hoc "enhanced cooperation" among members, of "variable geometry," were introduced into Maastricht to balance the supranational EMU regime. The renationalization continued with the popular recession-led backlash against Maastricht, the break down of the Exchange Rate Mechanism (ERM) in 1992 and 1993, the defense of national sovereignty by the German Constitutional Court in 1994, and later constitutional disagreements, involving blocking minorities, over enlargement to the East, and the profound split, domestic and external, over macroeconomic policy (macro) and the stability pact, free trade, relations with the US and over the Iraqi war.

Alongside the EU national regulation also proliferated to protect against globalization and Europeanization (Gelber, 1997). National imperatives and regulations still exceeded and superseded those of the EU with respect to price control, state aid and public services in France, environmental protection in Germany, and macro and social policy in all the larger states. More important than a mechanical counting of laws was the far greater salience of national decisions in daily life and the popular mind compared to those of the EU, which remained invisible to the public and inscrutable even to European parliamentarians, the MEPs. So long as politics remained tied to national cultures, institutions, personalities, and issues, little legitimacy could be gained in a new constitution by naming either a one, two or four-headed presidency to a fragmented, missionless and opaque EU.

EU studies attracted some of the best social scientists and raised important issues of national sovereignty in the face of neo-liberalism and globalization but it received undue attention especially in Britain where committed Euroskeptics outnumbered Europhiles four to one (*Times*, January 7, 2004) and the US where the government and public were increasingly indifferent to European concerns. The EC played, as we shall see, an important reinforcing but essentially negative role in pioneering globalization and neo-liberalism by undermining the national control and regulation of economic life without restoring them on a continental level.

In the 1990s neo-liberalism became the explicit doctrine, inscribed in the Maastricht treaty, of the EU and its member-states. Maastricht made "the allocation of resources through the competitive market" (art. 103) the guiding principle. The aim of the EU according to the draft constitution of 2003 was "a competitive single market without [state interventionist] distortions." Neo-liberalism differed from nineteenth century liberalism to the extent that it required strong EC action through its laws, institutions and principles to dismantle the aids, regulations and controls of the encrusted welfare state. It dictated tight money with low inflation, reduced social and public spending, deregulation, free trade and the commercialization and privatization of public concerns and services even as its economic and social consequences in slower growth and productivity and mass unemployment and job insecurity produced a growing popular backlash and disaffection from both national institutions and the EU.

Europe itself was a contestable ideological construction, possessing no obvious geographical, historical, religious, cultural, or economic unity. Spain, Portugal, Greece, and Eastern Europe not to speak of Turkey were peripheral to the original Christian Democratic conception. Britain has since the Reformation defined itself in opposition to the Catholicism, insularity and statism of the continent (Risse-Kappen, 1997; cf. Spiering, 2004). The shatter belt of Eastern Europe would always be torn between West and East, America and Europe, free markets and socialism. Spain would always dream of its Latin American empire. Could Greece and Turkey ever become friends? Neither would the core states of France and Germany ever be on the same partisan cycle. The notion of the concert of Europe emerged in the eighteenth century among national monarchies struggling for power and influence in the world. The EC palpably failed to transform national identities and interests.

The literature overrated and misinterpreted the function of positive integration in areas of social, labor, regional, and industrial policy. The only social policy the EC originally had was fostering labor mobility, which the French originally considered antisocial, because it was contrary to worker and national welfare. Social policy was viewed by the first Commission simply as propaganda bait for the working class. It was first introduced after the French general strike of 1968 and under Jacques Delors in the mid-1980s as legitimating compensation to labor for the damage anticipated under a single market and currency. The only accomplishments were a statement of principles known as the social charter and series of minimalist provisions and directives that tended to favor individual over collective employment rights and enterprise over sectoral and national bargaining where unions were strongest. What workers gained in the way of a few directives, they lost in the general deregulation, privatization and marketization of society and the ideological subordination of their unions to the EU's neo-liberal project (Chapters 3, 7).

Measures of positive integration were undermined by more basic market principles and forces if not actually designed to foster them. EU regional and technological funds may have loomed large as novelties – leading scholars thought they threatened the integrity of the nation state (Marks *et al*, 1996; Sandholtz and Sweet, 1998) – but they were nothing compared to state expenditure. The EU budget was held at less than 2 percent of state budgets or 1.26 percent of EU GDP in the 1990s. Since the literature tended to treat each EU policy sphere in isolation from others (e.g., Wallace and Wallace, 1977, 1983, 1996), much as it was institutionally done in the EC, students never noticed how market principles nullified interventionist policies. Regional aid, for example in Southern Italy, was decimated by a decision of the European Court of Justice (ECJ) that barred local procurement on fair competition grounds and by the Maastricht criteria, which limited national spending (Martin and Stehmann, 1991). Assistance to high tech research and development (R&D) was tailored to open up public utilities to multinationals, to commercialization and privatization. Employment policy, introduced as a concession to the French in 1997 and lauded by a leading authority (Dyson, 2002, 5) as a leap to social dialogue and expansive macro coordination, was made nonbinding and subordinate to deflationary economic policies.

Once upon a time the European Left, Communists as also most Socialists outside the founding states, were Euro-critical. In the 1970s Prime Minister Olaf Palme, paraphrasing a former German Socialist leader, warned the Swedes of the perils of the four Cs contained in the EC. The EC, he said, was conservative, capitalist because competitive markets across borders were bad for labor, clerical because it was dominated by Christian Democracy, which was anti-statist and anti-collectivist, and colonialist because it helped restore French and Belgian control in Africa. Because he was a social democrat Palme forgot a fifth C that was highly motivating – the EC was anti-Communist.

A more pragmatic evaluation came from the British Labourite Barbara Castle, who made an investigative trip to Brussels when Harold Macmillan applied for British membership in 1961.While told by officials that the EC was not hostile to Labour's program of planning and nationalization, she found that the whole spirit of the EC revolved around markets and free enterprise. The restrictions on state aid and public monopolies would prevent Labour from aiding industry or regions. The treaty prohibited the use of exchange controls or import duties to correct trade imbalances. The coordination of economic and monetary policy would impose monetarist Treasury restraints on growth and jobs while social security could fall under the axe of competition rules. Castle noted that the vaunted European Social and Investment Funds were mere trifles and that European social policy was more conservative than that of the Conservatives (*New Statesman*, March 30, 1962).

These insights from the European Left were missing from academic scholarship, which regarded the EC as class, politically and ideologically, neutral, economically effective, and socially beneficent much as many later regarded the "third way" of Tony Blair, who influenced EU policy after 1997.[6] It was hard to deny, however, that the aim of the EU was a Smithian or Hayekian free market utopia or that EMU, the single currency regime whose only aim was price stability, was monetarist. It was based on the same disinflationary principles with the same results that drove the Bundesbank after 1974, and Paul Volker, head of the American Federal Reserve Bank (the Fed), and Mrs Margaret Thatcher after 1979 to deepen recession, slow growth, and to generate mass unemployment and job insecurity *en permanence*.

Monetarism was not a foreign graft on the EC merely introduced to deal with growing trade interdependence, capital mobility or the crisis of profitability, but was contained in the neo-liberal logic and terms of the Rome treaty. Maastricht made this logic explicit by creating a central bank, the ECB, devoted to price stability that was independent of national or democratic control and by embracing the market allocation of resources as its guiding philosophy. The Maastricht criteria on debt and deficit aimed to compress wages and benefits and maintain sufficient unemployment, what was known technically as NAIRU, to keep wages within the bounds of productivity, prevent inflation and weaken the force of organized labor. To maintain long-term market credibility the ECB had to be insulated from popular or governmental pressures to lower interest rates and expand the money supply for the sake of growth and employment. Since governments still controlled budgetary and fiscal policies, the stability pact imposed an enforceable deficit limit of three percent per annum to be offset over the medium term to prevent them from diluting the currency and reflating through borrowing. EMU contained in vitro the essence of monetarism and the neo-liberal assault against the social or public regulation of the market (cf. Arestis, 2003).

Monetarism was the policy of making a currency harder, scarcer and more valuable by raising interest rates and limiting money supply in order to: (1) increase purchasing power over foreign goods and assets and leverage over governments with budgetary, trade, or payments deficits; (2) obtain the rental premium or seignorage that comes from possessing currency that is used as a reserve by other countries; (3) secure the value of loans, usually held by the wealthiest rentier class, against debtors; (4) reduce the margin for working class action, organization, and the real wage gains that price inflation affords; and (5) to prevent the redistribution of incomes and power to labor that usually comes from long-term and rapid growth. Monetarism was already enshrined in the national banks and treasuries of most major countries. While the major powers, France, Britain, and Germany, initially focused on the first two objectives, they along with the others became increasingly concerned with the last two in response to the labor mobilization and wage price spiral that exploded after 1968.

Monetarism was used after 1974 to check the labor mobilization and wage–price spiral that took off after the French general strike of May–June 1968 and the Italian "hot autumn" of 1969. Strikes and/or unionization, particularly strikes since 1947, were associated with inflation as both cause and effect. In the 1960s and 70s prices rose on the average a half year after wages, inducing further mobilization, a wage–price spiral and real wage gains that after generating boom conditions eventually squeezed profits and investment. The sign that capitalist discipline had broken down was the strong correlations between strikes, union growth and nominal and unit labor costs on the one hand and the rate of inflation on the other.[7]

The inflationary gains and mobilization of the working class were normally checked in the absence of national protectionist coalitions and regimes by the global capital or currency market controlled by the dominant world power (Herr, 1997, 134–5). The hegemonic country used hard money to keep its own working class in check and impose interest rate penalties on soft money states, those that relaxed fiscal and monetary discipline to accommodate labor. In the 1930s protectionist regimes that went off the gold standard like the US and Britain minimized wage and price deflation and gave extra scope for labor mobilization (Forsyth and Notermans, 1997). This could not happen under the free trading EC, however, because its rules precluded the formation of protectionist regimes such as the one Mitterrand considered in 1983 to save his program of nationalization and reflation from recessive global market forces.

With half the world's industrial production and gold after the Second World War, the US took over from Britain as the monetary hegemon, the enforcer of wage and spending discipline under the rules of Bretton Woods and the International Monetary Fund (IMF), backing relatively fixed exchange rates with gold. The hard money Fed was pitted together with the more conciliatory State Department, against Lord Keynes, who pleaded for more liquidity to help states like Britain with trading and payments deficits to achieve full employment. The international monetary system raised global and domestic class issues (Apple, 1983; Skidelsky, 2000).

The EC would later see the same clash of interests between the hard-money Germans and soft money states led by France. Though the IMF enabled the US to impose austerity or "structural adjustment" programs on spendthrift nations in the third world, the US did not exercise wage and spending discipline in Western Europe where the priority was not the increase of profitability but the defense of the entire capitalist system against Communism. This required a net outflow of dollars for economic and military assistance, especially the Marshall Plan and Mutual Security Pact of 1955. The payments deficit was at least initially the product of the Cold War. The US had no deliberate policy of macro expansiveness to foster national growth as implied in the notion of "embedded liberalism" (cf. Ruggie, 1982). European money supply merely kept up with the needs of corporate financing and growth punctuated with periodic tightening against wage-led inflation (Epstein and Schor, 1990; Edelman and Fleming, 1965).

To the US balance of payments problem was added declining productivity growth relative to Europe and the enormous sums spent on welfare for the Great Society and on the Vietnam War. Leakage into the Euro-dollar market outside of federal control and De Gaulle's aggressive conversion of dollars into gold forced the US to devalue in 1968 and 1971 and float in 1973, thus ending the fixed rates of Bretton Woods and contributing to inflation and the wage–price spiral. It was not until the Carter–Volker interest rate jolt of 15 percent in 1979 that dollar supremacy and the role of the US as European disciplinarian was temporarily restored (Block, 1977; Keohane, 1985; cf. Helleiner, 1994).

West Germany took up the slack as the monetary hegemon and wage disciplinarian in Western Europe (cf. Lankowski, 1982; McNamara and Jones, 1996; Herr, 1997). The state had been founded after 1948 on ordo-liberal principles that mandated price stability (ch. 5, Peacock and Willgeracht, 1989; Nichols, 1994). Profoundly disoriented by the experience of class and world war under Weimar and Nazism, the new business-oriented leadership adopted an abstract market philosophy that was foreign to national statist and socialist traditions captured by the East, but one consistent with American requirements in the Cold War. Possessing a virtual monopoly in capital goods, machinery, and chemicals in Europe, and thus having the ability to keep up prices without losing custom, the Germans became by far the largest EC exporter and holder of reserve currencies (Milward, 1984; Giersch *et al*, 1992).

The government and Bundesbank, the central bank, achieved wage stability with the help of accomodationist unions that rarely struck. German unions were strong and centralized but they bargained under severe Cold War ideological, legal, political, and monetary constraint that initially kept wage gains lagging below those of productivity (Chapter 5). The greatest fear was that inflation imported from trading partners like France and Italy would stir labor agitation and social instability. Consequently, West Germany used its economic power to press for free trade, currency convertibility, and wage and spending restraint on its partners, aims that were pursued through the treaty of Rome and the EC. In the final analysis, one might say that the EC was constructed on ordo-liberal lines in order to assure West German social stability (see Pittman, 1993, 467; Dickhaus, 1996).

The treaty of Rome owed more to the market philosophy of Adam Smith and Friedrich Hayek than to the pragmatic interventionism of Jean Monnet. The idea of constructing a single competitive European market under supranational supervision came from the Dutch international financier and foreign minister Johann Beyen as a compromise between Dutch global free traders and European integrationists (Griffiths, 1997b). It arose in the context of a resurgent capitalism that had triumphed over the labor movement in the immediate post-war period, that could exploit abundant labor reserves at relatively low wages combined with American assembly-line technology and achieve unprecedented leaps in productivity, wages, and profits with the help of a multilateral trading network around the West German hub. The EC was created in a climate of capitalist optimism, monetary expansion, and German economic dominance that obviated the need for Keynesian fiscal deficits or state intervention (Epstein, 1990; Armstrong *et al*, 1991; Brenner, 1998).

The EC drew upon the anti-interventionist sentiments of the Germans and business community that had blocked the development of Monnet's European Coal and Steel Community (ECSC) and other attempts to negotiate common agricultural, transport, industrial, and commercial policies (Gillingham, 1991; Trausch, 1993). Interventionist regimes like the ECSC only exacerbated national and class divisions whereas the capitalist security imperative was for a Europe united against Communism. What was needed was a leap to a new liberal trading order in which the gains and losses for countries, firms, industries, and classes were lost in the invisibility and objectivity of the market (Müller-Armack, 1957, 534). The invisible hand of the market was superior to the political planner, said Adam Smith ([1776] 1975, 456), not only because it could find the most efficient solution but also because it did not draw attention to itself and politicize relations.

The EC was supported not only by exporters looking for outlets (cf. Moravcsik, 1998a), but by the entire capitalist class, financiers, merchants, employers, large and small, because it was the optimal regime for the exploitation of labor free from state interference (see Aron *et al*, 1957).

The exploitation of wage labor has been reinforced by the extension of competitive markets in Europe since the Middle Ages (Braudel, 1972; Sweezy, 1978). Capitalists saw the expanded competitive market of the EC operating under sound money as a prophylactic against wage-led inflation and a guarantee of labor subordination.

Capitalists formed the only class that offered the EC sustained support (Chapters 2, 3, 5). Labor was divided between left-wing Socialist and Communist adversaries and right-wing Socialist and Catholic enthusiasts. French and German farmers preferred the bilateral agreements they had already concluded. In France only the CNPF, the employers' confederation, of Malthusian or protectionist reputation, gave unconditional endorsement once it realized the EC's potential to check and reverse state intervention – to lower taxes and social charges and end credit and price controls and subsidies to producers. Business backing brought with it that of many nationalist conservatives, notably in France, who had previously opposed European integration (Bjöl, 1966, 197–207; Guillen, 1980, 16–19; Mioche, 1993, 242–55).

The trademark party of Europe was the Christian Democrats, the governing party everywhere but in France. They acclaimed the larger competitive market as a generator of wealth and property ownership (Haas, 1958, 24, 115) and less overtly as a safeguard of personal autonomy, responsibility, and spirituality against the collectivist materialist tendencies of the democratic state (cf. Hanley, 1994). Europe was not for them the expression of citizen equality and popular sovereignty but of a charitable communion of souls committed to the market. They were joined by the Socialists of the Six, who saw the EC as an alternative to Communism, an expression of proletarian internationalism and a framework both for growth and prosperity on the American model and for a future socialist society. It was usually the most market-oriented, pro-American Socialists who were the most European (Marks, 1999; Marks and Wilson, 2000).

The treaty was a triumph of German ordo or neo-liberalism over remnants of French interventionism. It drew upon the Spaak Report (1956), chiefly of German inspiration, which envisaged a single competitive market without the social regulation demanded by the authorizing Messina Resolution of June 1955. In comparison with previous plans it was ultra-liberal. The French feared competition from low wage and benefit countries like Germany. French requests for a monetary union to aid the weaker currency countries adjust to competition were denied. Negotiations turned on French demands for the upward harmonization of labor standards to their level. The impasse was overcome, after the Hungarian and Suez crisis exposed French diplomatic isolation, with nominal social concessions and aid to colonies (Chapter 2).

The treaty was mostly about negative integration, the abolition of tariffs, and other restrictions on free trade. Negative integration was made automatic and self-executory, especially after the ECJ arrogated the right to enforce it. There were few provisions for positive or interventionist integration (Tinbergen, 1965). Missing were social and industrial policy. Transport and agriculture were left in abeyance subject to veto. The macro emphasis was on fighting inflation, achieving price stability and trade balance with relatively fixed exchange rates and neutralizing the competitive devaluations the French and Italians used to stimulate growth. The Germans got their way on the rapid and automatic elimination of tariffs, low external tariff, restriction of state aids to business, competition law, and the right to revalue to maintain Deutsche Mark (DM) supremacy (Küsters, 1982). Competitive market principles were also enshrined in provisions barring national tax and business discrimination and authorizing the harmonization of all national standards.

The basic competitive principle, the four freedoms of goods, services, labor, and capital, operating on a level playing field without national discrimination, ruled out state action to regulate market forces, which was necessarily selective, directive, and discriminatory. The treaty pointed, as the Commission noted, toward the creation of a single market with a sound currency on the model of a national one (Kapteyn *et al*, 1989, 76; Dyson, 1994, 67–8). The aim according to Commission President Walter Hallstein, a German law professor who had served the steel trusts before government service, was a "natural" competitive market enforced by a supranational authority free from the distortions of state interference (Hallstein, 1962, 29–45). The second action program of the Commission in 1962 called for the completion of the single market by removing capital controls, harmonizing indirect taxes, abolishing state aids and public commercial monopolies, enforcing competition law and moving toward fixed exchange rates and a centrally determined macro policy. It also urged the introduction of social policy, albeit contrary to the treaty's market principles, to win over worker loyalty from the nation state.

Just as the creation of a market economy out of feudal and mercantilist institutions required state action to remove social regulations and controls (Polanyi, 1956) so did the completion of the single market need a supranational authority capable of overturning nationally-based social regulations and protections. Supremacy over national law was achieved by the fiat of the European Court of Justice (ECJ), which went beyond words and intent by reference to the spirit, logic and general design of the treaty, the requirements of a free market and closer union (Chapter 2). Without the supremacy and uniform application of the law, the EC would become a mere inter-governmental body subject to continual negotiation. Member-states would interpret it to their advantage leading to cheating, reprisals, trade wars, and break-up, said the ECJ in *Entel* [1964]. The treaty had created a new juridical order impinging on national powers that would if invoked in the immediate national interest lead members in a neo-liberal direction they had never fully intended (cf. Pierson, 1996; Moravcsik, 1998a; Gillingham, 2003).

Based primarily on ordo-liberal principles of market competition and sound money, the EC acted as regional enforcer of labor subordination and wage discipline much as Friedrich Hayek, the Austrian-born economist-philosopher, had advocated. After the Second World War Hayek had rallied liberal economists and policy makers to challenge Keynesianism and the welfare state in his elite Mont Pelerin Society (Hartwell, 1995). Unlike social democrats, who supported the welfare state as a barrier to Communism, Hayek perceived the danger of communism arising from within, from the spiraling inflationary demands of labor backed by the democratic state. He was a neo-liberal because he recognized the difference that laws and political institutions could make to market outcomes. Having seen the inflationary demands of labor lead to civil war and dictatorship in Central Europe, Hayek advocated a single market and currency under a European federation as the way to discipline labor without recourse to force.[8]

The nation state strengthened the hand of organized labor against capital and raised wage share by restricting competition through tariffs, immigration and capital controls, protective worker and union legislation, social benefits, the public sector, expansionist devaluations, and macro policy (Rader and Ulman, 1993). It reinforced union power with benefits and labor protection in a rising tide and insulated unions from deflationary market pressures in receding ones (Western, 1997, 102). Strikes, unionization, and labor party votes augmented the size and income share of the state (Schmidt, 1982). The social democratic nation state fostered worker solidarity and organization by providing a common language, heritage, institutional relations, protections and benefits.

If the nation state strengthened worker solidarity, a federation would weaken it by cutting across national class solidarity and popular sovereignty. Labor movements with different heritages, partisan cycles, and institutional linkages would find it hard to concert forces against mobile capital (cf. Visser and Hemerick, 1995). A hard single currency would prevent employers from ratcheting up prices to pay for concessions, forcing them to resist wage and other worker claims. The free movement of goods, services and capital market would punish those employers or states that accorded higher wages or benefits. By creating a product and labor market that was larger than the organized national labor market, the single market would subject individual workers to the full blast of market forces (Rader and Ulman, 1993).

The benefits lost to workers on the national level could not be restored on the federal one either because of the difficulty of achieving unanimity from states with different traditions and cycles, or because such constitutions as the US, West German, or EC could reserve social legislation to the states. In the absence of strong federal legislation, employers and states would race to the bottom to reduce business taxes, quality standards and practices, wages and benefits to lower costs, and attract investment. Hayek (1976) turned against the EC in the 1970s when it began discussing a social dimension, but when it came in the 1980s it was at the minimalist level of a common denominator that constrained employers very little in a few states as his theory would have predicted.

Federations or confederations like the Holy Roman Empire had always been used to protect privileged elites, the Church, aristocracy, and the wealthy, against the leveling tendency of democratic majorities and the centralized state (Pentland, 1973; Harrison, 1974). Hayek's federalist logic was the same that secured property rights and financial interests against debtors and popular majorities in the US Constitution as elaborated by James Madison in the Federalist Papers (Beard, 1913; Dahl, 1998), the same that underlay the Basic Law of West Germany and the EC. It was a logic that undercut class solidarities and the excercise of popular pressure and sovereignty. Lacking a center of direct representation and decision-making, the decentered and fractured EC was an open sesame for business lobbies and breakwater against mass democracy and wage-led inflation in the nation state (cf. Risse-Kappen, 1996; Kohler-Koch, 1999).

Through his Mont Pelerin Society and British Institute for Economic Affairs Hayek influenced economists and politicians who were destined to turn Europe in a neo-liberal direction: the architect of the German economic miracle Ludwig Erhard and his advisor Armand Müller-Armack, who gave his imprint to the treaty of Rome; Jacques Rueff, the Poincarist economist who stabilized prices in Gaullist France; Milton Friedman, the American monetarist, who persuaded the Germans and Americans to float their currencies and control money supply; and Mrs Thatcher, who turned monetarism after 1975 into a full-fledged neo-liberal offensive against organized labor and the state (Hayek, 1972, 1991; Tomlinson, 1998). Guided largely by ordo-liberal principles, the EC fulfilled, especially after the end of the long boom, the functions of a Hayekian federation by compressing wages and benefits, the wage share of value-added and monopoly rents, and eliminating those public or collective institutions that sheltered workers from market forces much as the Enclosure Laws did the village commons that protected peasants in early modern Britain (Marx, 1967).

The EC did not apparently serve this function in the expansionary 1960s when it allowed the growth of organized labor and the welfare state but this was before the implementation of treaty provisions for internal liberalization vitiated state macro capacities. Governments saw little reason to yield sovereignty over their internal regimes while they were prospering from increased EC trade and so resisted Commission entreaties for the removal of capital controls, technical and health and safety standards, state aids to industry, national preference in public contracts, and commercial and public service and transport monopolies. Still, the EC pressed for price stabilization, financial de-regulation, external tariff reduction, and the commercialization of public services even in a Gaullist France that was so defensive of sovereignty in other realms. (Chapter 6). It was not until the domestic neo-liberal realignments of the late 1970s and 1980s aided by the Carter–Volker jolt and the ERM that conditions were created for the full implementation of the single market and currency, which consolidated domestic neo-liberalism.

Starting with the events of May–June 1968 the balance of class forces on many levels – demographic, economic, union, political, ideological, and governmental – shifted against profitability and capital. Governments initially accommodated the labor upsurge by expanding money supply and according new rights and benefits, which only fueled further mobilization and added benefits to the wage–price spiral (Marglin and Schor, 1990; Armstrong *et al*, 1991). The mobilization, spiral and real wage gains were greatest in those countries like France and Italy that had Communist-led class struggle unions and expansive semi-protectionist macro regimes linked to them and were most subdued in Germany where accommodationist unions negotiated under mobilization constraint in an open economy. The resulting profit squeeze and disinvestment faced labor movements with a choice, not clearly perceived or taken at first, of self-restraint or a move forward to nationalization and public control of investment. While German Social Democrats and Italian Communists both chose restraint, the transformative path was pursued by French Communists and Socialists in the Common Program, by the British Labour Party with its contested Alternative Economic Strategy, and the Swedes with the Meidner pension plan for the union takeover of industry (Chapter 5).

Banks and finance were more likely to suffer from inflation because of their fixed assets than manufacturing, but in the major EC countries France, Germany, and Italy, where they were fused, finance shared in the expansion and profit squeeze of industry (Epstein and Schor, 1990). Except in Germany employers bore the cost of the quadrupling of oil prices in 1974. Coming on top of the wage–price spiral the oil shock united financial and industrial capital against further inflationary growth. By 1978 UNICE, the European employers' confederation, was demanding fiscal and monetary restraint. The restriction of money supply would make it more difficult for employers to make wage concessions and for governments to borrow to pay for higher social costs. By shaking down excessive costs the monetarists hoped to achieve a sustainable non-inflationary growth that had never been attained under capitalism.

Monetary restriction required a political will, societal consensus, and union discipline such as existed in Germany to work. In Britain with a large public sector and undisciplined unions, the new Conservative leader Mrs Thatcher was persuaded by Hayek and Keith Joseph, an MP from Manchester, that monetarism had to be accompanied by a whole-scale assault on the state and unions, particularly the public sector unions that lobbied for expanded welfare. With Mrs Thatcher monetarism became a full-blown strategy of neo-liberalism attacking progressive taxation, welfare benefits, nationalized industries and union power (Chapters 5, 7).

Official opinion followed the business turn to monetarism. A 1975 study published by the Trilateral Commission, a private association of politicians and trade unionists with multinational executives, claimed that the excessive demands of workers, consumers, and citizens were causing a crisis of democracy, a code word for capitalist profitability (Sklar, 1980). The 1977 McCracken Report of the OECD, the body that advised Europe, urged that the power of organized labor be reined in by monetary restriction, the de-indexation of wages from prices and the end of centralized bargaining, an agenda largely fulfilled in the 1980s. The monetarist tide reached the Commission with the appointment of the Vicomte Etienne Davignon, a Catholic Belgian diplomat close to the multinationals, to the directorate of industry in 1977, and of Tomasso Padoa-Schioppa and Michael Emerson in 1979, two economists trained in the US, to D G II, the Directorate of Economic Affairs, where they switched accounting from a national to community basis, later becoming leading advocates of the single currency (Maes, 2002, chs 5–6).

In the past crises of profitability had been resolved by long and deep depressions that shook out jobs, labor costs and living standards and set the stage for a new recovery. This happened to some extent in the US after 1973 under Nixon and in 1981 under Reagan where unions and social benefits were attacked and the wages of the average male manual worker reduced long term for the first time in the history of capitalism (Schor, 1985; Brenner, 1998, 159; Madrick, 1997). With the help of a lower dollar and looser monetary and fiscal policy the US experienced an industrial recovery in the late 1980s and a high tech boom and bust in the late 1990s sustained by foreign money (Brenner, 2002).

In Europe the retrenchment begun in Germany in 1973 and 1974 was only applied half way by France and Italy in 1976, which preserved aid to industry and the growing numbers of unemployed. Countries contending with labor mobilization, rising welfare expectation, and menacing socialist alternatives resisted the stark terms of German disinflation and monetary union. The late seventies were thus a twilight period of stagflation, rising unemployment with inflation, of stop and go and half-way measures, which was not resolved until the definitive monetarist turn of the US and Germany in 1979 and 1981 (Epstein, 1990).

The German Social Democratic governments of Willy Brandt and Helmut Schmidt, unconstrained by a radical labor movement, were the first to exercise fiscal and monetary restraint and to limit the growth of the welfare state with the help of the Bundesbank and downwardly flexible wages – contrary to common belief (Grande, 1988; Heylen and Poech, 1995). While other governments and employers accommodated the oil shock, the Bundesbank began strict money targeting in 1974, which made unions choose between jobs and wages, turning them to less costly qualitative demands like the reduction of working hours. Under conditions of societally enforced monetary constraint, wage rises in excess of productivity would be punished by diminished output and jobs. Cutting the growth of money supply by more than half, the Germans imposed the highest interest rates, least responsive to unemployment, in the EC. The relative situation of German workers, who appeared well-heeled compared to their British counterparts, deteriorated after 1974. Through the 1980s they suffered net job losses, the worst welfare cuts relative to GNP, the greatest decline of unit wages, and the lowest wage share of value added next to the Dutch.[9]

The Germans used the EC and monetary union to drag their partners down to their low level of inflation and wage share. The first projects for monetary union came as a response to dollar depreciation and the wage hikes of May–June 1968, which increased the inflation differential between France and Germany. Negotiations opposed the hard money Germans, who favored price stability over growth, to the French and others who needed a higher rate of growth and inflation in order to accommodate the rising power of labor. French Gaullists and liberals shared the ultimate German goal of wage and price stabilization but they needed adjustment assistance for wage settlements and social benefits to achieve reconciliation with accomodationist unions, particularly the Catholic-based CFDT. The French wanted the Germans to aid the weak currency states to grow and stabilize and to reflate their own economy when the DM became too strong. Whenever German governments offered monetary facilities to the French as did Schmidt over the ERM in 1978 or Helmut Kohl in 1987, they were vetoed by the Bundesbank, which, backed by industry, upheld the constitutional and class duty of price stability (Heisenberg, 1999; Howarth, 2001).

The first EMU initiative came in 1969 from the French Commissioner Raymond Barre, a notably liberal professor of economics and translator of Hayek, who recommended a gradual adjustment to German macro norms. This was translated by the Commission into a proposal for a narrow band of exchange rate fluctuations known as the snake and by the Werner Report, written with national treasury officials, into a project for a ten-year transition to a single currency with prior convergence to German norms and a supranational government with economic and social competence responsible to the EP. This project achieved a broad consensus of capital and social democratic labor, including the liberal Gaullist cabinet of Jacques Chaban-Delmas. It was only vetoed by the neo-Gaullist President Georges Pompidou on grounds that it threatened national sovereignty and the governability of the working classes (Chapter 6). Despite a new agreement about monetary union in 1971 the only result was the snake in the tunnel, which tried to maintain collective dollar parity until 1973. But with raging inflation Italy and France soon departed and the Germans carried on a joint float with the

Dutch and occasional others willing to deflate their economies to German standards (Tsoukalis, 1977; Kruse, 1980; Dyson, 1994).

The snake gave the Germans the first chance to exercise their monetary hegemony and class discipline. They offered to share their huge foreign reserves with governments with payments deficits if they stayed in the snake and agreed to reduce their budget deficits and money supply. They used loan leverage through the EC to prevent the Italians from levying import taxes and forced them with the assent of the Communists (PCI) to adopt austerity budgets (Lankowski, 1982, 392–8, 464). The blocking partnership of the Bundesbank, EC, PCI and Christian Democrats (DC) slowed the wave of worker mobilization, but not inflation, which had been built into the social compromise with wage indexation, nearly full replacement wages for the unemployed, and rank and file mobilization (cf. Chapter 12).

The Germans also supported the efforts of Barre, appointed prime minister by President Valéry Giscard d'Estaing in September 1976, to impose a wage and price rise ceiling and align the franc with the DM in view of monetary union, but the inflationary differential continued due to increased social wages and industrial credits necessary to avert a left-wing electoral victory. Schmidt initially offered France and the weaker currency states more facilities in the ERM negotiated in 1978, a divergence indicator and European cooperation fund with the reciprocal duty of Germany to reflate when its currency rose above the average, but these concessions were either vetoed by the Bundesbank or rendered moot by the Carter-Volker interest rate jolt (Heisenberg, 1999).

Worried about their first trade deficit since the post-war period in the world downturn of 1980 the Germans emulated the Americans and passed on the higher interest rates to their trading partners via the EC and ERM. The German-led ERM thus tipped the balance of forces against labor toward national realignments around Catholics and liberals wedded to neo-liberal policies. This happened in the Netherlands and Belgium in 1981, in Denmark with the Socialist surrender of government to conservatives in 1982, with the French Mitterrand turnabout of 1983 and the de-indexation of wages in Italy under the modernist Socialist Bertino Craxi in 1984 that ended the last elements of resistance to ERM monetarism. Christian Democracy, which had always been economically conservative, was pivotal in this neo-liberal turn, abandoning its concern for social justice and the plight of the poor even in the Low Countries where they had made a difference. Right-wing Socialists appealing to aspirational middle-class voters supported the move while many left-wingers disoriented by the turnabout acquiesced in favor of a more integrated Europe. Monetarism and Europeanism reinforced each other, making national liberals and Gaullists more European and internationalist socialists more monetarist, especially when promised a social dimension by Delors in 1988 (Chapter 6).

The new neo-liberal governments aligned their currencies with the DM and imposed austerity programs, which doubled the rate of unemployment from five to ten percent, stabilized social costs and reduced the wage share of national income by between 8 and 12 percent between 1981 and 1986. By the late 1990s unit labor costs had been diminished by 13 percent since the 1970s. From 1980 to 1993 taxes on corporations fell by 10 percent while those on wages increased 20 percent.[10]

Inflation could also have been tackled through investment and productivity but that was not possible with real short-term rates at 6 percent and long-term rates double those of the 1960s. The EC as a whole grew only 1.9 percent per annum from 1981 to 1987 with industrial production at 1.3 percent, real wages 1 percent and investment at only 0.8 percent. Premium ERM interest rates raised the return on financial paper thus encouraging self-financing and mergers and acquisitions especially in the US and heightened with unemployment the rate of labor exploitation through job shedding, union repression, wage compression and subcontracting. There was little sign of the technological modernization promised by the Commission and governments; on the contrary productivity growth over the long haul declined. Neo-liberal policies restored rates of profitability but not those of investment, productivity gains, and growth, which remained at half the level of the golden years (Husson, 1996; Oatley, 1997, 147–50; Duménil and Lévy, 2000).

When Mitterrand was elected president in 1981 with a Communist-inspired program of nationalization, job creation, and enhanced welfare spending he posed a direct challenge to the Germans and the ERM if not to the existence of the EC itself. EC integration could go nowhere so long as Mitterrand pursued his program. While France was growing by 2 percent in 1982 and holding unemployment steady, the rest of the EC following Germany was deflating with declining wages, growth, and employment. Mitterrand ignored restrictions on state aid not to speak of the liberal spirit of the treaty and increased trade and payments deficits as well as the inflation differential with the Germans. They applied pressure on the French to halt their reflation, possessing an ally in Delors, finance minister, who had always opposed Mitterrand's program and who was joined in 1982 by the moderate Socialist prime minister Pierre Mauroy. The first major turnabout came in June 1982 with wage de-indexation, which, approved by the EC Monetary Committee before it went to French cabinet, reduced real income by nearly 2 percent (Moss and Michie, 1998, 66; Centre, 1989, 20, 43; Lecointe *et al*, 1989, 146–8).

The crunch decision came in Spring 1983 when Mitterrand considered a plan to leave the ERM and erect protectionist barriers in order to pursue his program of reindustrialization. He was blocked by pro-EC marketeers in cabinet, led by Delors and the Catholic-inspired "second left", who represented the margin of electoral victory. In order to obtain a small

German re-valuation he had to accept an austerity package of higher taxes and budget cuts that reduced domestic consumption by 2 percent of GDP. In order to encourage private investors to replace the public, Mitterrand did a complete turnabout with financial de-regulation, public sector wage and budget cuts, partial privatization, and alignment of the franc with the DM at premium interest rates.

The turnabout was taken to prove the impossibility of Keynesian socialism in one country, but it really exposed the fault in Mitterrand's majority between the working-class oriented Marxian left and the "second left" of Catholic origin, which appealed transversally to professional and managerial personnel, the aspirational middle classes. While the former had been hit hard by unemployment and looked to the state for help, the latter still held expectations of rising income and status generated by the golden years. They were culturally liberal, emancipated from traditional Catholicism but economically conservative, opposed to nationalization and the Communists. It was the differential class experience of the 1970s economic crisis between working and middle classes that underlay ideological divisions over nationalization and European integration and that ultimately defeated Mitterrand's program (Chapter 6, cf. Callaghan, 2000).

European integration replaced socialism as the grand project that justified his turnabout. As president of council in 1984 Mitterrand found the easiest way to advance integration was to implement treaty provisions for a single market, eliminating non-quantitative barriers to free trade: health and safety, compositional and technical standards, border controls, and national preference in public procurement. National standards were supplanted by the principle of mutual recognition by which each member-state was bound to accept goods sold legally in any other. According to Hayekian logic, this implied a race to the bottom, to the goods from the country with the cheapest and presumably lowest standards. Accompanying the initiative were plans to open up public utilities and transport to commercialization and privatization on the Thatcher model, to restrict state aids, adopt and enforce merger legislation, and end voluntary export restraints, vital to the car industry, which was accomplished by removing intra-EC border controls in December 1992 (Hanson, 1998).

To maintain DM parity the French still had to pay an interest premium because of their well-deserved reputation for laxity and rebellion. They wanted to move toward monetary union, but only on the basis of a softer common currency pegged to existing currencies for international exchange. As the monetary hegemon, the Germans defended the ERM status quo, which allowed them to undervalue the DM slightly for export purposes. With the alignment of all currencies with the DM after 1984 and the removal of capital controls in 1986 and 1990, the ERM became a system of virtually fixed exchange rates that guaranteed balanced budgets and wage restraint. Since everyone had come to share the monetarist belief in the ineffectuality of national macro policy and the economy was on the uptake in the late 1980s, nobody foresaw the possibility of the ERM crisis that occurred in 1992 or the need for a single currency to achieve the permanent stabilization of wages, prices, and exchange rates (Bakker, 1996; Balleix-Banerjee, 1999; Howarth, 2001).

The single currency was the work of Mitterrand, a failed socialist, convinced of the vanity of national macro policy, who wanted to leave a monument of European construction to posterity. When he accepted a proposal for it from the German Liberal Foreign Minister Hans-Dietrich Genscher in February 1988 and then reached an understanding about it with Kohl in June he acted in the foreknowledge that France would have to bow to the rigorous fiscal and monetary terms of the Bundesbank. Having swallowed these conditions, Mitterrand allowed his ministers to defend traditional policies and the need for a democratically responsible ECB in order to please the socialist gallery and win negotiating chips for other issues. In December 1988 he instructed the governor of the Bank of France to accept German convergence criteria in the Delors Committee that set the terms for EMU and later even outbid the Germans in rigor, demanding a 1 percent deficit limit. The EMU that emerged at Maastricht in 1992 was the result of prior undertakings between Mitterrand, Kohl, and the Bundesbank in Spring 1988 (Chapter 7).

The antilabor thrust of EMU was announced in both the Delors and specialist Emerson Report, which was endorsed by UNICE (Dyson, 1994, 118). While UNICE officially spoke of savings in transaction costs and risk premiums they thought the best advantage of EMU was that it would put downward pressure on wages and social costs (Verdun, 1996). The burden of adjustment for differences in competitiveness under a single hard currency would fall on wages and organized labor. As product markets became more competitive across borders, national unions would lose the power to set wages to local factor markets (Emerson *et al*, 1992, 24, 102, 147; Dyson, 1994, 250). Employers could rely on the neo-liberal consensus, the mass unemployment required by the NAIRU, new restrictions on strikes, bargaining, and wage increases and EC recommendations to keep wage increases below those of productivity (Hassel and Ebbinghaus, 2000; Featherstone, 2002).

The rise of unemployment and inequality coming after the growth blip of the late 1980s, contrary to Commission predictions, caused a crisis of popular confidence in national governments, private employers and the EU that became known after the near referendum defeat of Maastricht in France as the social divide between the people and the governing and ruling class. Philippe Séguin, Gaullist leader of the French Assembly, correctly identified Maastricht as a "social Munich", the greatest abdication of democratic responsibility by the governing and ruling classes since the capitulation to Hitler. The social divide was manifested everywhere in electoral abstention, the rise of the extreme right – and left in some cases – and nostalgia for the welfare state. Protest votes proliferated in the 1994 euro elections. More than half the electorate abstained in the elections of 1999 and 55 per cent in 2004. In 2001 a majority of those polled though favorable in principle to the EU were unhappy with its functioning. In spring 2002, as unemployment rose again, a majority in all but three countries said they would not care if it disappeared tomorrow. Less than half supported the Euro or expressed confidence in EU institutions (Eurobarometer, Spring 2002, 42–4; *International Herald Tribune*, January 22, 2004; *Le Monde*, February 26, 2004).

In a cumulative process an EMU created by market-oriented Catholics and Socialists drove them further to the right, making them indistinguishable to the voter and vitiating their propulsive role in European integration. The pro-EU left was more hurt by its policies than the right, which had less policy objection but little affective attachment. The Maastricht criteria made it virtually impossible for Social Democratic governments to meet expectations and pledges on wages and spending or on the chimera of a social Europe, which is why they were defeated after 1999 in Spain, Portugal, Italy, Denmark, and France, virtually so by a record low turn out in Britain and nearly so in Germany in 2002. Christian Democracy lost its propulsive force due to secularization, its own neo-liberal turn and overshadowing by more traditional conservatives like the British Conservatives, the former-Francoist Popular Party of Spain, Silvio Berlusconi's Forza Italia, or Bavaria's CSU (*Die Welt*, January 7, 2004; *Le Monde*, January 16, 2004). It was the right-wing government of Chirac that most directly challenged the Commission over the deficit limit and the German Social Democrat Gerhard Schroeder, who introduced Agenda 2010 for social cuts at the cost of his popularity in a sign of compliance. The main resistance to supranationalism in the constitutional negotiations of 2003 came from conservative leaders, notably Blair, Aznar and the Poles, defending neo-liberalism, national identity, and the US connection (Stuart, 2003, *Le Monde*, January 16, 2004).

The measures of positive integration initiated by the Commission were either undermined by EU market principles and forces or helped release them. Aid to high tech R&D opened up telecom and other public utilities and services to multinational penetration. Weakening national industrial policy, the EC became more technologically dependent on the US and Japan, falling further behind them in productivity and R&D despite the exhortations of the Lisbon summit.[11] Regional aid or structural assistance, doubled by Delors as a political-payoff and compensation for expected losses from the single market, was offset by ECJ rulings barring national discrimination in public procurement and by the budgetary constraints of monetary union (Moss and Michie, 1998, 152–3).

Despite the resounding statement of principles known as the social charter, which Delors used to win British labor over to the single market, the social dimension consisted of relatively consensual and costless measures – on health and safety, part-time employment, consultation, and so on – that were aimed more at individual rather than collective worker rights regarding unions, strikes, and pay. The Maastricht criteria reversed the growth trend of public spending relative to GNP by 1996. Social spending relative to GDP declined after 1993 as entitlements became leaner and meaner with means testing, reduced benefits, income linking, and capitalization, the investment of funds in financial markets, the "third pillar" of EU social policy. Often imported from the US these reforms made it even less accurate to speak of a more redistributive European social model (Daley, 1997; Rhodes, 2002; cf. McNamara, 2001).

Financial globalization had a greater effect in undermining regional policy and union bargaining power, membership, and centralization, in the EC than it did elsewhere because its borders were so open (Verdier and Breen, 2001, 242–57). The only positive EC interventions that went beyond those of member-states concerned environmental protection, a post-materialist concern with a transborder dimension ripe for EC picking, and equal pay for equal work for women, introduced as a token treaty gesture to the French in 1957. Both policies were overtaken by market pressures in the 1990s – for lower pay for most women and less environmental regulation (Chapter 3).

Far from stimulating growth and employment, as the textbooks would have it, the EC fettered productive forces. An econometric comparison of sixteen advanced capitalist countries between 1951 and 1989 shows that excessive intra-EC exports and German-led monetarist policies led to 2.8 percent average annual per capita income growth among EC members, 20 percent lower than the 3.5 percent for non-members, with 4.4 percent more unemployment per annum and further cumulative job losses. Performance worsened with the onset of EMU in the 1990s. The EC gave an export bias to national economies leading to enlargement to cheaper contiguous markets, which weakened nationally organized labor, rather than to a deepening of their own, which might have strengthened it. Intra-EC trade soon reached its limits. Manufacturing trade stagnated from the 1970s among founding members and from the 1980s among the newcomers. Investment did so from the late 1990s (ch. 8, Lafay and Unal-Kesenci, 1990, 1997, 133; *International Herald Tribune*, January 22, 2004).

Members gained little from lower costs because of trade diversion from cheaper non-EU sources or from economies of scale, which were already optimal in most cases on the local and national level. With the possible exception of Belgium and the Netherlands, the greatest EC enthusiasts, few benefited from the comparative advantages of the division of labor since most EC trade growth was intra-sectoral, affecting quality range and brand appeal, rather than inter-sectoral, which would have caused national redistributional conflict and protest (Fontagné *et al*, 1997). The minor trade gains were more than offset by income losses due to the restrictiveness of monetary union after 1979. The slowdown of French growth occurred, for example, when they switched from the more flexible interest rates practiced by the Americans to disciplinary German ones (Chapter 8).

Standard accounts attribute the triumph of monetarism in the EC to US-led globalization, especially the currency and capital mobility unleashed by the breakdown of Bretton Woods (cf. Moravcsik, 1998a). The initial effect of this mobility was to encourage labor mobilization and the wage–price spiral but the Germans began to retrench as early as 1973 and apply leverage as regional hegemon on trading partners, notably France and Italy in 1976. Though Republican administrations turned antilabor, they generally pursued expansive macro policy. It was only when the Fed raised interest rates in 1979 and the Germans, true to ordo-liberalism, chose to follow, that effective pressure was brought to bear as ERM members reduced the growth of money supply by half with convergence to high real interest rates, low inflation, nominal wage growth, and exchange rate stability.

The ERM countries were the pioneers of monetarism, the only ones to master inflation and to fix high interest and exchange rates, also the only ones to suffer mass unemployment and job insecurity, in the 1980s (Oatley, 1997, ch. 4 esp. table 4). EC monetarism preceded and exceeded in rigor that in the rest of the world. Capital mobility did not diminish inflation or the volatility of exchange and interest rates elsewhere in the 1980s. Long-term interest rates remained high due to the flight of capital from industry to financial investments bearing greater risk (Block, 2000). With greater macro and exchange rate flexibility the US managed an industrial recovery and high tech boom in the 1980s and 90s; so did the British with the less solid Lawson boom in the late 1980s and moderate growth in the 90s. Monetarism triumphed early in Western Europe because of the EC and monetary union.

Excessive trade interdependence within a German-led ERM certainly limited the effectiveness of national expansionism as Mitterrand discovered, but it was his decision to remain in the ERM and follow EC rules, a choice dictated by social and ideological divisions in his left majority. The macro regimes of France and Italy were better able to check deflationary global forces than the open economies of Germany and the Netherlands only so long as they were backed by protectionist coalitions. Neo-liberal business forces took advantage of the ideological and social cleavages between right Socialists, including former Catholics, favorable to the EC and the market, who appealed to the aspirational middle classes, and the diminishing number of left ones, who defended the traditional working class against unemployment and poverty.

The Mitterrand turnabout signalled an EC-wide Socialist shift in attention from workers and unions to the middle classes, from macro expansion to austerity and central bank independence and from national development to European integration, which helped motivate and justify the shift (Oately 1997, ch. 4; Marks, 2000; Callaghan, 2000). Monetary union yielded more unemployment and welfare retrenchment after 1990 contrary to EC assurances and expectations, touching the middle classes for the first time. It produced disenchantment with the EC and the social divide, that inchoate rebellion against the ruling and governing classes, most dramatically in France, but not any coherent political alternative because by that time left parties and programs had been so marginalized and demoralized by the neo-liberal consensus, the *pensée unique*, that they were incapable of resistance (Chapters 6, 7, Moss, 1998).

Constructed around competitive market principles and supported primarily by employers, especially large exporters and multinationals, the EC could only develop in a neo-liberal direction (cf. Gillingham, 2003). Its provisions for internal liberalization were invoked by domestic capital to dampen labor mobilization and resolve the crisis of profitability that broke out in the 1970s. The European Round Table of multinationals and UNICE became the chief lobbies for the single market and currency. They were supported electorally by professional and managerial personnel, who saw advantage in the competitive market, and opposed by workers, who felt threatened by it. Reinforcing declining wage share and growing inequality the EU became increasingly seen as an instrument of globalization, less clearly as a capitalist one. It created a backlash that extended the anxious, insecure, and protesting working class, most manifestly in France, to middle-class wage-earners, public, professional and even managerial personnel, who had remained immune to the crisis of the 1970s (Chapter 6).

The EC advanced in moments of market optimism – the 1950s, 60s and late 80s – and stalled in periods of crisis and doubt – the 1970s, 90s and after 2000. The monetarism and neo-liberalism of the EC, ERM and EMU helped halt the expansion of wages and benefits in the long boom and put downward pressure on wages and benefits in the long recession, slowing the growth of nominal and real wages, reversing the growth of public spending and forcing governments to commercialize and privatize public utilities and services. Despite the stickiness and opaqueness of national markets it began to exercise downward pressure on wages through product competition in the late 1970s and again after 1995 much as wider globalization would later undermine the bargaining power and protections of labor and the wage share of export rents in all advanced capitalist countries (Rodrik, 1999; Andersen *et al*, 2000; Arestis, 2003). As the strictest disciplinarian and enforcer of wage and price stability, the EC, ERM and EMU restored profitability at the expense of investment, productivity, employment, and wages. A pioneer of globalization, it fulfilled the neo-liberal function of a Hayekian federation in compressing wages and constraining labor.

Notes

1. For the sociology and politics of academic Euroenthusiasm see Moss, 2001b, for earlier critiques Jaumont *et al*, 1973; Holland, 1980; Moss and Michie, 1998.
2. Cf. *id.*, McNamara and Jones, 1996; Moravcsik, 1998a; Moss, 1998; Hay, 1999; Gillingham, 2003.
3. E.g. Wessels, 1997; Mény *et al*, 1996; Cowles *et al*, 2001; Hodson and Maher, 2003.

4. Eighty per cent of their salaries for three years, British Secretary of State for Education.
5. Lafay, 1990, 1997, 133; Glyn, 1998; Andersen *et al*, 2000; *International Herald Tribune*, January 15, 22, 2003.
6. Anthony Giddens, 1998, head of the London School of Economics, was the leading exponent.
7. Hibbs, 1987, ch. 3; Franzese, 2002; Friedman, personal note; Marglin and Schor, 1990; Freeman, 1994, 318; Heylen and Poech, 1995; Busch, 1993, 52–3.
8. This argument, based on later writings, 1972, 1991, elaborates upon an article written in 1937, Hayek, 1949; Tomlinson, 1998.
9. Grande, 1983; Epstein, 1990, 141; Marchand and Thélot, 1991, 585; Oatley, 1997, ch. 4.
10. Aeshimann and Riché, 1996, 48; Oatley, 1997, ch. 4; Huemer *et al*, 1999, 63; Hassel and Ebbringhaus, 2000.
11. Friedman, 1998 ch. 10; Fontagné *et al*, 1997; Bourry, 1993; Lafay and Unal-Kasenci, 1997, 133; *Times*, January 15, 2003.

Part I

History of the European Community

2
The Neo-liberal Constitution: EC Law and History

Bernard H. Moss

The EC was founded on a vision of a market economy untrammeled by the social and public regulation arising from or sustained by the nation state. It was a vision much closer to that of the ultra neo-liberal Friedrich Hayek than that of Jean Monnet, putative father of Europe, who initially opposed it as too market-oriented for his compatriots. It was not merely about external trade, but about transforming national domestic regimes for integration in a single competitive market. The drive for an "open market economy with free competition" (Maastricht Treaty, arts. 3a and 102a) was fundamental for employers and other capitalists because it assured the exploitation of labor under optimal conditions for profitability. State regulated or welfare state capitalism was a second best compromise forced on business by exceptional circumstances like war and the mobilization of working class power. The lineaments for a new competitive market order were traced in the EC's charter documents – the Beyen Plan of 1953, the Spaak Report of 1956, and the Rome Treaty with its provisions, principles, and logic as interpreted and enforced by the Commission and the European Court of Justice (ECJ). The project was neo-liberal rather than simply liberal because it required the intervention of strong executive and judicial EC authority to break the power of the nation state to regulate markets and capital and to enforce the competitive market allocation of resources.

The Rome treaty was all about negative integration the breaking down of barriers to the free flow of goods, services, capital, and labor. It sought to eliminate or commercialize all forms of national and public protection, including nationalized industries and public services, state aids and preferential procurement, discriminatory taxation, and product standards, and by implication competitive devaluations and counter-cyclical macro policy, which stimulated growth and fuller employment. Negative integration, the removal of state barriers, was made self-executory, but provisions for positive intervention or constructive integration like the social fund and investment bank were much diminished, omitted like social and industrial policy or subjected like transport, commerce, and agriculture to the rule of unanimity. The turning point of the negotiations occurred when the French conceded to the Germans the principle that social advances would have to come primarily from the functioning of the market.

The EC embodied the long-term interests of those chiefly responsible for its principles and design (*contra* Pierson, 1996, 34), the West Germans, the exporting and monetary hegemon, Christian Democrats, who governed in most member-states, the US, who patronized and indirectly financed it, and business, which supported it, not just large exporters, but the entire employer and capitalist class (Fligstein, 1995; cf. Moravcsik, 1998a). Like the neo- or ordo-liberal economists who espoused their cause, business endorsed the enlarged competitive market under sound money as a means to prevent wage-led inflation and check and roll back labor gains under the interventionist welfare state.

With its principles of competitive allocation, non-national discrimination, and the four freedoms of goods, services, capital, and labor the treaty set integration on a neo-liberal course that precluded the development of truly social, regulated or planned economies. Once the ECJ quite unilaterally determined the supremacy of European over national law, the EC became an instrument for the liberalization of nation states. This liberalization went beyond the intentions of most of the signatories and butted up against the rising power of labor and the welfare state in the EC's formative years. Member-states were free to resist full implementation of the treaty, as they did in the 1960s, but could only invoke it to move society in a liberal market direction.

Despite the neo-liberal spirit and letter of the treaty few commentators anticipated fixed exchange rates, the single currency or the attack on the mixed economy including such features as state aids and preferential procurement, subsidized public services and nationalized industries, product standards, and counter-cyclical macro policy (Machlup, 1976). The attack on the interventionist state and organized labor was a response to the unanticipated crisis caused by the breakdown of Bretton Woods and the worker mobilization, which accelerated inflation and led to a profitability squeeze (Armstrong, 1991; Helleiner, 1994; Brenner, 1998). This polarized social forces and impelled a choice between deepening socialism and a monetarist turn to German-type neo-liberalism. The EC and monetary union provided the external constraint and ideological justification for moving society in a market direction.

The EC is usually discussed as a supranational project without reference to political or class orientation and purpose. The issues debated were not those of class or ideology but of supranational or inter-governmental power. The claim was made for the EC's political neutrality as between the liberal and socialist tradition, either because it represented a median social democratic or technocratic third way or because it was deemed completely adaptable, reflecting the political preferences of its national constituents and the existing balance of forces within them. Blindness to the neo-liberal orientation and constraint constituted by the EC was linked to an apologetic view of a capitalism that was supposedly transformed after the Second World War by the interventionist welfare state.

Since the EC largely adopted the institutions and supranational ideal of the European Coal and Steel Community (ECSC), it was easily mistaken as a mere continuation of it. Extrapolating from the frustrated interventionism of the ECSC, Ernst Haas (1958), the American founder of EC studies, predicted the EC would become a social democratic suprastate within ten years. Alan Milward (1984, 1992), historian of post-war reconstruction, explained it as the product of mixed economies, of nation states pursuing mercantilist, welfare, and redistributive goals. A leading constitutional authority stressed the primacy of its free market principles, but noted the authorization of public ownership and scope for public intervention and planning (Kapteyn, 1989, 80–3). Few could miss the liberal orientation of the single market and currency, yet still perceived the EC as contested terrain between free marketeers and redistributive interventionists (e.g. Hooghe and Marke, 1999; Gillingham, 2003). Nobody outside the old Left saw that the EC constituted in itself, apart from other factors, a barrier to social and public regulation, social democracy, and socialism, that its principles, institutions, and practices militated in favor of monetarism and neo-liberalism in Europe.

The Rome treaty was understood not as a radically new free market departure from previous plans for constructive integration, but as a successor to the ECSC, a compromise between the statist French and liberal Germans. Was not Monnet, an American-oriented French merchant and financier, a pragmatist willing to use state planning, regulation, and trade union collaboration to rebuild Europe (Duchêne, 1991)? Did not the Christian and Social Democrats, the driving political forces, want to achieve the kind of social partnership and reform in the EC that had eluded them at home? Was not it prologue to a fully planned socialist society according to André Philip (1957, 250–4), leader of the Socialist European Movement?

The first Commission charged with removing tariff barriers set up the Medium-term Committee under the French Robert Marjolin to explore on the margins the possibilities for planning and trade union participation. The first EMU outlined in the 1970 Werner Report was a project for a single currency under a parliamentary state with a recognizable social and regional dimension. These were also essential components of Delors' plans to achieve class reconciliation in a federalist Europe. The minimalist achievements of social Europe were, however, vitiated by EC market principles and forces if not actually designed to foster them. Social Europe was a powerful myth, deployed by the Commission and others, to disarm union, worker, and social democratic opposition to the free market agenda.

The myth of social Europe was linked to misconceptions about the nature of post-1945 capitalism. Bedazzled by the contrast with the Depression years and anxious to present their system in the best possible light in view of the Cold War, Western scholars talked of a modern or late capitalism that had been transformed by the changing balance of public and private power.[1] State regulation, planning, collective bargaining, welfare spending, and Keynesian demand management had supposedly achieved both sustainable growth and social equity, wages rising with profits, moderating the business cycle and unemployment and thus reasons for class conflict. Five years after Andrew Shonfield (1965) of the LSE proclaimed the end of class conflict under modern capitalism in the text of reference he had to call for restricting union rights in order to arrest the strike upsurge in Britain (Panitch, 1976, 232). The sanguine view even rubbed off on the European Left. It mistook its political defeat for a change in the nature of capitalism, leaving it ill-equipped to understand the enduring crisis that began in the mid-1970s.[2]

The role of state and union power in promoting growth was vastly overblown. The same levels of wages and employment could be both a stimulus and inhibitor of investment at different phases in the long and short business cycle. The sources for the exceptionally high rates of growth in the takeoff after 1948 were classical, a high rate of exploitation made possible by the combination of large labor reserves, low wages, and a weakened labor movement with new technologies of assembly-line and continuous process production previously tested in the US (Gordon, 1982; Armstrong, 1991). The post-war miracle in Europe was both a catch-up to the US and a continuation of the growth and intra-European trade that had been cut short by depression and war (Carré, 1981; Bouvier *et al*, 1982, 1382–3; Moss, 1993). The EC was born after the defeat of the post-war labor upsurge and cutbacks of the welfare state after 1947–48, in the Cold War during the "economic miracle" of the 1950s presided over by business-oriented conservative governments, largely Christian Democratic, that had little time for planning, demand management, union rights, expanded welfare, or income redistribution (Brenner, 1998, ch. 2; cf. Milward, 1992).

The great performers of the golden years were those countries that disposed of cheap reserves of unskilled labor, Germans fleeing Communism in the East, Dutch youth, underemployed artisans and peasants from the south of Italy or the countryside of France (Kindleberger, 1967; Walker, 2000). The poor performers were those like Britain with labor shortages, especially of the skilled, which drove costs up even without union power. Having been divided and defeated by the onset of the Cold War, unions were weak and on the defensive both in France and Italy where the majority of Communists were blacklisted and collective bargaining virtually non-existent and in Germany and the Netherlands where Communists were purged and wage demands kept below unprecedented leaps of productivity. Wages remained below those of 1938 in France until 1955 and fell relative to national income in Germany. Parisian workers faced a high rate of job turnover and insecurity without unemployment insurance until 1958. The age of mass consumption, of the automobile in every worker's garage, was yet to dawn when student radicals denounced it in May–June 1968.[3]

The 1950s saw a reaction against income redistribution, demand management, union rights, and planning. The French plan, so much vaunted by Schonfield and others as a solution to the British disease of capital flight and industrial disinvestment, had been used to reconstruct basic energy and transport infrastructure but became merely indicative or suggestive after 1952, having virtually no effect on government spending or private investment (Chapter 6). The fiscal burden was shifted from corporations to workers with the introduction of the value-added tax on consumer items in France in 1954, which was eventually standardized in the EC. Welfare expenditure had doubled since before the war, but was still only half the level of the 1970s. It was more of the conservative Catholic-type in the EC, linked to income, occupation, and gender than the re-distributive variety found in Scandinavia (Esping–Anderson, 1990; Carpenter and Jefferys, 2000, 47, 100).

Keynesian demand management was taught, often as a substitute for socialism – Keynes himself feared wage-led inflation and sought long term fiscal balance – but it was never really applied. It was deployed only erratically in France, more to subsidize business than to increase consumer spending and not at all in Germany, Italy, and Belgium where monetarist central banks tried to rein in inflation. In France and Italy, governments fought inflation caused by pent-up wartime demand and goods shortages and spending on reconstruction and industrial investment and on the Korean and French colonial wars. The British practiced fine-tuning within the basic parameter of wage restraint (Panitch, 1976) but more to slow the economy because of balance of payments problems rather than to stimulate it. Governments expanded the money supply to accommodate real growth not to increase popular demand. Italy was the only country to run fiscal deficits. It was not until the end of the long post-war boom in the 1970s that governments accommodated labor with monetary expansion and produced small fiscal deficits.[4]

The country that most shaped the EC was West Germany, the dominant exporter, which held a large trading surplus and foreign reserves. It was guided by the ordo-liberal philosophy of wage and price stability, free trade, and the sanctity of the market process (Peacock, 1989; Giersch, 1992). The currency reform of 1948, which restricted bills in circulation, and mass migration from the East, which augmented joblessness, weakened and demoralized the socialist labor movement, which was forced to adjust to the "social market" economy. Because German Social Democracy was originally Marxist it was more interested in ownership and control, in codetermination, than Keynesian macro regulation, but the loss of the 1951 referendum on works councils tempered its militancy and made it submit to market forces. Labor peace was essential as Germany was on the front line in the worldwide struggle against Communism. German workers rebuilt strong and centralized unions, but they were subject to Cold War constraints, ideological, juridical and monetary, that made the country practically strike free (Jacobi, 1986; Moneckonberg, 1986; Streeck, 1994).

The Bundesbank, given an independent status in 1957, practiced tight money polices and sterilized foreign reserves by selling bonds to prevent imported inflation. The government ran budget surpluses that slowed growth (Epstein, 1990, table 3.5). Keynesian counter-cyclical policy was virtually unknown until the Brandt government of 1969 when it was not needed. The great fear of the establishment was that inflation imported from its trading partners – American financiers probably had a better memory of the runaway inflation of 1923 – would stir up labor agitation and social instability, which is why it wanted to extend domestic discipline via European integration and the EC (cf. Pittman, 1993; Dickhaus, 1996).

Though the mainsprings for growth in Europe were domestic, trade was necessary to obtain German capital goods and for further expansion, but trade alone does not explain EC principles, institutions, and design. European trade could have been arranged otherwise through bilateral or multilateral, selective or transitional agreements, or through a free trading area that did not directly challenge internal domestic regimes as advocated by Erhard and major German exporters. Why did it take the form as Pierre Mendès-France, former French prime minister, complained, of the nineteenth-century competitive market economy rather than the managed trade that he – and the French generally – preferred (Marjolin, 1986, 293; Bossuat, 1996, 138–9, 217, 226, 256)?

The answer is that the EC was not simply the expression of export interests (cf. Moravcsik, 1998), but the result of a constellation of concerns and interests, export, macroeconomic, European federalist, security, and Cold War geo-politics (Moss, 2000). Through the compromises and complexities of the treaty, one economic logic and vision shone through. It was the German ordo-liberal one of a single competitive market under a sound currency free of social or public regulation (cf. Gillingham, 2003). The free market agenda announced clearly in the Spaak Report and Commission programs was welcomed by Christian Democrats, the US, and business as a check on the inflationary demands of organized labor and the interventionist state.

The EC was a radically liberal departure from previous constructive schemes for European integration. It drew on the anti-interventionist sentiments of the Germans and business community that had blocked detrustification, industrial reconversion, and the power to fix prices and quotas in the ECSC (Haas, 1958; Gillingham, 1991). The clash of mercantile interests had scuppered attempts at constructive sectoral integration over tariffs, transport, and agriculture (Trausch, 1993; Brusse, 1997). Since the Common Market had first been mooted in 1953, the Six had assumed that the removal of tariffs would be accompanied by common policies on wages, employment, and social policy (Milward, 1992, 189–98). A common market had the advantage of hiding the clash of interests in the invisibility and objectivity of the market place following the dictum of Adam Smith (Chapter 1, Müller-Armack, 1957, 534). The Messina resolution that relaunched EC negotiations included the sectoral integration of transport, energy and communications and common economic, financial, and social policy (Gerbet, 1983, 200). These projects for positive integration were dropped, probably under German influence, in the Spaak Report written by Pierre Uri (cf. 1989, 114–17), Monnet's assistant, and Hans von der Groeben (1987), a German financial official.

Far from advocating mixed economies, the Report adumbrated the neoclassical utopia of a single competitive market with low external protection minus the distortions caused by national taxes, price controls, social security, devaluation, or legislated working conditions. Unlike previous projects it did not demand political, budgetary, financial, or social integration. Aside from a modest market-oriented Investment Bank and Social Fund, it relied on the market and labor migration to promote structural change and to harmonize wages and benefits. Employers could only maintain competitive prices within the enlarged market if unions respected productivity limits. Above all, the report called for an independent Commission with the power of initiative and the responsibility for enforcing market rules against recalcitrant states and for eventual qualified majority voting (QMV) rather than unanimity, which would create a truly supranational state. It suggested a single currency as a form of external discipline against excessive wage and price hikes. The EC was viewed as a transitional regime laying the economic foundations for a truly united Europe (Spaak, 1956).

The driving political forces behind European integration were the governing Christian and auxiliary Social Democrats, who formed a third force in France between Communists on the left and Gaullists on the right. Pursuing restrictive policies at home in coalition with conservatives, they embraced the European project as a trademark of centrism, as a substitute for internal social reform, an alibi explaining domestic failure and as a psychological escape from it. As the left-Catholic dean of French political science Maurice Duverger put it: "The myth of supranational Europe was the way to escape unbearable reality by taking refuge in imaginary worlds" (cited in Lemaire-Prosche, 1990, 35). "We are the party of Europe," said one delegate to the French Catholic MRP conference, "out of revenge for the failure and difficulties experienced in our social policy" (cited in Irving, 1973, 187).

Despite its charitable posture, a solicitude for the poor and family welfare, and respect for the person, more as a soul than as a citizen, Christian Democracy was wedded to the defense of property, markets, and sound money as guarantors of individual autonomy and responsibility against the intrusions of the collectivist democratic state.[5] Catholics acquired their attachment to property in centuries of struggle against the emerging democratic state with its leveling materialistic and collectivist – socialist or Communist – tendencies (Moss, 2001a). The personalism of Emmanuel Mousnier gave some Catholics a socialist tilt in collaboration with the Communists after the war (Hellman, 1981), but most reverted to form with the onset of the Cold War, becoming the group most hostile to Communism.

In defense of balanced budgets Christian Democrats usually opposed social spending and income redistribution, siding with employers on the crucial issues, notably in the European Parliament (EP).[6] They advocated a corporatist form of social security linked to income and existing hierarchies of profession, wealth, and gender (Esping-Anderson, 1990). Catholic devotion was highly correlated to right-wing voting and property ownership in France – as a bulwark of social order and perhaps also a prepurchase on heaven (Michelat and Simon, 1985).

The ideological rationale and rhetoric for the EC came mostly from Christian Democrats. A large competitive market, they said, was better equipped than the state to guarantee prosperity, create more property owners and therefore ensure more equal distribution of wealth (Haas, 1958, 24). They imparted to the EC spiritual values, born of the Middle Ages, that were consistent with the liberal pluralism of the expanding middle classes (see Chapter 4): guild corporatism, the familial partnership of workers and employers, subsidiarity, the respect for local prerogatives, and federalism, three doctrines that were used to check the power of socialist unions and the democratic state. Catholics could recognize in the fragmentary and decentered structure of the EC their own Holy Roman Empire preserving spiritual and property values from the encroachment of the nation state.

While Christian Democrats used the EC to preserve the status quo, Socialists endowed it with hopes for a more egalitarian future. Their European commitment was the result of the 1947 break with Communist Parties, which thrust them to the side of anti-Communist conservative governments. European federalism became a substitute for national social reform, which was justified in Marxist terms by growing economic interdependence and proletarian internationalism. The French Socialists joined the wage-cutting government of René Pleven in 1950 because it was pro-European. The enemy, said Philip, was the state. The contradictory reasoning made sense only in the long term. The EC would yield prosperity on the American model by creating a larger competitive market while providing instruments for eventual regulation on a larger scale. It would work with America to defeat Communism and also allow European initiative in case America faltered. It was almost always the most right-wing Socialists, the most anti-Communist and market-friendly, who pushed EC integration, throwing doubt on their rhetoric about a socialist Europe.[7]

West Germany gave the strongest imprint to the EC because it concentrated those economic, ideological, and class forces that lay behind it. The constitutional duty of price stability was imposed both by the savers who financed German industry through the big banks and by exporters who wanted to keep labor costs and prices low. As the capital goods hub of the West European trading network, Germany had by 1955 accumulated a huge trading and reserve currency surplus, which it could use as leverage against its weaker currency partners (Milward, 1984; Pittman, 1993; Dickhaus,

1996). Governed by Christian Democracy it could count on the support of ruling parties elsewhere that shared its spiritual and "social market" values. Its liberally ordered "economic miracle" was an inspiration and model for European capital everywhere. The person who invented the slogan of the "social market economy" for the 1948 elections was also the chief German architect of the Rome treaty, Erhard's advisor Armand Müller-Armack, who tried to make it as liberal as possible. The EC replicated the "intermeshing" features of German ordo-liberalism: a federalist structure for a competitive market with low external tariff and sound currency – the ECB was later modeled directly on the Bundesbank – and a presumption against state interference in the market process (cf. Risse-Kappen, 1996).

Chancellor Konrad Adenauer wanted a Europe that would keep the Soviets out, the Americans in and France on his side. Erhard was more interested in global free trade or at least a zone including Britain and Scandinavia. German employers in the BDI, the Bundesverband Der Deutschen Industrie, and financiers in the Bundesbank had their heart and purse with Erhard but their reasoning with Adenauer because he offered a security guarantee in partnership with the French for maintenance of the ordo-liberal regime. Fearing imported inflation, Müller-Armack (1957, 534, 1971, 10) and the Bundesbank (Dickhaus, 1996) were looking for an international regime that would set tight budgetary and trading deficits among its partners.

The Foreign Office and Erhard agreed on a common objective of a single competitive European market enforced by national administrators and a supranational executive. Both the Germans and French feared too strong a Commission, the Germans because it might be too interventionist, the French because it might be too liberal. The treaty established a strong Commission wanted by the Benelux countries for the enforcement of competitive rules, but satisfied most other German desiderata: the rapid and automatic abolition of internal tariffs and high external ones as required by the American-dominated OEEC and General Agreement on Tariffs and Trade (GATT), competition policy, the restriction of state aids, a minimalist market-oriented EC investment and social fund, an adjustable currency peg permitting them to revalue the DM, disciplinary macro policy coordination, and the avoidance of French-style industrial or social policy. The treaty thus tilted toward the Germans and away from the French and Italians, who wanted more positive integration, including aid for countries with payments problems and weak currencies (Küsters, 1982, 273–6, 362, 372–3; Lee, 1995).

The French held a different socialistic view of Europe that proved to be more of an ideological overhang from the Liberation than a viable alternative. Nearly everyone in government and the administration opposed the Common Market on the grounds that it would allow states with lower wages and benefits, notably Germany, to undercut French producers (Bossuat, 1995). Older industries like textiles were fearful of competition, but newer ones like auto and electrical were, contrary to Malthusian legend, enthusiastic about finding new markets as was the peak employers' association, the Confédération Nationale du Patronat Français (CNPF). A cabinet committee made a submission for a fully planned and regulated system that would redistribute wealth to wage-earners much like the Soviet's trading system Comecon in the East (Marjolin, 1986, 186–8). The Foreign Office warned that the recommendations of the Spaak Report threatened French sovereignty and industry. They suggested a more "positive integration" of state holding companies and cartels with a monetary union to aid weak currency states (DDF, 1956, 11, 636–40, III, 103–5, 473).

Interest groups insisted that the reduction of tariffs be accompanied by the parallel upward harmonization of labor regulations and charges, safeguard clauses, and a French veto over passage to a second stage. These conditions stipulated by cabinet were overridden by Mollet, a fervent European, who thereby became the real father of the EC (Kocher, 1989; Bossuat, 260–352). The CNPF was the only interest group to favor irreversible integration. Once the die was cast it offered its support in return for lower taxes and charges and the abolition of price and credit controls and subsidies to meet the new competition. It could use the enlarged market with greater competition under a single currency to block and possibly roll back labor reforms, as a "disciplinary force against demagogic initiatives" (*CNPF Bulletin*, February 1957, 98), and to consolidate capitalism by binding labor and the Left with an external constraint.[8]

Business backing brought with it that of many conservatives and centrists who had previously opposed European integration, notably the European Defense Community, on nationalist grounds (Mahant, 1969, 77–96, 135–50, 196–4). German business also demanded an end to state interference, including the state aid they received. Employers, financiers, and merchants elsewhere welcomed the EC as a way to check and roll back the gains of organized labor and the interventionist state (Aron, 1957). Employer organizations and capitalists generally, contrary to common belief (e.g., Gough, 1979; O'Connor, 1979), never really accepted state capitalism or the welfare state. While labor was divided on the EC between Communists and social democrats and farmers skeptical – the French preferred existing bilateral arrangements – capitalists – not only exporters – were the one class that consistently supported European integration.

Negotiations reached an impasse on the social question in October 1956, specifically the standardization of overtime pay, which would have raised Germans costs by four percent. The Germans feared that it would fuel an inflationary spiral and jeopardize social stability. Negotiations were not resumed until Mollet and Adenauer reached a diplomatic understanding at the height of the Suez crisis when the US forced Britain and France to retreat from the Egyptian canal. France and Germany had already settled border questions and were undertaking a common defense, including missiles capable of carrying nuclear weapons (Bossuat, 1996, 337–47, 376). The EC settlement was strongly motivated by their desire to rollback Communism in both Eastern Europe and the developing third world. They would have doubtless sought compromise on the social question in any event, but the Suez crisis by exposing French isolation swung other ministers and deputies around to the EC. In return for formal social concessions, mostly hidden away in protocols that were never invoked, and aid to colonies, the French conceded the principle that social advances would have to come primarily from the functioning of the common market.[9]

Like the Spaak Report the treaty was mostly about negative integration, clearing away national barriers to free trade, or standardizing national laws to facilitate such trade (Kapteyn, 1989, esp. 76). The aim was to create a single market on the model of a national market without state distortions or discriminations – aids, taxes, regulations – in other words, a level playing field in a mythical state of nature (cf. Polanyi, 1956). Negative integration was made self-executory: (1) by courts, mostly as a result of subsequent ECJ jurisprudence, (2) by Commission decisions regarding tariff reduction, competition, state aid to industries and public services, price discrimination in transport, and trade negotiations with third parties, and (3) by its economic and monetary recommendations to member-states to maintain fiscal and monetary discipline presumably German style.

Provisions for positive or constructive integration like industrial and social policy were either absent from the treaty or so vague and undefined as to require unanimous council action, which was the case for agriculture, transport, and commerce. Actions under article 175 for the failure of the Community to act were far rarer than actions to overturn state regulation; even where the ECJ found failure it could not command the detail of action to be taken (Hartley, 1994, ch. 13). In any event, the ECJ held that treaty provision for industrial, transport, or social policy was too vague, undefined or unsubstantial to be justiciable. No policies except perhaps agriculture, the details of which were left in abeyance, could be allowed to distort competition.

Unlike the Spaak Report, which noted the twin danger of deflation, the treaty emphasized the fight against inflation and trade and payments deficits through the coordination of fiscal and monetary policy. Macro policy and exchange rates were to be treated as matters of common concern. Growing trade interdependence was expected to limit the independence of national, especially countercyclical macro policy. A provision neutralized the trade effects of devaluation, which France and Italy relied upon to stimulate growth. Implicit in the logic of the treaty drawn by the Commission and ECJ, which outlawed floating exchange rates in 1977 (Snyder, 1996, 96), were fixed exchange rates leading to a single currency. Contrary to the neofunctionalist argument that the EC was groping through trial and error and accidental spillover toward greater unity (ch. 4), the treaty and Commission (1962) announced its agenda and goal, moving toward a single market and currency under a supranational parliament and government, from the beginning (Chapter 1, Hallstein, 1962, 3–45; Dyson, 1994, 67–8).

The treaty required much more internal liberalization than the signatories except perhaps Germany had intended or could reasonably hope to implement without a domestic revolution.[10] Only ultraliberals like Hayek, who inspired German policy makers, could have imagined such a shift. The treaty was concluded with such haste that the French and Germans barely had time to read it. Like many others Mollet never believed it would be implemented in detail. Many Socialists expected to use it for social regulation and planning on a grand scale. The Commission surprised member-states by its determination to advance the supranational liberal agenda, which explains why most supported the antithetical Fouchet Plan of General de Gaulle to set up a supervening inter-governmental directorate (Soutou, 1993). Nobody foresaw the constitutionalization of the EC with an ECJ capable of imposing its decrees on recalcitrant governments. The signatories did not realize that they were creating a new liberal economic order with primary jurisdiction over member-states.[11]

The treaty had been signed in the halcyon days of rapid growth in order to expand trade among the Six. Despite the spirit and letter of the treaty few leaders or experts anticipated fixed exchange rates, the single currency or the single market assault on the mixed economy with its state aids and procurement, nationalization, and countercyclical intervention (Machlup, 1976, 1977). These were unanticipated consequences (cf. Pierson, 1996) of the treaty in an economic environment transformed by labor mobilization, profit squeeze, class polarization, and the choice posed between further socialization or monetarism.

The Commission established a series of committees – short-term, budgetary, monetary, and medium-term – composed of its own and national financial officials to achieve coordination but members experiencing strong growth from EC trade saw no need to change their distinctive macro regimes. The Marjolin committee recommended the use of industrial and regional planning on the French indicative model to achieve convergence and envisaged a common currency by 1970. The Commission wanted to give ECOFIN, the council of finance ministers, control over national budgets. The Germans, who preferred price stability to growth, opposed planning, while the French, who were reaching their growth stride in the 1960s, objected to a single currency (Denton, 1969; Moss and Michie, 1998, 14).

Despite his hatred of supranationalism General de Gaulle had been forced to go along with the EC because of employer and public support, the Franco-German entente and the need to torpedo negotiations over a free trade area with Britain (Bossuat, 1996, 380–419). De Gaulle wanted to confront the supranational pretences of the Commission, but waited until it abused its power before cutting it down to size. In 1965 the Commission went over the heads of governments to appeal for more taxing power for itself and parliament. De Gaulle reined in the power of the Commission and gave each member-state a virtual veto in vital matters under the Luxembourg compromise.[12] During the economic crisis of the 1970s members went their own way. Supranational integration was effectively halted until the hard ERM of 1981 and the 1984 single market initiative.

Until then the Commission had accommodated the neo-mercantilism of member-states regarding capital mobility, non-quantitative restrictions on trade, state aids, public procurement, and commercial monopolies. France and Italy were given exemptions on state aid. So were public utilities, the main sector for public procurement. Above all, public services were spared any scrutiny under article 90, which could require them to show why their non-competitive behavior was necessary in the public interest. All but Germany had wanted to retain capital controls to encourage domestic investment (Bakker, 1996, 19–25). Under the 1960 and 1962 directives members could still control short-term flows. Complete freedom for capital movement was not obtained until 1990. During the first decade of growing trade interdependence the withdrawal of the state from the commercial sphere was replaced by more state regulation in others. Member-states responded to the oil shock and economic downturn in divergent ways, the Germans and Dutch with austerity, the French and most others with inflationary growth rendering economic and monetary coordination untenable (Taylor, 1980; Hodges and Wallace, 1981).

Neither the member-states nor the treaty's judicial committee ever intended to set up a court possessing supreme and preemptive power over national jurisdictions, yet this was essential for its implementation (Moravcsik, 1998a; Heisenberg and Richmond, 1999). But once established the ECJ went beyond its remit and asserted its own independent power over the member-states with the supremacy of EC law. The ECJ justified going beyond the words of the treaty by reference to its spirit and general design and the requirements of a common market and closer union. It held in *van Gend en Loos* (1963), *Entel* (1964), and *ERTA* (1970) that EC law trumped all previous or subsequent national legislation and that it preempted national action in areas of EC competence.

Without the supremacy and uniformity of EC law, member-states would interpret it to their advantage, leading to cheating, reprisals, trade wars, and break-up, said the ECJ in *Entel*. It would become a mere intergovernmental regime subject to continuous negotiation. In the enthusiasm generated by the opening of the common market nobody seemed to notice these judicial assertions of supranational power. States never protested when rulings went against them because the balance of their interests were being served by the common market and its mechanisms of adjudication, monitoring, and enforcement (cf. Moravcsik, 1998, ch. 1). To the doctrines of supremacy and preemption was later added absorption, barring member-states from exercising their rights, for example over education, because it overlapped with an EC competence, in this case vocational training. With its doctrines of direct effect, the supremacy of European law, preemption, and absorption, the ECJ became a powerful instrument for trade integration and national deregulation (Stein, 1981; Weiler, 1981, 1991; Dehousse, 1998).

The judges, mostly European law professors appointed for a six-year term, who had a professional interest in task expansion, were guided by "a certain idea of Europe" (Judge Pascatore cited in Cartelier, 1996, 58) that incorporated the treaty's free market logic and agenda. They recognized that fundamental rights to property and enterprise and equal treatment constrained government action (Mertens de Wilmars, 1993, II, 10–14). Universalist law is better at removing barriers to free trade than at selective protection. It was a major vector of capitalism in doing away with the remnants of the feudal and mercantilist state in early modern Europe. Courts of general jurisdiction rather than administration are better equipped to enforce universal rules and poorly qualified to make the individual exceptions and discrimination that are usually required by intervention in the market, which resembles the level playing field of universal justice.

Enforcement was achieved through the doctrine of direct effect, which enmeshed the national courts in the process (cf. Burley, 1993). EC measures that were clear, precise, and self-evident were held to have direct effect in national law. *Van Gend en Loos* (1963) gave individuals the right to challenge national regulations in state courts under the preliminary ruling process of article 177. The ECJ extended individual rights far and wide. Although article 119 on equal wages for women was directed against states, the ECJ made it illegal for anyone to discriminate against them in employment matters. States were held liable to individuals for damage caused by the failure to transcribe a directive. While individuals could attack state power based on EC law, there was no symmetrical right for them to challenge the EC's action or inaction.

The EJC could expand EC competence by relying on the spillover built into treaty articles 100 and 101, authorizing the harmonization of national policies for the smooth functioning of the common market, articles 52–58 and 95 barring national tax, professional and business discrimination, and article 235 by which extra powers could be granted the EC to achieve delegated functions. With the force of law and economic logic behind it the EC could spillover its tasks into any area affecting the common market: (1) the largely uncontroversial regulatory domains of the environment, consumer protection, and health and safety, (2) mutually beneficial aid to R&D to improve competitiveness, (3) and even some income re-distribution in the politically contentious areas of regional, economic, and monetary policy (Pollack, 1994).

The ECJ made the EC a more unitary state than the US or Germany in juridical terms. There was no countervailing doctrine of rights reserved to the states as in the US Constitution. The principle of subsidiarity written into Maastricht set practical criteria for the extension of EC competence, which was already very broad and subject to task expansion. It has never been invoked and is probably not justiciable. There was no identifiable judicial camp or jurisprudence of states' rights. The anonymity of decisions and absence of dissent made it difficult to identify supranationalist judges though Kohl failed to renew the appointment of one in 1993. The apolitical magistery of the law made it remote and removed from the public, but difficult to challenge. Though rulings were reversed by council, the tradition of *acquis communautaire*, of irreversible achievements, made it difficult to do so. Once the market was deregulated, it was very hard, though not impossible, to reregulate. Charged with an arbitrating function over states' rights, the ECJ acted as both poacher and gamekeeper, encroaching upon national sovereignty for the sake of that "certain idea of Europe" (Rasmussen, 1986; Dehousse, 1998). That is why Britain and others periodically demanded a countervailing legislative body to defend states' rights.

If the EC did not become a unitary state despite the assertion of juridical supremacy, it was because the ECJ could only operate in the gray areas of the law as an auxiliary institution subordinate to council, Commission, and the EP and subject ultimately to the sanction of member-states. Judges were careful to act along with the Commission as "purposeful opportunists" (Winicott, 1995, 584), announcing audacious encroachments on sovereignty in theory, but treading warily in practice, often ruling for states on technical grounds. They waited until the general political climate had turned neo-liberal in 1979 to assert the doctrine of mutual recognition contained in the treaty by which each state was compelled to waive its own standards and accept the goods that were sold in any other member-state. After endorsement by the Commission and struggle within council the doctrine became the basis for the deregulatory single market program (Alter, 1994).

The judges worked in tandem with the Commission approving 86 percent of its contested measures (Stone Sweet and Caporaso, 1998, 121). Their ruling that mergers could constitute anti-competitive behavior in *Phillip Morris* (1987) forced council to adopt the 1989 Merger Regulation, which was used to abort alliances of industrial merit on simple competition grounds. Their reversal of the burden of proof regarding competition and public service – in air transport and telecommunications and later post, rail and energy – was the catalyst for wholesale commercialization and privatization (Pollack, 1998, 232–7). Yet, in the national and antiliberal backlash against Maastricht they for the first time recognized special states' rights – for Britain on Sunday trading and Ireland on abortion – and even under French pressure some notion of public service. Liberalization had reached a point of provoking objection and protest, which the Court in its quest for legitimacy as an impartial arbiter wanted to avoid (cf. Dehousse, 1998).

The Court and Commission took the initiative in completing the single market by proclaiming the principle of mutual recognition and inaugurating programs of aid to high tech R&D that invited private participation in public markets (Chapter 3). They acted in conformity with neo-liberal realignments in member-states. When Mitterrand as council president in 1984 canvassed members for a new integration project, he found agreement on the single market and appointed Delors as Commission president to pursue it (Moravcsik, 1991). Lord Cockcroft (1994), a businessman appointed by Mrs Thatcher, drafted a white paper with 300 items for eliminating barriers to competition – border controls, technical and compositional standards, indirect taxation, and public procurement. To remove barriers the Commission relied on the principle of mutual recognition, the setting of standards by private professional bodies, and a minimalist approach – only the essential requirements – to the harmonization of health and safety standards (Chapter 3).

The Single European Act (SEA) overcame the veto problem by allowing the harmonization of standards by QMV. In the absence of harmonization the principle of mutual recognition obtained, which is what happened in most cases. Notionally, this meant that the cheapest regulation, presumably the poorest, would prevail in most cases. The confiding of standard-setting to trade professionals, who normally worked for private industry, without affording opportunity for public investigation or judicial review removed all public consumer protection in the EC (Chapter 3, *contra* Majore, 1991, 1996).

The new consensus surrounding the single market facilitated the passage of other deregulatory measures that had been bottled up in Commission. The Commission's White Paper on telecommunications in 1987 endorsed the Thatcherite solution for the commercialization and privatization of public services. The Commission sought to end preferential public procurement, which served regional, technological, and employment functions amounting to 15 percent of EC GDP. New directives provided for monitored compliance and open awards based on the lowest price or most economically advantageous. This was strengthened with court rulings and council agreement to end national preference. One such ruling resulted in a huge loss of income for Southern Italy. The EC was so insensitive to local growth and employment concerns that its directives made negligible impact on actual practices (Martin, 1996, esp. 45–8, 1991).

A more liberal industry commissioner began to enforce the prohibition against state aids, encouraging states and companies to make complaints and demanding refunds from companies that did not fulfill commercial criteria (Pernin, 1996). In return for the recapitalization of Renault the French government had to promise to impose commercial criteria of profitability (Cohen, 1995, 42). The Commission tended only to approve short-term relief that reduced capacity rather than long-term plans for expansion. It was ruthless toward aid for the public sector. Under the merger regulation several acquisitions of industrial merit like that of the Canadian De Havilland aircraft manufacturer were denied on pure competition grounds (Bourgeois and Demeret, 1995, 72–5). Steps were also taken to end voluntary restraints on exports, enforced by border controls under article 115, of particular importance to European carmakers (Hanson, 1998). Under the single market program the EC began to tear at the fabric of European industry.

One rule of conduct common to Christian Democracy, Delors, and the Commission, was to accompany large concessions to private industry with token social measures either as side-payments to get labor on board or as compensation for their anticipated losses. Delors, who had traveled from Catholic unionism and politics to Mitterrand's new Socialist Party, was a master at posing neo-liberal policies in the guise of social democracy and justice (Chapters 3, 6, 7). He doubled structural funds to help those peripheral regions that might suffer from the new competition and extended them for political reasons to blighted industrial areas in the wealthier countries. To gain labor backing, especially in Britain where it had always been Euroskeptical, he reintroduced the "social dialogue" of the ETUC, the European trade union confederation, with the employers' UNICE, which had no authority to negotiate, and took up an ETUC draft for a workers' charter. Renamed the social charter, this was merely a declaration of principles that lacked the force of law. Finally, the SEA gave special status to environmental protection and speeded the passage of relatively consensual health and safety legislation by QMV (Moss and Michie, 1998, 145).

The Maastricht Treaty took a bold leap toward supranationalism with the single currency balanced with steps backward toward renationalization. The EMU regime instituted a hard single currency with controls on public finances that further restricted the functions of the EC and its members to those of the liberal state, which was at variance with the goals of employment and social cohesion (arts. 2, 102a). The allocation of resources through the competitive market became the guiding principle not merely a principal value of the EC (art. 103). When combined with the principle of proportionality in article 3b, this made it incumbent upon regulators to show that exemptions from competitive practice were clearly justified (Snyder, 1996, 39–40 [Verloren van Thematt]).

While supranationalism advanced with EMU it was restrained by the doctrine of subsidiarity and the recourse to variable geometry, relieving some states from responsibility for policies they did not like. For the first time the EC reserved a certain competence, education, for the states. Opt outs were granted to Britain and Denmark and exemptions to Ireland on abortion and to Britain for week-end trading as well as to countries not wishing to implement defense policy. Instead of a unitary structure the new EU covered three separate pillars, the EC, and two others, police, immigration and justice on the one hand and security and defense on the other, neither of which were subject to ECJ jurisdiction.

National interests reasserted themselves on the morrow of Maastricht. Ratification proved difficult in several countries chiefly because of a business downturn and rising unemployment that voters could blame on the tight money policies required by monetary union. Public support for the EU slumped even in such Europhilic states as Spain and Portugal (Cameron, 1996). The ruling Conservatives in Britain were split over the treaty. The Danes only approved Maastricht after receiving serious serial derogations from it. Mitterrand, the leader who had launched EMU, almost lost his referendum in

France, finding himself deserted by working-class supporters (Chapter 6). The resulting crisis of confidence forced Britain and Italy to leave the ERM in September 1992. The Maastricht decision of the German constitutional court challenged the supremacy of EC law as did constitutional proposals from Britain and Germany. Even the ECJ began to show deference for states' rights.

The post-Maastricht period was also one of retreat from EU activism. Delors' hopes of accompanying EMU with social reforms and proactive industrial policy were dashed. After establishing a few worker health and safety standards and minimal rights of consultation in European companies, the Commission abandoned active social policy and endorsed UNICE employer demands for work flexibility and lower public expenditures, social wages, and overall wages relative to productivity. Delors' proposal to create jobs via the funding of trans-European transportation, communication, and energy networks was rejected by the member-states, led by Germany, which were compelled by Maastricht to reduce expenditure. Under Jacques Santer the Commission recommended budget cuts and deflation as the way to increase investment and employment (Moss and Michie, 1998, 158–9).

When conservative French and German governments held fast to currency parity for the sake of EMU, they lost popular support and were replaced by governments with a socialist orientation. Jospin pledged to revise Maastricht but fell into line right after election in June 1997. The Social Democratic Schroeder government in Germany appointed a Keynesian finance minister Oscar Lafontaine, who challenged the monetarist orthodoxy of EMU before being obliged to resign. The commitment to European unity prevailed as governments cut public expenditures and social welfare, privatized and commercialized industry and public services, and restricted union rights in order to meet the convergence criteria (Chapter 3).

A reaffirmation of national competence and reluctance to delegate further power characterized the treaties of Amsterdam (1997), Nice (2001) and the constitutional Convention of 2003. Under a complicated formula at Nice QMV was extended to external trade, industry, environmental protection and eventually structural and cohesion funds, but not to the key one of taxation, which Britain continued to block. Precautions were taken against the new members from Eastern Europe by giving the major states a blocking minority in council, making sure the QMV of 74 percent represented at least 62 percent of the population.

Each state was still entitled to one commissioner, making for an unwieldy body of twenty-five members. Even under QMV consensus had always been sought. It would be much more difficult to achieve with Eastern states that had such different orientations, for the moment pro-American, ultra-liberal and very nationalistic, and much lower living standards – Polish wages were one fifth of the German – especially with new restrictions on EU resources for persuasive side-payments. The larger states could not hope to impose new integrative measures on the newcomers but demanded a blocking minority to protect existing advantages – CAP for the French, structural funds for the Spanish, and immigration controls for the Germans, Dutch, and Austrians.

The Convention of 2003 under the direction of former French president Valéry Giscard d'Estaing aimed at making final arrangements to accommodate the new states, demarcating national and EU powers and consolidating previous treaties in a single constitution that incorporated the declaration of fundamental rights approved at Nice. The preamble attempted to construct European values out of a pastiche of Catholic personalism, Western Enlightenment, American individualism, and ecology. The aim clearly stated in the third part was to complete the single competitive market without the distortions caused by public regulation while at the same time paying lip service to social policy and cohesion.

The major institutional innovations were designed for efficiency and to preserve some power for France and Germany especially in the realm of foreign and security affairs. the election of a Council president for two years and of a minister of foreign affairs and limiting representation on the Commission to fifteen countries, a streamlining that contained potential conflicts of power and authority. The draft codified existing law while innovating as had Maastricht in both supranational and the intergovernmental directions. On the one hand, QMV was extended to new areas, including culture and criminal justice, with a Passerelle Clause facilitating further extensions, while a reference to competences voided ECJ jurisprudence restricting the exercise of national powers. Under the denomination of the German term "social market economy" it codified the principles of neo-liberalism and the free market economy. While constitutionalizing the supremacy of European over national law, it also set up the EU as a highly visible target for national and class critics to assault, an attack made more likely to succeed by the impromptu decision of Blair in April 2004 to hold a British referendum on it.

The draft was challenged in the Inter-Governmental Conference (IGC) by Spain and Poland, which had received more council votes at Nice, the smaller states excluded from the Commission, and by Britain, which wanted clearer red lines drawn on taxation, social security, foreign and defense policy and the EU budget if not a return of some powers to the member-states (Stuart, 2003; Federal Trust, 2003–4,a,b). National interests were re-asserting themselves, paradoxically most strongly in those states on the periphery that were least bothered by the EU's neo-liberalism but where governments lived under the fear of defeat in a referendum. Acknowledging the impasse, governments abandoned treaty negotiations on 13 December, for the first time in EU history. The terrorist attacks in Spain and election of a Europhilic Socialist government there in March 2004 revived prospects for agreement, but the Blair announcement of a referendum made sure there would be no supranational breakthroughs, increased the pressure on member-states like France to hold one and heightened the chance of ultimate defeat at the hands of the electorate in several.

The European elections of 13 June 2004 expressed the decline of popular enthusiasm for the EU in older states and lack of engagement in the new Eastern members. National issues and protest against incumbent governments in defense of the welfare state took precedence over EU questions. The participation rate reached a new low of 45 percent. Eurosceptic parties made a breakthrough especially in Britain where UKIP, the British independence party, called for a withdrawal from the EU and in the Eastern accession states where turnout was an abysmal 19 percent. Even the normally optimistic Europhilic *Le Monde* (June 15, 2004) had to admit that this was a sad day for European integration.

Defying negative public opinion, EU governments nevertheless went ahead and made a series of complex compromises essentially between large and small states to secure a draft constitutional treaty on 18 June. Though the supremacy of European over national law had long been established by the ECJ, the constitution codified the emergence of the EU as a self-standing political community. The constitution incorporated the charter of fundamental rights, including social rights, making them available for reference in ECJ decisions. The only return of powers to member-states consisted of a provision allowing national parliaments to question the constitutionality of Commission proposals under the principle of subsidiarity. The constitution added to the fundamental rules of the "open market economy where competition is free" rhetorical flourishes about equality, justice, social dialogue, and solidarity that lacked means of enforcement.

Supranational power was further enhanced by extending QMV, qualified majority voting, to another thirty subjects – culture, education, criminal justice, immigration, asylum, etc. – with red lines drawn by the British under taxation, social security, defence and foreign policy. QMV was set at 55 percent of the member-states and 65 percent of the population, which gave greater weight to the major states with a large population but a blocking minority to smaller ones.

The constitution authorized a European Council president for two and a half years and a foreign minister sitting on both Council and Commission, thus creating a two-headed executive. The Commission was to be streamlined by 2014 to allow only a rotating two-thirds of countries voting power. The European parliament was given equal power with council in all matters subject to QMV and final authority over the budget.

A new Commission with a distinctive liberal flavour was put into place under the Nice treaty. The new president José Manuel Barroso, chosen by the twenty-five member-states, was pro-Atlantic and very market-oriented. He promised to fulfil the competitive terms of the Lisbon growth strategy. The new Commission he appointed relegated the French and Germans to minor positions. It contained a liberal Dutch business woman, Neelie Kroes-Smit, at Competition and the Blairite Peter Mandelson, a self-declared globalizer, at foreign trade. The way was clear for a free trading Commission and EU in the line of anti-liberal fire.

The institutional arrangements, the two-headed executive, the greater power of the European Parliament and the balance between small and large states, contained the seeds for policy paralysis, especially on foreign affairs and defense, but for a greater consensus on free-market reform. Under the previous regime the Commission and Council had represented the slightly more regulatory approach of center-left governments on worker consultation and environmental protection, which was resisted by the conservative majority in Parliament. Now that the Commission and Council reflected a majority of center-right governments there would be no EU impediments to free-market integration (Hix, 2004).

By 2004 the problems raised by enlargement, the constitution, and the stability pact appeared to have ended the secular dream of a free market suprastate. The main constitutional trend since Maastricht with its opt outs, demarcations, variable geometry and doctrine of subsidiarity, domestic backlash and ECJ retreats had been the reassertion of national power. The constitutional and monetary crisis of 2003 may have marked the triumph of centrifugal over centripetal forces, of the disintegrative over the integrative and the national over the supranational, a crisis intensified by enlargement and the economic crisis. In 2004 the Constitution was headed for defeat in at least one major country, probably France, most certainly Britain.

Differences were widening between the core founding nations, France and Germany, often joined by the other majors, Britain and Italy, and the smaller and medium-sized states, which were more open to the global market and American alliance, over the stability pact, monetarism, and the constitution. Enlargement to the much poorer East with its consequence in tax dumping, plant relocation and migration to the West was causing a backlash against the EU in Western opinion. These differences, creating bipolar and variable divisions over vital matters, could no longer be contained by the older unifying forces of anti-Communism, American sponsorship, Christian Democracy, Franco-German dominion, and a secure trajectory of growth and rising living standards. Under the pressure of economic crisis the EU and monetary union were dissolving into conflicting nation states, political economies and social classes as was the utopia of a free market suprastate.

Notes

1. Galbraith, 1956; Maier, 1981; Maddison, 1964; Shonfield, 1965; Boltho, 1982, 3–20.
2. For New Left, Regulationist, Communist and Trotskyist views Mandel, 1970; CME, 1971; Mazier, 1984; 1999, Lash and Urry, 1987.
3. Jeannenney, 1991, 180–7; Bouvier *et al*, 1982, 1078–90,1289; Rioux, II, 1983, 274; Moss, 1993; Brenner, 1998, ch. 4.

4. Hall, 1986; Epstein, 1990; Milward, 1992; Garrett, 1998.
5. Pentland, 1973, 151; Hibbs, 1987, 297; Burgesss, 1989, 149–52; Kersbergen, 1994, 31.
6. Haas, 1958, 24, 43, 419; Mahant, 1969, 111–35; De Vos, 1989; Huber and Stephens, 2000, 91–5, 103–5; Berstein *et al*, 1993.
7. Bjöl, 1966, 60–2, 71, 96, 272; Quilliot, 1972, 291–308, 347; Pinto Lyra, 1978; Newman, 1983, 23–32; Bellers, 1993, 22, 79; Griffiths, 1993; Marks and Wilson, 1999, 2000.
8. Bjöl, 197–207; Mioche, 1993, 194–6, 242–55; Guillen, 1980, 16–19; Szokoloczy-Syllaba, 1965, vii, 54, 92–8, 237; *CNPF Bulletin*, esp. August 1956, February–March 1957.
9. The evidence on the importance of Suez is overwhelming, Müller-Armack, 1957, DDF, 1956, III, 198–200, 231–2; Elgey, 1972, 599–620; Küsters, 1982, 147–302, 1989, 233–7; Kocher, 1989, 147–302, 135–205; Serra, 1989, 283, 289, 309, 324; Bossuat, 1996, 260–352; Hitchcock, 2002.
10. Holland, 1980, 64 n. 23; Marjolin, 1986, 286, 356; Guillen, 1988, 331; Milward, 1992, 215; Moravcsik, 1998a.
11. Pineau and Rimbaud, 1991, 275, 298; Moravcsik, 1998a, 109, 157; Heisenberg, 1999.
12. Camps, 1967; Couve de Murville, 1971, 326–38, 360–8, 373–4, 382; Peyrefitte, 1997, I, 60–70, 106–11, 129, 302–3; Vaisse, 1998, ch. 3.

3

Raisons d'être: The Failure of Constructive Integration

Bernard H. Moss

The EC was justified on grounds of peace, prosperity, social justice, and public favor. This chapter evaluates these claims and explains why despite the negative liberal logic of the treaties, the EC had limited success intervening in some areas like environmental protection rather than more basic ones like the economy. By success we mean adding some positive regulation that would not have been provided otherwise by member-states. In broad survey we cannot possibly hope to cover all aspects of policy, but to investigate essential claims that are rarely subject to critical scrutiny or empirical investigation. Studies have looked at the transposition of EC policy and directives into national laws, but virtually none on the differences they made on the ground.[1] Most positive integration or constructive intervention as in social policy was minimalist and inconsequential except for the poorest and most backward states, more effective as propaganda for legitimization purposes than as reform, undermined as it was by EC market principles and forces or intentionally designed to foster them.

The strongest argument for the EC and the one that doubtless underlay the permissive consensus it enjoyed was that of preserving the peace in Western Europe, notably between the ancestral rivals France and Germany, the motors of integration. Affective support for the diffuse goal of European unification was always much greater than committed instrumental backing for particular EC policies. It was the peace factor more than any other that initially motivated the sacrifice of national public interest and identity for the sake of European unity. So many different factors operated in preserving peace however, that it was difficult to weigh the role of the EC, which is beyond the scope of this book. European integration was more the result than the cause of the Franco-German entente. The great leaps forward in integration were made possible by prior Franco-German accord (Willis, 1968; Simonian, 1985). At best the EC reinforced bonds that had deeper foundations. Once the peace factor faded as generations forgot about the Second World War and the long post-war boom ended, economic problems came to the forefront besetting the EU with major macro policy and geo-political divisions.

The other justifications for the EC proved problematic. The literature presumed that the EC promoted growth and employment, but this was not the case. Contrary to received wisdom, EC members experienced lower growth and higher unemployment than comparable non-members did because their putative trade advantages were more than outweighed by regressive EC-sponsored monetary and fiscal policy (Chapter 8). As for social reform, it was not in the EC's original mandate but was primarily tacked on as a side payment to obtain labor's assent to further integration. It was minimalist and inconsequential – much of an alibi and illusion (Vogel-Polsky, 1991) – except in the realm of equal pay for women, secured quite accidentally by treaty concession to the French (cf. Pierson, 1996; Hoskyns, 1996), and environmental protection, which was a new transnational policy area that the EC could capture as its own. Regional aid was mostly a payoff to countries as an inducement to join a larger or deeper union. It was almost entirely controlled by national governments and did not entail an EC regional policy.

But social and regional aid was peripheral to the main business of market integration and was doubtless undermined by it. For example, Italy received one billion ECU's in EC structural funds, but it lost 24 billion when the ECJ on competition grounds voided preferential Italian procurement awards to the South (Martin, 1991). The only places where EC aid made significant difference were in Portugal and Spain where it constituted 5 percent of the budget, a privilege that was partly lost in enlargement to the Eastern states (Verdier, 2001, 254–8).

The permissive consensus was more in favor of the EC as an ideal than a reality. There was trust in the elites who ran it during the peace and prosperity of the 1960s, but little specific knowledge of or commitment to it (Lindberg, 1970, 39–41, 98, 251–61; Inglehart, 1987). As the chimera of liberal "modernization" via the 1980s single market gave way to the reality of low growth, technological lag, and unemployment in the 1990s so did the permissive consensus turn for most to disenchantment and disaffection.

I The myth of growth and prosperity

One of the first neo-classical dogmas taught to beginning economics students and generally left unquestioned by them is that free trade is conducive to growth and employment. This dogma does not fit historical facts. For example, Britain, before the abolition of the Corn Laws in 1846, Germany and the US became industrial powerhouses behind high tariff walls. Industry and technology in most countries developed behind protective walls before they were able to come out and compete in world markets. Of course, once protected producers began to export to gain monopoly rents, they had to consider reciprocity with potential importers, who without freer trade would not have had the wherewithal to purchase their products (Milner, 1988).

Nevertheless, the removal of tariff barriers led invariably to declining growth as the experience of the EC and countries undergoing GATT liberalization demonstrated (Bairoch, 1996; MacEwan, 1999; Chang, 2002).

Protection allowed producers to perfect their methods, learning by doing, and to realize economies of scale and of scope in a familiar environment. These domestic efficiencies set off a cumulative growth pattern that could be regulated and coordinated, features that were not available in the heterogeneous and anarchic global or European market, which limited the effectiveness of national steering and where the risks of credit, speculative and imported crisis were far greater. The costs of intra-EC trade in terms of trust and reliability were considerable (Berger, 2002, 10). The free trader David Ricardo had advised Portugal and Britain to make and export what they were relatively best at doing for comparative advantage, wine for Portugal and textiles for Britain, but the German Friedrich List, who advised his nation to protect infant industries against British competition, foresaw that this would lead to underdevelopment in Portugal and overreliance on textiles in Britain.

The founders of the EC hoped to create a large market conducive to growth and productivity on the American model. They forgot that the US had first deepened its internal market behind closed doors before taking on the world after 1945 and possessed factors not present in Europe for market deepening, including labor mobility, regional specialization, economies of scale, cultural, institutional, and political homogeneity, and fiscal redistribution to declining and poorer regions (Eichengreen, 1994; Boyoumi, 1999; Chang, 2002).

The EC had none of these advantages. The treaty required a lowering of tariffs below the level one might expect from a customs union and contribution to global tariff reduction. In a series of GATT rounds led by the US the EC lowered the tariff on manufactured items to an average of 6 percent in the 1994 Uruguay Round, which was one half that of the US. The firms that took the greatest advantage of the common and single market, including R&D aid, were often American and Japanese rather than European (Hine, 1985, 75–9; Tyson, 1992, 255–9; Prate, 1995, 92–103). Free trade in the EC produced few efficiency gains and little contribution to growth – perhaps 1 percent per annum before 1975 (Belassa, 1975). Despite enlargement, the EC share of world trade fell from 17 percent in the 1960s to 15 percent in the 1980s (Lafay, 1990, 17). Free trade may have been more of a damper than a spur to growth and had a negative effect on popular feelings of security and solidarity.

After the Italian emigration of the 1950s, EC labor mobility across borders fell to less than 1 percent of the population (Faini, 1999). This was likely to change with enlargement to the poorer East, which had a long tradition of Westward migration. The growth in intra-EC trade had little effect on national specialization and thus comparative advantage except perhaps in

Belgium and Holland, the greatest enthusiasts, since it was overwhelmingly intra-sectoral, relying for advantage on differences in quality and brand appeal, mainly at the upper end of the market (Fontagné, 1997). Producer opposition to the EC would have been much greater had entire sectors been destroyed by competition. Little economy of scale was realized either because national markets were already adequately large or because firms obtained greater efficiency from multiproduct plants, plants in several countries or from flexible production methods involving local outsourcing, zero defects, and reduced inventories (Chapter 8, Cutler, 1989).

The treaty incorporated the neoclassical assumption that by reducing costs the competitive market would increase demand, productivity and growth. This was how the so called "best economists in Europe" justified the single market in the Cecchini Report (1988). They predicted five million more jobs within five years, 6 percent added growth and "an upward trajectory of growth through the next century" (id., xviii). Cecchini's figures were wildly over-optimistic. They anticipated the elimination of all non-quantitative barriers including preferential procurement, which resisted all EC injunctions, and the cultural costs of cross-border trade, arising from uncertain expectations of risk and enforcement, estimated as the equivalent of a 37 percent tariff (Berger, 2002, 10). Second, they made the neoclassical assumption that all the losses of protected jobs and income would be recovered. Third, they did not foresee further cyclical downturns that made such recovery impossible. The single market program was probably not foreign to the deep recession of the early 1990s.

The single market initiative certainly stimulated anticipatory merger and acquisition activity, which was more national and transatlantic than European (Haywood, 1995, 7–8; Salesse, 1997, 170–4), but it had no apparent effect on the upward trajectory of intra-EC trade, which benefited foreign as much as European firms (Allen, 1998; Phelps, 1997). In the event, the five-year target of Cecchini coincided with a serious recession, which produced the opposite of the predicated result, 1 percent lower growth and seven million more jobless. The Commission's claim of an additional 1 percent growth with a half million more jobs could only have obtained with negative growth before and after 1993 (cf. Chapter 8, Monti, 1996).

Despite the single market and currency an integrated market was not achieved. Manufacturing trade among the original six had declined since the 1970s and stagnated since the 1980s among the others (Lafay, 1997, 133; Andersen *et al*, 2000, 116–17). The overall growth of intra-EC trade fell in the 1990s and turned negative in 2002. The increasing share of intra-EC trade came from enlargement to new members as a statistical artifice. A major aim of enlargement, in addition to finding new sources of democratic legitimacy, was to find new markets rather than deepen existing ones with positive integration. Enlargement weakened the bargaining power of domestic labor whereas deepening might have strengthened it. However the enlarged market did not lead to an equalizing or lowering of prices – not after 1998 in the opinion of the Commission – only that of wages. Price variation on similar or identical items averaged 15 percent in 2002 (Corcoran, 1998; *The Times*, January 22, 2004). Product competition weighed on wage increases with nominal growth falling since 1975 and converging since 1995 (cf. Flanagan, 1993, 177; Andersen *et al*, 2000).

The common market eliminated firms oriented exclusively to the national market and strengthened those with an EC purview. This led to greater concentration on the EC level. Between 1972 and 1986 the top firms increased market share from 24 to 29.5 percent (Jong, 1988, 5, 13–14). There was no regional convergence of firm structures, unemployment rates or export propensities before the Euro (Pivetti, 1998) nor that of basic national indicators, inflation, unemployment, deficits, or business cycles, afterwards (Arestis, 2003; Arestis and Sawyer, 2003, 131–2; Mayes and Viren, 2003). American economists long knew that the EC was not an "optimum currency area" (Eichengreeen, 1992, 1994).

Putative gains from free trade were offset by the losses due to restrictive fiscal and monetary policy that came with monetary union. Monetary union, the snake in the tunnel in 1972, the ERM after 1981 and the single currency, followed the Germans, who refused intervention to kick-start an economy in recession. German interest rates were the highest and most unresponsive to downturns and unemployment in the EC (Chapter 8). In order to remain in monetary union weaker currency countries had to keep up with the Germans by raising their interest rates and restricting their budgets, further slowing growth. Like the Americans the French had been more Keynesian than the Germans in adapting their rates to the level of employment, but when they joined the ERM in 1979 and especially after 1983, they had to raise their rates above German levels. This increased unemployment from 6 to eventually 12.8 percent in 1997 with an estimated loss of annual GDP of 1 percent from 1989–97 (Chapter 6). The ERM helped block the way to socialism, to reduce the wage share of production approximately 10 percent and to forestall the type of industrial recoveries or technological boom as occurred recurrently in the US.

An econometric analysis comparing EC members with OECD non-members from 1951–89 shows a loss of 20 percent in annual per-capita income and an annual increase in unemployment of 4.7 percent. This did not include the feedback effects of unemployment and lost trade, which were particularly severe for France, Italy, Denmark, and the Netherlands. The EC gave an export bias to national economies leading to enlargement to cheaper contiguous markets, which tended to weaken nationally organized labor. Intra-EC trade soon reached its limits. Members gained little from lower costs because of trade diversion from cheaper non-EU sources or from economies of scale, which were already optimal in most cases on the local and national level. With the possible exception of Belgium, the Netherlands,

Spain and Portugal, the greatest EC enthusiasts, few benefited from the comparative advantages of the division of labor since most EC trade growth was intra-sectoral, affecting quality range and brand appeal, rather than inter-sectoral, which would have caused national redistributional conflict and protest (Fontagné, 1997, Chapter 8).

Putative trade gains were more than offset by income losses due to the restrictiveness of monetary union, the French Barre Plan in 1976, the hard ERM of 1981, and the Mitterrand turnabout of 1983. The slowdown of French growth occurred when it switched from practicing flexible interest rates as the Americans did to disciplinary German ones. The convergence criteria of EMU kept growth below 2 percent from 1990–97 and 1 percent after 2000 with that of wages going even lower. Overall, EC economic performance was mediocre when compared to that of other OECD or Asian nations (Peridon, 1996, Chapter 8).

II Positive intervention: social, regional, technological, environmental

Social policy

Where the EC succeeded in negative integration, the removal of most national barriers to trade, it failed in positive integration (Tinbergen, 1965, 146; Pinder, 1969; Scharpf, 1996), market intervention to promote social justice, industry, or technological progress. This failure was written in the market principles of the Rome treaty, which left social legislation to member-states, barred nationally discriminatory taxation and limited aid to industry and public services. Nevertheless, significant advances were made regarding women's work and wages and environmental protection. Why and how were these advances made contrary to the market principles and logic of the treaties?

The basic answer is that the EC, led by the Commission, in order to establish its power and legitimacy vis-à-vis the member-states had to acquire attributes of those states. To attract popular support it needed a social program even if contrary to market principles (Commission, 1962, 42–4). The EP set up a social committee, but this only considered the rights of migrant workers in order to encourage labor mobility. The leading political party, the Christian Democrats, could not be seen embracing the market without a social dimension. Social Democrats dreamt of making the EC a fully planned and regulated state. When the French reformist government of Jacques Chaban-Delmas and the German Social-Democratic one of Willy Brandt tried to assuage worker discontent after May–June 1968, this was reflected in a more social democratic vision of an EC suprastate (Gillingham, 2003, 87–97). But the first social action program on worker representation and the harmonization of labor standards introduced in 1972 yielded only two minor directives on collective redundancies and transfers of undertakings.

The only social provision in the Rome treaty concerned equal pay for women. Little happened to this provision until the Belgian lawyer Eliane Vogel-Polsky (1991) decided to take the case of a prematurely retired Sabena stewardess to the ECJ. Her case was helped by the climate of social protest arising out of the May–June discontent and the rise of the women's movement. She got the Belgian ministry of employment and trade unions to campaign for an EC equal pay directive, which extended the meaning to all compensation, and one on equal job opportunities and social security. The ECJ made individuals liable for employment discrimination against women and widened the meaning of the same work to equivalent work in blatant acts of judicial treaty making (cf. Hoskyns, 1996).

The Commission sought to capture a popular cause and create a new clientele by setting up an advisory committee and funding research, but it was not really sympathetic to the feminist movement or to its links with labor. The ECJ confined its interest in women's equality to work and left implementation to the states. When it left open the possibility of giving women retrospective pension rights, involving huge sums from companies that had discriminated, it was foreclosed by a protocol to the Maastricht treaty. When the women's movement declined in the 1990s, so did EC interest in the question. Without the backing of a social movement and support from the Commission women, constituting 80 percent of the working poor, continued to suffer the same level of relative wage discrimination after 20 years of ECJ jurisprudence (Hoskyns, 1996; *Le Monde*, January 16, 2001; March 7–8, 2004).

The EC could expand competence over health and safety in the workplace and the environment in task-related or spillover terms under article 100 on the approximation of national laws necessary to create a common market. After unemployment increased in the 1970s and 80s, social and regional aid could be justified as compensation for workers and poorer regions that suffered from the competition unleashed by the common and single market. Regional and social policy were used by Delors as side-payments to get unions and poorer states to support the single market and currency. Delors' personal ambition was to construct a supranational Europe that reconciled the interests of labor and capital (cf. Ross, 1995).

Under the influence of Christian Democracy the EC incorporated Catholic notions of corporatism, subsidiarity, and qualitative or "dignity of work" issues into its social and labor policy. As a Christian Democrat who had joined the Socialist Party in order to liberalize it, Delors[2] preferred negotiation or "social dialogue" to coercive strikes or state action and qualitative demands around working conditions to adversarial materialist wage demands. Social dialogue was a value in itself and the best reforms were costless to employers. Delors re-started talks between the European union and employers' confederations (ETUC and UNICE), which never got very far since neither was authorized to negotiate and since the monetarist turn left little surplus to redistribute.

The first issue he took up was the relatively consensual one of work-place health and safety, the first one to be dealt with by the nineteenth-century state because it was of mutual interest to workers and employers. His first accomplishment as social reformer was the directive on safe machinery. By relying on experts linked to the multinationals he was able to set a high standard without protest largely because the Germans, the main suppliers and users of machinery, already had one (Eichener, 1992).

To firm up trade union support for the single market, notably among skeptical British labor, he took up an ETUC draft for a Community Charter of Fundamental Social Rights. It was watered down and changed into a charter of workers' rights to please the British, who still refused to sign. It was merely a statement of principles that did not extend EC competence as promised and was hedged with a subsidiarity clause that weakened it. It was followed up with another social action program. Progress was impeded by British vetoes with only 6 of 24 proposals, mostly dealing with workplace health and safety, adopted by 1991 (Silvia, 1991, 634–9; Ross, 1993, 52; Streeck, 1995, 403).

Delors tried to extend EC competence to social policy in the Maastricht treaty, but had to settle for a protocol that allowed a British opt out. The protocol extended QMV to laws on working conditions, information and consultation, and equal opportunities, but excluded questions involving collective rights and power, pay, association, and strikes. Again it was hedged with a subsidiarity clause and a stipulation that the EC was only to provide minimal protection, which might conceivably threaten higher levels of protection in member-states. The treaty also contained provision for laws negotiated by employers and unions, which Delors preferred to government intervention. The "social dialogue" produced only a handful of directives, on parental leave, part-time and night-shift work, and so on. In these areas the desire of employers and the Commission to make working time more flexible coincided with the unions' interest in protecting those already in marginal work (Shaw, 1994; Szyszczak, 1994). EC legislation was pitched at a level that could only help workers in countries with the lowest standards like Greece and Portugal and might lower those where they were higher.

Social measures were notorious for taking a long time and being diluted upon arrival. A minimal provision for consultative works councils took 24 years to arrive. It was first incorporated into the Fifth Directive, a proposal for a European Company Statute. That Statute was passed after 34 years minus the worker-codetermination. The Vredling proposal to establish councils in trans-European companies was defeated in 1982 after heavy lobbying by multinationals, especially American, that swung Christian Democrats against it (De Vos, 1989). It was revived as part of Delors' social dialogue and passed in much diluted form despite employer opposition in 1994. With a high threshold for participation – firms with at least 1000 workers and plants in at least two countries with 100 workers each – a preference for negotiated over legislative rules and minimal requirements including only one hour of consultation a year, the directive on worker consultation was hailed as a great victory by the ETUC, but was only partly implemented and had little effect. By 2004 only 40 percent of companies covered had European councils, mostly meeting just minimal requirements.[3]

When the Renault plant at Vilvoorde Belgium was closed, there was no consultation and no effective judicial sanction. One contradiction disclosed was that infringements of European labor law could only be pursued under national law, which posed a problem for the plants of one company located in another country. The emotion generated by Vilvoorde persuaded the Commission to accelerate a more general directive on information and consultation, but it left much room for employer discretion and the marginalization of unions (Scott, 2002).

After Maastricht the Commission abandoned active social policy, relying on nonbinding recommendations and the market for the improvement of pay and working conditions. Delors' White Paper on employment and competitiveness while proposing a very ambitious program of trans-European public construction endorsed employer demands for labor flexibility, work sharing, the diminution of social charges, and wage reductions relative to productivity. Council in 1993 recommended policies of pay moderation, decentralized bargaining, lower social expenditure, and more flexible forms of work organization. To reduce unemployment to a noninflationary minimum of 6.1 percent the Commission in 1994 recommended the diminution of the social wage and work sharing. Job insecurity was deemed essential to meet the demands of global free trade (Bempt, 1999). The Santer Commission adopted the monetarist logic of EMU recommending budget cuts and deflation as the way to stimulate investment and create jobs (Moss and Michie, 1998, 158–9).

As a condition to signing up to the stability pact, the French demanded a full employment policy. What they got at Amsterdam in 1997 was a resolution inspired by for Blair that left job creation to the market to be encouraged by work-time flexibility and the lowering of taxes, social charges, and wages. Under the "open coordination" of employment policy each country submitted to deflationary market conditions in its own way without fixed targets or prescriptions (*Le Monde*, June 18, 1997; Milner, 2003).

The EC, ERM and EMU put governments under pressure to reduce wages, public expenditure, and corporate taxation and to de-regulate the labor market. They created a deflationary environment in which nominal and real wage growth relative to productivity was driven down regardless of local demand pressures. The open external and enlarged competitive market weakened unions and centralized bargaining (Verdier and Breen, 2007). The Belgians passed a Competitiveness Act in 1995, which limited wage and benefit increases to those of their neighbors, a process of wage dampening that was followed in several other member-states. The Commission and council considered wage guidelines to accompany the Euro in 1999. The ETUC opposed wage reduction, but even the militant IG Metall conceded the sharing of productivity growth with employers (*Transfer*, 6, 2000, 71; Andersen *et al*, 2000).

It was possible to obtain union assent for wage and bargaining restraint because of the wholesale conversion of members of the ETUC, including even the French Communists, to the integration process. Spanish unionists signed up to pacts facilitating dismissals, cutting pensions and centralizing bargaining in 1995 and 1997 much as the Italians had done earlier. Italian resistance to pension reduction faded as the former Communist PDS moved to defend EMU. Above all the ETUC endorsed the Lisbon process, the competitive strategy outlined at a summit of 2000, of deregulating markets and public services, increasing the work force by raising retirement age and downsizing the welfare state, including the capitalization or investment of pensions and other benefits in financial markets. Rhetorical flourishes about the pursuit of social cohesion kept labor on course for the marketization of public services (*Bastille, République, Nation*, March, 2003; Featherstone, 2002).

Governments used EMU to reduce welfare payments, particularly in Italy, Sweden, and Finland, which experienced the biggest reductions in history. Despite provoking a general rail strike and losing office Alain Juppé of France got most of what he wanted in social security cuts. Greek cutbacks were finally accepted when Greece joined the Euro. To meet the convergence criteria Italy had to reduce spending by 14 percent and raise taxes by 5 percent. The shortfall was made up by pension cuts and privatization, which the pro-EU PDS, the former Communists, justified as blows against vested privileges and the oligarchies (Featherstone, 2002; Abse, 2001)!

Social expenditure as a percentage of GDP declined after 1993 especially for sickness, disability, and unemployment benefits (Rhodes, 2002). Entitlements were made leaner and meaner and costs shifted back to wage-earners (Daley, 1997; Huemer, 1999, 63). Benefits were made less redistributive and universal depending more on means testing for the poor and linked with pay contributions and returns from the capital market, the third pillar of EC social policy (Friot, 2003). Unemployment, disability, and single mother benefits were lowered in Britain to force people to find work however low-paid or precarious as was also the case in the Netherlands, which became the model for EC employment policy despite low productivity. Waves of privatization undertaken either to meet competition rules or convergence criteria reduced the social advantages of the public sector, relieving pressure on the private one.

Competition and factor mobility tended to undermine national social provision. Migrant workers were entitled to carry their social insurance with them depriving the contributing country of consumption benefit. Under the right of establishment a dentist in Germany could move to Holland and charge German patients lower fees there. Patients could shop for the best value and free ride on better health services thanks to the taxpayers of another country – Britishers going to France for example. Under an ECJ ruling German employers could pay Portuguese workers the lower social wages they were entitled to at home rather than higher German ones. They did not even have to pay minimum wages for temporary workers. The EU favored wage competition to lower costs and encourage mobility (Leander, 1997, 136). Inducements to migration did not work, but might for workers from poor Eastern states with a migratory tradition. The massive influx of unskilled workers to the US over the last 25 years has driven down wages, burdened social provision, and enriched employers (*New Statesman*, January 6, 2003, 18–19).

The tax burden was also shifted to wage-earners. According to the Commission, from 1980–93 taxes on wages increased 20 percent while those on capital fell 10 percent (Aeschimann and Riché, 1996, 48). The part of corporate taxes in total revenue decreased from 23.6 percent in 1980 to 9.1 in 1995 whereas the part of wage earners rose from 30.5 to 34.7 percent (Leander, 135). The Commission and ECB preferred cuts in government expenditure to tax increases because it shared the neo-liberal view that the European economy needed a shakeout of labor costs, taxes, and rigidities.

Regional funds

Far more important in budgetary terms than social policy were regional structural funds. While the Rome treaty referred to evening out regional disparities, its only provision for regional policy was the limited aid of the European Investment Bank and Social Fund, which went almost entirely to migratory Italian workers. Once again reducing disparities was left to market forces and the hope that capital drawn to regions of cheap labor would speed up development. Regional funds were introduced primarily as a side-payment for enlargement first to Britain as the European Regional Development Fund in the 1970s, second to France, Italy, and Greece as compensation for Spanish and Portuguese entry, and then more massively to the poorer regions of Ireland, Spain, Portugal, and Greece to gain their acceptance of the single market and currency. It was feared they would suffer under the single market the backwater effects of competition from richer members endowed with more skills and technology. A special cohesion fund was set up for them under Maastricht to accompany EMU. Though the funds had an economic rationale they were treated by both donors and recipients primarily as political handouts and were not accompanied by a sustained EC policy (Allen, 1996; Pollack, 1998).

Delors doubled the structural funds in 1988 to a level of one quarter of the budget and later 35 percent replacing equivalent agricultural funds. To backward regions found mostly in the four poorest states were added declining industrial areas, youth, and long-term unemployment, which gave richer governments a share in the pork barrel. Ninety percent of the funds were administered by member-states. But the Commission used the remaining 10 percent to encourage local participation, in one case to impose the condition of additionality, that EC funds not replace previous government expenditure, on Mrs Thatcher. This local empowerment led to speculation about a multi-level assault on the nation state from above and below (cf. Marks, 1993, 1996), but after Maastricht national governments strengthened their control over the funds (Pollack, 1998, 224–9).

Despite the requirement of additionality EC funds often replaced national ones. They helped rich areas much more than poor ones, but this may be because financial openness advantaged rich areas in the first place. They only countered recessive globalization effects, according to one calculation, in Spain and Portugal. The natural process of poor regions catching up to richer ones stopped in the 1980s. Given the difficulty of disentangling natural from policy-aided catch-up and calculating recessive globalization effects, it was by no means certain that the funds narrowed the gap between poor and wealthy regions.[4] Finally, they faced cuts with enlargement to much poorer Eastern regions.

Industrial and technology policy

The EC under liberal employer and German influence always refused proactive industrial policy. When it did act to promote high tech electronics, the assistance to large companies was linked to an assault on the public sector. In 1964 the Committee on Medium-Term Policy discussed the technology gap with the US, but the Commission ruled out aid for sectors or nations. The French sought changes in commercial and tax law to facilitate intra-EC mergers, which were only 13 percent of the total in the 1960s. The Commission responded in 1966 with the European Company Statute on the German model. In 1970 the Colonna Report urged the EC to encourage industrial cooperation and mergers in order to narrow the productivity and technology gap with the US, but the only industrial policy acceptable to UNICE and the German majority was the completion of the single market (Hodges, 1977).

In 1979, however, with the neo-liberal turn the Commission, the industry commissioner Vicomte Etienne Davignon saw an opportunity to link the technology gap to its single market agenda. Davignon was a Catholic Belgian diplomat, who had worked with big oil and steel companies. He managed the shutdown of EC steel capacity in 1979 and began the EC's high tech and commercialization programs in 1983. He left the EC after 1984 to preside over the multinationalization of Belgium's largest investment bank and headed up the European business association for monetary union in 1987. The Commission, especially the industry directorate, often served as a stepping stone to lucrative jobs with multinationals.

Davignon linked programs of aid to high tech R&D with the completion of the single competitive market. In 1979 he formed a task force of 12 electronic companies with a view toward challenging national standards and monopolies. In 1983 these companies asked member-states to contribute to Esprit, a program to assist joint R&D ventures on integrated circuits or telematics. Esprit was launched right after the defeat of Altieri Spinelli's supranational constitution in parliament, which suggests political motivation for the program. Member-states were not eager to contribute because they had their own programs, but Esprit claimed its research would avoid duplication and establish common EC standards. It excluded public firms while including foreign subsidiaries and restricted research to the pre-competitive phase contrary to a French proposal to directly aid production, exclude foreigners and raise external tariffs – a truly European industrial plan (Pearce, 1985, 5–15, 71–3, 155; Hayward, 1995, 5–8; Sandholtz, 1998).

Davignon's IT task force formulated the project, awarded the funds and participated in 70 percent of the projects, a form of self-dealing that nobody questioned in the new age of neo-liberalism. Esprit was followed by Brite for textile machinery, RACE for telecommunications and annual framework programs. Davignon's task force squeezed out the postal authorities from RACE on grounds that they lacked transnational markets and the investment capital of the multinationals. RACE was prelude to the commercialization of telecommunications recommended in the green paper of 1987 (Junne, 1988, 224–43; Dang-Nguyen, *et al*, 1993; Sandholtz, 1998, 234–8).

The Commission displayed clear preference for the model of commercialization applied by Mrs Thatcher to British Telecom – the separation of regulation and execution and of infrastructure from operation. The sell-off of operating services to private companies had no technological justification because they used already existing public infrastructure with little investment risk but with a greater ability to save on labor costs. The sell-off of BT and the divestiture of ATT in the US provided the EC with a model of universal service based on ability to pay that was very different from the French conception of public service (Cohen, 1992; Cartelier, 1996; Sandholtz, 1998, 217–23).

The green paper of 1987 urging the commercialization of public telecommunications was a prelude to that of air transport and other public services for which there was also no technological justification. Public services had been exempted from competition rules under article 90, but the Commission sanctioned by the Court reversed the burden of proof. Henceforth, public services had to justify their mission in terms of the "general economic interest" and prove that their restrictions on competition were necessary to fulfil it (Sandholtz, 1998, 153–60).

Commercialization and privatization were part of the neo-liberal program driving the Commission, pressed by the multinationals, Britain, and Germany and sanctioned by the ECJ. The only muted opposition came from small consumers, public service groups, and trade unions. Once France abandoned interventionism in 1983 and 1984, political resistance vanished (Cohen, 1992, 248; Dang-Nguyen *et al*, 1993). In 1984 Davignon organized the CEOs of the largest European multinationals into the European Round Table (ERT) to act as a business constituency and lobbyist for the single market. The ERT took the standard business position that Europe was burdened with excessive wage and benefit costs, overregulation, bureaucratic government and inefficient public services (Wisse Dekker, Phillips, speech January 11, 1985) and that it needed the scale and standardization benefits of a single market unhindered by technical, fiscal, physical, and public procurement barriers (ERT, "Changing Scales", June 1985). This was the program that Mitterrand picked up in his search for a new European project in 1984 and that was incorporated into the single market initiative by the Delors Commission in 1985 – the removal of nonquantitative barriers to trade, including national technical and compositional standards, border controls, VAT differentials, and preferential public procurement. The ERT, which conducted a tiny proportion of EC business, became the chief interlocutor of the Commission and council and the most powerful group in the EU (Cowles, 1995, 1999).

EC technology policy turned out to be a contradiction in terms. The EC lacked the constitutional power and managerial and technical capacity to carry out effective industrial policy. It could not put together integrated systems because it lacked coercive power over industry. It failed to develop high-density television because it did not control satellite and network providers and broadcasters and could not commercialize products under competition restraints (Cohen, 1992, 308–40, 1995, 154–6). The EC's technology programs did nothing to narrow the gap with the US and Japan. US subsidiaries got 40 percent of RACE funds. Europeans often used the aid as a step toward more global ventures. Of all European joint ventures in telematics 59 percent were with Americans and only 18 percent with other Europeans (Junne and Tulder, 1988, 212–43, 1994, 84–7; Barreau, 1990, 129–30).

The EC programs ran up and up against the national budgetary restraints that the EC itself had imposed. Only 4 billion ECU were spent for the framework program and Eureka, the defense-linked intergovernmental program, as against an estimated 67 bn spent for industry by member-states in 1990. EC spending on R&D was less than what was spent by France or Siemens, the German company. In 2003 EU spending constituted only 6 percent of all public funding in member-states (*Le Monde*, March 3, 2004). Restricted to pre-commercial projects, the technology policy was vitiated by the turn to neo-liberalism at all levels – privatization, deregulation, restrictions on state aid and procurement, and the new merger regulation. Despite 10.3 bn dollars put into semiconductors under the intergovernmental Eureka program, EC world market share fell sharply between 1978 and 1988. The trade deficit in electronics grew. Despite the framework programs EC industry became more than ever dependent on US and Japanese technology.[5]

Under Article 130 of Maastricht the EC was required to enhance industrial competitiveness, to speed up adjustment, to assist smaller firms and to foster industrial cooperation and innovation in all areas. How the EC could do this without violating competitive market principles was hard to see. The German Liberal industry commissioner Martin Bangemann tried to square the circle by relying on the private sector and restricting EC intervention to the pre-competitive environment of research, training, and infrastructure. Since industrial policy was limited to the pre-commercial stage, there was no consumer feedback for further development. But even this potential was stymied by the anti-interventionism of the Commission – its communication of November 1994 – by the unanimity principle and by constricting national budgets. These factors doomed Delors' ambitious 400 million ECU scheme in 1993 for trans-European networks in transport, energy and telecommunications, a scheme actually backed by the ERT (Bourgeois, 1995, 72–3)!

The EC chose the Thatcherite model for public services because it was the only one consistent with its market principles (Dobbin, 1993). The French rated public services above the market and possessed the administrative, educational, and industrial capacity to outperform the private sector. In French law a public service has an obligation to provide continuous service to all users at equal and reasonable rates (Cartelier, 1996, 89). In most cases personnel possessed a special statute that guaranteed job security. Built up after the war by the state, the French railways SNCF was able to develop new technology for high-speed rail (TGV), to investigate and generate new markets, to raise money in both public and private markets and to sell its new system internationally. Under EC law France would have been guilty of discriminatory noncompetitive behavior and the TGV never built.

The EU lacked the structural prerequisites to launch its own companies: research networks, public procurement, fiscal intervention, commercial promotion, and a cohesive industrial leadership and culture – all of which remained in the hands of member-states (Cohen, 1992, 383, 1995, 37). It lacked the political will, institutional unity, and constitutional competence to carry out directive industrial or technology policy. It was not accidental that the EC rejected proactive industrial solutions and promoted, when the political atmosphere permitted, the devolution of public infrastructure to competitive tendering and privatization. Nor was it surprising that the greatest European industrial successes – Airbus, Eureka and Ariane – relied upon national networks of production and finance and inter-governmental agreements rather than the EC.

Environmental

The only EC policy that raised standards in a proactive way was environmental. This was due in part to the spillover effect, the tendency of the EC to extend its competence over trade-related tasks especially in an apparently costless regulatory way (cf. Pollack, 1994; Majone, 1993). It was impossible to create a common market without some approximation of health and safety laws. A directive on dangerous substances was passed in 1967 and one on car emissions in 1970. The Paris summit of 1972 followed up with an action program that put environmental protection on the agenda. The EC adopted the principle that the polluter pays and did not hesitate to regulate matters of water and air purity that had nothing to do with trade. More than 100 laws were passed before the environment was even brought within the scope of the treaty in 1987 (Vogel, 1995, chs 2–3).

The reason for this activism was the heightened concern about the environment in public opinion particularly in the three green states, Germany, Holland, and Denmark, which took strong measures against the pollution of air and water, car emissions, and solid waste. Social protest often took a green form in these countries because there was little outlet for labor radicalism in these countries for the '68 generation. Radicals like Joschka Fischer, later German foreign minister, turned to green issues after facing an impasse with Maoism and violence. Environmentalism appealed broadly to the educated young and middle class who could not identify with the materialist issues of pay and profit that divided labor from conservatives (cf. Inglehart, 1977, 280–8). Already in 1973 the environment was the number one concern of public opinion, which had not yet been taken up by the nation state. By the 1980s the Green Party became an electoral force in all but the poorer Southern states. People naturally looked to the EC for help as the pollution of air and water had a cross-border dimension. The EC could gain in legitimacy and support by pressing the issue.

The first exceptions to the sacrosanct freedom of trade were environmental. In 1981 Denmark required that all beer and soft drinks be sold in approved reusable containers. Even though this discriminated against foreign producers, who could not easily recycle their containers, the ECJ in 1988 found the Danish program was legal in the absence of an EC equivalent. Environmental protection it held was "an essential aim of the community" capable of limiting the application of article 30 on free trade. The Danish decision emboldened the Germans to pass an even more Draconian law on recycling plastic bottles and then in 1991 all packing material. The resale of German waste material destroyed recycling in other member-states, applying pressure on the EU to take action. It did with the packaging directive of 1994 that required member-states to achieve the recovery of one half of all waste material. EC regulation of solid wastes was a perfect example of spillover. The Treaty of Maastricht confirmed the right of member-states to adopt more stringent measures than those of the EC (Vogel, 1995, ch. 3).

The SEA made provision for legislation on environmental and consumer protection at a high level by qualified majority and extended environmental concerns to all policy areas, the only issue so universalized. Under article 100A the new directorate for the environment DG XI was able to get its way in the Commission against those linked to industry with the help of parliament under the cooperation procedure and the three green states. Environmental ministers could often demand higher standards in the EC than they could in their own country because they did not have to balance their claims against other ministers in a coherent governmental program. By threatening to undertake unilateral action that would block goods from dirtier countries, the green states could persuade them to adopt higher standards that would reduce their cheaper cost advantage.

EC environmental legislation ran up against neo-liberal resistance in the late 1990s with heightened concerns about cost and the preference for self-regulation and regulation by the market – selling the right to pollute (Golub, 1998). The shine came off the Greens because of their participation in government in France and Germany in the late 1990s and their innumerable divisions. A major problem with EC environmental policy – perhaps greater in this area than in others – was implementation, both in terms of the transposition of EU directives in the member-states and in the effectiveness of the law. The EC Environmental Agency collected information about implementation, but lacked powers of enforcement. The EU lacked the administrative instruments to monitor compliance, test results, and adjust policies accordingly (Grant, 2000, 199–207).

EC environmental policy seemed to contradict Gresham's law of social dumping. This law predicts that firms in countries with lower costs and presumably standards will drive out those from countries with higher standards. This did not happen. Instead there was a "California" effect, named after the American state that established high standards for the control of exhaust emissions, in which countries with the poorest standards aligned themselves with those of the most costly producers (Vogel, 1995). This was best explained by the political salience of environmentalism as a consensual issue that became associated with the EC and by the leading role played by the green states, especially Germany, which constituted both the largest market and the model of economic success to follow for other members. Since the economic crisis of the 1990s little has been heard about environmental initiatives from the EU.

III Popular disenchantment, labor and the democratic deficit

The EU was a myriad of inter-governmental and supranational authorities with no real center for decision-making or accountability. The Rome treaty was rightly called "Byzantine, – a maquis, a labyrinth, a brain twister, a puzzle" (cited in Lindberg, 1963, 43). It provided for (1) an independent Commission, which was composed of national political appointees and fractionated into separate nationally held directorates, to which were attached 300 quasi-national technical committees known collectively as Comitology, (2) a court that acted both as constitutional arbiter and supranational advocate, (3) an essentially consultative parliament with enhanced powers of co-decision, which promoted its own supranational power as the conscience of the community, (4) councils of ministers representing the member-states, which decided by a qualified majority in all but the most vital areas, and (5) since 1977 the European Council, consisting of the heads of member-states, which furnished overall direction.

There was no clear separation of executive, legislative, and judicial power. Policy-making was "headless, porous, unpredictable and chaotic (Peters, 1994, 19)", allowing for a multiplicity of actors, problems and solutions wide open to business influence peddling (Kohler-Koch, 1997, 1999). The product of innumerable diplomatic deals, the EC bore greater resemblance to the Holy Roman Empire, a constellation of large and small principalities and bishoprics, than to a modern nation state, whose power the EC and Papal-led empire were both designed to check.

The EC was a head without a body because it relied on member-states to collect taxes, disburse aid, implement, enforce, and evaluate the law. While absorbing or destroying many state functions, it had none of the attributes of sovereignty, which confers a monopoly of the legitimate use of force over a territory with the active consent of the governed in a democracy. Member-states lost functions to the EU but not sovereignty, which is indivisible and backed by military force (*contra* Wallace, 1994). It is because sovereignty is indivisible that we have wars and revolutions whenever it is challenged. If a state were to withdraw from the EU because it judged the harm caused outweighed the benefits, how many nationals would fight on the side of Brussels to stop the secession? Only a minority in most states would regret the dissolution of the EU (*Eurobarometer*, Spring, 2002, 42–4).

The complexity, technicality, and opacity of EU decision-making defied the understanding of all but the hardiest lobbyists and made the EC appear elitist and remote from people. Only the Commission and veteran lobbyists knew where decisions originated or traveled since no two decisions took the same paths (Page, 2001). The secrecy of council, Court and Commission deliberations and the absence of minority reports did nothing to instill confidence. The first theorist of European integration realized that the EC would have to walk a tightwire between politics and technique to succeed (Haas, 1964). If its processes and decisions were too political, they would provoke opposition to integration, but if too technical and obscure they would not attract loyalty. The EC strove to appear politically impartial and fair to all parties, but in doing so failed to attract loyalty and commitment. Attempts to make the EC more democratic failed because they could not reconcile different national views and interests without making it even more complicated and obscure to the public as Maastricht and the constitution of 2004 demonstrated.

The European Parliament was not about to replace national parliaments as a source of legitimacy and power. European elections were of a "second-order" with a low turnout – below half in 1999 – an incentive to punish national incumbents and preoccupation with domestic issues. They were de-motivating because they did not lead to a change of government or tangible legislation (Schmidt, 1999, 3–5, 161, 265–6). The lack of transnational media, a common language and real power and responsibility made the EP into a gesticulating sideshow, which is one reason why the election turnover of MEPs – composed earlier of "has beens", later of "wannabes" – was 50 percent.

Parliament was run by an arrangement between the Socialists (PES) and Christian Democrats, the European People's Party (EPP), who alone together had the votes to approve a budget. The extreme left and Greens were too small and divided to offer the PES any alternative left majority. The PES and EPP chose the powerful heads of committees and rapporteurs and took transnational positions, but national groups reserved the right to dissent. Debates in chamber were abbreviated – often limited to five minutes per member – and laws often passed without discussion (cf. Jacobs, 1995, 7, 90–3). The PES ran the gamut between market-oriented Blairites and leftist French while the EPP, which had a social face in the Low Countries, invariably sided with capital on economic, monetary, and labor questions. Challenged by both the anti-immigrant and traditionally nationalist right, the EPP eventually incorporated pro-business Euroskeptics from outside Christian Democracy in Britain, Spain, Italy, and the East (cf. Hix and Lord, 1997).

Parliament displayed the cross-cutting class and regional consensual politics of post-war Belgium (De Winter, 1993, 202), a state in a constant state of recomposition and dissolution, rather than that of France and Germany in which Socialists and Christian Democrats presented more or less alternative programs on the class divide. The consensus around EMU and social neo-liberalism muted trademark distinctions between them. It obfuscated political debates, gave resolutions an idealistic deracinated character, and fostered the illusion that integration was ideologically and class neutral (cf. Ladrech, 1996, 292–6). The victory of the EPP in the 1999 elections, repeated in member-states, made little difference to the operation of the EP.

The technicality and complexity of decision-making gave advantage to business lobbyists, who were well informed and knew all the stops, over trade unions or other civic groups, which had difficulty being heard otherwise than in the directorate of social affairs. These factors made it difficult to activate popular movements and mobilize public opinion on a European scale. Increasingly decisions were made by professional standard-setters and technical committees with close links to private firms. When directorates initiated decisions the first people they usually consulted were business lobbyists who possessed the requisite technical knowledge. UNICE was the best-financed lobby in Brussels. Business associations and firms greatly outnumbered unions and other groups (Streeck, 1991, 136–8; Greenwood, 1997). While labor was weak, divided and poorly represented, employers were united in opposition to European industrial and social regulation.

Through their influence on Christian Democrats in parliaments and governments they retarded and diluted works council legislation for twenty-four years (De Vos, 1989, 175–9; Lemke, 1992, 16).

Large exporting firms and multinationals, more interested in global trade than European construction, became the predominant influence in national employers' associations and the EU. Their influence was disproportionate to their interest (cf. Fligstein, 1995). Multinationals never really needed the EC because they had the capacity to circumvent national barriers themselves (Jaumont *et al*, 1973). Rival medium-sized interloping firms, which benefited most from the single market, and smaller firms, which were probably harmed by it, had little influence. The ERT, the semi-official business constituency composed exclusively of multinationals, was regularly consulted by the Commission and presidents of councils preparing their agendas (Cowles, 1999).

With power diminished, labor was still much better organized for political action in the nation rather than in the EC, which was a free space for capital (cf. Caporaso, 1996, 47–8). Unions depended on social norms, ideology and institutions that were not available on the European level where they were divided by linguistic, cultural, and political barriers (Lemke, 1992). The power of organized labor was inextricably tied to the growth of the democratic state from which it derived its rights and character. Labor used the protections it conquered in the state to ward off the dissolving effects of global competition. The history of union, socialist or proletarian internationalism is strewn with national barriers (Moss, 2001a). Because labor movements and institutions developed in different national contexts, they were barely comparable in form and function. A French strike and trade union served very different functions from the German in our period – for purposes of agitation and mass mobilization in the first instance rather than for targeted negotiations and social peace in the second, making coordination nearly impossible (Ebbinghaus and Visser, 1994, 1999, 195–202).

The ETUC was a cumbersome and bureaucratic confederation of national confederations, which was remote from individual unions and unknown to the rank and file. It served as an annex to the Commission, integrating formerly radical unions into its neo-liberal program. When European dockers were faced with an EU directive threatening their employment protection, they had to go outside their official European transport federation in order to coordinate strikes against it (*Bastille, République, Nations*, March 2003). Whatever labor gained from EC training schemes, works councils, and health and safety legislation it lost through EC-sponsored deflation and deregulation. Globalization had a greater debilitating effect on unions and centralized bargaining in the EC than elsewhere because of its open borders and monetarist policies (Verdier, 2001, 239–44). Deregulation might have occurred to some degree without the EC – it was part of a profound sociopolitical transformation – but the EC provided an alibi and justification for governments, particularly Christian and Social Democratic ones, disinclined to act alone. Rather than accept responsibility for regressive economic and social policy, they chose to tie their hands with EMU.

Many social democrats hoped that the discontents created by EMU would induce popular demands for European economic government such as the French made, but the idea was anathema to other members. Enthusiasm for extending the co-decisional powers of Parliament at Amsterdam and Nice was limited. Nothing new emerged from the eurogroup demanded by the French to serve as "an economic government" for Europe or from the coordination of employment policy (Puetter, 2003; Milner, 2003). While organized opposition to supranationalism and the constitutional draft of 2003 came mostly from Conservatives in Britain, it came increasingly on the Continent from both the old left and new social movements, who judged the EU by results (Aspinwall, 2002).

Further transfers of essential state functions were unlikely because the EU lacked (1) constitutional and institutional foundations for a constructive, effective or sovereign government, (2) democratic legitimacy, the primary support and loyalty of a European people or demos, and (3) consensus over political economy and foreign and defense policy due to variant traditions, institutions, geopolitics and political cycles. States reached the limit of transfers of competence beyond which they would lose their coherence as constituting bodies for society. The major powers possessing a degree of economic and military autonomy from the US – Britain, France, Germany, and Italy – resisted yielding to the EU more control of social, economic and defense and foreign policy, main sources of power and legitimacy. In an age of global physical and economic insecurity citizens were more inclined to seek protection from the nation state rather than delegate more power to an obscure, unaccountable, and splintered supranational authority (PEW, 2003).

Europeans still looked to the nation state for their physical security and social welfare. Everywhere primary loyalty was to the member-state and only secondarily to the EU (*Eurobarometer*, March 2003, 58, 90). In the early 1990s only 20 percent polled said they felt European (Gabel, 1998, 20). Europe was supported as an aid to rather than a replacement for the state, which remained the main forum of democratic expression and framework for market regulation. It remained the particular sphere of the public realm. Only in the national community was there sufficient collective solidarity and mutuality of identification and interest as to overcome some kinds of social division and induce minorities to submit to majority rule (cf. Bourdieu, *Le Monde diplomatique*, December 1998).

Globalization, ruining individuals, families, firms, industries and regions, made the nation state even more important as a protector of economic and social well-being. It increased national protective legislation alongside EC regulation (cf. Gelber, 1997). This was not to deny the pressure of international market forces, but to recognize the power of national governments based on popular coalitions to block, channel, and conceivably reverse them. Even with globalization the state preserved the capacity to secure markets, employment and industry, and attract long-term investment. Accelerated capital flight to and imports from poorer nations, especially China and India after 2002, created enormous pressures on governments to re-impose capital, investment, and import controls, that is, systems of managed rather than free trade. France and Germany began to regret the delegation of industrial and competition policy to the EU, resulting in the loss of national champions to foreign ownership and relocation to Eastern Europe (*Le Monde*, April 25, 2004). The state remained the most powerful institution to regulate markets for the purpose of employment, education, research, health, financial integrity, job training, labor relations, infrastructure, and justice. It had no peer as a source of public power for economic and social governance.[6]

Forty years of integration did not produce a transfer of loyalties, expectations, and political activity from the nation to the EU. The federalist movement, which was important in the formation of the EC, had practically disappeared 40 years later. The EU did not, as the German Constitutional Court noted in its Maastricht decision, create the sense of a European people or demos bound together by a common culture, identity, or destiny. The common adherence to market values and diverse forms of democracy did not bring nations together. Despite all the official cultural exchanges between France and Germany there was much less mutual knowledge and understanding in 2000 than there was on the eve of the First World War – fewer French and Germans studied each others' languages than ever before. As in the 1960s European elites were more familiar with America than with each other; indeed Americanophilia was often confused with Europhilia if only because of the international status of English.

The EC disposed of a fair weather or permissive consensus around goals of peace and prosperity, but without much specific commitment – the more specific the program the less support there was for it. Only 20 percent in polls said they felt well informed about it in the 1990s. Nor did citizens show much discrimination between alternative European programs. Despite his defiance of the Commission and belief in a union of states General de Gaulle was still treated by the French as a good European (Bahu-Leyser, 1981). The most committed came not from the Southern nations, which obtained the most subsidies, but from the founding states, which were still motivated by past experiences – memories of world war and Catholic antagonism to Communism. As these memories faded, the EU came to be judged in more instrumental economic terms.[7]

Attitudes toward the EC were increasingly determined by perceptions of national economic performance (Gabel, 1998, 99–100). It was blamed by many for the deep recession that followed upon the single market and

Maastricht. The biggest loss of favor took place in those countries Spain and Portugal, which had benefited most from EC largesse and its mantle of democratic legitimacy, as well as among the founding states France and Germany with instrumental judgments prevailing over the affective. In 1994 only 32 percent of those polled felt their country had benefited from the single market (Cameron, 1995b, 148–9, 1996, 350–7; Milner, 2000, 4–11).

Positions were determined by class differences over the market opportunities or threats the EC presented. Business executives and better-paid professionals, who benefited from the higher salaries and greater job opportunities the neo-liberal economy afforded, were the most favorable. The one group for whom the single market was a reality were corporate executives, who could bid up salaries and stock options. Workers from the wealthier states, particularly the better paid, were the least enthusiastic because they feared product and labor competition from poorer ones while workers in the poorer states hoped the single market would bring more investment. Managers were almost 50 percent more likely to support the EC than workers (Inglehart, 1987, 145; Gabel, 1998, 38–92; Green, 1999).

Support for the EC declined after the false dawn of the late 1980s when it produced growing unemployment and job insecurity. Voters fled to dissident lists in 1994 (Perrineau, 1994). More than one half abstained in 1999; only 45 per cent voted in 2004. Though the idea of the EU was still popular in 2000, the majority were unhappy with its functioning, particularly with regard to jobs and growth (*Le Monde*, January 16, 2001). In 2002 a majority, especially the young and working class, in all but three states said they would not care if the EU disappeared tomorrow; only about one third of all respondents, notably managers, showed concern (*Eurobarometer*, 57, Spring 2002, 42–4, 58, March 2003, 50, 69). In 2003 less than half of those polled in the EU thought it was good for their country or that the Euro was better than their former national currency. The peoples of Europe were no longer willing to sacrifice resources or well-being for the sake of the EU. With failing legitimacy it was vulnerable to a major shock such as a prolonged European depression, international war, or continuing institutional paralysis.

Notes

1. An early exception was the EC Membership Evaluated Series, e.g., Dreyfus, 1993.
2. He was portrayed by George Ross, 1993, 61, 72–3, 1995; Helen Drake, 2000 and Charles Grant, 1994, as a social democrat. Grant, 1996, corrected himself.
3. De Vos, 1989, 178–9; Hall, 1992; Hall and Gold, 1994; *Le Monde*, April 29, 2004.
4. Dignon, 1996; Fagenberg, 1996; Pivetti, 1998; Verdier and Breen, 2001, 254–8.
5. Bourry, 1993; Sharp, 1993; Cohen, 1995; Saint-Martin, 1996.
6. Boyer, 1996; Epstein, 1996; Streeck, 1996; Hirst, 1996.
7. Lindberg, 1970; Perrichon, 1989; Perrineau, 1994, 156–69; Gabel, 1995, esp. 20.

4
Theories of Integration: American Political Paradigms

Bernard H. Moss

The EC owed much to the United States not only materially through the Marshall Plan and diplomatically through the brokering of the ECSC and EDC, but also philosophically as an inspiration by example and as a source of academic legitimacy. From 1947 the US promoted the idea of a European community both as a unified market for its exports and as a bulwark against internal and Soviet Communism. The US was willing to sacrifice short-term commercial interest, notably in agricultural exports and its payments balance, for the geopolitical sake of European unity (Romero, 1996). As a federal state with a continental-wide market that encouraged the free movement of labor, goods, services and capital, and economies of scale, the US was the model of success to follow. The US also provided academic legitimation by establishing EC studies as a social scientific field and giving it initially a progressive social democratic thrust.

Because of their engagement in the Cold War, the cultural heritage and ancestral and émigré links, American scholars were the first to define a disciplinary field of European or European Community studies. Fascinated by the attempt to go beyond the nation state, which American liberalism tended to blame for wars and revolutions, they applied paradigms or models drawn from the pre-1914 Progressive tradition, which bore only a tangential relationship to pertinent European ones. The founding paradigm of interest group pluralism or functionalism, which entailed some political regulation of the market, was sometimes supplemented and later replaced with that of a neoclassical economics that foresaw market forces eliminating remaining national regulations and barriers. Missing from the American tradition were conceptions of class, politics, ideology, or the state that might structure markets or interests, order their priority, transcend, or overturn them.[1]

I Functionalism and neo-functionalism: the founding paradigms

The founding paradigm inherited from Progressivism was interest group pluralism, which saw government as the direct expression of organized, chiefly economic interests, firms, trade unions and the like. Pluralists preferred to see labor and capital, buffered by third parties, in bargaining equilibrium rather than conflict. The future supranational state would arise as "spillover" from economic groups pursuing their interests on a larger scale with the encouragement of transnational institutions. Labor would achieve on the supranational level the kind of reforms it had failed to obtain in the nation state. This social democratic ideal for Europe was linked to the idea of the end of ideology and class conflict in capitalism.

EC studies were founded in the Eisenhower years of peace and prosperity in which social scientists proclaimed the end of ideology and blanked out the turbulence of the 1930s. They returned to the more comforting paradigms of the Progressive Era in which political science as a discipline had been invented as a middle or third way between socialism and corporate capitalism. It was the science of a new society that stood above violent and irrational conflicts by evacuating concepts of power, the state, ideology, and class associated with the old. The major text was about what happened in government, procedures and processes, rather than causes material or intentional (Lustig,1982).

The United States was then still a vast continental-wide federation, which reserved all powers, notably social legislation, not delegated to Washington to the states. Lacking a dangerous enemy on its borders and with limited constitutional powers it had not built up a large standing army and bureaucracy. Living beyond the strong centralized states of Europe Americans found it hard to conceive of state power or any distinction between government and civil society. They conceptualized their own collective structures in functional terms, much influenced by medieval Catholic political theory, as corporations or guilds that fused public and private power and united master and servant (Lustig, 1982). It was the same convergence of medieval theology and middle-class "third way" aspirations after the Second World War that spiritually drove the EC project.

American interest group pluralism was more fluid and democratic than that of the Middle Ages, but it preserved its sense of balance, the conflation of classes, the crosscutting identities and the notion of government as an unmediated expression of civil society. As Alexis de Tocqueville had noted in the 1830s, before the growth of corporate capitalism polarized classes, the multiplicity and variety of groups in American society defused the class struggle and muted the levelling tendency of democracy. Giant corporations were to be judged by their efficacy, their functionality, not by any abstract standard of justice. Government was valued best as regulator, using scientific criteria much like an engineer to weigh and arbitrate differences – much as the EC and Commission were later viewed by American political scientists.

These preconceptions about American society were applied to international relations in the interwar years when the US spurned the League of Nations and entangling alliances. America was the new society expressing universal values free from the irrational ideologies of the old. Americans could not comprehend the nationalist ideologies that had led to so much bloodletting in the world war. They had gone to war only to defend democracy not for selfish nationalistic reasons. They had built a stable peaceful democracy out of practical commercial transactions. If only interstate relations could be structured in the same way around trade, transport, or communications, there would be no reason for wars.

This view was first expounded by David Mitrany, a Roumanian working for the British foreign office. He believed that the extension of trade and communications with other countries would create real interdependencies and generate functional supranational organizations that would prevent war. He later served as consultant for the first truly multinational company – British–Dutch Unilever. His motto was that of IBM, the computer giant – "world peace through world trade". During the Cold War Karl Deutsch (1957) extended the argument to politics, values, and culture, which would also be homogenized, he claimed, by international organizations such as NATO. He was not the last American to believe that the communication of their ideas irrespective of the context in which they were received would transform the world (Harrison, 1974).

With the ECSC Monnet hoped to achieve the same functional transcendence of national interests in the sinews of war, coal and steel, making it impossible. Monnet was a Frenchman who had acquired an American outlook – anti-national and functionalist – in many years of working and living with Americans as an international trader (Duchêne, 1991). Indifferent to partisan politics and ideology, even that of European federalism, his aim was to develop transnational ties and organizations. The ECSC that he negotiated was given interventionist powers over decartelization, social assistance, and prices and quotas in an emergency. He anticipated spillover from coal and steel to related sectors of energy and transport, but the ECSC provided more evidence of spillback than spillover as employers and the Germans resisted its interventions, leading to his resignation (Haas, 1958; Gillingham, 2003). Monnet nevertheless went ahead in 1955 to propose Euratom, a regulated market for nuclear energy, which he thought more acceptable to his compatriots than a common market in everything.

The neo-functionalism of Ernest Haas differed from functionalism in recognizing the proactive role of transnational institutions in promoting functional connections. A German Jewish refugee writing in the 1950s he had to mask his social democratic aspirations for the EC in the language of American engineering or managerial problem solving. The logic was self-evident and banal. European construction would be driven by the spillover that occurred when initial measures created problems that required new ones. But this could only happen if there were something wrong or incomplete with the original plan or if the real objective was hidden. Most integrationists hid their plan. Monnet thought you could advance toward European unification through a chain of technically related measures without ever announcing the goal. The Hallstein Commission was challenged and defeated by de Gaulle because it openly proclaimed its supranational project. Jacques Delors was also discrete in seeking a supranational state with "intentions masked", but this palpably failed to create a European identity.

The reasoning behind spillover was never clarified beyond managerial speak. The reason spillover to greater liberalization seemed necessary to solve problems created by the removal of tariffs was that nobody considered antiliberal spillback. Why would the unification of the market for coal and steel lead to that of energy and transport? All kinds of market segments existed in national economies (cf. Weber and Rigby, 1996). Regulated agricultural and competitive industrial markets coexisted in countries without any technical or economic contagion occurring. The answer was that spillover in neo-functionalist theory was not a material connection, but an ideological or "psychological" bias in favor of free markets as Commission president Hallstein (1972, 29) admitted. In other words, a cumulative chain of liberal market solutions, which did not necessarily correspond to a real socioeconomic process, was built into the integration project from the start (cf. Moravcsik, 1998a).

Haas (1964) saw the need for a proactive supranational authority to construct functional ties, to construe political issues as technical ones, upgrade them as common interests and draw interest group activity and popular loyalty away from the nation state. Such an authority would have to walk a tightrope between the political and technical. If issues appeared too political, they would provoke dissent and resistance to integration, but if too technical they would fail to elicit interest, support, and loyalty. The EC fell mostly over the latter side of the tightrope.

Haas (1958) was inspired by union proposals for European collective bargaining under the ECSC and Monnet's hopes for spillover to new domains and sectors. He knew that his theory would only work in a consensual society as he imagined America to be and Europe becoming. In the absence of class and national feeling, economic groups would transfer their loyalties to the supranational level where the factors of production could circulate more widely and where collective interests would be better served than in the nation state. Though neo-functionalism was deterministic and teleological – Haas predicted a supranational state by 1968 – it was highly sensitive to dramatic political events like de Gaulle's boycott of the EC in 1965 and the French strikes of May–June 1968, which confounded his predictions. In the 1970s Haas (1975) repudiated his model because it did not take account of political contingencies or the forces of globalization that were widening the scope of transactions beyond Europe.

Haas' assertion about the end of class conflict and political partisanship was contradicted by his own evidence on the ECSC. It had created a wider, freer market for coal and steel, but not the accompanying social and industrial protection that Monnet expected due to German and business obstruction

(Gillingham, 1991). The only examples of spillover Haas could cite were efforts by unions and social democrats to obtain benefits on the European level that they could not get at home – on working time, social security for migrants, and collective bargaining. Noble resolutions on European collective bargaining passed by the Assembly were ignored by the decision-making Council of Ministers. These efforts failed but they generated a transnational labor reform ideology with the illusion that domestic blockages could be overcome on the European level (Haas, 1958, 209–39).

The Christian Democrats were basically happy with the status quo voting invariably with employers (Haas, 1958, 24, 43, 419) while the Socialists imagined that European integration could be made into something other than what it was. It was because unions and social democrats felt so marginalized in their own countries in the 1950s that they hoped for better in the ECSC. The truth was that they had even less leverage there because of its built-in checks and balances and employer and German vetoes than they had in their own countries where they disposed of empowering institutions, common traditions, and a mass movement. European ideology masked and accentuated labor surrender and impotence at home.

Leon Lindberg, Haas' student, cautioned that the spillover process was not automatic and that it would only shift loyalties if it enmeshed national officials and changed domestic regimes. In his study of the formative years Lindberg thought he detected spillover between accelerated tariff reduction, which was negative integration, and the Common Agricultural Policy (CAP) and plans for social reform, which were positive. Initial tariff reductions had been so successful in increasing trade that big business pressed for more, which demand the French linked to agriculture and the Commission to the completion of the single market with an expedient social dimension.

The growth of intra-EC trade was not exceptional on a world scale in the 1960s; for the French it was due not so much to the Common Market as to de Gaulle's firmly maintained 37 percent devaluation (Chapter 6). The reduction of industrial tariffs was linked by the French to the CAP as a *quid pro quo*, but this linkage was part of the original treaty bargain and not the product of spillover. Nevertheless it took 12 years of struggle, including boycotts and threats of withdrawal, before France obtained financing for the CAP. It took even longer for social policy to be addressed, faintly in the 1970s but only seriously in Delors' package for a single market and currency in the late 1980s. The Commission's conception of a social program in 1962 was propagandistic, simply designed to win over worker support. As for the enmeshment of national politicians in the European project, they certainly began to spend more time on it, but even as more functions were transferred to Brussels, the politicians became more removed from the supranational faith that motivated the founding fathers (*contra* Wessels, 1997).

Lindberg became more skeptical about integration after de Gaulle's boycott and May–June 1968 challenged neo-functionalist assumptions. He noticed that the "permissive consensus" that allowed the delegation of state functions to the EC contained very little commitment, loyalty or knowledge, little sense of solidarity or of a common destiny. The working class remained parochial and nationally-minded. Indeed the resurgence of class struggle in France and elsewhere would threaten the essentially middle-class consensus around the EC unless national leaders – like Delors – could be found to offer symbolic compensation for the material losses workers suffered from it. The EC was in a race with nation states for loyalty that was not being won.

The possibilities for spillover were contained in the words and implicit design of the treaty and in its expansive interpretation by the Commission and Court, which established the supremacy of European over national law (Chapter 2). The goal of a single "natural" free market operating without national restrictions under a sound currency was spelled out by the Spaak Report, Hallstein and the first Commission. Spillover was contained in treaty provisions and logic. For implementation all that was needed was enforcement by the Commission and ECJ and the assent of member-states, but the latter required domestic regime change. The major steps toward internal liberalization were the result of domestic neo-liberal realignments. The transfer of state functions to the EC was driven not by technical necessity, market forces, or corporate lobbying, but politically and ideologically by domestic realignments aided by the free market agenda of the EC.

II Inter-governmental liberalism: the export interest

Established primarily to facilitate trade, the EC was dominated by large exporting and multinational companies and their peak associations, including UNICE, the European confederation of employer federations, and since 1983 the ERT, composed of the CEOs of the largest European multinationals.[2] Large exporting firms strongly influenced the large and small bargains that made up the EC in treaty negotiations, the Commission, council, parliament, and court. The great exporters however formed only a small proportion of the business community most of whom relied on domestic markets. Business interest in the EC went beyond access to new markets. Businessmen were also owners of capital, lenders, borrowers, and investors, national party partisans, usually conservative, and employers of labor. West European trade could have been organized under many regimes from the global free trading favored by Germans to the managed protectionism of the French. The choice of a supranational liberal regime reflected more than simple export interest. It represented a complex of geopolitical, ideological, political and economic interests and ideals that helped consolidate and maintain capitalism in Western Europe against both the threat of Communism and of a resurgent labor movement and expanding welfare state.

The case for the primacy of export interest was made by Andrew Moravcsik, (1998a; cf. Moss, 2000), who tested his model of interest formation, governmental aggregation, and international negotiation in a study of five major and several minor bargains that made up the EC. Though nationally centered, he used the same paradigm of interest group politics as the neo-functionalists minus the labor–capital distinction. Industry, represented by peak employer associations, was imputed to have an export interest in an undervalued currency and fixed exchange rate and wage-earners to share their employers' concern while banks and finance preferred a harder adjustable appreciating currency.

Moravcsik conceded that besides the direct pressure of exporters – for which he offered little evidence – governments were influenced by their conception of the public good and such objectives as national competitiveness and fiscal and monetary responsibility. The latter considerations gained more salience with the capital mobility released by the breakdown of Bretton Woods and help explain the turn toward monetary union in the 1970s. The precondition for monetary union was the convergence to low inflation, which for Moravcsik was the only rational choice in the face of capital mobility. He suggested that monetarism was the result of domestic political realignments, which were motivated to put downward pressure on wages and benefits and shift resources from the public to private sectors, but denied the EC's autonomous role in that redirection.

Moravcsik insisted that the pooling and delegating of power to the EC was controlled by national governments in rational pursuit of domestic interests. He rejected claims that self-aggrandizing EC institutions engaged in task expansion or that there was an underlying logic to the EC project that limited national capacities far more than governments intended. He found only one case, the single market initiative, where the Commission set the agenda. He admitted of a cumulative process of liberalization in which corporations were empowered by the removal of national barriers to seek greater freedom of access but this process was foreseen and willed by governments; there was no unintended logic of development, no spillover of EC functions or institutions and no unanticipated external changes giving a different twist or direction to outcomes than the ones intended. Successive governments reacting to the pressures of producers and markets merely decided that further liberalization was the best way forward.

To arrive at his conclusions Moravcsik had to bend over backwards to minimize the role of European ideology, EC initiative and constraint, and class, political and geopolitical alignments. Thus he denied the impact that defense cooperation and Hungary and Suez had on the resolution of differences between the French and the Germans over the Rome treaty or the class interest that turned French employers away from protectionism toward the EC as a useful weapon against the interventionist state. The main arguments used in the French parliamentary debate over the Rome treaty, Moravcsik to the contrary, were political, dealing with the need to overcome French diplomatic isolation and tame Germany; even if they were sometimes rationalizations of economic motives – employer support for the EC swayed conservative deputies – they still became reasons for ratification. If large French employers simply lobbied on the basis of export interest, why were exporters divided regarding the EC and EMU along partisan Gaullist versus liberal lines? Moravcsik rightly denied the role of German reunification in the initiation of the single currency in Spring 1988, but forgot its later effect on the German public, who acquiesced in the Euro out of fear of going it alone (Moss, 2000, 263–5).

Moravcsik admitted that European ideology might have prevailed where export interests were divided or uncertain. The employers' BDI backed Adenauer rather than Erhard over the EC despite interest in global or European free trade because they had special links with Der Alter and trusted him to provide external security for the development of German capitalism. When export interests were divided and supposedly clashed with financial ones in 1990, Chancellor Kohl was able to exercise his geopolitical preference for France and the EMU. This way of putting it allowed Moravcsik to maintain separation between the political and economic whereas the reality was that business endorsed political projects like the EC and EMU that were consistent with its class interest while politicians incorporated capitalist interests into their projects – a free trading EC and monetarist EMU.

Like many others (e.g. Frieden, 1991) he postulated a conflict of interest between exporters interested in low interest and fixed exchange rates and bankers wanting high adjustable ones. The evidence for this distinction was scant and contradictory (Moss, 2000, 47), the thesis simplistic and narrowly economistic, because of variation in banking relationships with the state and industry and in the difference that the political conjuncture or balance of class forces made. The assumption made was that industry and banks were only interested in their immediate return and future value of their assets rather than maintenance of the regime, state, government, and macro policy that ensured a high rate of labor exploitation and profitability. In most countries banks had links with industry and the state that gave them wider concerns for system maintenance. German bankers had organic links with industry as owners and managers, the French and Italians as providers of long-term credit. The Belgians and Dutch were indeed more interested in immediate returns and future values because they were much more oriented toward international currency and capital markets (Kurzer, 1993; Talani, 2000; cf. Walsh, 2001, 5–8).

Finance and industry were practically interchangeable ways of making profit. Banks depended on the profitability of industry just as industry relied on them for credit. Even the ECB mandated for price stability was not completely insensitive to popular and government demands for lower interest rates in 2001 to revive the economy. Central banks independent of government were more likely to seek price stability than those responsible to macro regimes and democratic majorities concerned about jobs and growth. On the other hand, governments like the British, even a Labour one, might want to instruct their central banks to keep money sound in order to maintain a world reserve currency, which policy was a major cause of the British disease of domestic disinvestment.

Profitability could depend on very different macro and exchange rate regimes. The relationship that pro-EMU economists claimed between exchange rate stability and trade and growth was spurious (Feldstein, 1997; *contra* Gros and Thygesen, 1998). German industry had an interest in a system of low inflation and slight currency undervaluation that kept labor in check and exports booming while the French and Italians before the 1980s usually relied on a regime of inflationary growth. The views of large firms, which preferred fixed exchange rates for long-term planning and tolerated higher interest rates because they were self-financing, could differ from those of smaller firms that needed low interest rates and were flexible enough in production schedules to accommodate exchange rate volatility. To some extent this material difference was reflected in political divisions among French employers between Catholic and Giscardian liberals, and Gaullists (cf. Boisseau and Pisani-Ferry, 1998, 78–80).

The political conjuncture made a difference to employer attitudes to inflation. Capital had greater fear of inflationary policies under pro-labor governments such as Mitterrand's, which could threaten its survival, than under conservative ones like Chirac's, which protected it. Moreover, the effect of fixed exchange rates depended on the macro policy of the monetary hegemon regulating the system (Herr, 1997). It could be inflationary as was the Bretton Woods system when the US was running a large trade and payments deficit in the 1960s or disinflationary as was EC monetary union under German dominion.

The critical factor, which changed everything in the 1970s, was the balance of class and political forces. The mobilization of organized labor and expansion of the welfare state squeezed profits and posed a threat to capitalist survival, most seriously in France. This drove industry and the banks and parties linked to them to adopt strict monetarism. Divisions on the Left between working and middle-class wage-earners, represented more or less by socialists and social democrats respectively, allowed neo-liberal coalitions to triumph with the help of American and German monetary hegemony. On the continent, these coalitions could use the external constraint of monetary union to achieve disinflation and their triumph over labor.

British capital however did not need EC monetary union to check union and worker power. It was able to reverse the balance of forces by the mid-1970s under Labour (Artis and Cobham, 1991), then more decisively under Thatcher, because of divisions in the unions and Left and the subjection of all governments to Treasury and American-led IMF orthodoxy. Monetary union was only really advocated by the exporting multinationals, not always British, who took over the employers' CBI. But even the slight division over the ERM and EMU between the financial City and the CBI did not overshadow their mutual political support for an independent Thatcherite monetarism (Blank, 1973; Middlemass, 1994; Talani, 2000).

It was only when inflation reared its head again in the Lawson boom that the City seeking a more constant external constraint than the US offered began pressing the government for entry to the ERM, which was done at an overvalued rate in 1991. After the shake out of the economy in the deep recession that followed governments both Conservative and Labour followed a mix of fiscal expansion and monetary restriction that with favorable terms of trade – high export and low import prices – produced medium service-led growth at low inflation. Under these conditions British capital lost interest in monetary union, making an affirmative vote on Euro entry in a referendum unlikely (Blank, 1973; Stephens, 1996; Talani, 2000).

The move toward financial rather than productive investment called financierization that occurred after the 1970s did not represent the triumph of finance over industrial capital but rather the inability of both to make profits in domestic manufacturing under conditions of labor mobilization and relatively full employment and their reluctance to go elsewhere.[3] Foreign direct investment (FDI) did not take off in response to rising domestic wages as it had before the First World War and as it was to do after 1995 in the American bubble. It cannot therefore explain monetary union. The financierization of investment, which started in Britain in the early 1970s, was accelerated on the continent by the ERM raising interest rates, which encouraged large companies to become their own bankers, accumulate and loan money, purchase shares, and make portfolio investments abroad (Holman and Pijl, 1996; Duménil and Lévy, 2000).

There was no evidence of German export industry pushing the Bundesbank for a looser monetary policy or a more asymmetrical ERM because all German capital benefited from the external constraint against inflationary wage rises and labor mobilization. Short-term export interests in lower exchange and interest rates were trumped by the broader political class interest in sound money that united the Bundesbank, employers, and government, including most Social Democrats. The Bundesbank spoke for German capital as a whole when it restricted growth but protected a system that guaranteed sound money, labor subordination, and long-term export surpluses. Contrary to Moravcsik, German industry was not seeking lower exchange and interest rates with a single currency but was perfectly content with the asymmetry and flexibility of the ERM, which allowed them both to keep the D-Mark undervalued and to force austerity on their European partners (Johnson, 1998; Kaltenhalter, 1998; Heisenberg, 1999a).

After the profitability squeeze of the 1970s European business valued those institutions national or European that would quell inflation and restrain wages however much growth and employment suffered. In Germany that meant the Bundesbank, in France and Italy tying government hands with ERM and EMU, while in Britain where the City was an independent power with both governmental ties and global scope and the EC carried the risk of a more regulatory regime, it meant the ERM only when inflation got out of hand during the Lawson boom (Stephens, 1996; Talani, 2000).

Moravcsik assumed wage-earners had the same exporting interest as their employers. But worker preferences on monetary policy were determined less by commercial than by class interest, wages and conditions, union organization, and political ideology. Unions and labor parties had opposed the EC because free trade and monetarism were inimical to their wage and political bargaining position. When unions and socialist parties turned around to support the EC as in Germany, it was not because of export interest, but because they had been defeated at home and hoped to do better with social reform on the European level. Class position and understanding still determined attitudes toward the EC. German metal workers, the real proletarians, were far more critical about the inequalities generated by the single market than were unions like the printers representing the labor aristocracy (Markovits and Otto, 1993). In France the most proletarian, Communist workers, were anti-EC, while the health sector, which had no interest in export but was more middle-class, represented mainly by the formerly Catholic CFDT, was pro-EC (*contra* Frieden, 1998). When Swedish metal workers turned from opposition to support of the EC, it had little to do with export and more with the conclusion, however mistaken, that social protection could best be guaranteed on a European level. They realised their mistake when they voted against entry into the Euro in 2003 (Wiebe, 2003; cf. Bieler, 2000, ch. 13).

The claim that the signatories of the Rome treaty intended to unleash a cumulative process of liberalization is more than doubtful. Aside from the Germans, who were often unorthodox in practice, none shared the neo-liberalism that was written into the treaty and pursued by the Commission, ECJ, EP and transnational firms (Chapter 2). Nobody foresaw, as Moravcsik admits, the constitutionalization of the EC with a court claiming far reaching competence and imposing its liberalizing decrees on recalcitrant members with the help of business interests. Despite the letter and spirit of the treaty few economists or experts anticipated fixed exchange rates, the single currency or the EC attack on the mixed economy including state aids and procurements, nationalization, and expansive macro policy (Machlup, 1977).

The attack on unions and the interventionist state was unleashed because of events that were not foreseen. The labor mobilization after 1968 and breakdown of Bretton Woods accelerated the wage-benefit-price spiral, squeezed profits, caused class and ideological polarization, and forced a choice between the further socialization of the market or a monetarist turn. In this debate pro-business forces used EC instruments, particularly the ERM, to tip the scales in favor of sound money and fiscal responsibility and to tie government hands in the future. The creeping incremental integration that had occurred as spillover between treaties (Pollack, 1994) was little compared to the national regime changes consolidated by the single market and currency. The great leaps forward were decided, as Moravcsik says, primarily by the realignment of domestic coalitions and governments.

III The EC and globalization theory

With the fall of the Berlin Wall and collapse of Soviet Communism the EC lost one of its original reasons for being as a bulwark against Communism. The triumph of capitalism on a nearly planetary scale and the failure of various national socialist experiments, notably the French, left the impression of an irresistible liberalizing force operating on state and society summarized as globalization. The globalization of market forces tended to destroy nationally-based collective institutions and identities and imposed individualism, monetarism, and neo-liberalism everywhere. Extravagant claims were made about the end of the nation state and the emergence of an international capitalism, bourgeoisie or class struggle, in particular by the neo-Gramscian school of international relations.[4] The most salient lesson that Eric Hobsbawm (1998), the prominent British Marxist historian, could glean from the *Communist Manifesto* for its sesquicentennial was not about class struggle but about globalization.

It became an intellectual buzzword in the 1990s that tried to explain too much, economic change, political systems, ideologies, and future trends. The degree of globalization was exaggerated and consequences drawn reductionist. The globalization of markets and finance with its ebbs and flows had been occurring since the sixteenth century reaching its purest, most integrated, form in the liberal state and gold standard of the late nineteenth century. The American economy and multinationals reached the apogee of their domination of the world market after the Second World War. Historically, the globalization of trade and finance was as much cyclical as linear in character (Aglietta, 1995; Bairoch, 1996). It had been interrupted and reversed by war and economic crises, notably that of the 1930s, and in the recent post-2000 downturn. Calculated in terms of current prices, the proportion of EC member GDP going to export was not much greater in 1995 than it had been in 1913. Export share of GNP in these terms slipped after the mid-1980s especially when only manufacturing is considered.

There was relatively less FDI, particularly in the former colonial world, than there had been. One half of foreign investment was in mergers and acquisitions rather than expanded production. Two thirds of foreign trade was handled among multinational firms, one-third within internal company markets, but multinationals employed only 1.5 percent of the work force and their value added represented only one tenth of GNP (Wade, 1996;

Perraton *et al*, 1997; Sutcliffe and Glyn, 1999, 112–14). Over one half of FDI after 2000 went to China whence cheap goods were exported to the West. Here was the real threat of globalization to growth and jobs in Europe, but this occurred long after the apogee of the EU and cannot explain it.

Multinationals were really national firms with international branches in assembly or distribution; they did not form the basis of an international capitalism. Because of their relative size they disposed of more political influence especially in the EC than their output warranted. They were nationally structured as were their assets, shareholders, management, R&D, and market orientation (Wade, 1996). Of the top 100 companies in the world only three had truly global markets, i.e., more than 25 percent of their sales in at least three continents (*The Times*, September 2, 2002). A comparative study of US, Japanese, and German transnationals found national differences in ownership structure, investment horizons, profit targets, work organization, and personnel practice (Doremus, 1998). There was little interaction with the host country; only the Americans were inclined to purchase in foreign markets. The Japanese got almost all their parts and raw materials from home. Transnationals in Wales, which had practically no local linkages, were not affected by the introduction of the single market (Phelps, 1997). During the stock market boom of the late 1990s, which drew a lot of European investment, US corporations became the model to follow in terms of shareholder value, merger, and profit targets, but these influences did not change national management structures (cf. Farnetti and Warde, 1997).

What exploded exponentially was the flow of short-term capital, mostly currency speculation, due to the breakup of Bretton Woods and wage-led profit squeeze. It was a circular process aided and abetted by political decisions like the floating of the American dollar in 1973 and abolition of capital controls starting in 1979 (Helleiner, 1994; Andrews and Willett, 1997). The depreciation of the US dollar was an important factor behind the first plans for EMU and the ERM, which aimed at stabilizing both internal and external EC rates. The Germans wanted to use EMU and ERM to quell inflation, but it was not until after the turnabout of the Americans in 1979, when the Fed raised interest rates to 15 percent, that members of the ERM were forced by Germany to deflate. But while the US, Britain, and the rest of the world preserved the ability to reverse course at the end of the 1980s, ERM states were locked into a rigid system of high rates that stifled growth and created mass unemployment.

Higher interest rates made government borrowing more expensive, but room was still left in wealthier nation states for independent macro policy (Baker *et al*, 1990; Garrett, 1998). Until they traded in capital controls for the single currency France and Italy could defend temporarily against high eurorates (Bakker, 1996; Oatley, 1997, ch. 5). The history of the ERM located the real origins of deflation in domestic political and class realignments rather than in capital mobility itself. The links between short-term interest rates – often determined by speculation – and long-term investment were tenuous since most investment came from national sources. Real interest rates and capital costs showed greater convergence at the end of the nineteenth century than at that of the twentieth. The convergence of short-term interest rates in the ERM in the 1980s came about as the result of political choice; it did not occur elsewhere in the 1980s as a result of globalization.[5]

The big change that exposed society to greater global forces was the collapse of political opposition in the social democratic or socialist movement (Callaghan, 2000; Huber and Stephens, 2001). Neo-liberalism became *la pensée unique*, the only respectable way of thinking (cf. *Le Monde diplomatique*, January 1995). The Left had suffered a real defeat, but it was easier to attribute it to ill-defined global forces than to unpack the concrete reasons for it. Profit squeeze and manufacturing decline had diminished the size and concentration of the manual working class (Pontusson,1995b), the traditional core of opposition, but the triumph of neo-liberalism had created a much larger working class, including professional and managerial personnel, vulnerable to the job insecurities of the market place, who needed and wanted more state intervention. This enlarged working class manifested itself most clearly in the social fracture or division opened up in France in the 1990s over Maastricht and its deflationary consequences (Chapters 6, 7).

One reason this movement lacked force and consistency was because much of the left, including the Communists, had already given up the instruments of the nation state for the will of the wisp of new social movements and global or European solutions.[6] Globalization could be invoked with equal fervor by the extreme left to justify its hollow call for world revolution, by non-governmental organizations (NGOs) to sustain their lobby of international organisms and by right-wing social democrats like Blair to prove the vanity of state intervention (e.g., Giddens, 1998). The anti-globalization movement was ridden with contradictions between national and internationalist aspirations.

Globalization theorists on the left assumed that the strengthening of world market forces would yield new global solidarities and organizations whereas the reality was that it undermined collective action and forced a retreat back to the nation state for protection. The dominant trend at the turn of the century was disintegration, the weakening or re-nationalization of international organization from the former Soviet bloc to the UN, World Trade Organization, IMF, NATO and the EU, the return in the US to military unilateralism, and growing demand for tariff protection. The growth of global markets would not reduce national barriers and differences, but cause even more uneven political and economic development, making national reactions and revolutions more likely than international ones as Marx, Trotsky, Lenin, and Otto Bauer all realized at some point in their lives (Moss, 2001a; Schwartzmantel, 1991). Working-class solidarities, customs, ideologies, organizations, and practices were embedded in the nation state (Ebbinghaus and Visser, 1994, 1999). The weakening of the nation state by the EC and globalization helped undermine union strength (Verdier and Breen, 2001), destroying the basis for euro strikes or other forms of transnational worker solidarity outside of the bureaucratic ETUC, which was firmly enmeshed in the neo-liberal EC project.

Academics and intellectuals were swept up in the twin myths of globalization and Europeanization. Left academics, disillusioned with previous political engagement, withdrew into a critical- and post-materialist posture that stood above nationhood and class conflict (Moss, 2001a). The class position and attitudes of academics fluctuate, depending on national politics, disciplinary paradigms, the class and aspirations of their student and research clients, and so on (cf. Walker, 1978). They saw the construction of the EC and the neo-liberal triumph both as a threat and opportunity, attracted by its universality – and for an elite material advantages – and appalled by some of its consequences (Callinicos, 1989, 170–1; cf. Kelly, 1996, 114, 124). Academic acceptance of globalization and Europeanization had little effect on public opinion, but it deprived it of alternative socialist direction and leadership.

The dynamic of academic Europhilia differed from country to country. In the US European integration became a subplot for the triumph of markets over socialism and Communism that was consubstantial with American supremacy (e.g. Gillingham, 2003). In Britain where academics outside Oxbridge tended to be social democratic, they turned to the EC as an alternative to the strident nationalism of Thatcher and as the more human, non-American face of an inexorable globalization. In France, where intellectuals had lost traditional ties to working people through Marxism, Catholicism, and primary and secondary education, Europe was an escape as it had been in the 1950s from domestic failures to transform society (Moss, 2001a; cf. Todd, 1998).

Globalization was used to justify the EC in two ways, either as the expression of regional economic interdependence or as a defense against globalization. Both liberals and Marxists had foreseen forces of production outgrowing the confines of the nation state and requiring regional or universal governance, for liberals the minimalist suprastate, for socialists a more regulated one. This notion of outgrowing had led Marx to oppose Czech independence in 1848, Leon Trotsky, Lenin's companion in the Russian Revolution, to prefer a United States of Europe to socialism in one country, and Mollet, the French Socialist, to help found the EC (Moss, 2001a). But the assumption that expanding forces of production required larger units of political governance, however seductive in the abstract, had to be subjected to empirical proof, which in the case of the EC was wanting. Whatever economic advantages were gained via intra-EC trade – and even these were doubtful – were more than offset by the restrictiveness of monetary union built into the original project (Chapter 8).

One of the best accounts of the single market would argue that it was necessary to expand the forces of production in high technology (Sandholtz, 1992, 1998). EC integration, it claimed, was driven by large companies seeking to expand productive forces and markets by felling national barriers. Concerned about the advance of the US and Japan in computers, semiconductors and telecommunications, the Commission undertook programs of aid and market liberalization to develop these industries because they were beyond the capacities of member-states to finance and market.

The argument was seductive but flawed in many respects. It asserted but did not prove that high tech development was beyond national capacity, relying on a *post-hoc ergo proctor hoc* argument – because the EC took it up, it was beyond state capacity. Member-states supposedly lacked the capacity because the new technologies required huge investments with little certainty of return and larger markets to amortize the sunken costs of R&D and obtain it. The standardization of national technical, compositional, and health and safety requirements would open up public markets monopolized by national and public suppliers to private competition better able to make the new investments. The authors viewed the Commission as the servant of the productive forces and multinationals rather than as their instigators and organizers. In fact, the demand for the single market and EC aid to high tech development was partly self-induced by the Commission when it organized 12 private electronic firms into a liaison group in 1979 and the CEOs of the largest European multinationals into the ERT in 1983 to lobby and formulate the terms for these programs (Cowles, 1995).

In any event, the EC program was a failure insofar as Europe fell further behind the US and Japan in high tech development, probably further than it would have been if industrial policy had remained in the hands of the member-states, certainly the major ones. The EC program of aid to multinationals and standardization deprived public providers of resources and outlets, yet member-states continued to supply the bulk of assistance to high tech R&D; the French budget remained larger than that of the EC, its public telecommunications at the cutting edge in the field (Chapter 3).

The EC lacked the constitutional authority and managerial and technical capacity to carry out effective industrial policy, which member-states still possessed (Cohen, 1997). Whatever the pressures of globalization on tax revenues, public services were still better able to make the large initial investments required precisely because they were guaranteed a national market whereas private firms faced a heterogeneous, more costly and uncertain European one. French telecommunications, which for decades had dragged its heels on providing domestic telephone service, introduced an internet system, Minitel, long before the multinationals did (Cohen, 1992). While a few multinationals increased market share and profits, most firms probably ended up with a smaller share of the market than when they began. Private companies may have had the profit incentive to commercialize new products like mobile phones much faster than would have the public sector, but they were vulnerable to speculation and overinvestment. Their rush to market produced enormous wastage – only 5 percent of the Atlantic optic cable was used – and when the bubble burst in 2000 most ended up poorer than when they began (Brenner, 2002).

The authors mistook the larger political forest of the EC's neo-liberal agenda for the technical requirements of high tech development. Neo-liberal thinking was taking over both in the member-states and the EC in 1979 with Davignon at Industry and Emerson and Padoa-Schioppa at Economic Affairs and with the ECJ ruling on mutual recognition in *Cassis de Dijon* (Chapter 2). The first R&D program Esprit was organized by the Commission with the self-supporting backing of the ERT to relaunch the single market after the defeat of the federalist Spinelli constitution in the EP. Through its R&D program the EC decided against French interventionism in favor of the Thatcherite model of commercialization and privatization. The Commission was acting as an errand boy for the multinationals, but it was doing so on the basis of its own constitutional remit, domestic political re-alignments, and larger class forces mobilized against the labor movement and the interventionist state.

Conclusion

The theory of European integration was dominated by American paradigms of producer or interest group politics, which accorded little role to class, ideology, and the law, or indeed political parties, leaders, or geo-politics. They were determinist, if not teleological, and apologetic of the EC in conformity with the general aims of US foreign policy. They assumed that European integration was conducive to economic growth, technological development, and citizen well-being rather than a fetter on material standards and productive forces. Their social scientific claims derived from the American Progressive tradition of third way problem solving that stood above – and depreciated – the partisan political or class struggle, which is the only way to engage with and understand the economic, social, and political world and its conflicts (Chapter 5). Rich in information their accounts built upon relatively static monist models of explanation pitched at an intermediary level rather than a complex articulation in time of deeper structural causes.

The foundational neo-functionalist school idealized the ECSC and EC as self-aggrandizing but essentially rational arbiters, who could balance the interests of employers and wage-earners in a way that was not possible on the domestic level. The spillover or task expansion they anticipated as solutions to technical problems turned out to be market-oriented, driven by economic, class, ideological, constitutional, and juridical imperatives. Whatever its philosophical provenance, the ideology of European integration was capitalist driven by virtue of its reference to an essentially neo-liberal constitution and project.

Moravcsik reminded us that the EC was first about trade and that its pillars were the nation state in which preferences were formed, coalitions built and responsibility to international organizations like the EC delegated, but he downplayed geopolitical and domestic political ideas, events, and projects and denied the constraint of EC institutions and principles. He was blind to class issues, assuming the identity of interest between wage-earners and employers, a simplified conflict of interest between industrial and financial capital and capitalist disunity in the face of the working-class and socialist challenge. Governments, he thought, foresaw the liberalizing consequences of their delegation of power to the EC. There was no unintended or unanticipated spillover of EC institutions or principles and no unexpected external changes, namely class mobilization and polarization, to give the EC a directional role in deciding the outcome of the crisis.

Sandholtz and Stone Sweet extended the forces of production argument to high tech development under the single market program. Integration was driven by large companies seeking to eliminate national barriers to market enlargement. The development of high tech on a level with the US and Japan was blocked by national standards and procurement that limited the size of the market to finance and amortize R&D costs. It thus required technical standardization, EC aid and the opening of public markets to private firms – hence the single market program initiated by an alliance of the Commission with multinationals. The inadequacy of national industrial policy, however, was unproven and the EC program a relative failure insofar as Europe fell further behind the US and Japan in high tech R&D. The EC R&D and single market program was not driven by economic or technical necessity, but by the neo-liberal project arising from EC principles and logic, domestic political realignments, and capitalist mobilization against organized labor and the interventionist state. The missing economic, ideological, juridical, and political dimensions to the dominant EC paradigms arose essentially from a blindness to class interest and conflict.

Notes

1. Olson, 1971, a critic of pluralism, recognized that self-interested individuals would not form groups unless driven by some ideological or other external force.
2. Cowles, 1995; Fligstein and Brantley, 1995; Frieden, 1996; *inter alia*, Sandholtz and Stone Sweet, 1998.
3. I thank Gerald Friedman for this point.
4. Cox, 1987; Gill, 1993; Holman and Pijil, 1996; Bieler, 2006. Also, Robinson and Harris, 2000.
5. Banuri and Shor, 1992; Hirst and Thompson, 1996, 36–9; Wade, 1996, 66–75; Oatley, 1997, ch. 4; Alexander, 2003.
6. Hirst and Thompson, 1996; Cerny, 1997; Bieler and Morton, 2001b; Monbiot, 2003; *contra* Hay, 1999a.

5
National Labor Regimes: The EC in Class Context

Bernard H. Moss

I Method and argument

How could the historian contribute to the voluminous literature on the EC whose models and paradigms came from American political science? There were several good internal narratives (e.g. Dinan, 1994) and one that placed it in the global context of the triumph of markets over national regulation and control (Gillingham, 2003). Like Hegel's owl of Minerva the historian takes flight at dusk post-festum after the dust has settled and clashes of the day have been resolved but like Marx in his more engaged work he or she must remember the heat of the day, its conflicts and the roads not taken (cf. Moss, 2003a). To the models of the political scientist he can add richness of context, the salience of the event or personality, uncover long-term trends and wider patterns, the sequencing, hierarchy, and articulation of causes, and perhaps the underlying structural causation of it all (Carr, 1961; cf. Moravcsik, ch. 1, 1998a).

What social scientists contribute in analytic clarity and focus and statistical precision they often lose in longer and wider perspective. By identifying contextual anomalies and supervening variables the historian can reaffirm long-term trends, patterns and relationships, in this case long waves of growth and the balance of class forces, the Phillips curve trade-off between inflation and unemployment, the difference that pro-labor governments made to worker mobilization and the advantages to unfettered labor, ultimately subversive of the capitalist order, of inflationary growth. The historian can correct the inversion of cause and effect, showing, for example, the dependence of collective bargaining regimes or central bank independence upon wider political class struggles or on the contrary regime changes like the single currency triggered by an accident of personality, in this case Mitterrand's.

A natural synthesizer, the historian may prefer those economists who integrate their discipline with politics and sociology, who recognize the way in which social mobilization or political institutions can alter the operation of neoclassical or Marxian laws, whether that of supply and demand or the production of surplus value. A generation of radical economists, British, French, and American (Gordon *et al*, 1982; Mazier *et al*, 1984, 1999; Armstrong *et al*, 1991), who had grown up and acquired tenure during the golden years, discovered a major contradiction in the system in the 1970s – a profit squeeze arising out of the power of organized labor and the interventionist state. They were not the first to question the neoclassical assumption of constant returns to capital and labor or the secular Marxian law of declining profit, but they offered credible empirical accounts of the emerging crisis of profitability resulting from the wage squeeze. Depending on phases in the cycle wage hikes could be either a stimulus or an inhibitor of investment; there were Keynesian moments when they increased profits and Marxist ones when they squeezed them.

Blindness to EC neo-liberalism was linked to an apologetic view of a post-war capitalism transformed by the interventionist state. State regulation, planning, collective bargaining, welfare spending, and Keynesian demand management were thought to have achieved both sustainable growth and social equity. Forms of state capitalism had emerged from the shifting balance of public and private power chiefly between the government and business. In the turn toward neo-liberalism distinctions were drawn among varieties of capitalism between the US and Britain, which had taken the full turn, and the managed and interventionist types of Germany and France, which preserved a distinctive European social model (Albert, 1991; Hutton, 1995; Hall and Soskice, 2001).

In fact the role of the state in regulating capitalism and its variety were vastly overblown. Insofar as capitalism relied on expanding competitive markets to achieve labor subordination and profit, it was always liberal (Braudel, 1972; Sweezy, 1978). Capitalists as an interest group were almost invariably opposed to state intervention whether in the form of subsidy or taxation (Chapter 2). After the defeat of the post-war labor mobilization and the marginalization of Communists after 1947, pro-business governments in France, the exemplar of state capitalism, cleared the way for the operation of market forces even under de Gaulle, whose monetarism and deplanification conformed neatly to EC economic liberalism in the 1960s (Chapter 6).

The real resistance to EC liberalism and the pertinent varieties of capitalism came from the labor movement and the industrial relations (IR) and macro regimes it shaped in different countries. Contrary to received wisdom, revolutionary or militant Communist unions gained more immediate benefits for workers than did the moderates, the social democratic ones that restrained immediate demands for the sake of future trickle-down rewards from employers and Catholic ones that sacrificed material gains for qualitative ones and a place in heaven. Christian Democracy propounded a great rhetorical, electoralist myth in Germany and elsewhere about the "social market economy." In actuality it defended property, markets and sound money against the danger of socialism. Its welfare reformism was protective of traditional hierarchies of wealth, occupation, and gender. The political values it imparted to member-states and the EC, of federation, subsidiarity, the inviolability of the person and of corporatism, were derived from the age-old struggle of the Church against the materialist leveling force of the egalitarian democratic state. Once inflationary growth threatened profitability in the 1970s, it was instrumental in imposing the monetarist cure through the mechanisms of the EC, ERM, and EMU.

The globalization of trade and finance, exaggerated as it was in extent and political consequence, was a cumulative political-economic process (cf. Andrews and Willett, 1997) motivated by a philosophy of free trade and deregulation that could not be reversed at the time because of the temporary impermeability of the middle classes to the economic downturn. The EC in its neo-liberal orientation was a forerunner of globalization insofar as its excessively free trade and monetary union forced convergence toward high interest and exchange rates that preceded in time and exceeded in rigor that in Britain, the US and the rest of the world (Hirst and Thompson, 1996, 35–7; Oatley, 1997, ch. 4).

It slowed growth and caused mass unemployment weakening labor's bargaining power and undermining EU social and regional policies. The freer enlarged market operating under monetary constraint generated the disaffection of wage-earners, no longer limited to the manual working class, from governing elites and institutions, employers, governments, and the EC. This public malaise and alienation, most manifest in France, forced governments to resist EU supranational neo-liberalism. This resistance lay behind the EU fiscal and constitutional crisis of 2003 and put paid to conventional wisdom about the growing consensus around the third way (e.g., Giddens, 1998) and the end of ideology and of class-based history (Fukuyama, 1992).

Facts never exist or speak for themselves, but only in relation to an order, real, unconscious, or imagined. Structural explanations make explicit that order, provide the landmarks and framework for apprehending facts. In history they guide the selection and ordering of facts and finding the essence and turnings of developments. As in the whole picture on the jigsaw box they give us an idea of how the pieces of the puzzle may fit together subject to experimentation. Rather than reducing explanation to one-dimension, they allow for a complex articulation of causation, from underlying fractures to random events, or parallel or linked causes that may trigger the schism (cf. Althusser, 1979; Winicott, 1995).

Structural causes produce permanent effects, not always visible. They have a continuous flow that is captured in grand narrative, which is essential to the Western historiographical tradition (Callinicos, 1995). Structural theories cannot be disproved, as the empiricist Karl Popper (1945) maintained, only replaced by one that offers – in the historian's lexicon – a better account of observable relationships and events. It is precisely because structural causation is held constant that knowledge can be advanced about the complex whole by adjusting intermediary linkages and auxiliary assumptions to fit the observable evidence. Without the anchor of an unproveable and unfalsifiable premise social scientific enquiry turns around like a spinning wheel following the personal whim and intellectual fashion that finally sustains the *pensée unique* or dominant ideology (cf. Lakatos, 1970).

In mode of production, exploitation, and class Marx provided the tools – not an articulated theory – for structural explanations in history.[1] The EC was discussed as a universalist supranational project without reference to class orientation and purpose. The best models were built around trade and export interest and class fusion or equilibrium. The missing dimension from all the literature, one hidden by EU ideology and its academic certification, was the one that best explained its overall development. Class conflict, capitalist defense and ideological rationalization lay behind the original project of the EC, its constitution and development unevenly on many levels from its substructure in business cycles long and short and geopolitical frame in the Cold War to the upsurge of labor mobilization and capitalist resistance to it that allowed the consolidation – national, European, and international – of an unstable neo-liberal order.

The EC was a class project supported by nearly all businessmen, bankers, merchants, manufacturers small and large, few of whom were exporters, because they instinctively saw the advantage that enlarged competitive markets and sound money gave them over organized labor. Where previous plans for integration had contained provisions for positive intervention, the Spaak Report and Rome treaty laid out the prospect of a single competitive market with sound currency in a utopian state of nature free from public or social control. The liberal terms, spirit, and logic of its constitution inspired chiefly by German ordo-liberals, drawn out by the Commission and sustained by employers, were those of a Hayekian federation that safeguarded profit-making enterprise against inflationary labor and state demands. Constructed as a defense against rising labor and the interventionist state, it was projected and rationalized as a supranational universalist project.

In the distributional conflict between capital and labor, which generated inflation and squeezed profits at the end of the long wave, the institutions and principles of the EC, free trade and sound money, could only be invoked in one direction – monetarist and neo-liberal. Thus they were used to compress wages and benefits and commercialize and privatize public utilities and services and to prevent member-states like France from taking protective measures for countervailing policies. The single market and currency implicit in the treaty were implemented by the Commission and realigned neo-liberal governments to resolve a crisis of profitability, but they only deepened the crisis of investment, productivity, growth, and employment – which redounded in the public mind against them.

II Class, long cycles and labor mobilization

The basic substructure of EC development was the long wave of economic growth, crisis, and stagnation that traversed its history from the initial launch in 1957 in an era of capitalist expansion and optimism to the single market and currency, put into place to solve a crisis of profitability but which aggravated stagnation and institutional crisis. The post-war cycle produced an expansionary phase from 1949 to 1974 when the annual growth of GDP, productivity, and real wages in the OECD – larger than the EC – rose 5.2, 5.2 and 4.7 percent to a downturn from 1974 to 1994, when they were 2.6, 2.1 and 2 percent, that is half that of boom capacity (Husson, 1996, ch. 1). Productivity at the root of growth continued to decline, in France from 1.5 percent in the 1990s to 0.88 percent from 1995–2002, even more in Germany (*Le Monde*, February 15–16, 2004). Even when this decline represented a return to historic norms, it narrowed possibilities for class compromise and popular adhesion and invited the monetarist turn.

Class structure, mobilization, and conflict through the control of labor supply were both a cause and effect of the long cycle (Boddy and Crotty, 1975; Gordon *et al*, 1982; Marglin and Schor, 1990). The struggle between labor and capital over value-added powered the cycle, driving prices up and down. Organized labor pressed the state to increase wages and jobs by expanding the money supply (Rowthorn, 1980, 412–13). At the same time the cycle set parameters for the changing balance of class forces and redistribution of the product between wages and profit. Overriding phases of growth and stagnation was money supply, regulated by the hegemonic world and regional powers – the US and Germany (Herr, 1997). Debates over the expansiveness of monetary policy, national and international, with its employment implications, whether between the British Lord Keynes and the American Fed over the IMF or France and Germany over EC monetary union were never class neutral (Apple, 1983; Forsyth and Notermans, 1997).

The cycle generated resources for both class conflict and compromise as well as generational mental expectations of plenty or dearth that were socially differential. Middle-class wage-earners maintained expectations of rising income and mobility far longer after the downturn than did manual workers immediately confronted with job loss. The track that working-class interest took, in contrast to rational capitalist profit-seeking depended on ideology (cf. Weber, 1991; Kelly, 1996). The preference for conflict or compromise was largely ideological ranging from revolutionary Communist to solidaristic Catholic, a projection of material interests in autonomous ideas about the world that had their own life but also definite class consequences in particular conjunctures.

The EC was initially established on the growth trajectory of the post-war economic miracle or boom and took its monetarist turn in the 1980s in response to the enduring crisis of growth and profitability that ensued. The boom and crisis drew upon the classical features of the long price cycle known to capitalist economies since the sixteenth or eighteenth century – a take-off based on abundant labor and other resources leading to a sustained expansion and accelerating boom that exhausted labor and other reserves, squeezed profits, and eventually caused a crisis of disinvestment and unemployment. Statistical economists might dispute the timing and regularity of these cycles, traced in the nineteenth century by the Russian Nicholas Kondratieff, for the trace was often hidden by supervening variables and unique events, but the underlying pattern of cycles linked to shifting wage and profit shares of production remains.[2]

Phases of rising prices, about twenty-five years in length, characterized by relatively few and short recessions and fuller employment, were followed by downward ones yielding more frequent and serious recessions and mass unemployment. The cycles correlated with economic growth, debt, productivity, real wages, unemployment, and political class conflict. They tended to mould long term outlooks, expectations and behavior in terms of collective action and even birth practices, rising in the boom and falling in the downturn (cf. Lembcke, 1991). At the crest of long cycle arose an hysterisis whereby the expectations raised by the boom clashed with the disappointments of the crisis to produce a period of acute social tension, strikes and conflict threatening the system, as occurred in a complex mediated way in the French Revolution (Labrousse, 1947; Screpanti, 1984; Chevallier, 2001).

The single most convincing explanation for the regularity of cycles in capitalist economies concerned fluctuations in labor supply, the *sine qua non* of capitalist profitability, both in its demographic and politically regulated dimension. Baby booms, not unaffected by political and economic conditions, furnished industry with the extra factory hands and consumers needed for expansion (Megan, 1987, 184–9). The eventual exhaustion of cheap labor and other reserves, subject to political organization and regulation, led on to boom and crisis. Labor supply was regulated politically by strikes, unions, parties, and governments. Responding to the wage profit squeeze crisis of the 1970s, radical political economists deployed a model of political class struggle, regulating labor reserves, to explain both ten year business cycles (Boddy and Crotty, 1975; Weisskopff, 1979) and in conjunction with other social and technological factors the long cycles of accumulation or growth in American history (Gordon, 1982).[3]

The long cycle typically began with an abundance of cheap resources of labor, capital, and raw materials, and weak unions that kept wage increases below those of productivity and allowed profits and capital stock to grow. Economic growth was the greatest stimulus to strikes and unionization. As more jobs were created and labor reserves absorbed, wages began to catch up to productivity and workers felt empowered to make collective demands, to strike and unionize, usually led by ideologically driven activists. The rate of translation of strikes into union membership was tripled by the action of pro-labor governments acting to defend worker rights (Friedman, 2003). The sense of injustice heightened by ideology overcame the collective action problem of individuals risking their jobs for the sake of the group or collective. Ideology gave them a map of the world, links with the larger political movement and hopes for social transformation – whether Communist, social-democratic or Christian (Kelly, 1996, 52–64).

Moving from recovery to expansion employers made so much profit that they were willing to concede collective demands lest production be interrupted. Strikes of the semi-skilled diminished wage differentials and strengthened the sense of class solidarity. Employers compensated for wage increases with price hikes made possible by governments eager to further growth by increasing the money supply. Labor mobilization was translated into political influence either through the election of pro-labor governments (Schmidt, 1982; Hibbs, 1987) or by the preemptive action of conservative ones. By thus yielding to labor mobilization employers and governments generated the cumulative strike–wage–price–welfare spiral, which encouraged more strikes and unionization. The spiral eventually came up against the limits of profitability and crashed into disinvestment and mass unemployment.

The post-war boom in Europe began with the application of tried and tested American technology to large labor reserves, essentially unemployed or underemployed workers left over from the depression and war. Growth was exceptionally strong and enduring because of the fit between the newly acquired assembly-line production of consumer durables – refrigerators, washing machines, radios, TVs, cars, and the like, – and the American model of consumption that inspired purchase (Mazier *et al*, 1984, 1999). Growth turned on a model of production and consumption that absorbed large amounts of capital for factories, machinery, and raw materials while requiring the expansion of employment to meet the needs of both production and sales. Thus was created a long-term balance between the new technologies capable of absorbing available capital at increasing rates of productivity on the one hand and the effective customized demand for their products on the other, a balance that did not exist in the American high tech boom and bubble of the 1990s (Brenner, 2002).

Labeling this virtuous circle of production and consumption as "Fordist" is misleading because it depended for take-off not on high salaries but on low (Brenner, 1998; Brenner and Glick, 1991; *contra* Denison, 1967; Mazier *et al*, 1984, 1999). Wages took a long time to catch up to productivity. Profitability initially depended on the exploitation of the poorly paid and unskilled, the unorganized, and insecure – young people under thirty and migrants from the French countryside, the Italian South, and Eastern Germany. The countries with the largest labor reserves Italy and Germany grew the fastest and those with the smallest, Britain and Belgium, which had skill shortages, the slowest in the 1950s (Kaldor, 1964; Kindleberger, 1967; Walker, 2000).

In the take-off of the 1950s profits rose as wages tended to lag behind productivity, but once labor reserves were exhausted after 1960 wages, especially low ones, caught up and workers were empowered by the market to make collective demands, to strike, and join unions. In the early expansion of the 1960s employers were making so much profit that they readily conceded higher wage demands lest production be interrupted. The strike threat of the semi-skilled diminished wage relativities or differentials. Price mark-ups to cover wage hikes fed inflation, which encouraged wage-earners to make more demands, again to strike and unionize in a wage–price mobilization spiral (Boddy & Crotty, 1975; Marglin and Schor, 1990; Armstrong *et al*, 1991). Economic growth was the greatest determinant of strikes and unionization (Friedman, 2003), a process delayed in France until 1968 by authoritarian incomes policies.

By the early 1960s labor markets in EC countries were tightening up and governments were looking for ways to obtain consent for incomes policy in case monetary controls failed (Edelman and Fleming, 1965). Holland ended its strict corporatism in 1963, releasing pent-up grievances and strikes. Macmillan in Britain applied for EC membership under US pressure convinced that it would stimulate a stagnant economy. He tried to imitate the French with consultative planning in the hope of getting voluntary wage restraint ignoring the fact that French unions were effectively excluded from the process (Panitch, 1976, 43–50; Moss, 1993a). Italy, France, and Germany deliberately slowed down their economies in the early 1960s with the latter engineering a serious recession in 1965. The authoritarian regime of de Gaulle kept a lid on wages with its large parliamentary majority, control of the media, and requisition of public sector strikers. Delors, the Catholic unionist on the Plan, tried to get the secularized CFDT to agree to an incomes policy, but it wanted to use its new ideological freedom to challenge the CGT for blue-collar members with militant action and so launched the famous slogan – related to the Church doctrine of subsidiarity – of autogestion or self-management in May–June 1968, which represented a breakout from ten years of authoritarian wage restraint. The same revolt occurred from 1968 to 1974 in all EC countries (Panitch, 1976; Crouch and Pizzorno, 1978; Barkin, 1983).

Labor mobilization, strikes and unionization, were both a cause and result of inflation in a cumulative process. Strikes were clearly linked to wage increases and thus to inflation. Prices were raised to meet rising wage costs (Heylen and Poech, 1995, 583–4). Most studies of the late 1960s and 70s showed inflation rising several months after successful strikes, but there were period regime shifts and differences among states both as to the volume of strikes and as to their propensity to produce inflation. Strikes caused less domestic inflation before the breakdown of the Bretton Woods system of relatively fixed exchange rates that occurred after 1968. Under the system states were required to maintain relatively fixed exchange rates against the inflation caused by the wage–price spiral by buying up stronger currencies, which forced others to share the inflationary burden. This was because the purchase of stronger currencies raised the export demand for goods denominated in those currencies as well as the real price of goods sold to other countries. Thus the inflationary effects of strikes on a country were shared and blunted domestically under Bretton Woods. Once however the system broke down and currencies floated free, inflation could no longer be shared but was reflected in a falling exchange rate. Strikes thus had a greater effect on domestic inflation after the dollar was devalued in 1971 and floated in 1973 (Busch, 1993).

The ability of wage-earners to catch up with and surpass price inflation depended upon the militancy, bargaining power, and political resonance of organized labor. From 1950 to 1975 factory workers were able to keep up with prices and surpass them after 1968 in France, Britain, and Italy due to union militancy. The strikes and political crisis of May–June 1968 gave French workers 8 percent higher wages than they would have had otherwise. In the 1970s the rate of inflation was highly correlated to rates of strikes and unionization and growth of nominal and unit labor costs though union density in disciplined systems was negatively related to strikes. Depending upon the institutional factors of union centralization and discipline, legal constraints and long-term contracts, and ideologies, social democratic, Catholic or Communist, which spurred or constrained mobilization, labor could win or lose from inflation.[4]

III From labor ideology to industrial relations and macro regimes

Labor ideology shaped forms of action, strikes, and bargaining and impacted on party political and governmental policies (Shorter and Tilly, 1974; Korpi and Shalev, 1980; Schmidt, 1982). Pro-labor parties in government made a difference to rates of growth, employment, and inflation and also to strikes, unionization and income distribution (Hibbs, 1987; Franzese, 2002). Essentially, three worldviews vied for control of European labor movements – the revolutionary Communist, social democratic reformist, and solidaristic Catholic. Apolitical business unionism was marginal even in its American heartland (cf. Kelly, 1996, 52–64; *contra* Hyman, 1996). The Communists, pursuing social transformation, put theory into practice with maximum demands, agitation and mobilization. Fearing revolution, Social Democrats moderated immediate demands in hopes of rewards in the future while Catholics sacrificed material needs for the sake of participation, partnership and other qualitative changes. Labor politics, especially revolutionary, made a difference for wage-earners that could destabilize capitalism from within. Governments and employers developed responses to labor mobilization that were consolidated into long-term regimes, usually with a certain coherence between IR and macro policy (Herr, 1997; Iversen, 2000).

The most salient distinguishing feature of IR and macro regimes was their degree of elasticity toward labor mobilization and wage gains, the freedom they afforded to strikes and unionization and degree of monetary accomoda-tion, the expansiveness of money supply. The two polar opposite regimes in the EC were the ordered German one with its strike and bargaining constraints and monetary restrictiveness and the French and Italians, who unfettered class struggle and loosened state expenditure and money supply. The configuration of ordered regimes varied from the voluntary restraint of German unions in anticipation of future rewards and the Scandinavian trade-off between union discipline and state guarantees of full employment to the truly neo-corporatist tripartite regime of the Netherlands, which set wages and prices in the 1950s with the cooperation of unions and employers.

Contrary to conventional wisdom, it was the adversarial class struggle unions with their threats of regime change that gained more from employ-ers and the state than did moderate cooperative ones precisely because of the larger class and political resonance of their action (Cohen, 1993; Friedman, 1998). The divergent strategies of leading Communist parties, national and transformative in France, European and integrative in Italy, led to different national trajectories, a half-hearted socialism that failed in France, and a long road to austerity in Italy. While well-ordered Germany with its low inflation was always vaunted by official economists as the model to follow, France and Italy, the countries of class struggle, had a better record for employment and income growth in the years 1960–99, especially before they adopted German monetarist policies (Friedman, personal communica-tion, Marchand and Thélot, 1991).

The ways in which wage-earners exploited their enhanced bargaining power in the long boom depended very much on prevailing union organi-zation and ideology – Communist, social democratic, or Catholic. Because Communists sought the overthrow of capitalist systems their unionism was the most aggressive in making inflationary demands, fomenting local and general strikes and promoting political transformation. In opposition to the Communists after 1947 social democrats settled on class compromise and accommodation with collective bargaining systems that guaranteed moderate wage increases and state benefits in return for social peace. An older opponent of revolutionary unionism were the Catholics, who sought to divert attention away from material issues of wages and class struggle toward more spiritual ones of dignity, working time and conditions, and participative cooperation with management.

Union centralization cut both ways, toward constraint or activism, depending on type. The ideological and organizational conformity of Communist unions contributed to rank and file activism, maximalist demands and generalized national strikes, whereas the more bureaucratic one of Social Democracy imposed no-strike discipline and wage restraint down the line (Schmidt, 1982, esp. 183). Wages tended to lag behind productivity in the countries of constraint but more than kept up in those of freewheeling struggle where the strike–wage–price spiral yielded real gains in wages and production share. France showed perfect correspondence between rates of inflation and wage share of added value with a short time lag in the 1970s and 80s (Husson, 2001) as adversarial unions exploited the space of uncertainty opened up by price rises.

The reason that inflation tended to accelerate in the long boom had little to do with rational expectations and a lot more with the unexpected capacity of labor to make use of the fluidity, insecurity, and uncertainty created by inflation to strike and organize for a fairer share of the wealth created (Hibbs, 1987, ch. 3; cf. Friedman, 2003). As John Commons, the American Progressive founder of labor economics, observed, workers strike and unionize to catch-up to prices, the more so the higher the rate of inflation, the more aggressive are the unions and the more accommodating is the government. For strikes and unionization also strengthened the political clout of labor whether directly through pro-labor governments or indirectly by leverage and threats of exit from business-oriented ones.

By inflating the currency, lowering interest rates, and increasing the money supply, pro-labor governments encouraged employers to grant wage increases that were high relative to productivity and to pass costs on to consumers and back to employers. Gaining the upper hand over capital in government, labor was able to extract a larger share of value-added along with greater worker and union protection, progressive taxation, social benefits, and replacement wages for the unemployed, making it less dangerous to strike and raise the level of demands. But weak unions as in the US and disciplined IR and restrictive macro regimes like the German could make workers rather than employers bear the cost of inflation.

IV Partisan domestic and regime cleavages in the EC

The margin of choice within particular regimes between inflation and unemployment for parties and governments was represented by the Phillips curve. Despite many intervening variables and anomalies – Gaullists making concessions for the working-class vote, Socialists turning to the right in the 1980s – the Phillips curve was the foundation of party electoral and governmental policy cleavage within and between EC countries from 1948 to 1978. Left or worker-oriented parties accepted higher inflation in order to create more growth and jobs while right or capitalist-inclined parties tolerated higher unemployment, greater inequality, and lower growth in order to boost profitability. Generally, inflation was good for wage-earners, small business, and debtors, who benefited from low real interest rates, and bad for asset holders and large employers (Chapter 4). Wage-earners who could organize and strike to catch up to prices were more likely to favor inflation than those who were less able to do so as in the US where unions were scarce and dispersed on the ground. Knowledge of this self-interest determined votes for conservative or labor parties. Until the late 1970s with some national variation, Germans were always rather anti-inflationary, the preference was for inflation over unemployment especially among majority wage-earners (Hibbs, 1985, 1987, ch. 11; Franzese, 2002).

The cumulative effect of more jobs and growth and equality was to strengthen unions and labor-oriented parties, which fed into more spending, monetary expansion, and inflation. Labor governments spent more on health, education, and welfare, increasing tax share of national income, especially corporate tax, than pro-business ones. They funded larger public and nationalized sectors and higher fiscal deficits and debt, which acted as automatic stabilizers in recessions. Partisan differences were mitigated by the tendency of both parties, particularly the right, to stimulate the economy just before an election generating the so-called political business cycle. They tapered off in the stagflation generated by the breakdown of Bretton Woods in 1973 and after the 1979 monetarist turn. Still, in the US from 1948 to 1978 Democratic administrations generated 6 percent higher growth, double the inflation and more income equality than Republican ones, which created 2.6 percent more unemployment. Similar differences existed within EC countries between left and right parties and between hard and soft currency regimes where the Germans and Dutch played the part of the Republicans and the French, Italians and Southerners that of Democrats. Once pro-labor governments faced capital mobility with fixed exchange rates they had little choice but to accept central bank independence and tight money to compress demand (Hibbs, 1987; Garrett, 1998; Franzese, 2002, 394–411).

Conservative governments faced with the threat of Communist-led regime change in France and Italy yielded the most in the 1970s. The immediate effect of this accommodation was to generate greater consumer demand, business confidence, investment, and fuller employment – in short a boom. Real investment in France rose from 17 percent in 1950 to 26 percent in 1973 (Aglietta and Baulant, 1993, 504). Points were reached, however, in the early 1970s, associated with the exhaustion of productivity gains and the saturation of markets, when the combination of higher wages and corporate taxes began to squeeze profits (Mazier *et al*, 1999). The boom was sustained for a while by scrapping old machinery for new and skilled labor for unskilled, but investment limits again were reached when profits could no longer be realized at high prices, particularly in foreign trade. The quadrupling of oil prices in 1974 by adding production costs and diminishing consumer demand was the crowning blow that ended the boom and produced the first massive crisis of profitability and unemployment since the 1930s (Weisskopf, 1979; Armstrong *et al*, 1991; Marglin, 1991).

Whether wage restraint was good or bad for capitalist growth was a highly contingent cyclical question – good in the early boom and bad in the later – good for productivity in some industries bad in others, good in the short run but bad in the long – that was invariably answered by employers and liberal economists in the positive. Higher wages could both accelerate investment and growth and eventually depress them depending on phases in the cycle. Decades of wage restraint and high interest rates did not have happy consequences for the exporting champions Germany or Japan. Wage restraint could be self-destructive because it bred demoralization among workers, which hurt labor productivity, and complacency among employers, which diminished innovative investment. After the monetarist turn, it led to a relative spiraling down of wages, conditions, and productivity in the EC (Hibbs, 1987, 103, 293; Western, 1997; Huemer *et al*, 1999).

The same inefficiencies of concessionary bargaining obtained in battles over employment. Defending their own activists French and Italian unionists were able to save more jobs and investment and obtain better retraining and retirement packages by plant occupation and strike action because of their political resonance than were threatened workers wedded to cooperation with management (cf. Golden and Pontusson, 1992). Econometrically based historical studies overturned the received wisdom that moderate unionism was more effective than the militant revolutionary (Cohen, 1993; Friedman, 1998).

EC states had widely divergent strike and strike-led inflation propensities depending upon the degree of constraint built into their IR and macro systems. One can discern three patterns: the relative wage–price stability of the Germans, the strike-led inflation of the British, French and Italians and, the state-led inflation of the Scandinavians. Countries with free wheeling mobilization and politically responsive central banks like France, Italy, and Britain had higher strike rates and inflationary strike propensity than Germany, Austria and the Netherlands before 1963 and after 1974. IR and macro systems were largely the result of the dominant labor ideologies that had emerged from national experience – Social-Democratic, Christian Democratic or Communist. It was not collective bargaining regimes that determined union ideology, as a leading British comparatist (Clegg, 1976) claimed, but the reverse (Moss, 1984; Friedman, 1998).

Outside of France and Italy where Communist unionism prevailed after 1947 governments working with Catholics and social democrats helped construct dikes of centralized bargaining against collective mobilization and inflationary demands. These systems were called neo-corporatist because of the increasing role of the state in negotiations, but the term also invoked medieval and fascist regimes that forced the fusion of classes.

The aim was to obtain union assent to the wage restraint deemed necessary for investment and growth. Corporatist accommodation – so hard to attain – nevertheless became the ideal for most governments in the 1960s and 70s; even the EC tried its version with the 1976 Maldague Commission (Lankowsi, 1982, 409–18). In applying for EC membership in 1961, the

British hoped to import methods of continental planning and corporatism to restrain union demands (Panitch, 1976, 43–50). Incomes policy was defeated in Britain because of independent unionism and – sometimes – Communist shop stewards and in France and Italy by Communist unionism. Generally, corporatism worked to restrain wages in recovery periods like the 1950s but could not survive prosperity and booms when wage-earners demanded their due and employers a return to relativities, skill differential pay, or recessions when employers could circumvent unions.

The ordered corporatist regimes differed in degrees of state intervention and class bias. The Dutch had a truly tripartite neo-corporatist regime in which wages, prices, and benefits were negotiated among employers, unions, and coalition government on three levels. The system prevented strikes and kept wage increases well below those of productivity in the 1950s (Walker, 2000). After the monetarist turn of 1981 Dutch unions renewed their social compromise with an agreement that increased part-time work for women in return for wage restraint and the retirement of older men. Belgian unions were forced to accept steep wage cuts as a result of collaboration between the Catholic union, which had spread its wings in nationalist Flanders, and a newly appointed Liberal prime minister (Jones, 1995a).

In Scandinavian countries, notably Sweden, where strikes had been virtually eliminated in exchange for full employment, inflation was generated by working-class power channeled through the state and public spending. Sweden held on to its pro-labor welfare state later and to a greater extent than others because of its high level of working-class concentration and organization (Esping-Anderson, 1980). The German system was one of semi-voluntary wage restraint motivated by Social Democracy in hopes of future rewards under the bargaining constraint of highly centralized unions, a juridification of IR that virtually barred strikes, and after 1974 strict monetary targeting (Jacobi, 1986; Moneckonberg, 1986; Streeck, 1994). Even Germany and the Netherlands could be affected in its labor market by imported inflation from neighbors arising from the appreciation of imports and accumulation of reserves. Imported inflation caused an unofficial strike upsurge in the late 1960s and early 70s, which led these governments to take restraining measures, initiating the wider monetarist turn in the EC in 1973 and 1974. The greatest wage restraint in terms of unit costs after 1974 was obtained in Germany, Austria, and the Netherlands (Taxler, 1999, 125).

The greatest wage price spirals took place in the countries of unconstrained labor mobilization, Italy, France and Britain. In France and Italy the mobilization was the result of agitational, spark-plug Communist unions that encouraged rank and file activism, wage maximalism, and generalized strikes until the PCI began restraining action in view of the "historic compromise" with the Christian Democrats in 1976.[5] In Britain the revolt of rank and filers and independent unions and leaders against incomes policies produced more strikes and disenchantment with the governments, both

Labour and Conservative, that promulgated them (Panitch, 1976; Hibbs, 1987, chs. 1, 10). The long road to austerity in Italy was due to the zig-zag and Jesuitical conversion of the Italian Communists to social liberalism, that in France to the defeat of the PCF by Mitterrand, and in Britain by Labour ministers bowing to the IMF in 1976 and to the 1979 election of Mrs Thatcher, inspired by Hayek's monetarism.

V Germany and neo-corporatist regimes

The regional enforcer of wage and price stability and anchor of the EC macro regime was West Germany, which by the mid-1950s had grown by leaps and bounds and accumulated a huge export surplus and currency reserve. The West German economy had been rebuilt with American help under the guiding philosophy of ordo-liberalism, a synthesis of Anglo-Saxon free trade with social Catholicism. The ordo-liberals, close to Hayek, blamed the past catastrophes of war, revolution, runaway inflation, and Nazism on state intervention and labor and industrial monopoly. Germans like other pawns in the Cold War had been torn from their roots by civil war, dictatorship, and defeat and were ready for conversion to any philosophy that pleased their new occupiers. Ordo-liberalism represented a foreign graft of nineteenth-century laissez-faire under the supervision of law and a state that would police competitive markets and wage and price stability. The latter was inscribed in the Basic Law or constitution of 1949 and the 1957 statutes of the Bundesbank.

Mutually reinforcing federalism and sound money were the mainstays of the West German state. Federations tend to preserve existing hierarchies of wealth and privilege (cf. Pentland, 1973). West Germany was given a federalist constitution to prevent the polarization of class and political forces that had occurred under the Weimar Republic, the union militancy, inflation, and nationalization in the British and Soviet zones of occupation and the recurrence of German military aggression.

The Basic Law created a national government fractured into autonomous departments, a federal division of powers and a Constitutional Court – by later statute an independent Bundesbank – as a check on central power. The fractured state yielded more power to the administration, which with its ordo-liberal orientation, translated dominant business interests and political issues into seemingly neutral technical decisions. The federal constitution made it difficult for the Chancellor to mobilize tax resources, as he only controlled two-fifths of total public expenditure and the budget could always be vetoed by states in the Bundesrat. It was thus easy for the Bundesbank to defeat an expansionary federal budget in 1975 and 1978. German officials always felt at home in Brussels because the politics and institutions of the EC resembled their own fragmented or "intermeshing politics" that gave pride of place to business interests (Risse-Kappen, 1996).

The new ruling Christian Democratic Party made up of business-minded civic leaders mostly untainted with Nazism – Erhard Economics Minister, had supported Hitler's full employment policies – incorporated the traditional Catholic solicitude for the poor and a working-class wing within the framework of a free market philosophy – all of which was captured by the fetching 1948 electoral slogan, invented by Muller-Armack, later negotiator of the Rome treaty, of the "social market economy" (Giersch *et al*, 1992). The approach to welfare, represented by the 1957 pension law, was conservative of occupational, wealth, and gender hierarchies, depending on income contributions rather than redistributional progressive taxes as in Scandinavia (Esping-Anderson, 1990). Ordo-liberalism with its bastions in the ministries of economics, finance, and Bundesbank would not deliberately brook any interference with the market process or challenge established social hierarchies (Giersch *et al*, 1992).

It would be wrong to suppose – as social-democratic champions of ordo-liberalism did (Albert, 1991, Hutton, 1995) – that it transformed German society. In fact it only worked in conjunction with much older monopolistic structures that were blamed for past catastrophes – quasi-medieval professional guilds, a trustified heavy industry with interlocking directorates and fusion with the three leading commercial banks, regional networks of small contractors, and councils of worker codetermination experimented under Weimar (Streeck, 1994, 1997).

While German governments always opposed directive industrial policy and monopoly in the EC and elsewhere, they defended their own cartels against American and French trust-busting and gave as much aid to their own firms as the French but on a more ad hoc politically expedient basis. Rather than dismantle monopolies the Germans tried to integrate them into the European and world economy and to impose macro and IR constraints on wages and prices. German success was due not so much to ordo-liberalism as to traditional skills, resources, and production, which the British and French had previously blocked from world export. Eager to build up its strongest front line state in the Cold War, the US promoted German exports under GATT, going so far as to open its own markets to it. Just as the French did not practice the dirigisme they defended in principle in the EC so neither did the Germans implement at home the neo-liberalism it imposed on others.

The German labor movement dealt with the triumph of ordo-liberalism from a position of weakness. It had lost many of its leaders to Hitler and the East Germans (Neunreither, 1994). The deflationary currency reform of 1948, sharply reducing the number of bills in circulation, and the migration of millions from the East escaping Communism caused mass unemployment and further weakened the Social Democratic Party (SPD) and unions. In 1951 the unions lost a referendum, which would have given them power in all works councils and boards. Instead market conditions were used as a benchmark in awarding supplemental pay in nonunion councils, which served as a safety valve for worker discontent and as a social alibi for the West German state (Streeck, 1994). Labor law punished all interruptions of work, effectively banning strikes over issues covered in contracts, wildcats, public sector and political strikes. Germany had the lowest strike level in the EC; when strikes did break out they were isolated incidents that were not followed up by union officials. In the 1950s wages trailed behind productivity increases, which were very large, and wage share fell, as did union density until 1956 (Moneckonberg, 1986; Streeck, 1994; Brenner, 1998, 63–76).

The defeats of the unions in the workplace and SPD in elections led to the abandonment of socialist goals. The SPD had opposed European integration as capitalist and clerical in inspiration and contrary to its goal of national reunification. But after several defeats in elections and hopes of reunification, they abandoned the socialist objective and came to accept the EC as an anchor for German democracy. Whereas the Marxist background gave them an interest in codetermination, in worker participation, they had very little interest in Keynesian stimulus (Allen, 1989), which was only ambivalently tried by Willy Brandt in 1969. When a true Keynesian SPD leader Oscar Lafontaine reached the finance ministry in 1999, he challenged the EC stability pact and was forced to resign (Chapter 9).

The key to the success of German monetarism was a domesticated SPD, which embraced the social market economy in 1959, and an affiliated trade union movement that voluntarily accepted wage restraint in anticipation of rewards from the export-led economy. German unions became strong and centralized, but they bargained under severe Cold War ideological, legal, political, and monetary constraint. With high unemployment in the early 1950s and strikes virtually banned, union demands and wages had a hard time keeping up with the tremendous leaps of productivity that made Germany the world export champion, supplying capital goods for mass production in Western Europe.

The great fear of the German establishment was that inflation imported from its softer currency trading partners, notably Italy and France, would stir up labor agitation and threaten profits. By 1955 the Germans had become the hub of the West European trading network with an enormous trading and currency surplus. As economic hegemon, it used its power to construct a trading system along orthodox liberal lines with free trade, relatively fixed exchange rates, trade and payments balance, and wage and price restraint. These objectives were sought in the Rome treaty and obtained in the austerity program that the new government of de Gaulle and Jacques Rueff, his ultra-liberal advisor, imposed on France in 1959 (Pittman, 1993, 467; Dickhaus, 1996, Chapter 6).

When labor markets tightened in the 1960s the CDU government engineered recessions, a deep one in 1965 that forced the unions to accept a minimalist long-term contract. When the Brandt government came in with a reformist agenda in 1969 and American dollars flooded the money supply, inflation rose and wildcat strikes broke out. Finance minister Karl Schiller wanted to revalue the DM and reorient production toward domestic demand while the pro-EC Brandt and the exporters of the employers federation preferred to use controls to maintain parity with the franc. Like the government, the Bundesbank was split in two over how best to reestablish price stability whether by revaluing the mark and holding back wages or by forcing the French to converge toward German norms through EMU. Under the influence of Milton Friedman the DM was finally floated upwards in 1973 after controlling for money supply (Lankowski, 1982, ch. 6).

To arrest imported inflation and the wage–price spiral in 1974, the year of the great oil shock, the Bundesbank adopted a restrictive system of monetary targeting that raised the employment cost of wage increases in excess of productivity. Henceforth, the Bundesbank would announce monetary targets and monitor wage settlements; fearing job loss, the unions kept demands within the bounds of supply targets. Control over the economy passed to the Bundesbank, which vetoed expansionary government policy in 1975 and 1978 and effectively put the growth of the welfare state on hold (Grande, 1988). By cutting money supply growth in half, the Bundesbank led the way to contraction in the rest of the EC and ERM especially after 1981 (Epstein and Schor, 1990, 141).

Rebellious French, Italian, and British unions were capable of thwarting monetarist policies, but German unions constrained by law and self-discipline conformed to them, diverting their attention to questions of working time and, more divisively, to environmental and nuclear issues. German workers were organized into 17 large sectoral federations of which only five actually bargained, usually following the lead of a restrained IG Metall (Streeck, 1994). The coordination of collective bargaining within monetary parameters was only made possible by a comprehensive system of labor constraint (cf. Soskice, 1990; Iversen, 2000).

During the stagflation of the 1970s, with unemployment growing along with inflation, West Germany was the model to follow because it had mastered inflation by 1975 without apparently creating mass unemployment. The darker side of this accomplishment was ignored. Official unemployment was low because guest workers were sent home and married women were returned home. Actually, Germany from 1960 to 1986 was the only major country to lose jobs (Marchand and Thélot, 1991, 585 [table]). High interest rates caused a decline in fixed capital investments, with hardly any GDP growth from 1980 to 83 and less than 1 percent per annum in the early 1990s. Wage increases rarely exceeded GDP growth and peaked at only 65 percent of value-added – more than 10 percent less than its trading partners. After 1974 Germany had the slowest growth of unit wages in the EC (Rowthorn, 1980; Streeck, 1994; Oatley, 1997, ch. 4).

Except for an ambivalent Keynesian flirtation between 1970 and 1972 German governments after the 1950s were always willing to accept slower growth and job loss in order to maintain price stability and profitability. They had the most restrictive macro policy in the EC, responding to downturns with higher interest rates and less expenditure until a shakeout of costs achieved equilibrium and recovery but at an increasingly lower level of growth (Epstein, 1990, 132–7). German interest rates were the highest and the least responsive to unemployment in the EC (Chapter 8). In the 1980s German inflation and unemployment were half that of the EC average. But low wages relative to productivity hollowed out the domestic market while high interest rates and low EC demand caused by the export of German monetarism through the ERM discouraged capital investment, especially in new technologies. The EC model of the 1970s and 80s became the sick man of Europe after 1990 when exports dived (Rowthorn, 1995).

The Netherlands, which was Germany's closest partner in the EC, had the most comprehensive corporatist system until 1963. It was traditionally a free trading nation whose main interest in the 1950s was to keep trading doors open to both Germany and Britain under global American security protection. It supported a strong EC Commission not because it was pro-integration, but because it saw the need for the firm enforcement of free trade. The Netherlands executed the reverse of globalization; it went from being a global colonialist trader to a regional one. In 1947 a rising Dutch Communist Party making inroads in the unions was confronted with a coalition of confessional parties, Catholic and Protestant, and a socialist party, which under Catholic personalist influence became the Labor Party. To prevent strikes these parties established tripartite bodies on all levels – works councils, the semipublic Foundation of Labor and coalition government – to set wages, prices, and benefits. To obtain investment funds from unpaid wages, they kept increases below those of productivity chiefly by employing young people under thirty whose standard of living doubled in the 1950s despite higher rates of exploitation (Jones, 1995a; Griffiths, 1997b; Walker, 2000).

The system broke down in 1963 when employers demanded a return to market wage differentials and workers their share of productivity and export. The Netherlands rapidly became a country of strikes with wages rising faster than productivity and high unemployment benefits that cut into profits. In 1974 the government was grateful to be able to link the guilder with the strengthening DM in the ERM to justify its own turn to austerity. Thereafter, the Dutch returned to more corporatist ways by mandating wage ceilings and compressing relativities. While manufacturing fell from 26 to 17 percent of GDP from 1970–82, the Dutch made up for it by exploiting natural gas. Highly dependent on Germany and the EC for imports, exports, and capital investment, it could not afford to devalue or conduct a macro policy that was very different from that of Germany (cf. Jones, 1995a, Chapter 10).

Sweden had a labor-driven corporatist system that despite the prestige it enjoyed among social democrats did not function smoothly much longer than the Dutch one. It was driven by the Social Democratic Party (SAP) with a highly concentrated and organized working class in which the more militant workers from domestically sheltered firms accepted the lead of those from the large exporting ones (Swenson, 1988). In the class compromise of 1938, the Saltjabaden Pact, unions renounced strike action in favor of full employment measures, essentially public works and aid to exports. Following the war and split with the Communists, the SAP abandoned nationalisation and adopted the unions' Rehn-Meidner plan to achieve full employment without inflation. It involved a more pro-labor trade-off than existed elsewhere, that between wage and strike restraint imposed by centralized bargaining and state guarantees of export credit, active employment policy, and welfare protection (Stephens, 1980; Esping-Anderson, 1990). The size of the interventionist state everywhere was directly related to the left vote, union discipline, and density in that order (Schmidt, 1982, 153).

Higher and sheltered wages were sacrificed in Sweden for the sake of the lower waged and export sector. By levelling wages across sectors unions promoted higher productivity and industrial concentration and centralization. Wage ceilings were enforced by centralized industrial federations following the lead of metal. Both capital and labor benefited from the use of pension funds for private investment, export credits, and housing and from an active manpower policy that relocated redundant workers to areas of new employment (Martin, 1979, 1984; Esping-Anderson, 1980).

By the mid-1960s half of all investment was coming from public pension funds, which gave the economy an expansionary boost and inflationary bias, cutting into international competitiveness. Sweden too was visited with wage drift, strikes, and a squeeze on exports and profits. The SAP tried to respond with legislation on health and safety and workplace rights, but this did not prevent the first electoral loss to the conservatives in 1976. Made aware of the growing conflict between profits and wages, the union confederation LO came out with a plan for the gradual socialization of industry through wage-earners' pension funds. One-fifth of the profits each year would be placed in these funds until unions acquired majority control. The plan was fiercely combatted by the employers, who withdrew from centralized bargaining, was watered down by the white-collar union and swept under the rug by the SAP in the 1983 elections (Martin, 1984, 1986; Pontusson, 1987).

Sweden continued to maintain relatively full employment and social benefits with the help of five devaluations and real wage losses in the 1980s, but gave into multinational pressure and neo-liberal advice and began to deregulate financial markets after 1983. The removal of capital controls in 1988 was an open sesame for massive capital flight to the continent, which led to the austerity plan of 1990 and abrupt decision to join the EC in 1991. This cumulative process of deregulation and capital flight produced a deep recession and only increased Swedish dependency on global markets (cf. Chapter 13). Overall though, its was the system that best survived the monetarist turn in terms of unionization and the welfare state (Garrett, 1998). It preserved macro flexibility and growth by staying out of the Euro, a decision confirmed in the 2003 referendum, which saw a large working-class majority defending the welfare state.

VI Revolutionary challenge: France and Italy

The least corporatist regimes in the EC were those of the soft currency countries France and Italy. Italy had the most militant unions and highest rate of strike activity, some thirty times that of Germany, to which constraining model many Italian capitalists aspired. But beginning in 1974 the Italian Communists (PCI) sought to restrain that militancy and to accommodate itself to the needs of capitalist profitability. France, which aside from May–June 1968, had many fewer strikes than Italy, posed a greater threat to capitalism because of a Communist party (PCF) that continued to pursue class militancy and wage maximization in the work place and a national road to socialism via large-scale nationalization that nearly triumphed.

National legacies made a vital difference to the strategies of the two parties. Italy, as Antonio Gramsci, the early Communist leader, had observed, had been unified from the top down, from the kingdom of Sardinia down to Sicily, without popular participation. The PCI inherited regional differences in the Italian Left before 1914 from reformist socialists in Milan, who looked toward the German SPD model, to syndicalists in Genoa and anarchists in the South (Davis, 1989). Banned under Mussolini, it had not shared in the experience and debates of the Third International. It took to heart Gramsci's pessimistic prison writings about the weakness of national consciousness and the state in Italy and the parallels of underdevelopment to be drawn with Tsarist Russia. Khruschev's revelations about Stalin in 1956 reinforced fears that an Italian revolution because of political and economic backwardness would also end up in terror and dictatorship. The PCI thereafter subordinated the labor movement to European construction in imitation of the German SPD (Fouskas, 1998; Abse, 2001).The French party in contrast despite breaking with Moscow over the necessity for a dictatorship of the proletariat remained in the national revolutionary tradition, placing the transformation of France above European integration.

As early as 1959 when the PCI broke with the Soviets over its condemnation of the EC as a capitalist construction, it began to see it as a framework for progressive change. When massive strike waves broke out in the 1970s it acted as a restraining force, calling for union negotiations with the government, a "historic compromise" with the ruling Christian Democrats (DC) and austerity in 1976. In 1977 the Communist-led CGIL adopted the so-called Euro line – named after the Rome suburb where the unions met – whereby wages would be sacrificed for aid to the South and the unemployed. The New Left hailed this as a breakthrough for socialism as though higher wages were the enemy of employment and the labor movement. European integration and monetary union were part of the deal (Lange and Vannicelli, 1982).

From 1968–75 Italy had the most widespread and intense strikes and greatest wage–price spiral in the EC. Real wages rose 10.8 percent per annum from 1969–72 and 5.2 percent from 1975–78 when growth began to slow. The impetus was given by the opening of the DC government to the Socialists in 1963 and by the virtual fusion of Catholic and Communist trade unions in the late 1960s. This pan-syndicalism, which also fused their programs, took up the demands of lesser skilled workers from the South – lump sum or non-hierarchical wage increases, shorter working time, and better conditions at the factory level. Unions demanded direct negotiations with the government on issues like aid to the South and unemployment, which a Catholic government claiming to represent all classes could not refuse. The mobilization of the "hot autumn" of 1969 in imitation of May–June 68 led to the promulgation of a labor statute that institutionalized worker delegates and factory bargaining on a wide range of issues. The mobilization also led to negotiation in 1975 of the *scala mobile*, indexing wages to prices, and to the *Casa integrazione*, which compensated laid-off workers at 90 percent of their pay (*id.*; Reichlin and Salvati, 1990).

The PCI benefited from the mobilization in terms of members and votes, which reached 31 percent in 1976. Under the "historic compromise" it sought to enter the government and obtain social investment in return for wage restraint and an austerity budget. In the end the party got neither reform nor the place promised in government by the premier Aldo Moro. It was sanctioned in the elections of 1979 for its failure to do so. Trade unionists in the party were not happy with the politics of austerity, but were silenced by party officials pursuing the trans-class Euro line (Golden, 1988).

One PCI concession was the conditional acceptance of the ERM to which the entire Italian establishment turned in the late 1970s, private and public sectors, bankers and industrialists, as a backstop against wage-led inflation. Like the German SPD the PCI demanded a social and regional aid component to the ERM, but soon went along without it. When Italy joined the ERM in 1979 its inflation was 13 percent, twice that of others with unit wages rising 12 percent as against 2 percent in Germany. Even after wages were contained in 1984 deficits arose out of the large pension, welfare, and clientele programs sponsored by the DC. Inflation resurged after the second oil and Volker shock of 1979. With growing inflation divergence from its partners Italy had to devalue seven times within the ERM until 1983. When it finally moved into line on inflation with its partners in the early 1990s, it was forced out of the ERM because of the severe business downturn deflation caused. The social democratization of the PCI drew the fangs of Italian labor, making it unable to resist the Draconian cuts in jobs and social welfare made necessary by adherence to EMU (Talani, 2000; Abse, 2001).

France stood out as the reluctant partner in the neo-liberal EC construction because of its state capacity and socialist tradition of market control. The sense of a collective national will and destiny had its source in both the monarchy and the French Revolution, Bodin and Rousseau. The legacy of the Revolution was democracy from below and above, sans cullotish and statist, Communalist, Jacobin, and Napoleonic (Moss, 1999). The strong state was served by the separation of public from private law and by a talented administrative elite that was partially democratized and socialized after 1945. The Liberation consensus around collective values and institutions like social security, nationalization, and planning gave way after 1947 to a liberal restoration of capitalist power that left behind minimal standards and regulatory potential, but only the shell of intervention. Nevertheless, under Communist pressure, the collectivist tradition influenced the thought and conduct of leading liberal politicians from Chirac to Barre, translator of Hayek, and Giscard d'Estaing, proponent like his financier father of the single market and currency. Still, the French statist alternative to the EC proved only a shadow in the negotiation of the Rome treaty in 1956 and in the monetarist turn of Mitterrand in 1983 (Chapters 2, 6).

The French labor movement in contrast to the Italian had always been nationally unified and predominantly revolutionary. Moderate reformist unionism as opposed to the corporatist Catholic had always been marginal. Outside of Northern Coal routinized collective bargaining with no strike-pledges was practically unknown. As a result of the Popular Front and Liberation, the French Communist Party (PCF) took control of the CGT, the Confédération générale du travail, and appropriated the Republican tradition. The CGT linked local action with generalized and general strikes and political revolution, making up in militancy, public resonance, and ambition what it lacked in members and organizational strength. This explains why the weakest unionism in the EC was able to exercise the greatest leverage on conservative governments fearful of its mobilizing capacity especially after 1968. The student revolt of May–June 1968 with its post-materialist aspirations, which took a Green or New Left form elsewhere, was able to link up with the working-class and socialist tradition only because of the presence and action of the PCF (Moss, 1990, 1999).

The greatest loss of Communist support came in the countryside with the decline of the small peasantry traditionally allied to the working class, mostly in the South, and the relocation of Parisian-based industry to Catholic regions distant from Communist activity where workers joined the Catholic CFTC. Converted into the secularized CFDT, it challenged the hegemony of the Communist-led CGT by appealing to both blue and white-collar workers. These secularized Catholics – Delors was an exception as a practicing one – entered the Socialist Party as a "second left" that offered an anti-statist and anti-collectivist alternative to the Marxists in formerly Catholic regions like the West. Mitterrand drew upon this second left to overrun the Communists and gain a free hand in government that effectively marginalized them. Communism was defeated more by Catholicism than by rising living standards. Yet, even as the Communists disappeared as an electoral force, their legacy of direct action and anti-capitalism spread to middle-class wage-earners in opposition to tight money and free market policies, creating a social divide with the capitalist elites that was first expressed in the 1992 vote against the Maastricht treaty (Moss, 1990, 1998).

VII Class struggle and central bank independence

A large literature attributes the difference between weak and strong currency regimes to the independence of the central bank, one that will not take orders from government or monetize debt but will secure sound money either by targeting an inflation or exchange rate (Elgie, 1998). The assumption made, well founded in principle, is that banks controlled by governments and parliaments will tend to reflect the class interests of the majority in inflationary expansion rather than those of the rentier and large employer class in monetary stringency. Banks free from democratic pressure will give less attention to the public good in growth and more attention to the future value of their own assets made secure against inflation by policies of price stability.

Yet, however committed to price stability no bank can afford to ignore general conditions of growth and profitability without which there would be no borrowing and lending. Several paths to price stability may exist. Without the cooperation of trade unions, home buyers, and consumers, who determine the velocity of money, it may not be possible to meet money supply and inflation targets as was demonstrated in Britain (Chapter 10). Formal measures of independence do not tell us very much about how banks choose their path to price stability and make the trade-offs between stability and growth. They also ignore the informal political influences that determine policy. The Bundesbank was treated as the paragon of independence, yet it was supposed to support government economic policy and its council reflected rival political influences, from orthodox economics ministries to less orthodox Social Democrats and state savings banks (Johnson, 1998; Heisenberg, 1999). During the early 1970s it, like the government was split in two about floating or fixing the exchange rate. The Bundesbank was usually orthodox because the German political and IR systems were.

Independent central banks followed prevailing political trends restricting money supply to the rate of growth in the 1950s, expanding it in the late 1960s and early 70s to accommodate labor, then clamping down after 1979 (Epstein and Schor, 1990). The Danes, Belgians, and Dutch were expansionary in the 1960s and restrictive in the 80s. The Dutch finance minister and the German parliament had the power to veto bank decisions. There was no more political creature, rooted in the Republican Party, than Alan Greenspan of the Fed, which had a polymorphous responsibility for growth, employment, and inflation. It was his political flair, along with weak unions, that enabled him to make credible trade-offs between growth and employment, and price stability, that explained the greater responsiveness and flexibility of American interest rates to economic trends than those of the ECB. The ECB was bound by the strict constitutional and institutional imperative of price stability. But not even it could be indifferent to public and official protest against its hard money policy and so began to follow the Fed down, ignoring excessive deficits in major countries, landing at 3.5 percent in June 2003.

Unless backed up by political authorities central banks alone could hardly control inflation. In the early 1970s aggressive unions could force an expansion of the money supply by increasing wages and demand and thus the velocity of circulation. Pro-labor governments could prevent the central bank from squeezing bank lending and reserves (Gerald Friedman, personal communication). If the Bundesbank was able to rapidly disinflate the economy, it was because it was sustained by a complex of constitutional rules, labor market institutions and ideologies, and government policy.

The British government tried similar monetarist policies without immediate success in the 1980s partly because of structural impediments, skill and manufacturing shortages and the growth of financial and property sectors (Chapter 10) and partly because the political consensus that the Germans enjoyed was missing. Having plumbed to lows in popularity during the tight money recession of 1980–81, Mrs Thatcher knew she had to loosen up policy in order to win elections and so encouraged the Lawson boom, which kept incomes up enough to win two more contests (Stephens, 1996; Thompson, 1996).

Offensive unions, privileged employee groups, homebuyers, importers, and consumers could defeat monetarism by increasing the velocity or effective supply of money. Without the backing of political authorities and the electorate, central banks failed to quell inflation in the US before 1979, France before 1983, and Britain before it entered the ERM in 1992. It was not Volker, head of the Fed, who reversed the course of monetary history in 1979 but Jimmy Carter and a demoralized Democratic administration, not the Bundesbank but a reconverted Helmut Schmidt in Germany, not the Bank of France, but a born again Mitterrand in 1983, and not the Bank of England but Mr Major and the ERM that brought price stability to Britain after 1992. The backstop of last resort against inflation was the ERM.

An econometric analysis found that bank independence was only one among several factors determining inflation rates in the 1970s and 80s. The others were essentially the level of political class struggle – the volume of strikes, government instability and left participation in government with one outlier, the Netherlands, and one regime turning point 1983. Given the level of strikes and number of coalitions and socialists in government, the Netherlands was a premature converter to disinflation in 1974 because of its corporatist ideology and economic dependency on Germany. After 1983, the year of the Mitterrand turnabout, Socialists turned neo-liberal and so became less responsive to strikers and more to monetarist central bankers. It was the domestic political turn to the right entailing class realignments that gave salience to central bank independence and the globalization of finance in the determination of macro policy. The sharpest disinflation came from the corporatist states, Germany, Belgium, and the Netherlands. The ERM and European construction provided a rationale and alibi for the monetarist turn that disarmed the opposition of internationalist-minded Socialists (Oatley, 1997, esp. 26, 64, 87).

Another argument linked central bank independence and its influence over policy to globalization. A comparative study of Belgium, Holland, Sweden, and Austria (Kurzer, 1993) placed formal independence in the contrasting contexts of national industry and international finance. Belgian and Dutch central banks gained effective independence from the government because of their reliance on global markets whereas the Swedish and Austrian ones remained more dependent on government because of their links with national industry. Belgian and Dutch banks were more dependent on international markets, but these were expansionary until the Volker jolt of 1979. Not even the formally independent banks could ignore the imperatives of governmental policy, which was expansionary in the 1960s and restrictive after 1981. It was the neo liberal alignment of pro-business and centrist parties after 1976 and 1979 that decided the monetarist turn and thus encouraged and gave salience to bank independence and capital mobility, not the other way around.

VIII Barriers to socialism: the road not taken

The later 1970s were a twilight zone in which policy debates and classes became polarized resulting in mixed policies of retrenchment and expansion. The term of convenience stagflation did not accurately describe it because growth continued under inflationary conditions though wages, employment, and profits generally suffered. An ever-increasing rate of inflation was needed by governments to stem unemployment, but this caused negative interest rates, loss of asset value and eventually with escalating wage costs a squeeze on employer profits and investments. It was when the latter happened that the capitalist class in its entirety and official and semi-official organizations like the Trilateral Commission, D-G II of the Commission and the OECD turned toward monetarism. To reverse the accelerating inflation of the 1970s required slower growth and a great deal of unemployment brought about with higher interest rates and fiscal restraint bolstered by dollar and DM hegemony and EC monetary union (Chapter 1; Crouch, 1979, ch. 1).

Already after May–June 1968 there was recognition in some quarters of the European Left of a crisis of capitalism – or at least one of private investment and profitability – that would require social control over investment and public ownership of industry and finance. This recognition was contained in the French Common Program of Communists and Socialists, British Labour's Alternative Economic Strategy and in the Swedish union project for wage-earners' pension funds. These programs involving greater public spending and nationalization required a break with the principles of free trade and capital mobility enforced by the EC and other international institutions and markets dominated by the US.

The Keynesian-socialist alternatives to neo-liberalism in response to the wage–price spiral faced formidable problems. The maintenance of growth and employment in one country against the EC and global market trends required a radical break with their systems, carrying risks that the middle classes not yet radicalized by the crisis were unprepared to take. Socialist and labor parties had accustomed their followers to far less radical programs during the golden years and it was difficult to change orientation at the last moment to meet the crisis.

Siding with capital, Christian Democracy was determined to reverse inflationary growth, install austerity, and stop socialism. It was joined by the PCI, which feared terrorism and revolution, and by most Social Democrats, who had found a new constituency to replace declining numbers of manual workers in the expanding ranks of technical, professional and managerial personnel (Carpenter and Jeffereys, 2000, 73–4; Callaghan, 2000). These wage-earners were still invulnerable to the economic crisis that hit the manual working class in the 1970s and carried on with "golden age" expectations of increased income and upward mobility. Much like the 1968 generation they sought a better quality of life, more participation and cultural emancipation, safe social reforms, not the radical economic adventure proposed by the Marxian Left. They held themselves above the conflict between capital and labor, a posture theorized in terms of post-scarcity, postmodernist and post-materialist society among the Greens and New Left (cf. Inglehart *et al*, 1987). The politically fickle educated middle class, radical at times on cultural and social issues, could be turned against manual wage-earners and collectivism as Mitterrand did in overtaking the Communists in France, Thatcher in 1979, the Dutch Liberals in 1981 and Italian FIAT management in the strike of 1980. Pro-business forces could help tip the balance of forces against organized labor by invoking the transnational ideal of Europe and the rules and institutions of the EC and ERM.

The manual working class, larger, more concentrated and better mobilized than ever, fought off initial attempts at budgetary retrenchment, factory lay-offs and closures, resulting in a crescendo of strikes in 1978 (Korpi and Shalev, 1980). However, once workers realized they could not muster enough strength economically and politically to prevent job loss, once the Communists were overtaken by the Socialists, Labour by the Conservatives and remaining Socialists and Communists accepted austerity and the

European project, they lost heart and sense of direction, dispersing their votes increasingly to abstention and the extreme right (Moss, 1998; cf. Golden, 1988; Callaghan, 2000). The shake out of labor costs during a long recession was supposed to produce the conditions of a recovery in neoclassical theory, but wage and benefit cuts were never enough to stimulate investment while they slowed the growth of domestic demand. The popular resistance to cuts that came from the norms, expectations, and leverage acquired from previous mobilization constituted the real distinctiveness of the European as opposed to the American social model.

The most radical and credible solution was the Common Program of the Left in France backed up by a mass Communist party of 700,0000 and a potential electoral majority. It contained provisions for the nationalization of all banks and major industries, worker control, increases in benefits and minimum wages, and a notional return to tariff protection. It was incompatible with membership in the EC and ERM to which it posed a major challenge. Though the Common Program had arisen as a revolutionary response to May–June 1968, as a rupture with capitalism, it became a magical stable solution for both unemployment and unprofitability. As an ordo-liberal Catholic Delors, chosen as finance minister in 1981, opposed the program because he believed in monetarism and European integration.[6] The failure of Mitterrand's government to revive the economy without inflation and trade deficits was taken as proof that there was no alternative to monetarism, but the most that can be said is that Mitterrand went about implementing his program in a half-hearted and equivocal manner, finally choosing to remain in the ERM in order to keep the support of the pro-EC second left. In that sense French socialism – never really tried – was forestalled by European integration (Chapter 6).

A similar program of nationalization, directed especially against multinationals, was proposed by Stuart Holland of the British Labour Party (Wickham-Jones, 1996). The program was welcomed by trade unionists tired of decades of failed incomes policies to freeze wages. Approved by the NEC, the party's national executive, it became the basis for the election manifesto in the hapless campaign of Michael Foot against Mrs Thatcher in 1983. One of its consequences was the demand to withdraw from the EC. The program, the most radical the party had ever presented to the electorate, caused a split from the party of the pro-EC Social Democrats under Roy Jenkin. It was not widely understood or appreciated by backbenchers and party members. Neil Kinnock, the new leader in 1984, blamed it for defeat, renouncing one after another of its interventionist policies (Heffernan and Marqusee, 1992) until the party ended up in the hands of Blair, the closest British equivalent to a continental Christian Democrat. The logical conclusion of this evolution was the embrace of the EU and single currency, but the latter was a step too far for the British electorate and finance.

Finally, the Swedish LO proposed gradual socialization through the wage-earners' pension funds as a response to the wage–price spiral of the early

1970s. This caused difficulties for the white-collar TCO union and for the party, which questioned union control. Employers put up fierce opposition, which was never really answered by the SAP, already undertaking its own "third way" of financial deregulation in the 1980s. The entry of white-collar and professional workers into the unions and party destabilized the old blue-collar collectivist culture, but it cut two ways, both toward greater militancy and radicalism and more accommodation to capital. It was difficult for a party that had long ago abandoned nationalization to defend the wage-earners' fund for socialization especially when it was now advised by middle-class economists schooled in OECD neo-liberal thought (Martin, 1984; Pontusson, 1987).

The post-war boom like previous long cycles had inexorably produced labor mobilization, inflation, and profit squeeze, which polarized the social classes and forced a choice between retrenchment and austerity or further socialization. The forces that militated against further socialization were the expanding professional and managerial middle classes, which did not yet feel the pinch of unemployment, and the anti-collectivist legacies of post-war Christian and Social Democracy. The strength of corporatism binding the labor movement in Germany and the Low Countries and the conversion of the Italian Communists to it left no alternative in the EC to monetarism. In these debates and contests, pro-capitalist domestic forces could call upon the principles and instrumentalities of the EC, particularly the ERM, to tip the scales against labor in their favor.

Notes

1. These concepts underlay E.P. Thompson's, *The Making of the English Working Class*, arguably the greatest historical work in the English language, cf. Moss, 1993b, 2003b.
2. Labrousse, 1947; Braudel, 1972; Hopkins and Wallerstein, 1980; Chevallier, 2001; cf. Solomou, 1987.
3. This promising work was never fully developed or adequately theorized, cf. Kotz *et al*, 1994.
4. Hibbs, 1987, ch. 3; Schmidt, 1978; Friedman, 2003; cf. Freeman, 1994.
5. Shorter and Lilly, 1974; Moss, 1984; Hibbs, 1987, 3–5, 44–5; Lange and Vannicelli, 1982.
6. Before the 1978 elections the author heard Delors tell colleagues that the Socialists would continue with Barre's neo-liberal economic policies.

6
Socialist Challenge: Class Politics in France

Bernard H. Moss

Whereas Germany was the economic engine of the EC project, France after playing the spoiler of the European integration under Pierre Mendès-France in 1954, de Gaulle in 1965, and Mitterrand in 1981 became the pilot of the single market and currency after the latter's turnabout in 1983. As the great Western outcropping of the Eurasian continent, the biggest sized-country, fourth largest world exporter and only country willing to stand up to the US, France was the reluctant but indispensable EC partner. European integration could only go so far as France wanted and France had many reasons to resist it – a strong sense of national identity and destiny, great state capacity, a deeply rooted revolutionary socialist tradition, and an economy that usually ran on inflationary fuel rather than the sound money of a German-style ERM or EMU. France always represented a potential challenge to EC neo-liberalism.

Yet, despite the socialistic inheritance of the Liberation a liberal capitalist order, a dual economy with a small oligopolistic exporting sector that became highly competitive, was restored in the Cold War after 1947 and France despite many protests was able to adjust to the new market order of the EC much more easily than is imagined in the literature. Nevertheless, the French government or people always posed the greatest potential challenge to the EC project, no more seriously than during the socialist experience of Mitterrand, the collapse of which led on to the single market and currency.

The French opposed integration primarily because it was politically supranational and, more disingenuously, because it was economically liberal. In 1956 a French cabinet committee outlined a planned economy for Western Europe not unlike the Soviet's Comecon in the East and demanded that partners raise wages and benefits to their own high level but because of diplomatic isolation and secret admiration for the American model easily yielded to German liberal terms. De Gaulle welcomed the economic liberalization, accompanied by labor repression, necessitated by the Common Market, and only vetoed the arrogation of sovereign tax and monetary powers by the Commission and parliament. Giscard d'Estaing despite his liberal philosophy carried on in much the same inter-governmental way as de Gaulle advancing integration through the European Council and what he hoped would be a symmetrical ERM. Mitterrand's socialist program threatened the prospects of ERM and that of further EC integration, but he too succumbed to market, EC, and internal pressure to reverse course and realign himself with the Germans.

Because of a deeply rooted socialism, liberalization provoked popular resistance when government opposition to the EC faltered. May–June 1968, the greatest general strike in history, was also a reaction to EC-promoted liberalization and labor repression. It inaugurated an upsurge of labor mobilization and wage–price spiral, not only in France, that caused macro divergence with Germany and undermined the proposed remedy of monetary union. The Common Program of the French Left that resulted, proposing a national, socialist solution to the economic crisis, threatened the future of the EC. The failure of this program, of socialist reflation in one country, was used to justify the monetarist turn. Leading on to the single market and currency, the change in French direction did not meet expectations and generated more unemployment and disaffection not only with neo-liberalism but with the EU itself as manifested in the Maastricht referendum of 1992, opinion polls, the strikes of 1995 and 2003 and weakening of the center ground. French governments were caught between a rock and a hard place between their EU commitment and popular pressure defending the welfare state against neo-liberalism.

French resistance to neo-liberalism had little to do with the statist Napoleonic tradition – Mrs Thatcher showed it was compatible with a strong state – and much more with the revolutionary tradition inherited by the Communist Party (PCF). To triumph over monarchical, aristocratic, and Church resistance to tax reform, the middle classes in 1789 and 1792 had appealed to the popular or working classes on the basis of a social democracy that spilled over from property rights into egalitarian Jacobin or republican socialism The cleavage in French society thus opened was perpetuated in series of revolutions in the nineteenth century, 1830, 1848 and 1871, which gave the early labor movement a revolutionary socialist or syndicalist direction, one taken over by the PCF after 1936 and 1944 (Moss, 1999).

Some employers and governments might have liked to reach mutual accords with moderate unions, but aside from Catholic and yellow unions set up with the express purpose of class or employer collaboration, reformist unions were never representative enough to discipline the work force even after the CFDT, the Catholic union secularized in 1964, made a serious challenge to the Communist-led CGT. Class struggle unionism was reflexive and self-fulfilling for it reinforced the combative, authoritarian, paternalistic and class-conscious impulses of employers, who described themselves aggressively as bosses, *le patronat*, as well as of their representative right-wing parties (Moss, 1988; cf. Weber, 1991). The class-conscious CNPF was converted to the EC explicitly on the basis of the leverage it gave over the interventionist state and unions. The mutually reinforcing dynamic of union–management conflict made social partnership with reciprocal concessions, wage moderation and no-strike clauses untenable in France even under the Auroux laws introduced by Mitterrand, which blanketed the country with enterprise bargaining (Moss, 1988, 1998, 1999). The collective bargaining vacuum was filled by state intervention providing minimal protection, by the erruption of general strikes, and the formation of broad left governments with transformative goals. The marginalization of the PCF by Mitterrand disoriented the entire Left, but a legacy remained of conflictual social norms, of militancy, direct action, and anti-capitalism, that challenged the neo-liberal direction of centrist governments and the EU.

Even if not a harbinger of the future France was a good laboratory for the testing of social theories, first because its philosophically trained social scientists had a theoretical bent, but more importantly because France was the only country where social and industrial conflicts were almost immediately transformed into political issues, matters of state, and where individuals, classes, and parties had the credible option of an alternative to capitalism or at least since 1995 a rather inchoate anticapitalist, antiglobalization movement. The socialist propensities of different social and cultural groups, degrees of class-consciousness, could thus be measured in ways that were not possible where an alternative movement or potential regime did not exist.

The exceptionalism about France since the second world war that most American and British writers emphasized was that of a state capitalism, a capitalist economy in which a politically and class neutral state played a central role, a model to follow during the prosperous golden years that became an archaic barrier to progress with the triumph of neo-liberalism (Kuisel, 1981; Schmidt, 1996). Much of the credit or blame was attributed to the role in government, administration and business of the *hauts fonctionnaires*, the public servants trained at the National School of Administration (ENA) and elite engineering schools as technocrats to combine expertise with discourse on the collective good (Suleiman, 1974). The golden years also produced the widespread social democratic myth of a country that had achieved both growth and social justice, of wages rising parallel with profits, and of seamless and endless prosperity through the growth of the welfare state, state aid to business, and Keynesian demand management (cf. Mazier *et al*, 1999). Even the Marxists saw state subsidies forestalling the secular decline of profits and the inevitable crisis of capitalism on the eve of a real crisis (Mandel, 1970; CME, 1971). France since the time of Napoleon has possessed a state apparatus with a great technical coordinating capacity, which has always served the governing parties and the classes they represented. It has thrown up Napoleon-like leaders appearing to rise above the battle to end civil war and strife, but they too have always attached themselves to the dominant class (e.g. Moss, 2003a).

The French state after the Second World War was no different. After 1947 the governments of the Fourth and Fifth Republics were all subservient to business with the exception of the Socialists, Mollet in 1956, Mitterrand in 1981 and Jospin in 1997. The technocrats always worked for the government of the moment, but most of their hearts were with the upper classes from which they came (cf. Suleiman, 1974). After 1952 planning did not figure significantly in the French economy. The French used government funds and planning to reconstruct transport and energy infrastructure after the war, but almost immediately in 1952 made way for private enterprise and a suggestive "indicative" plan, which boosted morale but had little impact on investment and spending (Carré *et al*, 1972; Bouvier *et al*, 1982, IV, 1078–90). By 1967 de Gaulle, who always pursued monetarist orthodoxy, was phasing out the Plan and encouraging private national champions and commercialized public services, a process already started in the 1950s (Durand, 1974; Frost, 1991). The technocrats talked Keynesianism as a substitute for socialism and cover for Colbertism, aid to large companies, but were strictly orthodox in practice. Deliberate monetary or fiscal expansion to stimulate popular demand was unknown until the 1970s.[1] The social security system, entirely based on work and payroll contributions, left the unemployed and others unprotected and preserved special funds for privileged groups (Friot, 2003).

As for the sources of prosperity, it depended at least until 1968 on American-tested technology combined with low wages and long hours, high job turnover, and growing social inequality made possible by a reserve work force drawn mainly from the countryside. (Kindleberger, 1967; Carré *et al*, 1972). Wages lagged behind productivity and pre-war levels until the mid-1950s. The legal minimum wage was allowed to sink further below the average. Because of the ostracism of the majority Communist union CGT collective bargaining and worker participation were virtually non-existent in France. Despite formal regulations France had the freest labor market with the least equal outcomes in the OECD, so easily adjusted to the wage restraint and liberalization required by entry into the Common Market (Moss, 1993a).

Most of the social reforms of the Liberation except perhaps that of the Plan were due to the rising strength of the PCF, which was credited with resistance to the pro-Nazis Vichy wartime regime and to employers, who had collaborated with it (Lacroix-Riz, 1983, 1999). Together with left Socialists the PCF was responsible for the nationalization of energy, transport and some finance under union control in the public sector and of enterprise committees in the private; for a constitution that recognized the right to strike, to social security and unionization; for a comprehensive labor code that guaranteed overtime pay and equal pay for women; and for national wage bargaining based on mass mobilization. The mobilization behind the CGT, which involved almost the entire work force, was fed by the inflationary reconstruction policies chosen by de Gaulle over the monetarist restrictiveness advocated by Mendès-France, the first finance minister. Most of these reforms, certainly worker control, were vitiated after 1947, when the PCF was ousted from government and marginalized after its defeat in the November general strike and fiscal and monetary expansion halted (Bonin, 1987; Frost, 1991; Steinhouse, 2001).

French governments, composed of the "third force" between Communists and Gaullists that became increasingly conservative, presided over the restoration of employer and capitalist power. Communists were removed from control of public sector boards and purged from many work places. The Plan, honored more in the breach rather than observance after 1951, relied on the private sector and the commercialization of the public one (Bouvier *et al*, 1982, 1078–90). Embracing the free trading vision of the Marshall Plan, which already contained the EC in vitro (Bossuat, 1996), the third force reined in public spending on welfare and industry, restrained wages and deprived employee representation of any managerial role. Enterprise committees, relegated to administering social funds, became arenas of union contestation and struggle (Combe, 1969; Frost, 1991, 87–116; Steinhouse, 2001).

The majority of French workers continued to support a party and union that obtained gains via class struggle, by constant agitation and contestation in the work place. There were petitions, delegations, sit-downs, and harassment of management, generalized sectoral strikes, and one-day warning and general national strikes – notably in 1950 over collective contracts and the vital minimum, 1953 over public sector reform, 1955 in the metal trades starting from St Nazaire, and 1957. Whatever part was due to labor mobilization or market forces, wages began to catch up with productivity from 1955. Workers demonstrated by their votes for Communists in enterprise, social security, and political elections that they remembered the mobilizations of 1936 and 1947 and preferred class struggle to "cold," routinized and bureaucratic, collective bargaining.[2]

To preempt further mobilization the third force established a minimum wage floor or SMIG tied loosely to inflation and a law on collective bargaining that allowed industrial accords signed by one recognized national union, usually at the lowest acceptable level, to be extended to all those employed in the sector. These accords, which kept some wages below the SMIG, were never renewed by the CGT, while the SMIG itself was allowed after 1956 to fall further below the average wage. The French possessed an ideology and legal framework for "dirigisme," work and wage regulation, but so long as the PCF was excluded from participation, it remained an empty administrative shell (Jefferys, 2002, 2003a).

As elsewhere French growth depended very much on the increased employment of the unskilled at low pay with more and better machinery. Econometric studies attributed most of the average 5 percent growth to new machinery, but did not consider the deflation of labor costs due to abundant labor supply (Carré *et al*, 1972). Lacking unemployment insurance until 1958, French workers lived in a state of insecurity – the actual unemployment rate was not registered – with high turnover and job dissatisfaction in Paris, diminishing upward mobility and a fear of unemployment held over from the 1930s. Encouraged by government, employers purposely located new industry outside the Parisian "red belt" to avoid labor agitation. Working hours were extended from 43.5 in 1945 to 46 in the 1950s, the longest in Europe. Wages did not return to 1938 levels until 1956, and it was not until the end of the 1960s that workers could afford an automobile and join the "consumer society" that young middle-class radicals denounced in 1968. So the enunciation of the law of absolute impoverishment of workers under capitalism by Maurice Thorez, the PCF leader, did not seem as ridiculous to workers in 1955 as it has to middle-class commentators. Wages as a share of value-added in France only rose slightly before 1973 while consumption fell as a share of production. In 1975 even after the post-1968 wage rises, France was still the most unequal society in the OECD.[3]

The French had the ideological predisposition and the state capacity to plan and invest, but these potentials were barely utilized after the first Plan in 1952. Industrial policy always ran up against the financial orthodoxy of the Treasury, which usually ignored the Plan (Mamou, 1988, 95–115; Quenouelle-Carre, 2000, 172–86). François Bloch-Lainé, head of the Plan, who incarnated the Catholic spirit of social responsibility, was dismissed by Antoine Pinay in 1952 because of his insistence on it. Government subsidies to private investment through an array of credits, interest-rate reductions, tax advantages and grants, were indiscriminate and apparently unrelated to the plan (Margairez, 1991; Loriaux, 1991). Industrial policy was only effective where government was both the investor and consumer in military, nuclear, and grand projects like the Concorde or TGV (high-speed rail) (Adams and Stoffaes, 1986, 13–14, 44–45). Efforts to create a national computer industry with Bull continually failed. A glaring example of the lack of civilian planning was the absence of private telephone service in much of the country until the 1970s (Cohen, 1992).

The fiscal burden was shifted from corporations to wage-earners and consumers with the introduction in 1954 of the TVA, the value-added tax on consumption, which was later standardized for the benefit of the EC, and with the increase of social charges after 1958 (Bouvier *et al*, 1982, 1078–90). Once France joined the Common Market special incentives were given to firms supplying capital goods to merge and become national champions in world trade. France's greatest success in foreign trade was with the third world countries that bought its military equipment. But though French industry did not tend to monopolize vertical niche markets as the Germans did in capital goods, it did establish reputations where it counted in the EC for quality-range goods (cf. Stoffaes, 1991; Aglietta and Baulant, 1993, 534–41).

Despite ten wage freezes and price controls over thirty years, the French economy had an inflationary bias due initially to wartime shortages, government investment, and union catch-up and later to the Korean, Indochinese, and Algerian wars. No more than others did France use countercyclical Keynsianism as an instrument of policy until the 1970s. The 1951 elections returned a conservative majority oriented to small business. Governments pursued wage restraint and austerity budgets with such ministers as Maurice Petsche, Joseph Laniel, René Meyer and Antoine Pinay, the tanner from St. Chamond, who gave the green light to discussion of a common market at Messina in 1955 (Rioux, 1983; Bonin, 1987).

Mendès-France, later glorified by the Mitterrand left, spent his time reining in wages, deficits and inflation just like his predecessors. While advocating managed trade and planning, he was the sworn enemy of wage-led inflation, class struggle unionism, and the PCF (Bonin, 1987, 235–48; Margairez, 1988, 103–13, 346–53, 385–93). The only other left of center government was that of Mollet, the father of the EC, who increased social and public spending and extended the third week of paid vacation but was unable to induce unions into a social contract (Brunet, 1987). Luckily for third force governments, the long boom prevailed over short-term retrenchment (Bouvier *et al*, 1982, 1091–2, 1119–33).

De Gaulle's coup d'etat of May 13, 1958 was designed as much to restore financial balances as to keep Algeria French. De Gaulle had opposed the Common Market as an encroachment on sovereignty, but once in power temporized with it to secure German cooperation, thwart British plans for a free trade zone, satisfy business and public opinion and provide competitive stimulus to French enterprise (Bossuat, 1996, 376–419). De Gaulle submitted to French employer, German and EC-mandated liberalism. He named Antoine Pinay as economics and finance minister and the ultraliberal economist Jacques Rueff to head a committee that included CNPF representatives. It met CNPF demands for budgetary and wage cuts, transferring the tax burden to workers and consumers to meet EC competition (Szokoloczy-Syllaba, 1965, 368–9; Gauron, 1983, I, 60–8).

De Gaulle's military coup and electoral victory, which took one-fifth of the Communist vote and established a virtual one-party state, was enough to ensure social peace and wage freeze for two years. The entry into the common market was successful because of a devaluation of 37 percent over two years, which was sustained by austere budgets and labor repression. Wage increases were capped in 1961, striking railwaymen and miners requisitioned in 1959 and 1963, wages held back under a stabilization plan from 1963–67, and minimum wages allowed to fall 35 percent relative to the average (Jefferys, 2003a).

The CNPF became a great EC enthusiast because it gave a spurt to industrial exports, especially to Germany, and because it enabled it to leverage more liberal concessions from the government. Contrary to hoary legend,

French employers and capital were never "dirigiste", favorable to state intervention or the welfare state (Moss, 1988; cf. Weber, 1991). The only private sector linked to the state in the early 1950s was steel. In 1965 the CNPF promulgated the Liberal Charter, which aimed to do away with the plan, price control, corporate taxes and social charges and end EC restrictions on the free movement of capital. Its president called for a "truly European economy" (cited by Braun, 1969, 121).

Gaullist governments complied with CNPF directives. While de Gaulle quarreled with the EC over questions of sovereignty he raised no objection to the accelerated removal of tariffs in the EC or global free trade in the GATT negotiations. After the government stabilized wages with its 1963 austerity plan it looked to the formerly Catholic CFDT, represented on the Plan by Delors, to enforce a restrictive incomes policy, but the union used its new ideological freedom to challenge the CGT for blue-collar members with militant action. In 1967 de Gaulle began to phase out the plan, remove capital controls, and place public services on a commercial basis. He quashed union elections to social security boards, a source of influence and patronage, which was one of the triggers of the general strike of May–June 1968. With this supply-side encouragement to investment the French economy was able to grow at more than 5 percent per annum accumulating American gold without much inflation (Durand, 1974; Jeanneney, 1991).

The general strike of May–June 1968 was a breakout from ten years of authoritarian wage restraint. Though triggered by student activists, anarchists and Trotskyists, who hated the Communists, the revolt against de Gaulle was taken up and extended after May 13 by the Communist-led CGT, which negotiated at Grenelle a 35 percent increase of the minimum wage and eventually an average wage hike of 8 percent. A left alternative to de Gaulle was ruled out when Mitterrand, leader of the non-Communist-Left, proposed a government led by Mendès-France, bête noir of the PCF. With the Left split the public responded favorably to de Gaulle, who promised to restore order against the Communist menace after creating a terrifying void by disappearing mysteriously, then suddenly returning from visiting troops in Germany.

While de Gaulle restored order, resisted devaluation, and tried to contain wage-led inflation, he was defeated in a referendum, which included a proposal for union representation in a corporatist Senate. He resigned and made way for the more liberal and pro-EC presidency of Georges Pompidou, the prime minister who had negotiated the Grenelle accords. The wage hikes of May–June destroyed de Gaulle's strategy of attacking the dollar with a strong franc, thus suggesting a more collective EC effort. Pompidou was more generous than de Gaulle on both the financial and social fronts, expanding the money supply and encouraging collective bargaining within productivity limits. He accepted devaluation in November 1969 hoping that EC enlargement to Britain and better economic coordination with the Germans – the first EMU was proposed by the newly appointed French Commissioner Raymond Barre – would provide new resources for social reforms without destabilizing the franc (Jeanneney, 1991, 518–21, 526; Aglietta and Baulant, 1993, 505–7).

The Werner Report on the first EMU, which urged the creation of a single currency under a fullfledged supranational state, reflected the European idealism of Willy Brandt, the first Social-Democratic German chancellor. It called for the parallel convergence of German and French macro policy and a ten-year transition to a supranational state with an executive responsible to parliament and authority over social and regional policy. The plan received almost universal acclaim from both capital, employers and financiers, and non-Communist labor. It was apparently supported by a majority of the liberal neo-Gaullist cabinet, but was vetoed by Pompidou, who told it in December 1970:

> We cannot accept a brutal and unrestrained capitalism, which would bring on political revolt in member-states first in Italy and then France.... Europe can only be made gradually. It is not M. Malfatti [Commission president] who will have to confront the winegrowers of the Midi if there are troubles; it is the government that will have to send troops and if it turns nasty, it is the French government that will be overturned.... If there's a new May '68, it is not M. Malfatti who will speak to the Séguy [Communist leader of the CGT in 1968] of the moment (cited by Frank, 1995, 352–3).

Pompidou feared both for the nation state and governability of the social order in a period of labor unrest. In the end France accepted only a first step toward monetary union with a band of currency fluctuation against the dollar called the snake. Requiring convergence to hard-money German norms after 1973, the snake could not withstand the divergence of wage and macro policy among members in response to the economic crisis of the 1970s (Tsoukalis, 1977; Dyson, 1994).

Inflationary pressures in France, accentuated by American laxity, caused a resurgence of local strikes from 1970 and a wage-price spiral that lasted through the oil shock of 1974 until the Barre Plan of September 1976. Employers responded to higher wage settlements by scrapping old for new machinery and employing women at lower rates. Both employers and employees enjoyed a boom until the end of 1973 when profits were squeezed by the exhaustion of new sources of productivity, the depletion of labor reserves, and the higher cost of oil (Armstrong *et al*, 1991; Mazier *et al*, 1999, 110; Jefferys, 2002).

The neo-Gaullist government of Jacques Chaban-Delmas, advised by Delors on social matters, sought to win the adhesion of the CFDT to wage moderation combined with relatively costless qualitative reforms on training and working conditions thereby splitting the formerly Catholic union off from the Communist-led CGT with its maximalist across the board wage demands. But the work force energized by May–June rejected the *contrats de progrès*, long-term contracts including no-strike clauses signed by the CFDT in the public sector, which contained moderate increases adjusted for inflation and productivity.

The strikers in the early 1970s were mostly semi-skilled newcomers to factory life from the Catholic countryside. They were drawn to the local CFDT because of geographical proximity – few workers had any choice of union in their locality – and spiritual affinity with its qualitative and egalitarian demands. Whereas the CGT insisted on defending wage skill differentials in order to build a broad class front against employers, the CFDT demanded lump sum increases for the poorest categories, better health and safety measures, and reduced and flexible working time. During May–June the CFDT had also launched the slogan – derived from the Catholic doctrine of subsidiary or local prerogative – of autogestion, of worker management, a slogan that resonated with middle-class students seeking their own identity, and less radically so to professional and managerial personnel demanding more recognition from the top. CFDT slogans made sense to some employees in the post-scarcity boom, but imploded with the onset of unemployment and crisis. Lacking any tradition of struggle, the unskilled threatened with job loss faded into the woodwork while the CFDT leadership took fright at the revolutionary implications of their rhetorical leftism and halted militant action (Moss, 1984, 1990; Cours-Salies, 1988).

The strikes of the newcomers were relayed after 1974 by those of the skilled led by the CGT for more pay and job protection, which were initially accommodated by fiscal and monetary expansion. Benefiting from Chirac's fiscal stimulus in 1975 wages rose 4 percent in real terms and unit wage costs 17.4 percent, causing greater profit squeeze. With record wage share and unit wage costs driving inflation to a peak of 14 percent, France was forced out of the snake for the second time. The effective devaluation of the franc vis-à-vis the DM since 1969 of 45 percent did not prevent import penetration, which affected the old industrial Communist centers of the North. Strikes reached a crescendo in response to the threat of dismissals in 1976 with five million days lost and at least 200 factory occupations before Barre slammed on the disinflationary breaks in 1977.[4] This mobilization was transferred to the electoral arena in Spring 1978 when the PCF, after splitting with the Socialists on the interpretation of the Common Program, gained ground against them among the young and in the old working class (Moss, 1990, 56–7).

France was governed after 1974 by Giscard d'Estaing, an economic liberal trained in republican collective responsibility in the first post-war class of the ENA. Like his financier father he dreamed of an integrated European economy with a single currency. His plans in 1974 for budgetary retrenchment, privatization and deregulation were checked by labor mobilization and the rising threat of a Left electoral victory around the Common Program. He wanted to imitate the German ordo-liberals, but given the leftward drift of opinion had to present himself at the 1978 elections as a Swedish social democrat (Giscard d'Estaing, 1976).

The Barre government was appointed by Giscard in 1976 to disinflate and align macro policy with Germany. Barre stopped real wage increases and curtailed strikes via voluntary wage guidelines, public sector cuts and currency pegging to the DM. Investment and profits declined with growth approaching zero in 1979 and 1980 while inflation raged on, especially after price controls were lifted in 1978. Threatened with a Communist-inspired majority, the government could go only half-way toward austerity. It continued to subsidize 43 percent of business loans and to maintain unemploymet benefit. Raising social wages to 30 percent of the total returned unit labor costs in 1980 back to 1975 levels (Mazier *et al*, 1999, 116). Subsidies to the public sector and social payments to workers from declining industries, especially steel and shipbuilding, partly made up for the shortfall in private investment, but the franc was under pressure from the rising trade deficit and inflation differential with Germany of 14.4 percent (Gauron, 1983, 38, 57, 102; Zinsou, 1985, 119–21). The ERM project taken up from Roy Jenkins, Commission president, by Giscard was designed to prop up a seriously overvalued franc with German help, as a discipline against laxity and as a step toward a single currency (Jeanneney, 1991; Aglietta *et al*, 1993).

Giscard's hard money policies destroyed swathes of French industry, but he could not overturn sacred state welfare and industrial institutions entirely if he wanted to win elections. Giscard produced the pain of more unemployment without tangible gain for capital investment and profit, driving more of the middle classes into the arms of Mitterrand, who had broken with the Communists and who after a half-serious experiment with socialism turned about and accomplished Giscard's dream of a single market and currency.

François Mitterrand was elected in 1981 on the basis of Communist propositions of nationalization, welfare expansion and worker control that had been part of the Common Program of the Left negotiated in 1972. The program was initially proposed by the PCF in response to the revolutionary aspirations unleashed by May–June as a move forward to socialism, but became interpreted by the Left after 1974 as a definitive solution to the problems of stagflation besetting the economy. Blocked on the industrial front by plant closures and the Barre Plan, workers transposed their hopes to the Common Program. Approaching the threshold of a majority by Spring 1977, it was at once the most radical and credible alternative to neo-liberalism in Europe. The split over worker control and extent of nationalization between the PCF and PS in September 1977 also ruptured the social alliance between the older working class and its newer working class and middle-class allies, leading to Left defeat in March 1978 (Moss, 1990).

EC integration could go nowhere so long as Mitterrand pursued nationalization and industrial planning. The failure of Mitterrand to carry out his program and his neo-liberal turnabout in 1983 were taken as proof of the impossibility of countercyclical Keynesianism and socialism in one country. The apparent failure of socialism became a major reason for the pursuit of European integration, notably for Mitterrand, who picked up the baton of the single market and currency as a substitute grand project that was used as rationalization and alibi for his neo-liberal domestic turn.

The failure of French socialism did not really prove the impossibility of left Keynsianisn or socialism in one country because it was never seriously tried (cf. Halimi *et al*, 1994). Mitterrand did not come to power with a mandate for the socialist transformation contained in his program and to which he was never truly committed. Like the prince of Machiavelli, whose biography he planned to write, he was, above all his populist rhetoric and sensibility, an expedient politician, the youngest ministerial deal-maker in the Fourth Republic, with feet in all camps, clerical and anti-clerical, liberal and socialist (Nay, 1984). He borrowed the PCF's program and turned it against them by hitching on a second left, of Catholic background, who were determined to resist it. With the help of this left, notably Finance Minister Delors, he gave himself a free hand to change course when the going got rough. He approached socialism in 1981 as an improviser without preparation or commitment juggling liberals and socialists in his cabinet until under the pressure of the global market and German-led ERM he made a desperate bid to save his program before caving in to neo-liberalism.

Mitterrand's expansionary economic policies came under pressure from the EC and global markets in the form of trade deficits and a run on the franc during the recession engineered by the monetarist turn in the US, Britain, and Germany. Mitterrand could have anticipated these problems and found partial remedies with an immediate and substantial devaluation, purposeful nationalization and sectoral plans, especially for machine tools, and tariff protection for an industrial policy that needed five years or so to work. These measures, incompatible with the EC and ERM, were inscribed in the Socialist and presidential program, but advisors like Jacques Attali had a different agenda, keeping the economy open for a global upturn that did not arrive.

The monetarist turn – raising interest rates and taxes on average wage-earners, reducing industrial aid and welfare commitments, and deregulating financial markets – was not dictated by global market forces, the EC or any technical rationality (*contra* Moravcsik, 1998a), but was preeminently political. Mitterrand had failed to build a majority for socialism; only 39 percent wanted a radicalization of policy at the end of 1982. He was blocked in his plans by the Catholic-inspired second left, who were committed to European integration. It was represented in cabinet by Delors and Rocard, who had always opposed the Common Program, joined by the moderate Socialist prime minister Pierre Mauroy. Underlying the commitment to EC integration was the Catholic fear of collectivism and faith in property, markets and sound currency as guarantors of individual and group autonomy. French socialism was defeated not by external constraints, but primarily by the internal Catholic-bred opposition within Mitterrand's majority.

Mitterrand was able to outdistance the PCF and displace it as leader of the left by attracting many reformist groups but especially secularizing Catholics from the political Center and geographical West, the historic bastion of clericalism and aristocratic reaction. This included newly industrialized workers drawn to the CFDT as well as upwardly mobile middle-class personnel, who were as yet untouched by economic crisis. Mitterrand appealed to their brew of cultural liberalism and economic conservatism, the post-materialism – feminist, ecological, and participative – of the post-1968 youth cohort and the self-identity of teachers and academics, who had lost traditional ties to the popular classes via the PCF and Catholic Action (Todd, 1998, ch. 9).

Mitterrand wooed the second left, Delors, and Rocard, when he ran for president in 1974 without mentioning the Common Program. He kept it on board by breaking with the Marxian CERES in 1976 and standing up to PCF demands for a clarification and radicalization of the Common Program, which split the Left and snatched defeat from the jaws of victory in March 1978. In the middle of the campaign the CFDT, the idol of the New Left, declared its political neutrality and returned toward its Catholic corporatist white-collar beginnings, preaching class accommodation, wage and benefit restraint, and work-time flexibility. The new Socialist voters, mostly Catholic real property-owners, preferred the Center to the Communists on the second round in 1978 (Capdevielle *et al*, 1981).

Despite making inroads on the Socialists in the working class in 1978 the PCF was blamed by the media and middle classes for the defeat of the Left, suffering a revolt of its own intellectuals, notably in the Paris Federation. It responded by fabricating a neo-syndicalist strategy, the *stratégie autogestionnaire*, designed to present an anti-statist image, whereby gains would be made little by little outside politics by struggles in the work-place. By abandoning the fight for political influence in the state and Common Program to the Socialists and adopting a revolutionary pro-Soviet posture abroad, they facilitated the Mitterrand victory in 1981. Striking steel workers could not prevent the EC-ordered closure of their plants under the Barre government in 1979. The revolutionary external posture led Georges Marchais, Secretary-General, to announce his support of Soviet intervention in Afghanistan on French TV while he was in Moscow to declare his independence from the Soviet party, a public relations blunder that cost the PCF dearly (Hofnung, 2001, ch. 16; Moss, 1990).

Mitterrand won election in 1981 by drawing PCF votes on the first round with propositions taken from the Common Program and ecologists and Gaullists on the second, reassured by his defeat of the PCF on the first. He carried out his pledge of 1973 to the Socialist International to come to power by stealing PCF votes and breaking their hold on the French Left, but the result was a heterogeneous majority without a clear socialist mandate.[5]

Could Mitterrand or another Socialist – because Mitterrand was naturally a temporizing politician – have come to power under the Common Program in harness with the Communists on the left rather than by standing up and defeating them from left center ground? If he had remained united with them on the left could he have radicalized the new working class that supported the CFDT and the modernizing Catholic middle classes fearful of Communism that normally voted Centrist? Mitterrand probably had no choice but to appeal to the center against Communism because the new working class lacked the traditions of resistance of the old and the aspirational middle classes, as yet unaffected by economic crisis, wanted a safe moderate reformism that would allow them to continue their upward social trajectory. By the time the latter were thrown into the maelstrom of job insecurity in the 1990s, the PCF and socialist alternative had virtually disappeared as a structuring element of protest and labor mobilization.

In power Mitterrand nationalized the major firms and banks with some delay but reappointed most of the old CEOs, who carried on in the usual commercial ways. Mitterrand thus followed the capitalist course advocated by Delors rather than the directive planning perspective of Jean-Pierre Chevènement, who was forced out as minister of industry in March 1983. Nothing more was heard about the worker control mentioned in Mitterrand's platform. The infusion of an additional 240 percent of state aid, which nobody in Brussels questioned as a treaty violation, paid off huge debts and kept the large firms afloat (Rand, 1990).

With the turnabout of 1983 the nationalized firms were returned to profitability due mostly to labor shedding – 20 percent were dismissed from the large firms – worker demobilization and portfolio acquisitions with big companies becoming their own finance houses. Delors encouraged foreign rather than domestic investments and acquisitions, especially in the US. Mitterrand's pledge to reconquer the domestic market through national investment was forgotten despite symbolic gestures like the inspection of Japanese videos at Poitiers. French industry only returned to profitability with yields from financial assets. Production and consumption declined. Exports fell 20 percent between 1985 and 1989, when France had its first trade deficit in two decades.[6]

Under Mitterrand public expenditures were increased by 21.5 percent, social transfers by 13 percent, the minimum wage 18 percent and disposable income 6.3 percent, but the fiscal stimulus was only 2.3 percent, not much more than Chirac's in 1975. Since the crisis of the 1970s, the French have had only one political obsession – jobs (Cameron, 1996). Mitterrand created 240,000 jobs in the public sector and more in the private with the reduction of the working week by one hour to thirty-nine and the extension of paid vacation to five weeks. Despite a worldwide downturn France alone among

EC countries kept growing at 2 percent and halted the growth of unemployment. With all this state help the wage share peaked at 77.3 percent along with the inflation differential with Germany (Halimi *et al*, 1994, 101–3; Beaud, 1985; Fonteneau and Muet, 1985).

Mitterrand faced the opposition of the entire capitalist class and conservative parties with Delors pressing for a reversal of policy in the cabinet and a demobilized working class and disoriented PCF on his left. In 1981 and 1982 wage share and inflation were at their highest and profitability at its lowest while new taxes and the high dollar rate raised costs of investment. The shortfall in private investment could only be made up by government, but time was lost debating nationalization the purpose of which was never made clear (Rand, 1990). Also, the increase in consumer demand without the production to satisfy it drew in imports, especially German ones. Wealthy consumers deliberately chose expensive German cars like the Mercedes to sabotage Mitterrand's program. High American interest rates, the growing trade deficit and the rising inflation and interest rate differential with Germany caused a flight from the franc despite controls. The pressure was on Mitterrand to effectuate either a large devaluation and leave the ERM or a small one accompanied by budgetary retrenchment (Beaud, 1985; Fonteneau and Muet, 1985).

On three occasions the government sought devaluation within the ERM. Thrown into a serious recession by the second oil shock and high American interest rates, the Germans demanded severe cuts in the French budget and social programs, particularly social security. From October 1981 Delors echoed these demands calling for "a pause" – a reference to the phrase used by Leon Blum to signal the return in 1937 to financial orthodoxy. The turning point came in Spring 1982 when Delors and Mauroy after consulting with the Germans and Commission, proposed a wage and price freeze to accompany a ten percent devaluation. It was approved by the EC Monetary Committee even before going to the French cabinet. By de-indexing wages from prices it brought about a reversal of rising wage share. The government also undertook to keep the budget deficit under 3 percent of GNP, a magical figure that became the criterion for EMU.[7]

To avoid a third austerity plan Mitterrand considered floating the franc, leaving the ERM and bolstering industry, which would benefit from lower interest rates, more state aid, trade protection, and wage controls. He was tired, he said, of acting like a "dead dog carried down the stream" (cited in July, 1986, 96) by the Germans. He was finally dissuaded by the opposition of Delors and Mauroy, the EC faction, and by the political shift of his close aide and next premier Laurent Fabius. Fabius, displaying remarkable economic naivete for an ENA graduate, was apparently persuaded by the head of the Treasury Michel Camdessus that France lacked reserves and that a float would see the franc fall 20 percent, possibly into the hands of the IMF.

This time the Germans required a comprehensive austerity program in return for their 5.5 percent revaluation and large ECU loan – a tax surcharge, substituted for the German demand for lower social charges on employers, compulsory loans from taxpayers, an exchange restriction on tourists and budget cuts – altogether removing 2 percent of GNP from consumption.[8] Real interest rates of 5.7 percent pulled the plug on growth and employment. By halting the socialist experiment in France with the help of the Germans and the EC Commission and Monetary Committee, Delors probably did more for European integration as French finance minister than he did later as Commission president.

Most observers concluded that the outcome, crucial to the continuation of monetary union if not the EC itself, was dictated by international market forces. But like de Gaulle in 1958 Mittterand might have solved the trade problem by a large devaluation or float at the outset accompanied with tariff protection and a rapid purposeful nationalization of industry and finance, but all this would have been contrary to EC commitments. One econometric study showed that after initial exposure to political risk, devaluation in 1983 would have been more effective in righting the trade balance and reducing joblessness than in the past (Cameron, 1996, 81, n. 62; Petit, 1989, 260, 257; Blanchard and Muet, 1993, 38–41). Floating the currency would not have required large reserves, which were probably larger than made out to be by Camdessus, who went on to become the head of the IMF and eventually that of the Vatican's finances. The Treasury and Bank of France, bastions of monetarism, took revenge against Mitterrand by their veto (Mamou, 1988).

While most socialists hoped that austerity would only be an interlude, Mitterrand decided to make a vice into a virtue. If the state could no longer fund investment, he would have to convince private investors to do so and how better to show his seriousness than to open up all financial markets to competition and proceed with the European single market. Since he had failed to make his mark as a socialist, he would leave the legacy of a European. He was not to be outdone by New York or London in the creation of a unified financial market with exchanges for unlisted securities, non-voting and preferred shares, certificates of deposit and financial futures. The issuance of non-voting shares allowed the government to sell off 70 percent of nationalized subsidiaries by 1986. Banks were no longer to control the flow of credit to selective firms but to act as intermediaries between financial markets and industry in the German mode. Money supply and interest rates would not be fixed by government but determined in the open market. State subsidized loans to business amounting to 43 percent of the total in 1979 were curtailed. When the franc was threatened again in November 1985 Pierre Bérégovoy, the finance minister, resolving not to suffer another humiliation, raised rates and converted to sound money (Virard, 1993, 102–12, 228–9; Loriaux, 1991, 223–7).

The turnabout of Mitterrand destabilized the labor movement, already suffering from the loss of two million jobs since 1975, and stifled protest.

The PCF went from defeat to decline obtaining 7 percent in the 1988 presidential elections. Trade unions, which had slightly rebounded after 1981, plumbed record lows for rates of strikes and unionization – to about 8 percent of the work force. With labor demobilization, resignation and despair notions of "the working class" and "the left" also declined as did distrust of employers. When these notions were resurrected in the 1990s they were no longer associated with the influence of the PCF (Moss, 1998, esp. 235).

The results of Fabius' modernization were devastating to wage-earners. The sharp fall of inflation back to 2.4 percent by 1986 was directly linked to the rise of unemployment from 6 to 10 percent. Under the impact of rising unemployment and de-indexation, the average real wage per employee dropped 1.7 percent between 1982 and 1988 while public employees faced a loss of 5.7 percent in rates of pay. Profit margins, which had fallen to the lowest level of 13.3 percent in 1982, were back to normal levels of 18.4 percent by 1987. The tax burden was shifted from companies and financial profits to households. With real interest rates of 6 percent the asset values of property holders grew 50 percent while working-class families became more indebted. Between 1982 and 1985 the wage share of added value fell 8 percent, an enormous decline in a short time. The shakeout of the 1980s kept wage rises below productivity gains and stabilized social costs.[9]

The new Rocard government elected in 1988 stuck firmly to a policy of "competitive deflation" whereby a strong franc causing unemployment would drive down wages, interest rates and costs leading to a reprise of investment and export. The fixed exchange rate of the ERM gave added credibility to this policy because it guaranteed that governments would be punished with higher real exchange rates for allowing inflation. Mitterrand said there was no more trade off possible between inflation and unemployment; at least, corrected Bérégovoy, there was no political majority for it. Since Mitterrand had transformed France into a market society there was no longer any reason to object to capital mobility or permanently fixed exchange rates. The French approval of the 1986 EC directive freeing up short-term capital controls was a turning point for neo-liberalism in Europe (Bakker, 1996, 149–57). In May 1988 Mitterrand agreed with Kohl to give up remaining controls without conditions in return for the single currency that had been proposed by Hans-Dietrich Genscher, German foreign minister (Aeschimann and Riché, 1996, 48, 59, 83).

The long recovery of growth promised by liberal economists and believers in mechanical Kondratieff cycles (cf. Chevallier, 2001) did not happen. The econometric study that had cautioned against the strong franc proved not far wrong in predicting that recovery would take twenty years – a strong mini-recovery took place from 1997 to 2000 along with the American boom. From 1990 to 1996 French unemployment grew from 9 to 12 percent as high interest rates necessary to maintain franc parity with the DM reduced industrial growth by 5.6 percent and annual GDP by an estimated one percent.[10]

Between the 1970s and 1990s unit wage costs fell 20 percent. (*Le Monde,* September 9, 2003). Social benefits fell as a percentage of GDP after 1993 despite increased need (Lordon, 2001, 116). The number of half time, underpaid, precarious and temporary jobs grew, especially for women. Whereas three quarters of jobs in France were considered to be permanent under the law in 1970 only one half were by the 1990s. Youth poverty and the fear of unemployment and homelessness reached levels that had not been seen since the 1950s (Moss, 1998, 238–9; Rozès, 2002).

In France as in most EC countries profitability and productivity began to turn around in 1983 mostly as a result of de-indexing wages from prices, labor shedding, and the end of contestation and strikes. New techniques were introduced to eliminate waste, softer methods of lean flexible production and Japanese quality circles and harsher ones of repression and the dismissal of activist delegates. As always during depressions of demand increasing use was made of cheap subcontractors to bear the cost. The only sign of the technological modernization so vaunted by Fabius came in 1989 in time for the downturn of 1990. Another consequence of declining markets was the hypertrophic growth of sales and marketing departments in larger firms, trying to steal market share from smaller ones (Aglietta *et al*, 1993, 520, 542–7; Jefferys, 2003, 153–68; *contra* Hancké, 2002).

A major characteristic of the monetarist turn was the increasing dependence of large firms, including the nationalized ones, on financial portfolio profits through mergers and acquisitions, self-financing and foreign direct investment (FDI), which was directed primarily to the US. The financierization of investment appeared first in Britain then France in the 1970s as an escape from the diminishing returns from manufacturing. The Volker jolt of 1979 gave a further boost to financierization everywhere but in Germany, where profitability stagnated as a result. Financialization destroyed the macro coherence of national economies and thus undermined political projects based on growth (*Le Monde,* May 20, 2003; Holman, 1996, esp. 63–5; Duménil and Lévy, 2000).

The political enthusiasm for a second Mitterrand term and the single market and currency benefited from the micro recovery of growth and employment that occurred from 1986 to 1990. It was stimulated by pent-up demand, increased worker productivity due to dismissals and discipline and the negotiated fall of the dollar and thus of oil prices accompanied by the decline of interest rates. But starting from 1990 there was a growing divergence of profitability, which continued to rise, and investment, relative wages and productivity, which fell (*id.*; Husson, 1996, 2001b). The ERM aggravated a deeper structural problem as yet unfathomed. French exporters preferred to use lower wages to increase profits rather than markets (Aglietta *et al*, 1993, 533). The early nineties saw a long recession deepened by high German interest rates, which were extended to others by the ERM. While profitability in the EC continued to climb to levels unknown since the

1960s, French investment rates fell from 22.7 in 1990 to 15 percent in 1995 (Huang-Ngoc, 2001, 75; Rowthorn, 1995).

In France higher unemployment and greater inequality opened up the crisis of representation and confidence that presidential candidate Chirac, borrowing from Emmanuel Todd, called the *fracture sociale* or social divide between the people and the traditional parties and elites. The social divide described the alienation not only of manual workers – the traditional seed-bed of revolutionaries – but of all wage-earners, white-collar, even managerial personnel, facing the new insecurities of the market place caused by the neo-liberal turn. Since the 1974 crisis the one issue determining the outcome of elections and fates of government had been job insecurity. In 1992 one half of male wage-earners feared unemployment, by 1996 over a quarter of all families had been affected by it (Moss, 1998, 239).

Even as the PCF declined and imploded, the legacy of high social expectation, contestation and militancy in protest against market insecurity remained. The number of people participating in protest action rose considerably expanding among the wage-earning middle classes and especially among the young. Whereas one half of respondents reported they had never engaged in protest in 1980 only 28 percent said so in 1998 (Jefferys, 2003a, 167). More than half supported the 1995 transport and other strikes and occupations by the unemployed as well as the antiglobalization protests in Genoa and elsewhere. In 1997, 72 percent told pollsters the economic system inspired them with fear and revolt; 41 percent wanted radical change. A majority of wage-earners including managerial personnel thought striking was the best way to achieve their job objectives. French wage-earners were unwilling to defend those market disciplines of dismissal, wage and strike restraint, longer hours and benefit cuts that were necessary to maintain profitability. The flagging legitimacy of capitalism in France was noted by the U.S. State Department, which placed it on top of the danger spots for US interests in 1997.[11]

The social divide appeared obscurely after Mitterrand's turn of 1983 in growing worker abstention and votes for the National Front, but most dramatically in the near defeat of the Maastricht treaty in 1992. The referendum split both the Right and Left along class lines. Catholic regions were bastions of Europhilia. The largest no vote came from the "people of the left," workers and peasants from urban and rural France, who had voted for Mitterrand. This was not a nationalist vote but a class vote of protest that associated sound money and the single currency with unemployment. Two-thirds of well-paid professionals and managers voted for and two-thirds of workers against Maastricht; the richer you were the more likely, whatever your position on Europe, to vote yes. Departments with the highest unemployment voted no. Class lines subsequently hardened on the issue. Parallel dissatisfaction with governments and the EC followed the rising curve of unemployment during the recession of 1991–92 in France, Germany, Spain and Portugal – both founding and new member-states (Milner, 2000). Most French felt the government put European construction ahead of France. The trust in private management and the EC, which had risen with hopes for liberal "modernization," was undermined by the resurgence of unemployment after 1990 (Moss, 1998, 238–39).

Following upon the Danish rejection of Maastricht the publication of negative French opinion polls caused a panic in the market for the traditionally weak currencies, the English pound and Italian lira, which were forced to leave the ERM. The conservative French government of Edouard Balladur, which kept real interest rates above five percent after 1993, faced considerable internal opposition from smaller employers and Gaullists, notably the President of the Assembly Philippe Séguin, who called Maastricht "a social Munich" because it sacrificed the welfare state to German monetarism. In July 1994 another run on the French franc triggered by the devaluation of the Irish punt and Spanish peseta was stemmed by joint intervention by French and German central banks and by the widening of the fluctuation band to 15 percent.

Chirac tapped the malaise caused by the strong franc and social divide in his 1995 presidential victory over Balladur on the first round and the Socialist Lionel Jospin on the second. Always a juggler of contradictions, he promised to put finance at the service of the economy while pledging to respect the Maastrict criteria. Le Pen also exploited the discontent gaining the largest proportion of worker votes, 30 percent, including many disappointed with Mitterrand, who were still socialist in value orientation. Chirac's contradictions exploded into the 1995 general transport strikes that were supported by 57 percent of the population and by demonstrations in defense of employment and the public services, which were larger than those of May–June.

After conferring with Chancellor Kohl, Chirac had announced the need for budgetary cuts to meet the Maastricht criteria. Counting on the cooperation of the CFDT, the government of Alain Juppé introduced a reform of social security that hurt nearly everyone. The rail workers, the professional kernel of the strike, preserved their own special regimes, but most of the reforms and budget cuts went ahead. At the end of 1996 Chirac negotiated the EU Stability Pact, which imposed a stiff penalty for excessive deficits under Maastricht. The pursuit of the strong franc and Maastricht criteria caused a widening of the social divide, deepening dissatisfaction with the government, and a radicalization of all parties, but especially the Socialists, with respect to Maastricht (Moss, 1998, 240–5).

Chirac called a surprise election in May 1997 in order to get a mandate for further cuts in respect of Maastricht, counting on a division of the Left. The Socialists and Communists ran on similar programs of wage reflation, defense of public services, the introduction of the thirty-five-hour week to create jobs and the revision of Maastricht in an Euro-Keynesian direction.

The Left won a marginal victory by 47.7 percent to 46.2 to the Right by converting enough workers and young people who had voted for Chirac in the 1995 presidential race (Moss and Michie, 1998, 75–6).

Jospin went to the summit on the Amsterdam Treaty in June 1997 hoping to change the terms of the Stability Pact. Two weeks after coming into office on a slim majority without an anti-Maastricht mandate he was in no position to provoke a constitutional and European crisis over the pact, upheld by both the Germans and Chirac. Instead, he was forced to accept a nonbinding resolution inspired by Blair that made employment a goal, but only by encouraging more flexible labor markets, essentially poorer wages and conditions, lower corporate taxes and social charges, and a clause in the new treaty, subordinating employment policy to existing economic policy (*id.*, 77–80).

The French mini-recovery from 1997 to 2000 was in part a spring-back from earlier retrenchment and partly a response to the high-tech bubble drawing imports to the US. Jospin got unemployment down from 11 to 8 percent with the help of the 35 hour week, for which employers received credits, greater time flexibility, wage stability and more intensive labor, and of youth jobs in education and public security. Jospin did not have a European policy of his own but tried to balance his socialist and EU commitments.[12] Once his demands for a revision of Maastricht were refused at Amsterdam, he folded his tent and stopped opposing EU policy. Maastricht had made an expansionary policy almost impossible by requiring unanimous consent for any departure from orthodoxy so that the election of a German government with a Keynesian finance minister Oscar Lafontaine could make little difference. When it came to reconciling social needs with the Maastricht criteria, Jospin cut the apple in two, using half of the three per cent growth for expenditure and more than a third for tax reduction as recommended by the EU Commission. He also went back on a promise not to privatize France-Telecom and undertook more privatizations than had previous conservative governments, arguing they were required by the need for joint ventures in the global economy (Sterdyniack, 2001, 33, 39–49).

By 2000 the emphasis shifted to assuaging investors. Jospin declared that lay-offs at Michelin were no affair of government, deeply shocking popular opinion and reopening the social divide (Rozès, 2002). He gave executives tax relief for stock options, subsidized firms for hiring the low paid, and gave as much income tax relief to the rich as to the middle class (Sterdyniak, 2001). Running up to the election, he gave free rein to the "elephants," future presidential hopefuls in the party, Fabius and former finance minister Dominique Strauss-Kahn, to talk about privatizing pensions and part of EDF (Electricity of France). Much of this domestic balancing act between the "elephants" and the people of the Left was designed to please the EU where Jospin condemned the inflationary growth of the Irish, ignored the

Keynesian critique of the ECB by Lafontaine, and supported plans at the Barcelona summit, which called for further privatization and commercialization, a balanced budget by 2004, the capitalization of pensions and raising the retirement age by five years. The latter meant relinquishing one of the proudest Socialist accomplishments – retirement at 60 (Fondation Copernic, 2001).

Faced with a record number of protest candidates on his left, Jospin's presidential campaign in 2002 was indifferent and unprogrammatic, focusing only on the person and implied misdeeds of Chirac. The results of the first round were a shocker to those who thought Jospin had bridged the social divide: record abstention, the retreat of mainstream candidates, Socialists and the Right, and the proliferation of votes for the extreme left – and right – on issues of employment and social justice. Le Pen received the largest number of votes of workers and the unemployed – 30 and 38 percent respectively. Adding protest votes from the Greens and Chevènement to the 10 percent received by the Trotskyists, the 3.4 percent for the PCF plus a portion from the hunters and Le Pen might yield as much as one-third of the electorate in revolt against neo-liberalism, much more than ever voted for the PCF alone. Le Pen eliminated Jospin, who lost 2.6 million votes compared to 1997, especially among his core supporters, public sector employees. Chirac garnered only nineteen percent, the worst ever for the winner of the first round. Because of the splintering of the Left and the absence of any common program, the consolidated Right party of Chirac, the UMP, won an absolute majority in parliament on an extremely narrow vote of only 23 percent of the electorate (Martin, 2003; Perrineau and Ysmal, 2003).

When the new government of Jean-Pierre Raffarin moved to cut budget and social security deficits, capitalize contributions, and raise the retirement age in accordance with EU directives and recommendations, it met with a wall of popular resistance in strikes and demonstrations of teachers, transport, and energy workers applauded by majority opinion. The popularity of Raffarin fell to record lows. Despite support from the accomodationist CFDT on pensions the government was forced to delay liberal reforms of schools and universities, health insurance, union rights, and public services out of fear of losing control of public order and the regional and European elections of 2004.

The Left, led by the Socialists, swept to victory in the regional elections, gaining four percent since the last ones and winning all but one of the regions and a majority of departmental councils for the first time in history. Contrary to expectations, it contained the Naional Front on the first round and eliminated the challenge from the Trotskyist left on the second, reversing the trend toward abstention and marginal protest. The election forced Chirac to reverse or halt most of the neo-liberal program though he went ahead with the partial denationalization of French Electricity and Gas, which was more than necessary to conform with the EU directive on the commercialization of that public service. His government would increasingly use the EU as an alibi for domestic liberalization.

The French elections to the European parliament on June 13 were an expression of protest and indifference to the European Union with participation declining to a historic low of 43 percent of the electorate. The big winners were the Socialists, who led the Left opposition with 29 percent of the vote. The loser was the UMP, the umbrella government party, which gleaned only 16.6 percent, having to share the right-wing vote with the Catholic pro-European UDF on 12 and the anti-Europeans on 8 percent.

When governments bent their programs to satisfy EU policies, the French people wielded a shield in defense of the welfare and interventionist state implicitly set against the EU. With little hope of economic recovery, faith in the EU declined. Fearful of immigration and product competition, a French majority opposed enlargement to Eastern Europe. Though opinion was still in favor of the EU in principle, it was more in an intergovernmental than federalist way (cf. *Le Monde,* Nov. 5, *Bastille, République, Nations,* Nov. 2003). With the Left and extreme Right opposed and the Socialists divided the European constitution faced possible defeat in the referendum called by Chirac.

The French people and mainstream parties were caught in the contradiction between their dual commitment to the EU and to the interventionist welfare state. EU pressure for more commercialization of public services, budget and social cuts, and industrial competition was meeting resistance. The programs of both the Chirac government and Socialist opposition lacked coherence and credibility because of the EU commitment. With slow growth and burgeoning welfare expenditure, the government had little chance of satisfying the 3 percent deficit limit under the stability pact within the next few years.

The Jospin government that had introduced the 35-hour week and pledged to revise Maastricht had reversed course and given tax benefits to the rich in 2000 largely because of its EU commitment. In response to the rearranged Raffarin government in 2004, the Socialists promised more progressive taxes and higher benefits, but these were incompatible with competition under the single European market and currency. The Socialist Left representing almost half of the party, called for a radical refoundation of the EU, but this was utopian escapism from the real problem. None of the parties on the left were yet willing to demand recovery of those state powers delegated to the EU – for the regulation of markets and capital, for renationalization, planning and exit from the single currency – that would be necessary to accomplish their goals of workers' rights, job security, greater social equality and renewed growth.

The elections of 2004 were another manifestation of the social divide between wage-earners and the mainstream parties and capitalist elites that was opened by the hard ERM, EMU and Maastricht. EU pressure on wages, jobs, benefits and public services helped create an enlarged protest movement that included many middle-class wage-earners. The protest against EU-promoted neo-liberalism produced majority support for strikes and other action, for the transport strike of 1995, the occupations of the unemployed in 1999, the margin of young people and workers who elected Jospin in 1997, and those public sector workers who defected from him in 2002 as well as the Left victory in 2004. The working-class vote remained fractured with more votes in the North going to both the PCF and the National Front. The elections of 2004 were an expression of antiliberalism in defense of the welfare state rather than a vote of confidence in any left party or reconstructive program.

Whether the contradiction between EU commitment and the interventionist welfare state lead to a rethinking of the former remained to be seen. The opposition of the French Socialist Left and Fabius, second in party command, to the European Constitution was based on a commitment to a chimerical social Europe. Less direct and overt resistance in defense of the welfare interventionist state existed in all the member-states, contributing to the crisis of the stability pact and EU. The conditional No given by the second in command of the Socialists, Lauren Fabius, to the Constitution for social reasons virtually assured its defeat in the promised referendum. What seemed likely was that the French people would remain a core of resistance to free market integration in the EU.

Notes

1. Mamou, 1988; Rosanvallon, 1989; Garrett, 1998; Quenouelle-Carre, L., 2000, 172–86.
2. Combe, 1969; Barreau, 1976; Morel, 1981; Borrel, 1996.
3. Carré *et al*, 1972, 85–6, 531–6; Jeanneney, 1991, 180–7; Bouvier *et al*, 1982, 1289, 1350–74; Rioux, 1983 II, 202–10, 227–36, 267–76; Mazier *et al*, 1984, 1999; Bonin, 1987, 273, 331.
4. Korpi, 1980; Gauron, 1983, 34–90; Moss, 1990; Jefferys, 2003b.
5. Portelli, 1980, 122–200; Capdevielle *et al*, 1981; Lancelot, 1986, 20, 60–6; Christofferson, 1991, 11–64,
6. Zinsou, 1985, 245–7; Barreau, 1990, 45–80; Rand, 1990; Cotta, 1991, 49–77; Schmidt, 1997; cf. Hencké, 2002.
7. Bauchard, 1986, 98–103; Favier and Martin-Roland, 1990, 45–7, 412; Giesbert, 1990, 150–4; Oately, 1997, 117–19.
8. Beaud, 1985, 160–71; Bauchard, 1986, 144–7; Giesbert, 1990, 169–82; Attali, 1992, I, 417; Oatley, 1997, 121–4.
9. Centre, 1989, 20, 43; Lecointe *et al*, 1989, 142–7; Cotta, 1991, 49–77; Gélédan, 1993, 78, 156, 223; Virard, 1993, 234–6; Lordon, 2001, 116; Piketty, 2001, 704 (table G).
10. Interview, Jean-Paul Fitoussi, OFCE, January 5, 1996.
11. Todd, 1995, 1998, 13; Boy and Mayer, 1997, 14, 62; *International Herald Tribune*, May 21, 1998; Moss, 1998, 239.
12. Interview, Marc Nouschi, Jospin's European advisor, May 17, 1998.

7

From ERM to EMU: EC Monetarism and Its Discontents

Bernard H. Moss

The treaty of Maastricht signed by twelve member-states in 1992 established the Economic and Monetary Union (EMU) with a single currency controlled by an independent European Central Bank (ECB) and the exclusive aim of price stability. It established strict convergence criteria for membership in terms of national rates of inflation, budgetary deficits and debt. The stability and growth pact of 1996 set a deficit limit of 3 percent sanctioned by a fine of up to 0.5 percent of GDP in order to preserve the value of the Euro. The statutes of the ECB were modeled on those of the Bundesbank with an assured majority of German monetary satellites and prohibition of attempts of national governments or politicians to influence it from the outside.

Maastricht consecrated the German ordo-liberal rules and principles that were implicit in the treaty of Rome. The EC became the first public body, at least in Europe, to make neoclassical economics based on a competitive market and sound money its guiding philosophy. Though the French hoped for a more interventionist economic government, the model chosen for Europe was a Hayekian federation in which the competitive market allocated resources under the constraint of a hard currency and labor bore the cost of adjustment in job insecurity, wage restraint and unemployment (cf. Verdun, 2000, 205). EMU consolidated the reversal of class forces that had ended labor mobilization and profit squeeze in the late 1970s and early 1980s.

The politicians and economists who had lauded EMU came to regret it too late. When unemployment resurged and national growth dipped as a consequence of single market and convergence policies after 1990 and again after the launch of the Euro in 1999, it became obvious that EMU was a monetarist and neo-liberal regime. After claiming social democratic potential for the EC, for a social Europe, American specialists, notably the more historically minded, acknowledged that it was a liberal, if not a Thatcherite, construction (Moravcsik, 1998a; Gillingham, 2003). Its impetus came from business forces and neo-liberal realignments within member-states under the pressure of globalization, initially that of currency speculation, which supposedly undermined the possibilities for national macro policy. Specialists neglected the role that the juridical superstructure, the rules, procedures and economic logic of the treaties, had played in orientating governments to the neo-liberal outcome (cf. Pollack, 1994; Pierson, 1996). The monetarist turn in member-states had more fundamental causes in the social structure and long cycles of capitalist development but the EC and monetary union, invoked by pro-business domestic forces to resolve the crisis of profitability, helped and over-determined the turn in a free market direction.

Most accounts see monetarist union as the only rational response to the breakdown of Bretton Woods and financial liberalization. We have argued that the monetarist turn was primarily a response to the wage-led inflation generated by labor's breakout from income policies and restraint after 1968. Labor mobilization was fed by the breakdown of Bretton Woods and the depreciation of the dollar that was more the result of expansionist Keynesian rather than monetarist US policies (Boddy and Crotty, 1975; cf. Helleiner, 1994). EC monetarism preceded and exceeded in rigor that of the US. Through the mechanism of the Exchange Rate Mechanism (ERM) interest and exchange rates converged upward past the DM in the EC before they converged with the UK, US, or rest of the world in the 1990s (Oatley, 1997, ch. 4; Block, 2000).[1] Long-term interest rates remained at an historic high everywhere because of the financierization and internationalization, and thus the riskiness, of investment (*id.*). After the burst of the high tech bubble in 2000, the American Fed lowered its interest rates 4 percent while the ECB reduced rates only 2 despite a more enduring recession. Lacking effective control over external exchange rates, the ECB did nothing to temper their volatility.

Globalization consisted initially of short-term speculative currency flows, which did not necessarily affect productive investment, FDI, or interest rates because of their domestic stickiness.[2] A major reason for keeping investment at home was the cost or perceived difficulty of the enforcement of obligations in foreign countries (Berger, 2002). Under less business-oriented regimes, speculative capital flight could have been limited by capital controls, taxes, and proactive industrial policy. Until the Carter–Volker interest rate spike of 1979 and its relaying by the Germans and ERM most EC states maintained controls on short-term flows, offering them enough leeway in time to effectuate successful devaluations (Bakker, 1996; Oately, 1997, ch. 5). German, British, and EC emulation of the spike arose not out of necessity but out of political choice, philosophical inclination, and the availability of supranational institutions.

EC monetarism had its own antecedents, rhythm, and internal dynamics. As a weapon against wage-led inflation it was built into the treasuries and central banks of the member-states, German ordo-liberalism, French Poincarism, the liberalism of the Bank of Italy, and the orthodoxy of the Bank of England and Treasury in defense of a reserve currency. During the 1960s Christian Democratic and Gaullist governments had kept inflation under control by engineering recessions during prosperity, but May–June 1968 set off a strike-wage-price spiral that eventually threatened profitability and private investment.

The EC was constructed around the utopia (cf. Polanyi, 1956) adumbrated in the Spaak Report of a "natural" competitive market under the constraint of a hard currency, free of the distortions caused by social or public intervention or regulation by proactive governments or unions. EC treaties were constructed around the basic competitive principle, the four freedoms of goods, services, labor, and capital operating on a level playing field. This principle precluded state regulation or intervention, which was inherently selective and discriminatory, and pointed in the Commission's view to an EC macro policy of price stability obtained through a single market and currency (Chapter 1).

The constitution of the EC bore the imprint of West German ordo-liberals, who thought of using it to prevent imported inflation by eliminating the trade and payments deficits of their weak currency partners. They refused French requests for aid to the weaker ones via a symmetrical monetary union. Structural business and political philosophical differences lay behind the German "economist" insistence on prior convergence to low inflation, a neo-classical view, and French "monetarism," which sought monetary expansion to levels of productivity that would eventually yield price stability, a European Keynesian one (cf. Howarth, 2001).

Despite Belgian calls for fixed exchange rates and French preferences for loose money the Rome treaty settled on an adjustable peg that would permit the Germans to revalue against imported inflation (Küsters, 1982, 362–73). Provision was made for neutralizing the beneficial trade effects of devaluation. Articles for the coordination of macro and exchange rate policy through state consultation and Commission recommendations provided the legal basis for the ERM and EMU.

The first Commission, headed by Hallstein, had an ordo-liberal orientation. To coordinate macro policy the Commission set up a galaxy of committees, including national financial officials. The second action program of 1962 called for the completion of the single market and movement toward fixed exchange rates and a single EC macro policy. The committee on medium-term planning envisaged a single reserve currency by 1970. The Commission proposed giving the power to decide the volume of national budgets to the Economic and Financial Council (ECOFIN). In possession of the legal framework and philosophical inspiration for EMU the Commission waited for the opportunity to launch it after the completion of the common market in 1970 (Dyson, 1994, 67–8; Hallstein, 1962, 39–45).

The first EMU proposal was a joint attempt by the French and Germans to establish a culture of price stability against the inflationary pressures arising from dollar devaluation and the wage hikes of May–June 1968. Negotiations over monetary union pitted the Germans, the anchors of stability, against the French and others who wanted a higher rate of growth and inflation in order to accommodate the rising power of labor (cf. Rosenthal, 1975). French conservatives and employers – some Gaullists apart – and others shared with the Germans the ultimate goal of capital mobility with a single currency, but they needed more rope than did the Germans, more financial resources and incentives, with which to bind prospectively accommodationist unions. Pompidou vetoed the goal of a single currency out of fears for national sovereignty and social order (Chapter 6). The band of monetary fluctuation called the snake that resulted could not withstand divergent policy responses, hard German versus soft money states, to the profitability crisis intensified by the oil price shock of 1974 (Dyson, 1994, ch. 3; Kruse, 1980).

The trailblazer of monetarism was West Germany, the regional guardian of sound money and balanced budgets, which had pressed for currency convertibility in the 1950s, stabilization plans in the 1960s, and a hard money EMU, snake and ERM in the 1970s. The Germans were the first to turn the screws of fiscal and monetary policy against inflation at the end of 1972, capping it at 6 percent in 1974 when it was 14.5 percent in France (Lankowski, 1982, chs 5–6). The Germans refused French requests for monetary aid to the weak including the Fourcade plan to recirculate petrol dollars. Whenever German governments made reflationary concessions to the French as did Schmidt in the first 1978 ERM agreement or Kohl in 1987 they were vetoed by the Bundesbank, which upheld the constitutional and macro regime of price stability (Kalthenthaler, 1998; Heisenberg, 1999; Howarth, 2001).

The Germans used EC monetary union to impose austerity on others. They offered to share some of their $50 billion in reserves to governments with payment deficits if they stayed in the snake and reduced their budget deficits and money supply. Aside from the loyal Dutch, they failed to rally other EC members to the discipline necessary to remain in the snake. Italy agreed to withdraw threatened import controls, the first serious breach of the common market, and reduce consumption when the Germans offered a loan of $2 billion. This was converted into a medium-term EC loan in 1976 under which council set Italian interest and tax rates. The turn toward austerity was endorsed by the the Italian Communist Party (PCI) whose cooperation was needed in paring down municipal budgets. The disinflationary partnership between the Bundesbank and the EC and the DC and PCI, the so-called historic compromise, ended the long wave of working-class mobilization begun in 1968 (Lankowski, 1982, esp. 392–8, 464).

The Germans offered to prop up the franc if the French government cut its budget and restrained wages. This arrangement, refused by Chirac in 1975, was welcomed by Barre, who capped wage and price rises and made budget cuts when he replaced Chirac as prime minister in September 1976. But because of fixed macro regimes, class politics, and labor mobilization it took another eight years before the Germans using the EC and ERM were able to reverse the inflationary tide in France and Italy (Chapter 6; Aglietta and Baulant, 1993).

The British, who were always a bit Euroskeptic, came to monetarism on their own because of American dependency, the power of the City, and divisions in labor ranks. The first effective anti-inflationary measures, taken by Labour in 1975, were supplemented by the 1976 austerity measures, the most Draconian in history, dictated by the IMF. The government had inflation under control when it went to the IMF, largely to enhance international monetary credibility, the traditional goal of Treasury (Artis and Cobham, 1991).

Mrs Thatcher in her 1978 manifesto incorporated monetarism into a whole-scale assault on state intervention. Elected in 1979 because of disenchantment with Labour's incomes policies, which alienated both skilled and unskilled, Mrs Thatcher immediately removed exchange controls, raised interest rates, and targeted the M5 money supply, the same rigorous measure used by the Bundesbank. At the same time she reinforced the effect of monetary restriction by reducing welfare benefits and taxes on the rich, attacked public service unions, and began the commercialization and privatization of public utilities and services, providing a model for EC industrial policy under the Vicomte Davignon (Chapter 3; Michie, 1992; P. Stephens, 1996).

Mrs Thatcher, who initially supported ERM, became an enthusiastic European for internal market reforms, which opened up the continent to British financial services and achieved the deregulation and commercialization of public markets on a vast scale. She stopped at the hard ERM and EMU because she saw a danger to national sovereignty and wanted to preserve a margin of macro maneuver in order to maintain average incomes and win elections. The Thatcherites and the City saw no need to subject themselves to German monetarism and EC regulation so long as they could defeat the unions and master inflation themselves (Stephens, P., 1996; Thompson, 1996). Thatcher won the 1987 election but produced the inflationary Lawson boom, named after Nigel Lawson, the chancellor of the exchequer – she wanted an even lower exchange rate and frenzied boom than he did – which was only checked by recourse to the ERM. In the end, her macro flexibility served the neo-liberal cause because the TUC and Labour Party became so demoralized by defeat that they were converted to a monetarism barely disguised in social rhetoric. This was the social neo-liberalism first preached by Delors to the TUC on behalf of the EC in 1988 and then that of the Labour Party, which had renounced all forms of interventionism by the time of the Blair–Brown governing pact in 1994 (Heffernan and Marqusee, 1992; Strange, 1997; Holden, 1999).

The idea for the ERM was part of a project for EMU revived in October 1977 by the newly installed Commission president, the liberal Labourite Roy Jenkins. It was taken up by Giscard after he had beaten off the Left and diminished Gaullist representation in the elections of March 1978 (Verdun,

1996, Aspinwall, 2002). He saw the ERM as a transition to a single currency that would relax the discipline of DM parity while guaranteeing some external wage and spending constraint, also as a haven of stability against the depreciating American dollar (Aglietta and Baulant, 1993). Schmidt viewed it as a way to stop the appreciation of the DM and reflate the German economy over the head of the Bundesbank and as an assertion of independence from the US, which had neglected German commercial interests. The snake had been weighted in favor of Germany and strong currency allies because it was always easier for them to bring down their exchange rate by buying up foreign reserves and sterilizing or soaking them up to make them price neutral than it was for weak currency states to sell off the reserves that bolstered their rates. In 1978 Schmidt agreed with the French to make the ERM more balanced than the snake with a cooperation fund to assist weak currencies and a common currency ECU grid to make adjustments more symmetrical (Moss and Michie, 1998, 15–16; Heisenberg, 1999).

The initial arrangement was vetoed by the Bundesbank with the backing of German industry (Kalthenthaler, 1998). The ECU grid was changed to bilateral rates, which shifted the burden of adjustment back to the weak to buy harder currencies with their reserves, and the cooperation fund forgotten. The Bundesbank warned it would not prop up another currency if it threatened German price stability. Preference for responding to major imbalances was given to realignments, which would be subject to mutual, that is German consent. The Monetary Committee led by the Germans became responsible for the management of a state's finances in the event of a crisis. The Germans were rather lax about devaluations in the ERM until the effects of the Volker and second oil price shock were felt in their first trade deficit, in 1980. If they were to continue emphasizing export-led growth, they would have to bear down on domestic costs and imported inflation, which meant imposing similar discipline on EC partners. They raised interest rates to keep up with the re-valued dollar and forced their partners in the ERM to follow suit (Kurzer, 1993; Oatley, 1997, ch. 4; Heisenberg, 1999).

In 1981 the Germans applied pressure on the French Socialists to reverse their spending and wage increases, finding an internal ally in Delors (Chapter 6). When the Danish asked for a 7 percent devaluation and the Belgians for 12 in 1982, the Monetary Committee conceded only 3 and 8 percent respectively (Marcussen and Zolner, 2001, 8). The Belgians were given more credit than the Danes because the ultra-liberal Wilfried Martens V government pledged a wage freeze and budget cuts. The Danish Socialist government, opposed by its own central bank and the EC and denied its budget by parliament, resigned yielding power to the conservatives, who instituted social cuts, deregulation and privatization (Christiansen, 1994, 93–4). With the definitive turnabout of Mitterrand in 1983 and the Italian deindexation of wages from prices in 1984, the ERM became a system of fixed exchange rates by means of interest rates aligned above the German.

The ERM was used by pro-business forces as a grid within which to engineer the reduction of labor costs, unit costs and real wages, in order to restore profitability. By the end of the decade profit rates were restored to levels of the early 1970s in every country but Germany. This was achieved by setting real interest rates above 4 percent and doubling unemployment to 10.8 percent by 1985. On average two points more of unemployment, especially long-term, were needed to decrease real wages by one point. Much less was needed in Germany and the Netherlands, the corporatist monetarist states, where, contrary to common belief, wages were downwardly flexible as in the US (Heylen and Poech, 1995, 583–4). Real wage increases fell below those of productivity to an average of 1 percent per annum in the 1980s. Job insecurity rose dramatically frightening workers away from union membership and strikes.

Productivity recovered largely because of layoffs, lower wage increases, greater inequality, and the intensification of work, but because of declining demand and high interest rates investment was only 0.8 percent per annum and growth 1.9 percent in the 1980s. Low investment and manufacturing output, lagging productivity and overall growth combined with restored profitability became permanent features of EC economies. For the first time since the Second World War profitability appeared to be linked with the greater exploitation of and worsening conditions for workers.[3]

The Netherlands and Belgium, suffering the greatest loss of profitability, made the earliest and most Draconian turn toward austerity of the EC; member-states. This was natural as they were the most interdependent upon the EC and Germany: 59 percent of their GDP passed through the EC; Germany received 30 percent of Dutch exports and contributed 40 percent of its capital; 41 percent of Dutch inflation was imported. This left little room for independent macro policies, especially devaluations, which would cost as much in German imports as it would gain in export revenue. Both countries also had leading Catholic parties with a corporatist affinity with German ordo-liberalism, which came increasingly to prevail over socialism (Braun, 1987; Jones, 1995a; Oately, 1997, ch. 4).

The decision of the Dutch in 1974 and Belgians in 1978 to join the snake forced them to resist wage hikes though social payments continued to rise until 1981 when they adopted German real interest rates at 7 percent. Wages were frozen and budgets cut. Between 1982 and 1985 real wages declined 2 percent while unemployment rose to 12 percent in Belgium and 13.3 percent in the Netherlands, the highest in the EC, allowing them to undercut low trend unit wage costs in Germany. Between 1981 and 1989 they raised profit share by 15 percent, returning to the profitability of the early 1960s, but without stimulating more investment (Jones, 1995a, esp. 161–2, 198, 238–9, 277).

The big turnabout came in the Liberal–Christian Democratic government of Martens V in 1981 in Belgium and the Karl Lubbers government in the Netherlands. Catholics, moving rightward, were replacing socialists in government and the influential unions. The Catholic union chose the Liberal Martens as prime minister (Jones, 1995, 172). In both countries Catholic unions collaborated with the government on austerity measures. Socialists had always fought for redistribution, employment, and the public sector, but were weakened in the Netherlands by the emergence of the post-materialist, anti-authoritarian New Left, which switched from supporting Democracy '66 to the Liberals in 1981, and in Belgium by the industrial growth of Catholic Flanders and the rising salience of the regional question. Because of the role of Brussels in international finance Belgium felt the pressure from the IMF for cuts as well. With higher interest rates it accumulated a huge government debt – 105 percent of GDP by 1986. Persuaded that austerity was necessary for European construction and that there was no alternative, the Belgians and Dutch re-elected neo-liberal governments despite mass unemployment (Kurzer, 1993, 156, 161–2, 205).

In the 1990s Belgian unemployment and job insecurity caused increasing regional tensions and the rise of the extreme right in Flanders. By the end of the 1990s the Netherlands had reduced official unemployment from 13 to 6 percent and become a model for EC employment policy. The government had brokered the Wassenaar agreement with the unions in 1983 to obtain wage restraint in return for flexible employment. This involved retiring older workers and placing them on disability benefit, thus disguising the unemployment of between 10 and 20 percent of the workforce, and replacing them with part-timers, mainly women, who became 35 percent of the workforce, and subsidized workers, another 27 percent.

These techniques for disguising unemployment and underemployment were picked up by the British government, which omitted older men above 57 and the young from its official figures.[4] Because of the spread of low-paid precarious jobs industry was deprived of the incentive to upgrade work quality, to motivate personnel, and scrap old machinery for new. Britain and the Netherlands could boast low official unemployment in the 1990s but also poor rates of investment in machinery and overall productivity growth (Kitson and Michie, 1996).

Disinflation was a long drawn out process in Italy, the country that had the highest inflation for the longest time. Once the PCI accepted the need for austerity in accord with the Germans and EC in 1976, the trade unions fell into line with management on wage restraint at EUR, a suburb of Rome, in 1977. Formally opposed to ERM entry in 1978, under which the Italians were given a wider band of fluctuation than others, the PCI followed the German Social Democrats in demanding a social and regional dimension in compensation for the ERM. When the inflationary shocks of 1979 rekindled the wage–price spiral, the Bank of Italy, given more independence, raised interest rates to 20 percent. Wage indexing was greatly diminished in 1983–84 by a "modernizing" Socialist Party after a tightly fought referendum against PCI opposition. There were only three devaluations after 1983 and none after 1987, making ERM a fixed exchange system (Epstein and Schor, 1989; Oatley, 1997; Talani, 2000).

Still, because of commitments to a large electoral clientele – pensioners, small business, the South – the Christian Democrats continued to run deficits and put the currency at risk so that in the 1992 panic over the pound the government, after using the ERM to blackmail the unions into wage concessions, took the country out of it. The country had to climb a large mountain to qualify for the euro by cutting expenditures 14 percent, raising taxes, including a special euro one of 5 percent, and privatizing industry. After a successful general strike against pension reduction in 1994 opposition faded because of the support of the former Communists of the PDS, who led the unions, for the cuts required by Maastricht (Oately, 1997, 128–136; Talani, 2000; Abse, 2001).

Despite the monetarist shift French and Italian governments wanted to keep a margin for maneuver to finance entrenched social rights and industrial subsidies. The German standard of deflation was too stark for the stimulative policies necessary to reduce unemployment. Where acquired social rights were a precondition for governing because of the prior mobilization of labor an expansive macro regime became a matter of state policy. The Gaullists even more than the Socialists believed that austerity was just a prelude to another state-led expansion. Employers who had reason to distrust inflationary policies, devaluation, and lower interest rates, under pro-labor governments could support them under non-threatening conservatives (Howarth, 2001, 167–8; Moravcsik, 1998a, 412).

Both the French Right and Left remained suspicious of the ERM and EMU because they threatened the post-war consensus around devaluation and reflation that afforded credit to capital and social security to wage-earners. No matter how high the French raised interest rates they were still trumped by the DM in the global market. Even after drawing even with the Germans on inflation in 1986 the French continued to pay an interest premium to maintain parity with the DM because of their reputation for intervention and monetary laxity. They required a more symmetric monetary union in which the hard currencies from corporatist states aided the weaker inflationary ones to become strong like them (Howarth, 2001).

To achieve a single market in capital the Germans wanted to remove remaining restrictions on short-term flows. This was done by the British and Dutch in 1979 and the Danes and Belgians in 1982, but not by the French, Italians, Spanish, Greeks, and Portuguese before 1990. By restricting trade credits and the acquisition of foreign loans and assets the French and Italians limited the amount of currency that could be taken out at any one time thus conserving reserves at times of crisis or rumored devaluations. This allowed the French and Italians to keep interest rates 7.2 and 3.2 basis points below euro-rates in 1983 enabling them to carry out successful devaluations. None of the French parties favored removing controls until Mitterrand bartered them away to the Germans for the single currency in 1988 (Bakker, 1996; Oately, 1997, ch. 5).

The French and Italians would only consider a removal of controls if they got sufficient assistance from Germany. After an EC directive freed up controls in 1986 the Germans negotiated two accords with the French in 1987 that afforded some relief, but it was not enough to eliminate the risk premium and speculation against the franc. At Basel-Nybourg the Germans agreed to coordinate interest rates and to take responsibility for keeping weaker currencies afloat. This was a policy breakthrough but once again the Bundesbank set a limit of domestic price stability that led to an addendum to the Franco-German treaty of an economic and financial council to coordinate rate policy. Converted into merely a consultative body, this council did not abate speculation against the franc in 1988. Clearly there was reason for the French to seek new solutions, but the single currency was not one of them (Balleix-Banerjee, 1999; Heisenberg, 1999; Howarth, 2001, ch. 4).

The preferred French solution was increased use of the ECU as a common currency for international trade. Pegged to national currencies and thus weaker than the DM, it would allow for domestic policy relaxation while protecting weaker currencies from speculative runs. The French sold large ECU bond issues and encouraged its use in EC payments. The SEA of 1987 referred to both monetary union and the ECU as "the European currency" to Mrs Thatcher's dismay. When Edouard Balladur, the French prime minister, in his memo to the Germans in January 1988 talked of a "European currency zone with common central institutions;" Giscard's association of European multinationals, the AMUE, called for an independent European bank; and Mitterrand in his April 1988 Letter to the French wrote of "a reserve currency managed eventually by an ECB," they were all referring to the ECU, a common parallel not a single currency (Balleix-Banerjee, 1999; Howarth, 2001, 84–119, *contra* Collignan, 2003b). In 1990 as a riposte to the Delors Report Mrs Thatcher proposed a hard ECU designed to set a restrictive standard for national supply and to reconcile Tory Euroskeptics and Europhiles (Dyson and Featherstein, 1999, 618–30).

By 1988 the ERM had become a fixed rate regime pegged to the DM, which had achieved the boundless horizon of deflation with fiscal and monetary restraint. Governments had been convinced by pro-business forces that low inflation and exchange rate stability was most conducive to trade and growth (cf. Gros and Thygesen, 1998 with Feldstein, 1997). Nobody in power or close to power questioned its premises, capital mobility under fixed exchange rates, or its consequence according to the Mundell (1961) law of incompatibilities – the end to independent national macro policy. The German government and business were quite happy with the ERM status quo because it eliminated inflation while keeping the currency slightly undervalued. The Bundesbank feared any innovation like a common or single currency that would allow deficitary countries to dilute the currency (Heisenberg, 1999; Howarth, 2001).

Since all agreed with Mrs Thatcher about TINA – that there was no alternative to monetarism – and that monetarism would end capitalist instability, cycles, and crises, there was no need for governments to tie their hands with a permanently fixed ERM or EMU as suggested by Tomasso Padoa-Schioppa, from D-G II (Directorate-General) economic affairs (1987). His was a spillover argument that without further monetary union an economic downturn would provoke backsliding or spillback from the ERM to devaluations and controls. This is indeed what happened in 1992 and 1993 because tight money policies were not politically acceptable in a long and deep recession. The spillover argument became a *post-facto* justification for EMU, but it was not the trigger for it (cf. Verdun, 2000).

It was immediately the creation of Mitterrand looking for a monument of European construction much like the Arc at La Défense to leave for posterity. Ever since his domestic turn in 1983 European construction had become a substitute for socialism as his grand project and legacy, also an alibi for his turn. French opinion followed. His advisor Attali convinced him that expansionary policy was gone for good or at least as Bérégovoy said, there was no political majority for it. Mitterrand faced an impasse trying to reform the ERM the French way. The vice-chair of the Bundesbank told him in November 1987 that it would have to be the pivot of any European central bank. Thus when Mitterrand welcomed a proposal transmitted by Delors in February 1988 for a single currency from the German foreign minister Genscher, a Free Democrat and European federalist, he acted with the foreknowledge that he would have to meet the Bundesbank's rigorous criteria of balanced budgets, tight money, and central bank independence (Balleix-Banerjee, 1999, Dyson and Featherstone, 1999; Moss, 2000, 263–4).

Motivated by monetarist assumptions and European ambition he was willing to sacrifice traditional French policy and interests in order to obtain EMU, but he had to win his countrymen over slowly and not expose his hand too early. With a presidential and parliamentary majority including the Catholic Centrists and a platform commitment to the "United States of Europe" he disposed of a permissive consensus for further European construction in June 1988. The French bank governor Jacques de Larosière again spelled out German conditions for EMU to Mitterrand in May. An understanding about EMU was probably reached with Kohl at a pre-summit meeting on 2 June 1988, when the French abandoned capital controls without any obvious *quid pro quo*. but two and a half more years of negotiation were needed to iron out the details and persuade public opinion (Dyson and Featherstone, 1999; Moss, 2000, 263–5).

Mitterrand allowed ministers like Bérégovoy to defend traditional French principles on political control of the central bank in order to reassure domestic, especially Socialist, opinion and gain bargaining chips on peripheral issues with the Germans, but the final conditions of EMU at Maastricht in December 1991 were the same German ones Mitterrand had agreed to with

Kohl in June 1988. Lacking the power, legitimacy, and permissive consensus behind the French president, Kohl had a much harder job convincing the Germans, who were basically happy with the status quo and fearful of diluting the currency. He had to build supportive coalitions in his own party, government, parliament and opinion, and above all convince the ordo-liberal temple, the Bundesbank and the ministries of economics and finance, that the French were serious about sound money. The fear and danger of Germany going it alone in Europe after re-unification in 1990 persuaded many of the need for monetary union (Dyson and Featherstone, 1999; Moss, 2000, 263–5).

Mitterrand's haste to conclude on German terms can be seen in the appointment of the Delors committee to discuss the modalities, not the pros and cons, of EMU with central bankers, in admonitions to his ministers, interest rate signals, and early decisions of ECOFIN and the EC Monetary Committee that predetermined the final outcome. In April 1988 he told Bérégovoy to abandon savings tax harmonization as a condition for the free movement of capital saying "the Germans are with us [on EMU]. We have to go forward with them" (cited in Aeschimann and Riché, 1996, 48). Once re-elected he pursued tight money policies signaling his conversion to German ones by raising interest rates that had been lowered by Bérégovoy.

During the deliberations of the Delors Committee he got de Larosière to reverse himself and accept rigorous German convergence criteria. When Bérégovoy expressed skepticism about the report he told him "if the others are agreed so are we" (cited in *id.*, 88). In January 1991 when ministers were attracted by the British proposal of a hard ECU, chiefly as a way of stopping the German one, Mitterrand got them together to warn that Germany not Britain was their ally and that an independent bank would allow them to influence decisions (*id.*, 90). He was the one who suggested the 3 percent deficit limit, which was the arbitrary target he had set for the French budget in 1983, at one point outbidding the Germans in rigor by demanding 1 percent. Contrary to the French brief, which was to obtain a long transition period for the harmonization of currencies, Mitterrand was responsible for getting the Germans to accept the automatic starting date for the Euro in 1999 (Cameron, 1995b; Balleix-Bonerjee, 1999, esp. 302; Dyson and Featherstone, 1999).

The Delors Report (1989) was designed to bind the Bundesbank into the French–German understanding of June 1988. It recommended fixed exchange rates or a single currency under an independent central bank with strict convergence limits on deficits and debt upon entry and continuing control over national budgets. Like all integration projects it contained social and regional compensation for the losers. The burden of adjustment for differences in competitiveness was placed on labor, which had to keep their demands within the limits of productivity growth. The report was backed up by the *One Market, One Money* study, undertaken by Commission economists close to the employers' UNICE (Dyson, 1994, 118, 136). As product markets became more competitive across borders, they said, national unions would lose power under risk of unemployment to set wages and conditions, which would revert to local factor markets (Emerson, 1990, 24, 102, 147).

Once worries about EMU laxity and interventionism were relieved employers became its most enthusiastic supporters. Giscard's association of multinationals had lobbied for a parallel common currency to integrate capital markets (Collignon and Schwartzen, 2003). UNICE endorsed the Delors and Emerson reports. Like the reports they argued – with little justification (Feldstein, 1997) – that exchange rate stability was most conducive to trade and growth. While UNICE officially spoke of EMU savings in transaction costs and risk premiums, employers thought its greatest advantage was the downward competitive pressure it would put on wages and social costs (Verdun, 1996, 75–80). They could count on the neo-liberal consensus, mass unemployment, EC recommendations, and new restrictions on strikes and bargaining to keep wage increases below those of productivity (*id.*, Chapter 3).

Business attitudes toward EMU did not simply depend upon class or export interest, but also upon political affiliation and national macro regime. German business never intervened in the debate because it trusted the Bundesbank to defend the sound money regime upon which it relied. As the dominant exporter in the EC, it benefited from the status quo and was skeptical of both the single market and currency. Under EMU it risked losing not only the undervalued DM in the ERM, but also the whole culture of stability and wage monetary coordination that had safeguarded profits. The undervalued DM and wage monetary coordination were indeed lost under EMU (Huelshof, 1997; Franzese, 2000b).

French employers were almost unanimously supportive of the idea of a single currency in 1989, but many, especially Gaullists and smaller ones, lost faith when tight money contributed to the deep recession of 1991–93. The CNPF condemned EMU on the eve of Maastricht for political reasons as "monetarism and technocracy gone mad" (cited in Balleix-Banerjee, 1999, 141), but looked more favorably as the Right united behind it, especially when their support for the strong franc allowed Chirac to lower interest rates in 1996 (Boissieu and Pisani-Ferry, 1998).

British business attitudes reflected particular interests of firms and banks allowing the Tories to divide on sectarian lines for and against Europe. Increasingly under the influence of multinationals – not necessarily British ones – the CBI was pro-ERM and EMU because it was export-oriented (Blank, 1973). The financial City on the other hand favored entry into the ERM only briefly, in the late 1980s, as a means of dampening the Lawson boom. The City was an independent power, which had privileged relations with the Treasury and truly global reach. Having greeted Thatcher's "big bang" stock market deregulation with enthusiasm, it feared the EC would regulate its operations and parochialize its global trading. The Treasury and Bank of

England shared Mrs Thatcher's preference for macro flexibility and expansiveness, if need be, which helped her win her third election.

With union power broken and the Labour Party tamed, the danger of wage-led inflation had disappeared. The Treasury and the City only sought recourse to ERM austerity when the Lawson boom got out of hand. Once brief ERM membership plus lower import prices had deflated the economy for good after 1992, it was no longer necessary to have an overvalued pound linked to the ERM to keep wages and prices in check (Stephens, P., 1996; Thompson, 1996; Talani, 2000).

The basic decisions about EMU were made along Delors' lines even before the intergovernmental IGC negotiations opened at the end of 1990. In November 1998 ECOFIN decided on an economic policy coordination that would not permit the monetary financing of public deficits. In May 1990 five countries, including France, Germany, and Italy, agreed to use Bundesbank criteria to control money supply. In July 1990 the Monetary Committee rejected the French plan for a long transitional second stage during which the weaker currencies would be strengthened and the use of the ECU as a common currency promoted by the ECB. The final treaty provided for a short transition during which a monetary institute would serve merely an informational role (Balleix-Banerjee, 1999; Dyson and Featherstone, 1999; Howarth, 2001, ch. 5).

The official French draft submitted by Bérégovoy in January 1991 was a compromise between French inter-governmentalism and German monetarism (*id.*; *Projet*, 1991; Italiener, 1993). It set out a French version of federalism that could be used as a bargaining tool and as a new European ideal for domestic consumption. While accepting bank independence and non-inflationary growth in principle, it gave the power to set the parameters of fiscal and monetary policy on all levels, including the national, to the European Council, an economic government acting by a qualified majority together with a consultative assembly made up of national legislators. Almost nothing of the French draft was retained. Bérégovoy, who became prime minister in 1992, committed suicide after the Socialist defeat in 1993, partly in despair at the unemployment consequences of what he called "this hoax (*fumisterie*) of Maastricht" (cited in Aeschimann and Riché, 1996, 170).

The French draft was used to offset German demands for a political union with a stronger parliament and committee of regions and to obtain peripheral concessions. ECOFIN was given the power to set internal and external exchange rates in consultation with the ECB while ensuring price stability and fair competition. In actuality, considering the conflict of interests and powers between a more growth-minded ECOFIN and price fixated bank, the latter effectively set external rates, making coordination with other major currency powers nearly impossible (*Le Monde*, December 10, 2003, March 4, 2004). The French defense of looser convergence criteria, which had been abandoned in the Delors Committee on instructions from Mitterrand, was resurrected during the IGC in order to prevent a two-speed Europe, the exclusion of the Spanish, Italians, and Greeks, who were likely French political allies within but price competitors without. Overall, Maastricht represented French capitulation to German principles and conditions (cf. Dyson, 1999).

The French asserted that they would enjoy more control over monetary policy under EMU than they had under ERM. Whereas they still disposed of some influence and freedom of action under the ERM, where they had possessed capital controls and allies and could always devalue and float in the event of a crisis, they lost all once their money disappeared into an EMU with a central bank they could no longer influence. Yet, with typical braggadocio and insouciance Mitterrand claimed during the referendum campaign that "we will control the European bank" (cited by *Libération*, September 4, 1992). Much was made by Chirac of a deal in 1996 by which Wim Duisenberg, the first president of the ECB, would step down in mid-term in favor of the French Governor Bernard Trichet, who was in any event even more orthodox than Duisenberg, and by Jospin of the creation in December 1997 of a Euro-x council, renamed Eurogroup in 2000, which had no official standing but was supposed to function as the economic government of EMU. In fact, it merely served to police excessive deficits, not formulating expansive macro policy as hoped by the French (Puetter, 2003).

As realists with little respect for liberal juridical culture, the French supposed their raw geo-political and economic power and diplomatic aplomb would prevail over monetarist rules inscribed in treaties, agreements, and the general consensus. The EU was a rule-based regime, which did not exclude the exercise of national leverage, but under the crisis conditions of the stability pact in November 2003 the rules on budgetary discipline were suspended by the informal veto power of major partners as the French had anticipated they would be.

EMU is often seen as the *quid pro quo* for French acceptance of German unity (Grieco, 1995). The basic understanding about EMU had been reached long before reunification, but it was not without effect in getting Kohl, who believed a single currency to be contrary to German interests and opinion, to set a date for the Inter Governmental Conferences (IGCs) at Strasbourg in December 1989 (*Le Monde*, July 30, 1998; Heisenberg, 1999). Mitterrand had counted on the Soviet's Michel Gorbachev stopping reunification, but once it happened it became vital to harness the new Germany to France and the EC. Mitterrand could frighten Kohl and Kohl the German public about the dangers of going it alone in the post-Cold War world. After the fall of the Berlin wall Kohl pushed for supranational political union, deploying the security argument about the need for Western allies to overcome economic skepticism about the single currency (Dyson and Featherstone, 1999).

Germans remained skeptical about the anti-inflationary commitment of their partners. They pressed for a strict interpretation of the convergence criteria that would exclude the Southerners and argued for a delay. On the eve of entry in 1998 at a time when 60 percent of opinion was hostile, the ministry of finance warned the government not to proceed. The decline of the euro, 25 percent relative to the dollar in the first two years, did nothing to endear it to well-traveled Germans. Nevertheless, attempts of politicians like Gerhard Schroeder and Edouard Stoiber to exploit Euroskepticism in elections or of finance minister Oscar Lafontaine to defy the ECB had little resonance due to the weak sense of German statehood and identity and fear of going it alone. Like others Germany had to use creative accounting to meet convergence criteria and became the most delinquent of deficit spenders in the deep recession that followed (Heisenberg, 1999, ch. 7; Milner, 2000; Dyson, 2002).

The 1990s saw the breakdown of Germany as the export-leader, model, and economic driver of European integration. It had done nominally better than its partners on inflation and unemployment, but at the expense of capital investment – gross stock declined between 1973 and 1992 – and wage share of value added (Rowthorn, 1995, 33). Deepening the 1990 recession were the high interest rates set by the Bundesbank to check the inflationary effects of reunification. As a result, the trade-weighted exchange rate rose 15 percent and relative wage costs 20 percent, which reduced the trade surplus from 6 to 1 percent of GDP in 1992.

The crisis of German neo-liberalism was profound. Years of high interest rates and low capital investment, lack of technological innovation, and neglect of the domestic market made Germany vulnerable to Japanese competition on the high end and Eastern Europe and soon China on the low. Germany was the only EC country that did not recover previous rates of profitability probably due to its failure to renovate technology in manufacturing upon which it, unlike others who flew to financial speculation, depended (Rowthorn, 1995, 33; *Le Monde*, March 3, 2004). Overvalued in relation to the Euro by about 3 percent, the German currency did not benefit from the low Euro rate against the dollar in the late 1990s (Essex, 2003, 20–1). Relative export shares in the EC fell in the 1990s as did gross investment, domestic demand, and government spending after 2000. Corporate insolvencies rose to 45,000 in 2000, threatening the major banks, which had expatriated funds to the UK, US, and Eastern Europe. The stability pact that Germany had imposed on its partners came back to haunt it, making it impossible to conduct proactive counter-cyclical fiscal policy in a long recession that nevertheless subjected it to the excessive deficit procedure.

The German model of social partnership between unions and management, which had served as legitimation for the EU as a whole, broke down in this era of declining profitability, investment, and growth. The only immediate solution was to bear down on wages and benefits, but this destroyed incentives for worker and union cooperation with management that was the heart of the model. German workers began to resist plant and mine closures in the French manner. After a long fallow IG Metall, the pattern leader in collective bargaining, demanded and received wage increases that were two or three points above national income growth and elected a left-wing leader. Despite a severe recession East German members struck for the 35-hour week and other benefits enjoyed in the West.

In the face of recession and union militancy management reconsidered its commitment to works councils and sectoral bargaining. While resisting immediate compliance with the stability pact on technical grounds in complicity with the French, the chancellor Schroeder made a long-term commitment to trim the welfare state with Agenda 2010, which facilitated job dismissals and reduced health and unemployment benefits. Agenda 2010 gave a slight boost to business confidence but not enough to revive the economy, while alienating SPD members and voters.

The fall of the German export-driven model, misrepresented as a successful "third way" by commentators (e.g. Albert, 1991; Hutton, 1995; Dyson, 2002), was as inevitable as its rise. Germany was caught in the long-term contradiction that lay at the core of the EC trading network for which it produced one-third of the GNP. Beginning with its huge comparative advantage in the manufacture of capital goods, Germany maintained its dominance of EC and global markets through its constitutional and macro policy adherence to tight money and wage restraint. But whereas its growth was based on relative price stability achieved by means of central bank independence and union discipline, that of its EC trading partners was inflationary resulting from aggressive mobilizing unions and politically responsive banks, which propelled the strike-wage-benefit-price spiral. Germany feared for its social stability from inflation imported from its EC partners. By exporting its own wage and budgetary constraints to them through the EC and monetary union, it deprived itself of markets both at home and abroad, hoist with its own petard and that of the EC constitution.

The nostrum for the US and German governments, international finance, most economists, and the EU for this deflationary crisis was more austerity, capping wages, benefits, and corporate taxes to induce more private investment. Delors' White Paper on employment and competitiveness in 1994 echoed recommendations of the European Round Table and the OECD. It endorsed employer demands for labor flexibility, work sharing, the diminution of social charges, and wage reductions relative to productivity. Council in 1993 recommended policies of pay moderation, decentralized bargaining, lower social expenditure, and more flexible forms of work organization. The Santer Commission of 1996 abandoned active social policy and recommended budget cuts and deflation as the way to stimulate investment and create jobs. The Amsterdam summit and treaty of 1997 under Blairite influence made job creation dependent upon deflationary market conditions and lower taxes and social charges. Like Blair the EU adopted Thatcherism with a human face consisting of a factitious social dialogue and a "soft" macro coordination that was necessarily deflationary (Moss and Michie, 1998, 158–9; cf. Dyson, 2003).

Meanwhile, the EC pursued the commercialization and privatization of nationalized industry and public utilities and services begun around the single market program from telecommunications and air transport to rail, post, and energy (Chapter 3). This was the strategy proposed by the Lisbon summit of 2000 to produce "the most competitive and dynamic information age economy in the world by 2010." Other policies involved the expansion of the workforce by raising the retirement age and downsizing the welfare state with the capitalization on private financial markets of pension and other benefit funds. As a result of lower growth and job insecurity, welfare retrenchment was needed to maintain profitability (*Le Monde*, 8, June 11, 2003).

The so-called Lisbon process, which was declared a non-starter by the Commission in 2004 (*International Herald Tribune*, January 22, 2004), relied on information technology (IT) as the motor of growth in imitation of the US where it had sparked a speculative bubble with tremendous wealth effects from 1995 until 2000 when the bubble burst. The growth of IT could not sustain prosperity because unlike the mass production and consumption of the "glorious years" its productive base and market, representing 2 percent of the workforce and 8 percent of GDP for the entire information sector, were limited. Yet, even with its own leaps of productivity the IT sector took some time before it raised that of manufacturing but by that time the recovery was jobless when faced with Chinese competition. It may have raised long-term productivity growth. In any event, the EU with its *laissez-faire* industrial policy lost out on the IT revolution and continued to fall behind the US in R&D.[5]

The ERM and EMU with their high interest rates aggravated a deeper structural problem, which contradicted the laws of neo-classical economies, of falling investment and productivity despite lower wage increases and higher profitability (Rowthorn, 1995, 36). French exporters preferred to use lower wages to increase profits rather than markets (Aglietta and Baulant, 1993, 533). While profitability continued to climb – barely in Germany – to levels unknown since the 1960s, French investment rates fell almost 8 percent from 1990 to 1995 (Huang-Ngoc, 2001, 75). Wage increases were kept below those of productivity as the Commission had demanded. French wage share dropped from 70.8 percent in 1991 to 68 percent in 1997, lowering demand and making for a sluggish recovery (Sterdyniack, 2001, 32). The privatization and commercialization of nationalized industries and public services further reduced labor costs. By 2000 real unit wage costs in the EC had fallen 13 percent since the 1970s (Huemer, 1999, 63).

Economic simulations showed that lower wages would lead to a deflationary downward spiral toward lower growth (*id.*, 164–5, 185). The aim was to achieve a limited "equilibrium" growth that could increase jobs without wage share. In pursuit of this latent goal the ECB set the inflation ceiling at

2 percent, forcing the expansionary countries to slow down to the growth rate of the slowest ones, precisely the ones that needed an export demand boost from them (Husson, 1996, 71, 2001, 70–1; Sterdyniack, 2001, 32).

The EC helped reverse the growth of public and social expenditure and increase income gaps. GDP share for social expenditure was reduced after 1993, especially for health, disability, and unemployment insurance (cf. Rhodes, 2002, 312–17). Entitlements were made leaner, meaner, and less redistributive, linked more with payroll contributions and capital markets (Daley, 1997; Huemer, 1999, 31). Imported from the US, welfare to work, which cut benefits for those refusing to take any job, became the EC benchmark. Following the US example, a rising proportion of benefits were privatized in the form of tax credits for health and pension plans. The retirement age was raised and funds capitalized under the Lisbon process. The tax burden was shifted dramatically after 1980 from companies to wage-earners, reducing that on capital by 10 percent and increasing that on wages by 20 percent (Aeschimann and Riché, 1996, 48).

Welfare institutions and expectations had become so rooted in people's minds that even with the ideological and programmatic decline of left and labor parties, attempts by governments and the EU to make further cuts only created mass disaffection. It was resistance resulting from past labor mobilization and class political organization, not any particular national welfare institutions, that distinguished the European social model from the American. Contrary to predictions of the end of the working class and communism (*contra* Hobsbawn, 1978; Fukayama, 1991; and Pontussen, 1995b), the job insecurity and welfare cuts induced by the EU enlarged the aggrieved working class to include the young, public sector, professional, and managerial personnel (Moss, 1998, 238–41; Huber and Stephens, 2001).

This enlarged resistance to neo-liberalism was first expressed in the near rejection by the French of Maastricht in 1992, in the transport strike of 1995, and ensuing movements of protest, strikes, and elections. Anti-liberal EU sentiment was the broadest socially and most manifest ideologically in France because of the revolutionary socialist and republican tradition, but signs of it could be seen elsewhere, in Italy, Germany, and Austria, which held its first general strike since 1945 over the reduction of pensions and advancement of retirement, in the collapse of support for Schroeder because of his Agenda 2010 program, in Swedish and Danish rejection of Euro membership, and in the record levels of abstention – 41 percent in the 2001 parliamentary ballot – in British elections. In the absence of credible political alternatives on the left growing abstentionism and protest voting manifested a real crisis of confidence in both national governments and the EU (*Le Monde*, February 26, March 3, 2004).

The growing anti-liberal sentiment was more often directed at the distant phantom of globalization rather than at the EU as the cause of the problem. Most Europeans identified with the issues raised by the anti-globalization movement, which included after the European Social Forum of 2003 in Paris, the ultra-liberal character of the EU (*Le Monde*, December 3, 2003). The jobless recoveries that occurred after 2000 could be attributed to long-distance globalization, the outsourcing of jobs, relocation of plants, and the massive flight of capital, principally to China. But people were beginning to understand that globalization was also a product of political decisions, philosophies, and institutions that could be altered to regulate or even reverse it. The majority of nearly all mainstream political parties and unions remained pro-EU. Most of the Left believed it could be reformed. There were no mass movements or major parties demanding withdrawal, but with the threat of immigration and company relocation coming from the new, much poorer Eastern members, a dawning sense that the EU was also an instrument of globalization, job insecurity, and declining living standards.

The EU was increasingly judged in terms of economic performance, which was poor. When the hopes of liberal "modernization" raised by the single market program were dashed in the 1990–93 recession, public support for the EC plummeted. The disaffection was expressed in the 1994 European elections by protest votes (Perrineau and Ysmal, 1994), in 1999 by the abstention of half the electorate and 55 percent in 2004. The single market and currency were applauded by well-paid political, professional, and business elites and distrusted by wage-earners and small business. The majority was not opposed to the EU as such but to its policies. A majority in all but three countries told pollsters in 2002 that they would not care if the EU disappeared tomorrow (*Eurobarometer*, Spring 2002, 42–4). Support for membership fell below 50 percent everywhere in 2003 for the first time (*The Guardian*, December 14, 2003). Member-state divisions over the Iraqi war, the stability pact and new constitution, and economic stagnation resulting from an overvalued Euro threatened to turn permissive consensus into outright rejection of the EU (*Le Monde*, December 10, 2003).

As of 2004 EMU had not met its promise of monetary strength and stability and economic convergence and growth, and was under threat from the fiscal crisis of the stability pact. The Euro brought no external stability, falling up to 30 percent against the dollar and yen with a real decline of 15 percent in the first two years before overtaking its original position by more than 20 percent and causing stagnation three years later (Arestis, 2003, 107–8). The conflict of interest and powers written into Maastricht between the ECB and ECOFIN made coordination to control exchange rates with other major powers nearly impossible (*Le Monde*, December 10, 2003). With only 13 percent of world reserves the Euro did not rival the dollar, which increased its share to 70 percent. Even as a trading currency it was employed in less than half of all intra-EC transactions. Used for three-quarters of international loans, the dollar remained king (*id.*, January 1, November 25, 2003). The economic downturn in the US after 2000 caused a reversal of dollar flows back into the Euro, but this was a default strength due to the EU's deflationary environment and doubts about the large American trade and budgetary deficit and Iraqi war. (*id.*, January 5, March 4, 2003).

As for intra-EC exchange rates, EMU produced stability by abolishing national currencies, which removed the possibility of reviving stagnant economies with devaluations that reduced real interest rates, diminished imports, increased exports, and stimulated inflationary growth. One advantage it offered for weak currency countries was that when the Euro fell, their currency did not plummet in relation to the strong currencies as it had done in the 1970s. The governments of countries with trade deficits no longer suffered from external payment constraints in borrowing, but it was limited by the debt and deficit ceiling. Having given up recourse to devaluations and counter-cyclical policy, they had no way to prevent large-scale bankruptcies and layoffs during a downturn. The stability pact was a hindrance to the operation of so-called automatic stabilizers resulting from the reduced tax revenues and added social expenditure that stimulated recovery in a recession through deficit spending and increased purchasing power (Crowley, 2003b, *The Guardian*, May 8, 2003).

The Euro did not produce the convergence and coordination of national economies that was necessary for the functioning of a notional "optimal currency area" or the social efficiencies of the US market with its economies of scale, regional specialization, labor mobility, and fiscal federalism redistributing taxes to poorer and declining areas (Bouyami, 1993, 1999). National economies still differed in industrial and business structures and cycles, export propensities, rates of growth, and responsiveness to macro policy. Convergent budgetary deficit, interest and inflation rates – but not debt – were a pre-condition for entry, but there was no subsequent convergence of business cycles, deficits, inflation, unemployment, or growth rates not so much because of varying external shocks but because of internal structural differences (Pivetti, 1998; Arestis, *et al*, 2003, 125–6, 129–34; Mayes and Viren, 2003).

Since the Euro was created for divergent economies, it was not possible to find the money supply and interest rate that fit all. The ECB had to decide whether to help the high growth camp of Spain and Ireland or the low but more important one of Italy and Germany. Lacking a real national economy as a target it could only shoot in the air; according to its own account and on its own terms of reference in 2002 it undershot rates in seven countries and overshot them in three. Because exchange rates were pegged at levels that reflected German strength in the 1980s without considering the weakening effects of reunification or French deflation since 1990 they caused greater divergence between a depressed Germany with an over-valued Euro and inflationary Spain with an under-valued one. Since a Germany in recession required a much lower interest rate than inflationary Spain, inflation was allowed to exceed the limit, but interest rates were still not low enough to stimulate a sustained recovery.

After the bubble burst on Wall Street in 2000 the American Fed took remedial action, lowering its interest rates in twelve steps by 4 percent by 2003, which sparked semi-recoveries in 2002 and 2003, but the ECB only followed slowly, reducing its rates by 2 percent despite a prolonged recession. While George Bush, the conservative American president, provided a shot in the arm with front-loaded tax reductions and more unemployment insurance in 2003, which together with the huge expenses of the Iraqi war ran up the budget deficit to 5 percent, the Commission tried to enforce the 3 percent deficit limit against Portugal, Germany, Italy, and France.

With the prolonged recession producing excessive deficits in several countries, official voices were heard to make exceptions and bend the rules. In October 2002 Romano Prodi, Commission president, called the pact "stupid" because it was rigidly applied. The British chancellor Gordon Brown, more hostile in principle, wanted deficit mitigation for long-term investments and countries with lower debt like his own. Much like Mrs Thatcher he wanted a more flexible Europe in both macro policy and labor market terms. The French minister of economics Francis Mer asserted that national defense and industrial and transport development took priority over the stability pact and requested an exemption for a joint program of public works spending with the Germans while the Italians proposed their own. Running excessive deficits the four major powers demanded greater leniency during recessions, provoking protests from the smaller states that had sacrificed spending and growth in order to respect the rules.

Conflicts of interest emerged on a host of related issues between the four major powers, who still possessed independent military and macro policy capacity, and smaller and medium sized-states, notably Spain, who were more open to the global market and more dependent militarily upon the US. Smaller states like the Benelux always had an interest in strengthening EU supranationalism as a counter-weight to the major powers. The smaller states respected EMU rules because they adhered to neo-liberalism, to free trade, low business taxes, and wage restraint, with substantial regional kickbacks going from the EC to Spain and Portugal. The four majors had the interest and capacity not only to contest the stability pact but also to demand re-nationalization, the return of other sovereign functions delegated by treaty to the EU (*Le Monde*, November 25, 2003; Stuart, 2003). Britain and Italy were mixed polities, torn over welfare reform and spread-eagled between Europe and America. The core resistance came from France and Germany, the founding states, defending macroeconomic and military independence and the welfare state.

The failed attempt to enforce the budget deficit limit against France and Germany, which contributed half of total EU GNP, caused the first major breach in EMU and in the supremacy of EU law over state power. By continuously backtracking from their injunctions over deficits to France and Germany EU authorities demonstrated their helplessness in the face of major power non-compliance. In 2002 the European Council called for annual reductions of the deficit by 0.5 percent of GDP and balanced budgets by 2004. Having decided to take counter-cyclical measures against the recession by lowering taxes, France and Germany conspired to support each other against the Commission, which demanded specific budget cuts for 2003 and 2004. The French prime minister Raffarin asserted defiance of that "office" in Brussels but worked toward compliance by 2005 through over-optimistic forecasts. The Germans made greater gestures of obeisance arguing clemency on juridical grounds, but refused to go the extra inch, about 0.2 percent of GDP, to satisfy Commission requirements. In November 2003 ECOFIN, lacking a qualified majority, decided to suspend the penalty procedure against France and Germany altogether but not without extracting pledges of eventual compliance. The breach in the fiscal rules added to the sense of crisis created by divisions over the Iraqi war and NATO and the new constitution (*Le Monde*, June 25, November 4, 5, 26, 2003).

The EU was caught between a rock and a hard place. If it loosened stability rules and enforcement, it would create national incentives for even greater deficit spending, thus ruining the credibility and value of the Euro, while rigid enforcement in the face of national resistance might provoke open revolt with the same result. Revising the terms of the pact with exemptions for structural investments or low debt would only stir up resentments among those countries that did not qualify and a cause a jockeying for national advantage. Greater latitude for deficits for all in recessions would stoke up inflation again because governments were reluctant to raise taxes in good times in order to achieve long-term balance (Crowley, 2003b). The Maastricht criteria had been arbitrarily accepted by member-states because they shared at one moment in time the same illusions about sound money and market solutions. Once serious recessions and resurgent unemployment had made them aware of the risks inherent in Maastricht, they were not likely to find a consensus on reform, which is why the EU had to continue to enforce the rules.

The EU could not be radically reformed because it was founded on self-contained liberal principles and institutions. The integration project was based on the assumption that Europe could be made into a single political economy and an optimum currency area, whereas in fact it remained a juxtaposition of national economies with their own industrial and market structures, rhythms of adjustment, and policy requirements. To loosen the single market and EMU discipline would unleash all kinds of centrifugal national forces in EU countries, which were no longer bound by the old loyalties, solidarities, or imperatives that forced compromise and kept it going forward in the past – the long boom and expansion of intra-EC trade, Cold War anti-Communism, American encouragement, the Franco-German entente, the strength of Christian Democracy, European federalist ideology, and the fight against inflation.

To maintain EU discipline with occasional concessions to major countries would not hold the system together for long because state and cyclical partisan interests would always diverge even between the French and German core. The idea of a Franco-German union launched at the end of 2003 in order to leverage agreement from the Eastern states for Giscard's draft constitution was just as chimerical as that of the EU. With the irresistible force of national, popular, and partisan interests pressing for relief from the unmoveable object of EU rules and discipline, national revolt, and secession possibly but certainly a gradual loosening of federal ties could not be excluded.

The EC was founded primarily for trading and security purposes but they were largely achieved by the mid-1970s with détente in the Cold War and the peaking of intra-EC manufacturing trade. Once the single market and currency were sold as solutions to the economic crisis EU legitimacy rested on economic performance, that is, jobs, income, and growth. The great leaps forward in EC integration had taken place during periods in which people placed confidence in free trade, enterprise, and markets to produce the goods – the mid 1950s, 1960s, 1986–90, and 1997–2000. Halting or backward steps in EC integration occurred when liberal promises yielded inflation and/or recession and unemployment, 1973–83, 1990–97, and since 2000.

The single market, which was supposed by the Commission to produce a long trajectory of growth, combined with ERM and Maastricht disciplines to yield a long and deep recession in 1990–93, relative stagnation until 1997, and another long recession after 2000. By 2004 the founding decades of growth and prosperity had been replaced by three decades of economic insecurity that transformed generational social attitudes from confidence and trust to disaffection and alienation from capitalist institutions, especially those that seemed to represent an external constraint and threat like the IMF and World Bank, and those more directly imbricated into domestic regimes such as EMU and the EU. In a world of greater economic and physical insecurity people tended to turn back to the nation state for protection (PEW, 2003). The democratic state was the only community that people could rely upon to protect them against the insecurity and exploitation of the market place.

After Maastricht, as many American specialists recognized (Moravcsik, 1998a, 1998b; cf. Dyson, 2002), forward progress toward a supranational European state was halted. The resulting equilibrium of national and supranational power was conceptualized in terms of multi-level governance. The proposed EU Constitution with its national and institutional compromises, which was unlikely to be ratified by all, would not fundamentally change that equilibrium, which historians know cannot last forever. Meanwhile, real conflicts of interest and policy emerged between the major EU states, Britain, France, Germany, and Italy, who sought to retain independent macro state capacity within EMU, and the smaller states plus Spain and Poland, more dependent on the global market and the American alliance, who demanded respect for EMU and other market disciplines. Even these divisions were subject to unexpected domestic political changes like the victory in March 2004 of the Spanish Socialists or future turnabouts in a volatile Eastern Europe. The enduring crisis of growth, productivity, and employment put pressure on all governments to recuperate state functions delegated to the EU. If this analysis of past and present is correct, the likeliest prospect for the EU was the loosening of supranational ties and the renationalization of policy with a return to social or socialist democracy and intergovernmental cooperation.

Notes

1. Thanks to John Grahl for statistical series and comments.
2. Hirst and Thompson, 1996, 35–7; Andrews and Willett, 1997; Epstein and Gintis, 1995, 11–12, 326–8; Wade, 1996.
3. Glyn, 1990, 1995; Kitson and Michie, 1996; Oatley, 1997, esp. 150, 244; Michie, 1999.
4. Thanks to Regan Scott of the TGWU for his personal communication.
5. Husson, 1996, ch. 2; Mazier, 1999; Brenner, 2002; *The Times* October 29, 2003; *Le Monde*, May 16, 2004.

Part II

The Failure of the European Community Quantified: Monetarist Fetters

8
Has European Economic Integration Failed?

Gerald Friedman

I Economic policy and the origins of the European Community

Economic growth accelerated after the Second World War when per capita income growth accelerated to 2.9 percent per annum from 1950–89 compared with only 1.3 percent 1870–1950. Even without taking account of the benefits of increased leisure, social security, and improved health and social services, this acceleration in economic growth was a remarkable achievement. Although rapid growth has not been restricted to Europe, advocates of unrestricted free trade have credited the European Economic Community with raising European growth rates. Europe's slow recovery after the First World War had persuaded many that the existing national borders contained markets too small to realize gains from mass production and modern technologies. Repeating views popular among socialist critics of European capitalism, advocates of economic integration argued that Europe's businesses needed a larger scope to compete with continental powers like the US and the Soviet Union (Griffuelhes, 1910; Landes, 1949; Lorwin, 1958). Economic integration, it was hoped, would give Europe's relatively small states the wider scale they needed to compete with businesses from continental-sized countries. Business productivity would bring in its wake prosperity, peace, and the political influence that comes with economic success.

The EU has promoted trade, and Europe has been prosperous, reaching American levels of per capita income by the 1980s. This has made the EU a model for economic policy throughout the world, an argument that open markets lead to economic growth. But the claim that post-war Europe's success is due to economic integration and the EU has been supported by assertion and theory rather than data, and it has never been carefully tested. This chapter measures the impact of the EU on growth rates by systematically comparing annual economic growth rates for countries belonging to the EU with growth in countries outside the EU. As its founders hoped, membership in the EU boosts international trade. But, contrary to the conventional interpretation, EU membership is associated with *lower* rates of economic growth.

Advocates of expanded economic integration emphasize the benefits of international trade. But, I argue that among relatively homogeneous European economies, the gains from intra-European trade have been small, easily swamped by the much larger economic losses associated with the application of a single macroeconomic policy to different economies. Indeed, by redirecting trade away from non-members, the EU has reduced some of the gains from trade previously enjoyed by member-states with extensive non-European trade relations. Furthermore, the EU has done little to help European firms realize scale economies because existing markets in the larger EU member-states were already large enough to support efficient plants and firms. Nor has the EU conducted an effective anti-trust policy to reduce the losses from monopolistic practices. Instead, community-wide anti-trust has been inhibited by the goal of promoting larger establishment and firm sizes. In addition, growing barriers to trade with non-EU members, such as Japan and the US, have created anew little, Europe-wide monopolies.

The EU's relatively small allocative efficiency gains must be balanced against the significant costs of imposing deflationary and other inappropriate demand-management policies on different economic regions of the Community. Membership in the EU has been associated with higher unemployment and slower economic growth because EU member-states have pursued deflationary monetary policies to maintain stable exchange rates rather than seeking to maintain employment, economic growth, and aggregate demand. Evidence is presented showing that membership has been associated with higher interest rates and a monetary policy that is less sensitive to levels of unemployment. Poor macroeconomic performance has already produced extraordinary social and economic costs for Europe. It is likely that these costs will continue to rise with the implementation of a single European currency across a wider European Union.

II European trade in theory and practice: the promise of allocative efficiency

Hopes that a European common market would increase income came from applying simple neoclassical trade theory to an exhausted and demoralized post-war Europe. Advocates of trade integration objected that Europeans were poor and their proud states were supplicants in New York and Moscow because their small firms were inefficient and even lazy, surviving only behind narrow walls of national protection. Seen from Paris in 1947 or Rome in 1957, political divisions and subsequent trade barriers prevented Europe from competing successfully with the larger American and Soviet economies. The small size of Europe's national markets prevented European firms from realizing the scale economies needed to compete with their giant American rivals. By shielding local and national monopolies from competition, trade barriers allowed European firms to survive without seizing the new technologies applied in the US and the Soviet Union. A new political arrangement, a common market, would allow, indeed, it would force, European firms to apply new technologies and to reap scale economies otherwise denied them by the narrow bounds of their nation states. Stripped of monopoly protection behind national trade walls, European firms would quickly learn new technologies to make themselves competitive with the world's most efficient firms. And free trade would allow Europe's workers to concentrate on what they do best. No longer would French labor be wasted doing badly what German or Italian workers knew or had the tools to do well. Instead, expanded international trade would allow productive specialization, the reallocation of labor to exploit comparative advantage.

This last argument is based on theories of international trade dating back to David Ricardo. It was Ricardo who first demonstrated the economic gains possible through specialization and exchange, even between countries with different levels of efficiency. Ricardian efficiency gains come from specializing in products where a country has a *comparative* advantage that is where it is relatively more efficient than its trading partners even if it is less efficient than its partners in all products. Even if Britain is more efficient at producing both cars and fish, both Britain and Portugal, Ricardo showed, will gain if Britain imports Portugese fish in exchange for British-made cars so long as Portugal is relatively better at producing fish than cars. Even though it is more efficient at producing both cars and fish, Britain does better buying Portugese fish because Portugal is so inefficient at making cars that it must give up more fish to get a car than does Britain.

Ricardo provided the central argument for free trade but later trade theorists have added additional grounds for economic integration. The efficiency gains from trade can be greater, for example, where there are increasing returns to scale in production because specialization can allow trading partners to produce more efficiently by operating on a larger scale. Trade may also promote growth by undermining local monopolies. This will benefit consumers directly by eliminating monopoly profits. It may also promote technological progress by forcing producers to seek new production technologies and efficiency gains to survive international competition.

Unfortunately, none of these benefits appear to be very important when applied to twentieth-century Europe. Ricardo was certainly right that comparative advantage can lead to significant efficiency gains. It can explain, for example, why Massachusetts farmers abandoned wheat cultivation to produce textiles, shoes and, later, computers to exchange with wheat farmers in the Dakotas. These trade patterns reflect the comparative advantage western farmers had in grain cultivation because of the relative abundance of good agricultural land in the western states compared to the abundant manufacturing labor and capital found in Massachusetts. The EU's expansion to include Greece and the Iberian Peninsula may have opened up some areas for comparative advantage by including regions with climates and soil significantly different from those found in Northern Europe. But it is doubtful that comparative advantage has produced significant gains among the EU's member-states because there are relatively small differences in national factor endowments, the larger European countries are already large enough to realize within their borders many of the benefits of trade, and because the major European states had already reaped many of the advantages of comparative advantage through trade with the non-European world. Bordeaux vineyards, for example, have for centuries exchanged their wines for Normandy dairy products and manufactured goods from the French *Nord,* just as vineyards in the Rhineland exchanged wine for the Ruhr's manufactured goods. Neither set of farmers or manufacturers needed additional occasion to realize the efficiency gains coming from comparative advantage.

Before the EEC, European countries reaped the benefits of comparative advantage and productive specialization by trading manufactured goods with colonies and former colonies, importing agricultural products from tropical regions and land-abundant former colonies in Africa, America, and Oceania. Compared with this extensive trade across continents and climate zones, the EU, a free-trade zone among European neighbors, has added little to Europe's productive specialization. Furthermore, by restricting imports from outside Europe and subsidizing European agriculture, the EU has reduced the Community's gains from trade, raising the share of intra-EU imports from 37 percent of total goods imports for the 15 community members in 1960 to over 60 percent in 1987 (Monti, 1996, 83). Unlike trade with tropical or land-abundant regions, the growing trade among European Community members leads to little productive specialization because it is largely intra-industry, the exchange of like-for-like rather than the exchange of products produced using comparative advantage in different industries utilizing different productive factors.

Some intra-Community trade does produce efficiency gains from comparative advantage. In 1996, for example, France exported $760,465,000 of wine and $715,630,000 of cheese to Germany in exchange for only $21,261,000 of wine and $153,622,000 of cheese (United Nations, 1998, 1, 219; 1, 32–3). But inter-industry trade like this is the exception in the EU. Wine and cheese together account for only 3 percent of France's exports to Germany and most other traded products do not capture the gains from specialization predicted in the Ricardian model. Instead, most intra-EU trade consists of the exchange of products from the same industries. In 1996, for example, Germany, imported even more power-generating machinery than French wine, including $849,159,000 from France and $932,628,000 from the United Kingdom. This trade might be seen as a clear sign that Germany had a comparative disadvantage in this type of manufacturing except that Germany also *exported* $1,078,803,000 of power-generating machinery to France and $1,177,296,000 to the UK, producing small export surpluses on trade involving over 2 percent of Germany's commerce with its two largest Community partners (United Nations, 1998, 5, 7–8; 1, 4, 5, 8). Nor is intra-industry trade restricted to manufactured goods. France, for example, exported $8,125,000 worth of phosphates to Germany and $5,672,000 to the UK, in exchange for phosphate imports from these countries of $29,218,000 and $8,282,000 respectively (United Nations, 1998, 2, 145–6).

The European Commission estimates that intra-industry trade accounts for 60–80 percent of trade among EU members. Such trade among advanced industrial countries reflects product differentiation and niche marketing rather than any comparative advantage or gains from specialization in products using different factor endowments (Helpman and Krugman, 1985; Belassa, 1986, 1988; Feenstra, 1998). Within the EU, inter-industry trade accounts for a majority of trade only for two peripheral members, Greece (where it accounts for 69 percent of trade with Community members) and Portugal (63 percent) (European Commission, 1990, 41). Otherwise, perhaps because there is little differentiation in the factor endowments among the major European countries for much productive specialization, intra-Community trade has done little to capture the gains from comparative advantage. Indeed, in one area, Community policy has retarded industry specialization and the development of comparative advantage. To protect local farmers and landowners, the Common Agricultural Policy has inhibited regional agricultural specialization as well as diverting trade from the Americas and from former colonies to fellow EU members. By reducing specialization, the EU's agricultural policy has reduced the Community's gains from trade.

The large share of intra-industry trade reflects a general lack of regional specialization as compared with the US where different regions specialize in different products to take advantage of differences in regional factor endowments (Messerlin and Becuwe, 1986, 200). Reflecting the lack of effective specialization and the small gains from comparative advantage, there is less productive specialization within the EU than in the US. Textile and automobile production in the US, for example, are concentrated in the South and Mid-west, respectively, close to sources of raw materials. In Europe, by contrast, all four major European countries maintain large textile and automobile industries, and all produce large crops of staple grains and meat (Krugman, 1993, 250–1). Instead of trade leading to changes in the industrial distribution of national products and exports, there has been relatively little change over the last 40 years in the share of exports between manufacturing and other sectors, or even between manufacturing industries. Despite France's evident comparative advantage in viticulture and dairying, the agricultural share of French exports dropped from 1955–57 from 15.2 percent to 14.1 percent in 1977 before rebounding back to 15.3 percent in the late

1980s. By contrast, the manufacturing share of French exports rose from 70.3 percent up to 74.7 percent in 1967, 78.5 percent in 1977 before slipping to 76.2 percent in the late 1980s. The lack of industrial specialization after 40 years suggests that there has been little productivity gain from exploitation of comparative advantage in Europe.

It is not surprising then that economic reallocation has contributed little to increase European output since the Second World War. Angus Maddison (1991, 162–3) estimates that labor reallocation increased economic growth rates by 0.29 percent per annum for five major economies besides the US 1950–73, but most of this gain was in Japan, a poor and heavily agricultural country in 1950. The gains from labor reallocation have been small in Europe, averaging only 0.09 percent per annum in France, Germany, the Netherlands, and the UK; after 23 years, labor reallocation raised income in these countries by only 2.1 percent. Among the Europeans, the gains from reallocating labor were greatest in France, which still employed 28 percent of its labor force in agriculture in 1950 (*id.*, 248). But even there, moving labor out of agriculture raised income by only eight percent over a 39-year period from 1950 to 1989. The gains from reallocation are even smaller after 1970 because few workers remained in less productive sectors and because the productivity gap between sectors has fallen. From 1970 to 1989, labor reallocation had almost no effect on income in Germany, the Netherlands, and the UK and only raised incomes by +0.01 percent p.a. for France (*id.*, 158–9). Despite the Common Agricultural Policy, few workers remain in European agriculture, and their productivity has grown faster since 1950 than has the productivity of workers elsewhere (*id.*, 150). If every worker remaining in French agriculture (where relative productivity is 68 percent of productivity elsewhere) shifted to manufacturing (with relative productivity 122 percent of the national average) then output would increase by only 3.7 percent or $516.[1] This is an upper-bound estimate because it assumes no change in relative productivity as workers are reallocated.

Nor have EU members realized efficiency gains from increasing firm size and the size of industrial establishments. Historically, European firms and establishments have been smaller than their American or Japanese counterparts. Arguing that these smaller firms and establishments are less efficient, trade advocates blamed low European industrial productivity on small firm and establishment scales blaming small firm and establishment scale on the small size of European national markets constricted by national protection. They argued that European establishments were too small to realize the efficiency gains from large machines and specialized labor on long production runs. Expanded markets coming from free trade would then lead to increased productivity by giving European firms the scope to enlarge their scale of operations.

Smaller scale due to narrow markets has been associated with the loss of competitive positions for some European industries, including automobiles and trucks, aluminum, computers, and aerospace where the minimum efficient scale of production is large relative to the market size in individual Community member-states (Table 8.1). But most member-states are large enough to support minimum efficient scale production in most manufacturing industries and in most activities outside of manufacturing (also Zeitlin, 1985; Sabel and Zeitlin, 1985). Even where European industries need larger scale than can be supported within one country, there are alternatives to a general free trade zone. One alternative, used in aviation to develop the Concorde and Airbus, is to build cooperative ties between firms in Community members and non-members; inter-firm cooperation allowed Europe's aerospace industry to realize necessary economies-to-scale even

Table 8.1 Products for which the minimum efficient technical size (METS) is superior or equal to 20% of the production of the UK

Product	Minimum efficient technical scale as percentage of production in		Extra cost at 1/2 METS
	UK	EEC	
Cars	200	20	6–9
Cellulose fibers	125	16	3
Rolled aluminum	114	15	8
Trucks	104	21	7.5
Computers	>100	n. a.	5
Electric typewriters	n. a.	33	3–6
Aircraft	>100	n. a.	20
Dyes	>100	n. a.	17–22
Tractors	98	19	6
Refrigerators	85	11	4
Steel	72	10	6
Titanium oxide	63	50	8–16
Electric motors	60	6	15
Washing machines	57	10	4.5
Large turbine-generators	50	10	5
Telephone exchangers	50	10	3–6
TV sets	40	9	9
Rayon	40	23	5
Marine diesel engines	30	5	8
Cigarettes	24	6	1.4
Synthetic rubber	24	3.5	15
Petrochemicals	23	3	12
Fertilizers	23	4	n. a.
Wire netting	20	4	n. a.
Ball bearings	20	2	6–8

Source: Emerson (1988, 133).

without general free trade. The Concorde was built by cooperation between firms in an EC member (France) and a then-non-member (the UK). In other cases, such as automobile or computer production in the UK, Germany, and France firm scale economies have been realized by admitting foreign companies, such as Toyota, GM, and IBM, from outside of the EU. Targeted industrial policies have thus helped European firms to achieve scale economies without general free trade.

Free trade within the EU has led to efficiency gains in some industries, including refrigerators and washing-machines where expanded intra-European trade allowed a larger, and more efficient, scale of production (Owen, 1983, 142–53). But there are other cases where free trade reduced productivity growth by undermining the ability of national firms to achieve efficiency gains from learning-by-doing and discouraging capital investment. Italian refrigerators, for example, were produced in the 1950s and 1960s at a large cost advantage compared with British and French refrigerators. Competition with Italian producers forced refrigerator producers in these countries to reduce their costs dramatically by technological innovation and by consolidating their operations to realize economies to scale in production. Declining refrigerator prices for consumers might make this industry a prime example of efficiency gains from trade except that the price of this success was the near destruction of the French refrigerator industry. Because France was in the EC, its refrigerator manufacturers were denied any protection from Italian competition. Unable to innovate in time, French refrigerator manufacturers were driven under, losing their investment in productive plant and trained personnel as French consumers shifted wholesale to Italian-made refrigerators. In Britain, however, Italian competition came *before* EC entry when British producers were still shielded by a 15 percent tariff.

Although conventional trade theory would predict that the British producers would have less incentive to innovate than did their more exposed French counterparts, it was the British producers who made dramatic gains in production efficiency in the 1960s, using the tariff advantage to invest, to increase the scale of their production, and to achieve efficiency gains through "learning-by-doing". "But for the tariff", an English advocate of EC membership acknowledges, "it is doubtful whether much of the British refrigerator industry would have survived" (*id.*, 1983, 124). Because it remained outside the EC, the UK preserved an industry, which by the late 1970s had equaled or even surpassed the productivity of its Italian competitors (*id.*, 1983, 125).

The European Commission compiled a list of 25 products where national markets are less than five times the minimum efficient technical scale of production (METS) to argue that, in these industries, international trade is needed to produce at an efficient scale (see Table 8.1). But even this makes only a weak case for expanded trade. In several cases, such as aerospace and automobiles, the efficiency gains from scale were realized outside of the EU.

Furthermore, for many of these products, the cost of producing below the METS is small. At half the METS, the extra cost of producing is usually under 10 percent and reaches 20 percent for only two products, dyes and aircraft. But spread over the whole economy, small efficiency losses in a few manufactured goods do not amount to much. And, for these products, the gains from producing at a larger scale for a larger market could be realized outside of a free-trade zone.

By focusing on economies to scale, furthermore, the Commission may be responding to the last period's economic problem. Unlike the Commission's planners, manufacturers in recent decades have been abandoning large-scale, big-batch production technologies to realize the economies on inventory and improved quality and response time from "flexible specialization" linking networks of related producers in small establishments. It is ironic, given the European Commission's evident concern to capture economies to scale through large scale production, that some of the most successful examples of flexible specialization have come from Europe where networks of linked firms have formed some of the continent's most successful industrial regions, without any producer depending on large markets to support massive investments in a single product run (Piore and Sabel, 1984). The European Commission makes a dubious argument that abandoning Europe's own success to invest in the American or Soviet technology of the past will promote growth for the future.

Nor is there evidence that trade-induced increasing returns have produced large efficiency gains. Using a generous estimate of the economy-wide returns to scale, Carré, Dubois, and Malinvaud (1975, 414–15) estimate that increasing international trade raised France's GDP by 4 percent from 1950–89, or only 0.1 percent per annum. Angus Maddison (1991, 158) also finds that scale economies from increasing trade were relatively unimportant, raising income by only 0.06 percent per annum for four European countries, 1950–73. He estimates that trade-induced increases in scale raised French income by less than $150 in 1973. Nor should the EU take credit for all of these small effects. Some of the increase in scale would have come without trade, and some of the trade-induced increase in scale would have come without membership in the EU.

Expanded trade could also promote efficiency by undermining local and national monopolies and oligopolies. This could be especially important for smaller states where national markets are too small to produce more than one or two firms at the METS. The wider markets made possible by international trade can reduce monopoly power by supporting more companies at an efficient scale, lowering prices to consumers, and encouraging further productivity growth.

The reduction in monopolistic power has been a goal of the EU, which has enacted a variety of specific rules to restrict anti-competitive behavior (Molle, 1994, 363–6; Jacquemin and Joug, 1977, 198–242). Competition has increased in some sectors; the share of the national automobile market held by the largest producers, for example, has fallen in all the major European states (Owen, 1983, 52–3). But it is unlikely that EU anti-trust policy has contributed to any significant efficiency gains. European markets remain highly inefficient; wide price differentials in near-by regions reflecting pockets of persistent market power. The coefficient of variation among average national prices is nearly 20 percent even for basic commodities like rice, noodles, or sugar, and it rises to 30–50 percent for less homogenous goods like pharmaceuticals. Despite energetic efforts to open the automobile market to competition, the same model car can sell for as much as 90 percent more between countries within the EU (Emerson *et al*, 1988, 278–85; Flam, 1992, 11).

Instead of undermining monopoly power, trade may have promoted concentration in many European industries. From 1972–89, the share of the EU market held by the 100 largest firms rose from 24.3 percent to 29.5 percent with increasing market shares for the top firms in almost all industries (Jong, 1988, 5, 13–14). Anticipation of increasing competition from expanded international trade led to a flurry of merger activity in the 1960s and again in the mid-1980s when national firms sought partners to consolidate their operations to increase efficiency and to secure a steady cash flow from their national operations to support foreign investments. This response to reduced trade barriers may have reduced competition by more than expanding trade and official EU policy promoted it (Jong, 1993; Jacquemin and Jong, 1977, 55–8).

III Estimating the net gains and losses from membership

Considering the small gains from reallocation, scale, and competition, there is little reason to expect large economic gains from EU membership. The European Commission estimated in 1990 that eliminating remaining trade restrictions would boost GDP by 6.4 percent (Table 8.2); and they predicted that full monetary integration would raise income by a further 5 percent (Emerson *et al*, 1988, 278–85; Monti, 1996, 105–6). These estimates far exceed those of independent economists (Grossman, 1990). Few agree for example, with the Commission's estimate that moving to a single currency will save a full 1 percent of national income from reduced foreign exchange transactions because it assumes that monetary union would eliminate the need for *any* foreign exchange transactions, conveniently ignoring the persistence of independent currencies inside and outside the EU (Taylor, 1995, 40). Nor do many agree that the Community has substantially raised income in the past. Bella Belassa (1975, 113) estimated that tariff reductions in the original six EEC members raised output by less than 1 percent, including 0.15 percent through increased specialization and by only 0.5 percent from economies to scale. Others put the welfare gains through the early 1990s

Table 8.2 Estimated gains from market integration as share of European Community Gross Domestic Product (GDP)

Source of gain	Anticipated GDP gain (as % of GDP)
Elimination of barriers to trade	0.3
Elimination of barriers affecting all production	2.4
Economies of scale from restructuring and increased production	2.1
Competition effects on X-inefficiency and monopoly rents	1.6
Total Gain:	6.4
Average GDP increase 1948–89 in 7 EEC members	3.8
Months of normal growth to achieve gains from market integration	20.2

Sources: Emerson (1988, 203). GDP increase estimated for Belgium, Denmark, France, Germany, Italy, Netherlands, the UK from Maddison (1991, 212–19).

from membership in the European Community in the 1–2 percent range – less than one year of normal economic growth (Owen, 1983, 155; Flam, 1992, 14). Two American scholars estimate that closer integration and full monetary union may raise the Community's income by 1 percent: "a modest return on a process riddled with risks and uncertainties" (Eichengreen and Frieden, 2001, 7).

Lacking evidence that the EU has raised income in the past, the European Commission has had to make its case by arguing that integration will have other, intangible economic benefits. The Commission argues, for example, that closer economic integration will increase competition (an assumption we questioned above) and would push European producers to be more resourceful and innovative. It predicts that these "intangible" productivity gains (or "x-efficiency") would raise income by 1.6 percent, accounting for a fourth of the 6.4 percent income gain expected from a single market (Table 8.2). Notwithstanding surveys of European producers reporting no efficiency gains from the Single Market, the Commission optimistically expects large future productivity gains, at least once there has been one more push toward economic integration (Monti, 1996, x, 99–100, 107).

One way to estimate the net impact of membership in the EU is to compare per capita income growth for countries in the EU with growth rates for the same countries when outside of the Community and for countries that never joined. Viewed in this way, the Community's record is not good. Using data for 16 advanced capitalist economies, the average annual per capita income growth for 1951–89 is 2.8 percent for countries in the Community, 20 percent lower than the 3.5 percent rate for non-members (including

Table 8.3 Per capita income and growth in EEC member countries. Growth rates in and outside of the EEC 1948–89

Country	Per capita income growth rate			Per capita income 1989	
	Outside EU (%)	In EU (%)	Change net of US (%)	Actual ($)	At non-EU growth rates ($)
Belgium	3.1	3.0	−0.1	12,876	13,281
Denmark	3.2	1.7	−1.1	13,514	17,180
France	4.9	3.0	−2.4	13,837	24,937
Germany	9.5	3.7	−6.5	13,989	88,902
Italy	5.8	3.7	−2.1	12,955	24,841
Netherlands	4.2	2.4	−1.8	12,738	22,256
United Kingdom	2.4	2.2	+0.1	13,460	13,898

Note: The "change net of US" is the change in the country's per capita income growth compared with US growth in that year when the country was in the EEC compared with when it was outside.
Source: Maddison (1991, 212–19, 232–5).

member countries when outside of the Community). Some of the growth deficit for EU members reflects high growth for Japan (6.2 percent), although this is balanced by the relatively slow growth in the US (2.0 percent, the lowest of the 16 countries). Even among the seven EU members in the sample, income growth is lower in all cases when in the EU than when outside (Tables 8.3 and 8.4).

Slow growth among EU members is not due to the general economic slowdown after 1973; the reverse is the case. When compared with the contemporary US, countries grew slower after joining the EU (Tables 8.3 and 8.4). Only the UK did better relative to the US when in the EU than outside, and there the difference is very small, 0.1 percent (Table 8.3). The EU growth slowdown is small in Belgium, and exaggerated in Germany by the strength of the pre-EEC, post-war recovery of the late 1940s and early 1950s. In Denmark, France, Italy, and the Netherlands, membership in the EU is associated with a slowing of annual per capita income growth by as much as 2 percent.

The logic of compound interest magnifies even small differences in per capita income growth rates. In France, for example, the difference between the pre-EU growth rate of 4.9 percent and the country's growth rate of 3.0 percent in the EU is $11,000 in per capita income in 1989. Had France continued to grow at the 1947–58 rate for another 31 years its real per capita would have been 80 percent higher, $24,937 instead of $13,837. If growth had continued at pre-EU rates, per capita income in Belgium and the UK would have been 3 percent higher, in Denmark 27 percent higher, 75 percent higher in the Netherlands, and in Italy 92 percent higher (Table 8.3).

Table 8.4 Per capita income growth and unemployment in the EEC and outside

Period/countries	**EEC 6**	**EEC 9**	**Never joined**
	Percentage growth in per capita income growth		
1947–59	5.6	2.4	4.2
1958–71	*4.0*	3.1	3.9
1972–89	*2.2*	*2.0*	2.5
	Unemployment rate (percentages)		
1947–59	4.45	3.53	2.50
1958–71	*2.25*	2.30	2.67
1972–89	*7.14*	*7.14*	4.00

Notes: EEC 6 countries include original members of the EEC: Belgium, France, Germany, Italy, and the Netherlands. EEC 9 include countries that joined in 1972: Denmark and the United Kingdom. Never Joined include: Australia, Austria, Canada, Finland, Japan, Norway, Sweden, Switzerland, and the United States. Numbers in italics are for EEC members.

Source: Maddison (1991, 212–19, 232–5).

Economic growth rates often decline as countries approach the level of the productivity leader because they exhaust the stock of readily available new technologies (Baumol *et al*, 1992; Barro, 1997). Some of the EU growth slowdown reflects a productivity growth slowdown as countries approach the level of the US, the technological leader. But EU membership is associated with lower growth even after controlling for relative income. Using regressions for annual per capita income growth rates, moving from half of the per capita income of the United States to three-fourths is associated with a reduction in annual growth of 1.8 percentage points a year, or about half of the average per capita income growth rate (Table 8.5). This large effect does not negate the negative effect of EU membership on growth rates. Membership in the Community is associated with a reduction in income growth of about 0.5 percentage points. The negative effect of EU membership on growth rates declines for larger countries, but there is no evidence here that even large countries benefited from EU membership.

Membership in the European Union has increased international trade. But there is little evidence that this trade expansion raised income. Exports were only 13.1 percent of GDP among countries outside of the EU compared with 20.0 percent among members. Comparing export ratios for EU countries, UK exports averaged 13.9 percent of GDP when in the EU, or 54 percent higher than 9.0 percent before joining. In France, 10.8 percent of output was exported as an EU member, compared with 5.2 percent before the EU. In regressions controlling for country size, the proportion of national income involved in international trade is over twice as high among EU members

Table 8.5 Regressions for per capita income growth, 16 countries, 1948–89

Variable	Mean	Model 1 coefficient	Model 2 coefficient	Model 3 coefficient
Intercept	1.00	0.083**	0.067**	−0.726**
Relative per capita income	0.69	−0.071**	−0.072**	−0.069**
EEC member	0.31	−0.005**	−0.005#	−0.047
Export share of GDP	0.16		−0.031*	1.019**
Year since 1920	49.81		0.0008	−0.002#
Year since 1920 squared	2614.70		−0.000007	0.000018#
Unemployment rate	3.99			−0.014*
Log population	9.86			0.074**
Export share × log population	1.47			−0.103**
EEC × log population	3.20			0.005
Number of country dummy variables		0	0	15
DW statistic		1.492	1.516	1.638
F statistic		64.575	27.358	9.256
DFE		612	609	590
R-square statistic		0.1743	0.1834	0.2735
Mean of dependent variable		0.03227	0.03227	0.03227

Notes:
** significant at 99%.
# significant at 90%.
* significant at 95%.

Table 8.6 Regressions for ratio of exports to GDP, 16 countries 1948–89

Variable	Mean	Coefficient	T-ratio
Intercept	1.000	2.2847	8.39
Unemployment rate	3.986	0.0018	2.44
EEC member	0.314	0.2799	6.70
Log population	9.858	−0.2088	−8.74
EEC × log population	3.196	−0.0268	−6.50
Year since 1920	49.805	0.0068	5.12
Year since 1920 squared	2614.700	−0.000012	−0.98
Number of country dummy variables	15		
DW-statistic	0.221		
F-statistic	275.476		
DFE	598		
R-square statistic	0.9070		
Mean of dependent variable	0.1548		

than non-members, although the effect drops for larger countries (Table 8.6). Greater trade did increase growth for small countries (Table 8.5), but large EU members benefited little from increasing exports (Table 8.6). There is no evidence that the EU and trade are strong engines for growth.

IV Why hasn't the EU increased growth?

Against the losses or small gains that might have come from EU membership and expanded trade must be counted the potential for substantial losses through the conduct of a common macroeconomic policy inappropriate for some individual members. An independent country could conduct independent macroeconomic policies to reduce unemployment or to restrain inflation. It could, for example, conduct expansive fiscal policy or lower interest rates to expand aggregate demand and reduce unemployment without concern for their policy's impact on foreign countries and trade. But in a world with international trade, any policy that expands a country's economy faster than its trading partners will lead to trade deficits and capital outflows. Countries with very large foreign exchange holdings, like the US and a few others, might ignore these deficits for a time and continue their economic expansion by buying their currency back from foreign exporters. But an over-supply of a country's currency on world markets will eventually force all countries to take measures to reduce imports, or to attract international capital flows. When their reserves are insufficient to protect their currency, countries must slow their economy, lower wages, institute trade restraints, or devalue their currency to make imports more expensive and exports more competitive.

The EU has lowered growth rates because it restricts members' response to trade deficits by forbidding trade barriers and discouraging currency devaluations. An economic theorem associated with Nobel-laureate economist Robert Mundell (1961) explains the EU's failure. Called the "impossible trilogy" principle, it asserts that only two of the three following features are mutually compatible, fixed exchange rates, full capital mobility, and independent monetary and fiscal policy. One element of the trilogy must be sacrificed: free trade, fixed exchange rates, or independent economic policy. The EU has not prevented expansive economic policy, but members can conduct such policies only until they experience rising trade deficits because the EU forbids trade restrictions and monetary union has largely eliminated flexible exchange rates. Members, therefore, can pursue expansive policies to reduce unemployment only if they can restrain imports and promote exports by driving down wages while the economy expands. This aspect of monetary and trade integration has been openly applauded by some, such as Ernst Welteke (2002, 66), President of the Deutsche Bundesbank.

Restrictions on economic expansion and a policy of wages restraint to inflate profits constitute a hidden agenda for advocates of close integration. Advocates of French or British participation in the European Monetary System openly favored trade and monetary integration "as a means to impose external discipline on inflationary forces in the domestic economy, in particular limiting government spending and aggressive wage claims." Once locked into a regime of fixed exchange rates and free capital and trade flows, governments would be forced to adhere to a deflationary economic policy that would ultimately raise profits by restraining wages. Conservatives appreciated the external political support foreign commitments gave them. But even socialists, such as the French in the early 1980s, were forced by their commitment to the EU and the policy of monetary integration to impose "une solution de rigeur" and a "franc fort" that raised profits at the expense of their own constituents.

A binding commitment to fixed exchange rates and free trade will, on average, be deflationary because it forces government to restrain economic expansions but will not require that they promote growth in economies in recession. When income rises during economic expansion, imports will increase more than exports. But because EU membership precludes the use of tools to protect a member's currency during an expansion, such as open trade barriers, countries have only two alternatives to economic slowdown, lowering wages, or devaluation. The EU has long discouraged adjusting exchange rates and since 1978, devaluation has been made more difficult because of the mechanism of the European Monetary System; and it is now impossible with full monetary integration for the 12 countries in the Eurozone. By establishing free capital flows and forbidding the use of tariffs and other trade barriers, EU membership fixed in place two elements of Mundell's trilogy. EU members are compelled to pursue economic policies of restraint, mitigating economic expansions that produce trade imbalance with a restrictive fiscal and monetary policy.

Note that the requirement that economic policy support trade balance at fixed exchange rates is asymmetric. Countries must deflate in response to foreign trade deficits because their currency reserves will be drained when foreigners seek payment for exports. Every trade deficit is balanced by a surplus in another country's balance, but surplus countries need not take action to balance *their* trade and eliminate *their* surplus; instead they can contentedly maintain surpluses by banking excess foreign exchange. The need to eliminate foreign trade imbalances, therefore, falls exclusively on countries running economic expansions and trade deficits. Only conscious political action can force surplus countries to balance their trade by expanding their economies and increasing imports. Like the Gold Standard of old, fixed exchange rates among EU members creates a deflationary bias, pushing all down to the rate of economic expansion found in the slowest-growing country (Temin, 1990).

The EU could avoid this deflationary bias by pooling reserves or by requiring economic expansion in surplus economies so that rising income would increase imports. Instead, it has used trade imbalances to impose deflationary policies on member-states. This deflationary bias reflects the privileged position of the German *Bundesbank*. Since the "snake" and the EMS of the 1970s, the *Bundesbank* has in practice set "monetary policy for Europe as a whole." Small countries like the Netherlands learned this quickly; but even "larger

European nations like France, Italy, and Spain, gradually realized that they had lost control of their domestic monetary policy" (Wyplosz, 1997, 5–6; also Oatley, 1997). Acting as Europe's central bank, the *Bundesbank* has extended to the whole continent a restrictive monetary policy that reflects what some have labeled a "German allergy to even moderate inflation" (Wyplosz, 1997, 25).

But there is more than a peculiar German psychology here. The *Bundesbank*'s restrictive policy reflects the different circumstances facing Germany and its European partners. Until the 1990s, strong corporatist institutions and a highly centralized labor movement allowed Germany to maintain high growth rates with relatively low inflation and social peace. Lacking such institutions or the social consensus on which they rest, other European countries had to rely on high unemployment rates to restrain inflation, giving them both higher inflation and higher unemployment rates than Germany. From the formation of the EU through 1989, for example, Germany had barely half the French unemployment rate and less than half of Italy's. Over the same time, however, German prices increased by only 184 percent compared with increases of 738 percent in France and 1238 percent in Italy. Through the 1980s, corporatist institutions spared Germany the inflation that would otherwise have accompanied its low unemployment; the lack of such institutions in Germany's partners has meant that they can sustain German levels of inflation only with high unemployment.[2]

There is more than fear of inflation behind *Bundesbank* policy. Germany has run large trade surpluses for decades but revaluing the DM, which would reduce inflationary pressures in Germany, has been rejected because it would threaten German exports. Instead, Germany has sought to place the burden of trade adjustment on its neighbors, shunning revaluation to protect its large export surpluses and the jobs and profits coming from these sales. In effect, by maintaining an undervalued DM, German has exported unemployment to its European neighbors (Moravcsik, 1998a, 240ff). Ken Couzens, Britain's representative to preliminary EMS negotiations during the Labour government of the late 1970s described EMS as "little more than a means of holding down the mark and imposing restrictive policies on Germany's partners." British Prime Minister Callaghan similarly labeled Germany's refusal to reduce its surpluses as "an act of German self-interest thinly disguised by a veil of Community spirit" (cited in *id.*, 1998a, 280).

In practice, monetary integration had by the 1980s reduced other European central banks to the status of local agents of the *Bundesbank*. French central bank governor Jacques de Larosière said in 1990: "Today I am the governor of a central bank who has decided, along with his nation, to follow fully the German monetary policy without voting on it." He called for greater monetary integration by adding that "at least, as part of a European central bank, I'll have a vote" (cited in *id.*, 1998a, 414).

The costs of inappropriate macroeconomic policy have been magnified in the EU because the Community comprises regions with disparate economies but lacks the tools to rectify regional imbalances. A common economic policy might be appropriate if the economies of the different EU member-states moved together or if there was easy factor mobility between member-states, or the means to compensate regions suffering from inappropriate common policy. Unfortunately, the EU does not meet any of these standards. Even in the well-integrated product and labor markets of North America, some regions suffer from the imposition of inappropriate fiscal or monetary restraint during periods of high unemployment while others suffer from accelerating inflation (Blanchard and Katz, 1992; Krugman, 1993). But migration and federal policy helps to alleviate distressed regions in centralized federal republics like Australia, Canada, and the US.

These problems of inter-regional maladjustment are even greater in Europe. First, there is greater disparity in economic fortunes across European regions than in different states of the US or between Australian or Canadian provinces. Furthermore, cultural, political, and linguistic barriers restrain inter-regional labor and capital mobility. Perhaps most important, there are no significant federal means to aid distressed regions (Taylor, 1995, 31). Advocates of monetary integration have pointed out that there is more correlation in key macroeconomic variables, such as unemployment rates and GDP growth, across European countries than between these countries and the US and Japan (Cohen and Wyplosz, 1989; Bayoumi, 1993). But this only makes the argument against establishing a single currency between Europe and the US and Japan; it hardly justifies a single European economic policy. Among EU members, there is only a weak correlation in the timing of changes in unemployment. For the 1953 to 1998 period, the correlation between changes in unemployment rates in France and Germany is only 0.41, and it is only been 0.06 between Germany and Italy. Large differences in unemployment rates persist even between adjacent EU members – such as in 1998, the 7-percentage point gap between Belgium's 11 percent unemployment and the 4 percent rate in the Netherlands or the 6-percentage point gap between Germany and the Netherlands (Maddison, 1991, 262–7; United Nations, 2000, table 32).

The correlation in the annual economic growth rates among EU members is stronger than that between changes in unemployment rates; but changes in the French GDP still explain less than half the variation in economic growth rates in Germany, a third of the variation in Belgian growth rates, and only a quarter of the variation in British or Italian growth rates (Maddison, 1991, 212–19).[3] Disparate regional economies experience disparate economic shocks requiring different macroeconomic policies. Tamim Bayoumi and Barry Eichengreen (1993) have found significantly less correlation in demand and supply shocks between EU members than between regions of the United States. Advocates argue that these correlations will increase over time; the different European regions will grow together and will harmonize their business cycles. Admitting that the "EU-12 (the present Euroland) is assumed not to be an optimal currency area as yet," economist

Paul de Grauwe (2002, 58) argues that "the dynamics of integration (which is stimulated by the monetary union itself) will move it toward an optimal currency area." It is unclear why this is a particularly desirable object, nor whether it will be worth the costs. But to the extent that EU members seek out comparative advantage through specialization, the composition of their national product would differentiate further, and this may cause *greater* divergence in their unemployment and economic growth rates and their vulnerability to idiosyncratic shocks (Bean, 1992; Krugman, 1993).

It is not possible to conduct a single appropriate fiscal and monetary policy for different regions with divergent economies. Inappropriate and deflationary policy has led to high unemployment for EU member-states. Unemployment in EU countries for 1948–89 has averaged 5.4 percent, compared with 3.3 percent for non-EU countries, and the gap has grown in the last decade. Unemployment rates are 35 percent higher for Belgium when in the EU, and twice as high in Denmark, France, the Netherlands, and the UK (Table 8.7). The problem of inappropriate policy is compounded by the leverage that open capital markets gives speculative investment flows. A foreign exchange crisis in the early 1990s shortly after joining the EMS led Sweden to dramatically raise taxes, cut spending, and to double interest rates overnight. This deflationary policy eventually raised unemployment to 9 percent, higher than the peak rate during the Great Depression of the 1930s. Sweden's experience was typical; the struggle to remain in the EMS led France, Italy, Spain, and others to adopt policies that brought on the depression-level unemployment rates found throughout the EU in the 1990s. In regressions for annual unemployment rates in 16 countries, membership in the EU is associated with a 4 percent increase in unemployment. In addition to the direct effect of EU membership, greater involvement in foreign trade also raises unemployment, reflecting the loss of policy autonomy (Table 8.8). The

Table 8.7 Unemployment in EEC member countries. Unemployment rates in and outside of the EEC, 1948–89

Country	**Unemployment per 100 persons in Labor force**	
	When in EEC	**When outside EEC**
Belgium	5.72	4.23
Denmark	7.02	2.71
France	4.71	2.12
Germany	2.99	5.61
Italy	6.57	7.64
Netherlands	5.12	2.59
United Kingdom	7.80	2.75

Source: Maddison (1991, 262–7).

Table 8.8 Regressions for unemployment rates, 16 countries 1953–89

Variable	Mean	Coefficient	T-ratio
Intercept	1.000	−37.28	−2.053
EEC member	0.326	3.984	1.550
Export share of GDP	0.160	7.657	3.202
Log population (population in thousands)	9.823	5.133	3.208
EEC × log population	3.320	−0.261	−1.024
Year since 1920	51	−0.878	−10.417
Year since 1920 squared	2715	0.009	12.231
Number of country dummy variables	15		
DW-statistic	0.336		
F-statistic	62.047		
DFE	570		
R-square statistic	0.6608		
Mean of dependent variable	3.9860		

indirect effect of EU membership, through its effect on trade, raises unemployment by more than two additional percentage points.[4]

A policy that is inappropriately deflationary for some regions is even worse in the EU than it would be for an integrated federal state like the US where a strong federal government redistributes income from more to less prosperous regions. In the US, for example, federal policy compensates for regional economic downturns, redistributing back to depressed regions about 30 percent of their reduced income through tax reductions and increased federal expenditures for unemployment relief and welfare programs (Sachs, 1992). No such counter-cyclical spending program exists in the EU. The Community's only redistribution program is the very limited structural adjustment funds. Barely 1 percent of the Community's income, these funds are too small to reduce significantly the cost of inappropriate economic policies, and they are distributed through a political process only loosely related to regional need. Without the tools to reflate a local economy through independent fiscal or monetary policy, depressed regions of the EU can only hope for relief from migration or by eventually forcing local prices and wages down enough to make local products more competitive. Either is an agonizingly difficult and slow process only exacerbated by Europe's highly rigid wages and the low propensity of Europeans to migrate.[5] The only relief offered by advocates of integration is to beat down wages. As de Grauwe (2002, 59) bluntly admits "flexibility is probably the only instrument available that allow euro area countries to adjust to asymmetric shocks."

V Restrictive policies have devastated Europe

A large literature documents American Exceptionalism, seeking to explain the lack of a strong labor movement in the US and the relatively conservative orientation of the American state (Esping-Andersen, 1990; Friedman, 1998). There is much to explain because the US has weaker unions than are found in any other advanced capitalist economy, and government welfare programs for the non-elderly are less generous in the US than anywhere else. And the US alone has never had a strong socialist political party.

Notwithstanding American Exceptionalism, the US has recently had a better record on counter-cyclical macroeconomic policy than its European counterparts in the EU. To cushion the effect of a decline in aggregate demand, monetary authorities lower interest rates to encourage investment and lower rising unemployment; and to mitigate inflation they can raise interest rates. These standard Keynesian policies were pursued aggressively by monetary authorities in the 1950s when every percentage point rise in unemployment was associated with a drop in interest rates of 0.6 percentage points. By contrast, reflecting a central-bank bias toward fighting unemployment rather than inflation, every increase in inflation was associated a much smaller increase in interest rates, of only 0.03 percentage points (Table 8.9, Franzese, 1999). But over time, economic policy has changed, especially in Europe, leading to reduced use of interest rates to combat unemployment. By the early 1970s, every percentage point increase in unemployment is associated with a reduction in interest rates of only 0.4 percentage points but increases in inflation were associated with increases in interest rates of 0.1 percentage points. Participation in the EMS is also associated with a reduced response to unemployment and greater response to inflation. By the 1990s, European monetary authorities hardly lowered

Table 8.9 Regressions for annual changes in long-term interest rates: 1953–98

Variable	Mean	Coefficient	T ratio
Intercept	1.000	0.360	2.588
Change in unemployment rate	0.078	−0.646	−3.749
Change in inflation rate	0.028	0.031	0.510
Participant in EMS/EMU	0.132	0.029	0.149
Years since 1953	26	−0.012	−2.363
Years since 1953 × Change in unemployment	2.630	0.012	2.798
Years since 1953 × Change in inflation rate	−3.43	0.003	1.310
Participant in EMS/EMU × change in unemployment	0.007	0.107	1.297
Participant in EMS/EMU × change in inflation rate	−0.042	0.407	3.708
F-statistic	10.702		
R-square statistic	0.1075		
Mean of dependent variable	0.006		
DW-statistic	2.175		
DFE	711		

Source: Interest rates are from the International Monetary Fund (1952–99).

interest rates in response to rising unemployment but raised them by nearly 0.6 percentage points for every 1 percentage point increase in inflation. European central bankers accepted the logic of their choice for fixed exchange rates and free trade. Membership in the EMS was associated with higher interest rates and more unemployment (Table 8.10).

For 35 years after the Second World War, European unemployment rates were substantially below the American level and rates of productivity growth far exceeded the American experience. Called on to help build Europe by joining the European Monetary System in the 1970s, Britain's Labour Party Prime Minister Callaghan refused, fearing that the UK would be "locked in at too high a rate which would prevent his dealing with unemployment" (cited in Moravcsik, 1998a, 283). France's Socialist President François Mitterrand said that he had two goals in life, "the construction of Europe and the promotion of social justice." Reluctantly, he too came to see that these conflicted: "The EMS is necessary to achieve the first, but limits my ability to achieve the second" (cited in *id.*, 1998, 333). One might add that this conflict is regretted only by those who share Mitterrand's (and Callaghan's) desire to "promote social justice" through state action. Conservatives might be delighted at the way European unity inhibits domestic social reform.

The drive for economic unity and trade liberalization has taken a toll on Europe. Unemployment rates have risen to and then surpassed the American rate, and European growth rates have drifted down to American levels. These are measures of how Europe's political authorities have abandoned the struggle for universal prosperity in their campaign to unite Europe. Instead of using economic policy to raise wages and fight unemployment, they have established institutions to insure that domestic authorities make it their highest goal to prevent inflation and maintain the value of their currency in international markets (Arestis, 2003c). Currency stability has become the goal of economic policy; ending Europe's period of slow growth, high unemployment, and social suffering has become secondary. Europe's citizens have paid a high price for economic integration.

Table 8.10 Effect of one percentage point increase in unemployment and inflation on nominal long-term interest rates, France and the US 1953–98

Country	Effect of 1% unemployment			Effect of 1% inflation		
	1953	1973	1998	1953	1973	1998
France	−0.65	−0.40	0.02	0.03	0.09	0.58
United States	−0.65	−0.40	−0.09	0.03	0.09	0.17

Source: Regressions in Table 8.9.

Acknowledgements

I am grateful to Bernard Moss for advice and encouragement and to Engelbart Stockhammer and participants in the conference on "Neo-liberalism in Europe" at the University of Nottingham, June 2002, for advice. Merrilee Mardon provided research assistance.

Notes

1. This is calculated as the percentage of the labor force in agriculture, 6.9 percent, times the productivity gap between agriculture and manufacturing, 122 percent 68 percent, or 54 percent × 0.069 = 3.7 percent.
2. Lange and Vannicelli, 1982; Wilson, 1982; Cameron, 1984, 143–78; Turner, 1991.
3. Economic growth rates are measured by the percentage change in the gross domestic product (GDP). The share of variation explained is the R^2 statistic.
4. Membership in the EU is associated with an increase of 0.2799 in the share of national income exported (see Table 8.6). Multiplying this by the coefficient on trade in the unemployment regressions (see Table 8.8) gives 0.2799 × 7.657 − 2.14.
5. Feldstein, 1997; Bayoumi and Eichengreen, 1999; Faini, 1999; Eichengreen, 2001.

Part III

Monetarist Turn in Member-States: Neo-liberal, Social-Democratic, and Communist

9

"Ordo-Liberalism" Trumps Keynesianism: Economic Policy in the Federal Republic of Germany and the EU[1]

Christopher S. Allen

Introduction

For more than three decades, governments of the Federal Republic of Germany (FRG) have repeatedly been asked by their allies to stimulate the economy in order to improve international patterns of growth and trade, but the Germans have been reluctant to do so. They have consistently resisted international efforts to secure a Keynesian-style reflation, whether in the context of their domestic economy or as the strongest economy in the European Union. As mysterious as this stance appears to some observers, there are strong domestic precedents for their position. Even during the center-left governments of Helmut Schmidt (1974–82) – the years of the German Model – and the center-right governments of Konrad Adenauer and Ludwig Erhard (1949–66) – the years of the Social Market Economy (Sozialemarktwirtschaft) and the so-called Economic Miracle – Keynesian ideas and policies were used sparingly in the Federal Republic. In fact, Keynesian policies were popular only for a brief period during the Grand Coalition (1966–69) and the early years of center-left government (1969–74) under Willy Brandt. Even in the wake of the slow growth in both Germany and the EU during the 1990s, the Red-Green government of Gerhard Schröder has not encouraged aggressive economic stimulus since taking office in late 1998. In fact, Schröder dismissed from his cabinet in early 1999 the one figure, finance minister Oskar Lafontaine, who was urging just such economic stimulus.

Therefore this chapter faces an unusual task. Rather than explaining the presence of Keynesian ideas and policies, so widespread in developed capitalist countries in the post-war period, the principal problem in the German case is to explain their absence. We can take our cue for doing so from the 1987 comment of a Canadian G7 Summit official on FRG economic policy: "They are always saying, 'Watch out for inflation,' but it's more complicated than that. They have a different idea about how economies function" (Kilborn, 1987). In short, I will argue that, in the FRG Keynesianism was effectively pre-empted by another set of organized capitalist or ordo-liberal policies, oriented toward the supply side and the social market economy, that was progressively reinforced – both institutionally and ideologically – over succeeding stages in the post-war period (Grande, 1987). While Harold James (1989) correctly characterizes the interwar period as one in which policy experimentation lacked theoretical foundations the post-war period was different. Rather than relying on more policy experimentation after the Second World War – of which Keynesianism was seen as one variant – postwar FRG policy makers took a different tack. They returned to an institutional pattern with roots in the late nineteenth century in which the state established a general framework for a powerful and self-regulating private sector. But they ideologically justified these policies with theories emanating from the anti-statist Freiburg school of the 1930s and 1940s, which arose in direct response to Nazi abuses of central state power. In other words, this was not the origin of *laissez faire* monetarism more common in Anglo-American countries; it was monetarism within the very structured context of ordo-liberal institutions.

This alternative economic paradigm became dominant during the Federal Republic's formative stage in the late 1940s and early 1950s when Keynesianism could not gain a foothold. Rapid economic growth subsequently reinforced the power of ordo-liberal and social market views in the minds of West German policy-makers during the 1950s and 1960s. By 1966, social market views had become so dominant that they even constrained the effects of Keynesian ideas during the brief period (1966–73) when such views had become somewhat more influential in FRG policy. Then with the perceived failure of Keynesianism beginning in the latter years of the Schmidt regime, the subsequent government of Helmut Kohl reverted to familiar ideas and policies – an updated "social market economy" – during the mid-1980s. Even in the 1990s under both Christian Democratic and Social Democratic-led governments, there was never any aggressive demand-stimulus economic policy. The billions of DM spent after German unification were presented as infrastructural investment, that is, economic *supply* rather than economic demand. Ultimately, this German architectural framework has proved to be so redoubtable among European economic policy elites that it has set the stage for economic policy – monetary, fiscal and, wage setting – that has provided an anti-Keynesian, monetarist model for the European Union.

My specific argument will be presented in four parts. Part I offers a structural explanation for the weakness of Keynesian ideas in Germany – and the strength of ordo-liberalism – that finds its roots in the institutional patterns first formed during the late industrialization of the nineteenth century. Part II provides an analysis of post-war FRG economic policy which sees it as an amalgam of general "framework" policies – rather than a more detailed Keynesian "management" – built around free market competition; investment-led and export-oriented growth strategies; tight monetary policy; and a paternalistic social welfare system. Collectively, these components comprised the "Social Market Economy" and served to pre-empt Keynesian ideas and policies. Part III reviews briefly the mild flirtation with Keynesianism in the early 1970s by Chancellor Willy Brandt and his economics minister Karl Schiller. And Part IV argues that the embedding of these constraining ordo-liberal economic policies – leavened aggressively with more neo-liberalism since the 1990s – have limited and pre-empted more stimulative economic policies not only for Germany but for the entire EU. How sustainable these policies are, however, remains to be seen.

My general argument is a path-dependent one (Thelen, 1999). Namely, the dominant economic paradigm guiding a nation's policy-makers, what Jukka Pekkarinen calls their "economic policy model," is built up over a long period of time on the basis of a historical legacy of policy experiences which cumulatively point in certain directions and gradually become institutionalized within the structure and operating procedures of the state (Pekkarinen, 1989). In the German case, this legacy began with a pattern of late industrialization in the nineteenth century, the effects of which persisted into the post-Second World War period but were modified by intervening experiences of failure during the Weimar Republic and the Third Reich. Together, these experiences gave rise to an ordo-liberal ideational legacy and institutional setting in which it was difficult for Keynesianism to take root. Moreover, the arrival of the EU – with its push for neo-liberal economic policy – has now implanted restrictive economic policies widely among European economic elites and thereby even further pre-empting more expansionary ones.

I Foundations of German ordo-liberal policy

The structural problems that Germany faced in 1945 of rebuilding an exhausted economy in the face of stiff international competition were not entirely dissimilar to those the nation had faced in the 1870s. In the face of this challenge, it was natural for post-Second World War German policy-makers to turn toward the same methods that had been used to create an industrial society out of an agricultural one 75 to 100 years earlier.[1] Those methods subordinated domestic demand to the needs of industrial capital and emphasized the importance of supply-side policies for the reconstruction of German industry. Similarly, the introduction of a program of social insurance – and pre-emption of the Social Democratic Party – had been central to Bismarck's strategy for securing social peace within the context of rapid industrialization during the Second Reich (Lidtke, 1966). This lesson, too, was not lost on post-war German policy-makers. Despite the free market emphasis of the "social market economics" that inspired them, the economic strategy of those policy-makers provided a generous system of social benefits, designed to offset the social dislocation engendered by industrial adjustment for rapid growth. Although free market economists in other nations often saw welfare state programs as measures that would interfere with the functioning of markets and the achievement of growth, the Germans had a precedent for believing that the two were complementary (Swenson, 1991). Finally, one of the least-understood, but most important, legacies of nineteenth century industrialization in Germany was a system of "organized capitalism" involving big business, the banks, and the state, that still gives all but the largest, transnational German-based firms a distinctive character (cf. Hilferding, 1981).

The language of "social market economics" stresses "freedom" and "competition" in terms that remind one of laissez-faire or the American system of free enterprise. But, behind this facade, German officials and businessmen take for granted a degree of industrial concentration and inter-firm cooperation that seems strange to American eyes and often goes relatively unnoticed (cf. Berghan, 1986; with Braunthal, 1965). The relatively organized nature of private capital in Germany is important, however, because it lends a degree of stability to the private economy on which the German faith in private enterprise is built. There are some dissenters, but, in general, when German economists think of the private sector, they do not see the same phenomenon that preoccupied Keynes.

Keynes was deeply concerned about the fundamental instability of the private economy. By and large, he saw it as a realm governed by market mechanisms that were not capable of ensuring equilibrium on their own, without some external efforts at coordination. By contrast, even when they perceive problems with market mechanisms, the German economists have come to believe that such "framing" coordination can be secured from within the private sector itself, through the coordinating activities of powerful industry and employer associations, as well as the massive universal banks, rather than through the more detailed "management" of the public sector. The banks are particularly important because – except among the largest firms and financial institutions (Deeg, 1998) – they still control large amounts of investment capital in the form of loans and proxy control of huge amounts of common stock (Shonfield, 1965; Couge, 1979). Many take these features of "organized capitalism" for granted, and they see them as an intrinsic part of the competitive economy rather than its antithesis.

Hence, the pattern of nineteenth century late industrialization left three important marks on German thinking that lasted well into the post-war period. First, the success of these early economic policies convinced many economists that supply-side policies – that is an emphasis on investment over consumption – were a crucial component of any economic strategy. Second, Bismarck's successful social legislation persuaded others that a well-developed welfare state was perfectly compatible with and even conducive to rapid economic growth. And, third, a pattern of industrial organization, whose roots lay in the nineteenth century, also left many German businessmen and economists with a conception of the private economy that cut against some of the most fundamental kinds of Keynesian concerns. All three notions survived the Third Reich and – combined with an institutionally bound, German-specific form of monetarism – had an important impact on German economic strategy in the post-war period.

These three interrelated points, suggesting a linkage between post-war patterns of economic policy-making and those of the late nineteenth century, resonate well with recent historical reassessments of the "exceptional" pattern of German industrial growth (Eley, 1980; Blackbourn, 1984). Most of what are now called "standard" accounts of early German industrialization have emphasized how a strong, militaristic state was able to pre-empt the formation of a "normal" Western pattern of bourgeois liberalism, thereby fostering a system of rapid industrial growth within feudal structures (Craig, 1965; Moore Jr., 1966; Dahrendorf, 1968). Under these formulations, the imperial period and the Third Reich – though fundamentally different – do have in common a powerful central state. Blackbourn (1981) and Eley have argued however that German business was much less the "junior partner" in its relationship with Bismarck's state than conventional wisdom would have it. These two "revisionist" historians have argued that just because Germany did not use the *laissez faire* Anglo-American model did not mean that its industrialization took place under the tutelage of the pre-industrial feudal state. They argue that the German pattern of organized, large-scale industrial growth was forward- and not backward-looking in that it was able to create a national market and form the Second Reich within fewer than forty years. Moreover, moving from disunity and underdevelopment to formidable industrial might took more than just a strong state. Public sector action was certainly crucial in this growth spurt, but also took a private sector that could raise and allocate capital, mobilize sufficient resources, harness technological innovation, and recruit – if not co-opt – skilled workers. It is in this context then that the continuities are visible between the organized private sector in the nineteenth century and its post Second World War counterpart. It also makes more understandable why the weakness and/or absence of the central state as a major actor in shaping economic policy in the Federal Republic did not result in greater demands for *laissez faire*, or for Keynesianism. The legacies of these earlier institutional and ideological roots – rather than those of the Third Reich – are visible in the following three sections of the paper.

II The growth of ordo-liberalism and the social market economy: Keynesianism pre-empted

The two decades after the Second World War in the FRG did not provide a supportive environment for the development of Keynesian policies. This section will show how a number of conditions combined to limit the influence of Keynesian ideas over policy and policy-makers and reinforce a German-specific, ordo-liberal form of monetarism. Among the most important of these were:

1. the perception that Keynesianism would intensify inflationary and interventionist tendencies in a country where memories of hyper-inflation in the 1920s and the rigidities of Nazi and Allied economic controls were still vivid;
2. a currency reform that was biased in favor of investment and export-led economic growth and was later reinforced by the restrictive monetary policies of a powerful Central Bank, the Bundesbank;
3. a deeply ingrained acceptance of highly organized industrial structures which assumed a measure of informal cooperation within the private sector that seemed inimical to the reliance that Keynesianism placed on state action and more formal quantitative economic targets; and
4. the political hegemony of a center-right government that articulated and supported these "Social Market Economy" goals, including a conservative, paternalistic and Catholic welfare state (Esping-Andersen, 1990), over a Social Democratic Party and trade union movement that were weakened by the Cold War and more interested in nationalization and worker control than in Keynesianism.

These factors were mutually reinforcing; they created an economic structure and culture that limited the impact of Keynesian ideas in the 1960s, early 1970s, and beyond. It was powerfully buttressed by the economics profession. The first – and most significant – economists who emerged from the Third Reich untainted by complicity with the Nazi regime were part of the "Freiburg School" of economics.[2] Few others in the economics profession were so influential just after the war.

The members of the Freiburg school were transfixed by concern about the political dangers inherent in interventionist economic policies and by fear of the disorder that might follow from any increase in inflation. They had lived through the centralized planning of Hitler and the Allies' controls, and they had vivid memories of hyper-inflation followed by depression in the 1920s. To many such economists, Keynesian ideas seemed to court such dangers. Its attempt to place responsibility on the state for giving "global-guidance" to the economy seemed to resemble the inefficient systems of planning with which Germany already had too much experience, and reflationary policies conjured up images of citizens carrying wheelbarrows full of Reichmarks along the streets in 1923. With these experiences in mind, members of the Freiburg school believed that the depression had been caused, not by a deficiency of aggregate demand, but by the state's experimentation with activist policies that led to a breakdown of the market order. What was needed then, they argued, was not the experimentation of the 1920s and

1930s (James, 1989), but a clear set of policies based on sound economic theory.

Thus, when a market economy was reestablished after the Second World War, the Freiburg economists wanted to ensure that an effective and "organized framework" policy would protect its operation from undue public interference and all inflationary tendencies. They put a premium on policy that was designed to foster a stable set of expectations in the private sector. Public policy was to be aimed at four major goals:

1. Upholding the primacy of monetary policy, on the grounds that a stable money supply would make anti-cyclical policy unnecessary. Hence, a strong central bank, the Bundesbank, was to be the guardian against any misuse of power by the political authorities.
2. Seeking an open international economic system, in reaction to the Nazi policy of autarchy. Hence, these economists supported greater economic contacts with the United States and Western Europe, and they saw exports as the key to German growth.
3. Favoring increased market competition, but within the context, described above, of an "orderly market framework." The latter could be provided by banks and industry associations in conjunction with limited action by the state. In a sense, Freiburg economists like Walter Eucken saw the whole nation as a unit within a setting of international competition. Hence, some cooperation among firms was quite acceptable in that it would lead to a positive sum outcome for the German economy.
4. Desiring a limited measure of state intervention. The role of the state was to provide a stable legal and social order, including an important measure of social security, as well as infrastructural measures to aid in the establishment of higher market equilibrium.

Perhaps the best words to summarize the "framework" philosophy of this school come from the economist Wilhelm Röpke (1982):

> ... (our program) consists of measures and institutions which impart to competition the framework, rules, and machinery of impartial supervision which a competitive system needs as much as any game or match if it is not to degenerate into a vulgar brawl. A genuine, equitable, and smoothly functioning competitive system can not in fact survive without a judicious moral and legal framework and without regular supervision of the conditions under which competition can take place pursuant to real efficiency principles. This presupposes mature economic discernment on the part of all responsible bodies and individuals and a strong impartial state. ...

Rather than the anti-statism of traditional Anglo-Saxon *laissez faire*, the Freiburg School saw the state performing a crucial and positive role in enhancing investment-led economic growth.

Reinforced by the economic successes of the 1950s, the Freiburg school occupied a dominant position within post-war German economics but it was also internally divided. The major line of cleavage was between the dominant "ordo-liberals," who favored the more organized capitalist portion of this program and the minority "neo-liberals," who tended to stress issues such as freedom, monetarism, and individual competition. Politically the ordo-liberals were primarily located within the Christian Democrats, the party of the large business community, while the neo-liberals were closer to the Free Democrats, the party of small business (Blum, 1969). Both groups belonged to a single school of thought, but this tension between its two branches helped to keep a vigorous economic debate alive. To the extent that the FRG economy can be characterized by a mix of large firms with networks of smaller suppliers, this tension has allowed both of these segments of the business community to have intellectual "representation."

The remainder of this section will evaluate the course of FRG economic policy and attempt to understand more precisely how such conditions inhibited the diffusion of Keynesian ideas.

For most of the first four post-war years (1945–49) economic policy in the three Western occupied zones of Germany was strictly controlled by the allies.[3] Many Germans saw the Allied controls as even more oppressive than those of the Nazis. It is often thought that the free market economists who gained influence in this period did so primarily in reaction to the disastrous experience with state intervention under the Nazis, and this is certainly true. But the hardships that Allied controls imposed on post-war Germany played an important role in reinforcing these views. They contributed to an atmosphere in which enthusiasm for state intervention was quite limited; and this is important here because Keynesianism was initially seen in Germany as a relatively interventionist doctrine.

In this setting, 1948 was a watershed year. It brought two important changes in policy. One was the introduction of Marshall Plan aid, which signaled a change in Allied thinking from a stance that stressed punitive measures to one that accepted German economic growth as an important bulwark against Communism in Europe (Hardach, 1980, 94–5). The second important change was a currency reform and partial decontrol of prices, which saw the old Reichsmark replaced with the Deutsche Mark (DM). On the surface, such moves might portend an opening for Keynesianism, but this was not the case. German officials saw currency reform primarily as a means to encourage investment. In their view, consumer goods and the satisfaction of demand would have to take second place. Accordingly, the reform rewarded large property holders and, in effect, redistributed wealth and income sharply upward in the Western Zones. The Allied authorities were generally supportive of these policies, but the determination of (West) German officials to rebuild the private sector was even greater (Hardach, 1980, 107). In fact, they took the Allies by surprise with the next step, which was to lift price controls altogether on all but a few key commodities (Ehrard, 1962).

It might seem surprising that German policy-makers, highly concerned about inflation in light of the 1920s experience, should move so swiftly to decontrol prices. But Ludwig Erhard and his colleagues were even more concerned about the distortions that an overly active economic policy might provoke in the underlying market system. Decontrol was selective so as to hold down prices on basic consumer necessities, but the principal object was to set loose the forces of competition in line with the view that the market could best send the proper signals about what goods should be produced (Wallich, 1955). This turn toward greater reliance on the market was a deliberate reaction against the unhappy experiences with both immediate post-war Allied controls and earlier Nazi economic policies. As a result of the latter, many German economists believed that state intervention and reflation could quickly lead toward a system of centralized planning and totalitarian politics. In their eyes, even Keynesianism seemed to lean too far in this direction (Dillard, 1985).

The economic results that followed currency reform, price control, and similar "social market" policies were highly encouraging. Inflation did rise for the first few months, but the relatively quick transition to the new currency and the arrival of Marshall Plan aid in early 1949 brought inflation below 2 percent by 1952, a figure that it did not exceed for the rest of the decade. Unemployment shot up because, under the system of price decontrol, it was no longer necessary to have a public sector "job" to get ration coupons and a wave of Eastern European immigrants swelled the ranks of the German labor force as the Cold War intensified. Hence, unemployment averaged 9.4 percent from 1950–54, but its effects were offset by a level of economic growth that averaged 8 percent during the 1950s, the low cost of such basic necessities as food, utilities and rent, and the introduction of a basic system of social security, which formed the "social" part of the Sozialemarktwirtschaft. It provided a floor under which working class Germans would not fall. Together, these policies proved economically viable and politically popular.[4]

This approach, which used public sector policy to shape the framework for market competition, with the exception of de-trustification, which was never carried out, was to become a hallmark of post-war FRG economic policy and is the context in which German monetarism must be seen. And the apparent success of this approach reflected in low inflation and high rates of economic growth, whether coincidental or not, reinforced the regard in which social market economics was held so strongly as to limit the room for experimentation with Keynesian ideas. The approach was so widely accepted by German economists that Keynesianism was rarely even given serious consideration as an option (Kloten *et al*, 1985).

These policies were politically as well as economically successful. The currency reform and price decontrol were ratified in effect by the election of the first FRG government at the founding of the Federal Republic in 1949 and the continuing success of the policies generated support for the center-right governments of Konrad Adenauer and Ludwig Erhard for over 15 years. The government and Germany's leading economists shared a comparable vision regarding the economy. They agreed that government policy should steer a middle course between the unpredictability of complete *laissez faire* and the distortions that central planning might introduce into market mechanisms for the allocation of goods (Kaltefleiter, 1968).

In short, during the 1950s and early 1960s, German policy-makers followed a strategy that relied on exports of capital goods to rejuvenate the economy. In retrospect, it turned out to be an extraordinarily fortuitous choice. The investment-goods sectors were well positioned to serve the growing needs of the industrialized world during the 1950s (Kreile, 1978). The strong export performance of these sectors provided key contributions to the economic infrastructure of other Western European countries. It also took advantage of the demand for such goods as a result of the Korean War boom. In fact, even the tight money policy established in the late 1940s began to seem desirable, as low rates of domestic inflation enhanced the competitiveness of FRG exports and generated high profits out of which further growth could be fueled. In all these respects, the policy formed a coherent package whose success reinforced support for each of its elements.

It is well worth asking, however, why the German trade unions and Social Democrats were unable to challenge the hegemony of social market economics and the Christian Democratic Union (CDU) in this period. After all, this stress on capital goods and exports left many workers without access to consumer goods and somewhat threatened by high levels of unemployment. Why were the German trade union confederation (DGB) and the opposition Social Democrats unable to put Keynesianism on the political agenda? Did they not favor Keynesianism or were they simply not strong enough to secure it? For the 1950s, the answer is the former, and since the 1960s the answer is the latter (Graf, 1976; Markovits and Allen, 1984). To begin with, the great success of social market policies proved a formidable obstacle for any segment in society that wished to challenge them. The influx of refugees from the east during the 1950s weakened the labor market position of the trade unions. The social welfare system provided tangible benefits for the working class, and an 8–9 percent annual rate of growth slowly raised wages in the FRG. In addition, the continuing tensions of the Cold War – in which the Germans were on the frontier – tended to weaken the left. The Social Democratic Party of German (SPD) was ghettoized at approximately 30 percent of the vote during the 1950s.

Of even more significance, however, neither the DGB nor the SPD were particularly disposed toward Keynesianism during the 1950s. Like German conservatives, the left also had a long tradition of interest in "supply-side" rather than demand-side policies. Accordingly, both the DGB and the SPD advocated supply-side policies at the macro and micro levels. Their macro policy derived from a straightforward interpretation of Marxism that saw nationalization and planning as the principal national level policy tools of the left. At the micro level, they pressed for systems of worker participation – both via codetermination or *Mitbestimmung* on company boards of directors and via greater union influence within the legally-mandated works councils *Betriebsräte* in all plants with at least five employees – in line with the long-standing concerns of the guild-based craft workers on whom the union movement was originally based.

The SPD and DGB did begin to move toward Keynesianism in the 1960s, but even then never completely relinquished their supply-side concerns (Markovits, 1982). In fact, even after Keynesian ideas had become deeply ingrained within the unions, the DGB pushed for policies that they termed "Keynes Plus" since they still embodied an important supply-side element (Markovits and Allen, 1981). In part, this can be seen as a natural response to the features of "organized capitalism" that characterize the German private sector. The unions believed that macroeconomic management alone could not deal with problems that might arise from the private sector mechanisms for coordination built into the German economy.

III The brief rise and fall of Keynesianism

Between the late 1950s and early 1960s, however, several changes took place that seemed to open the door toward Keynesian ideas in the Federal Republic. The initial impetus lay in two exogenous events: the opening of the FRG economy to the rest of Europe; and a sharp drop in the available labor supply with the building of the Berlin Wall in 1961. Three other factors in the shift toward Keynesianism during the mid-1960s were endogenous. They included: attempts by the SPD and DGB to incorporate demand stimulus policies into their economic programs; efforts by the Center-right coalition comprised of the CDU and the Christian Social Union in Bavaria, and the Free Democratic Party of Germany (CDU/CSU–FDP) to stress the "social" part of the social market economy and the creation of an independent Council of Experts to offer outside analysis on economic matters. Together, these developments contributed to a growing feeling that the conditions that had generated German growth in the 1950s had changed and new economic policies might be required to deal with the evolving situation. This belief reached a dramatic height in 1965 when the economy experienced its first post-war recession, but it had been gaining force for some time before then.

When the Common Market was created in 1958 and the DM achieved full convertibility, the Germans had to examine more closely the Keynesian premises that underlay their trading partners' policies (Kloten, 1981; Boarman, 1964). In an economically integrated Western Europe the Germans had to deal with Keynesianism more explicitly, even if it meant that imports from the more inflation-prone economies of their European partners threatened to drive domestic prices higher. The German preference for tight monetary policies came under slight pressure to continue easy access to European markets of the important FRG export-oriented industries.

Similarly, the construction of the Berlin Wall in August of 1961 had more than political effects. It sharply curtailed the influx of skilled workers from the GDR, which had fueled the economic boom of the 1950s by simultaneously raising levels of demand and showing to German workers concrete improvements in wages and fringe benefits could be attained. The Social Democrats had done poorly in the 1949, 1953, and 1957 elections which by the late 1950s caused the labor movement and the SPD to question the predominance of their left supply-side policies. Thus, the shortage of labor supply – and the resultant new found full employment – convinced them that other less exogenous factors favoring demand stimulus, that is., Keynesianism, might be an effective tool in the future should unemployment return.

Specifically, the unions and the SPD themselves became more open to Keynesianism as a policy option. Until the early 1960s they had tended to give little emphasis to Keynesian policies although the latter had been a subject of some discussion at least since 1953 (Schiller, 1964; Böhm, 1982; cf. Held, 1982). The SPD moved toward Keynesianism decisively only in 1959 and the DGB four years later. The SPD seemed to have moved on this issue primarily because they were seeking a new programmatic appeal that might bring them the kind of electoral success that had hitherto been elusive. The more straightforward Marxist-oriented approaches of the 1950s – nationalization, planning and worker control – had been unable to rally enough electoral support to give the party a chance at participating in government, let alone winning a majority.

In roughly the same period as well, the governing center-right coalition began to put more emphasis on the ways in which the social market economy could serve the nation's social needs. In part, this was a response to a growing atmosphere of prosperity in which the old focus on savings and self-sacrifice seemed misplaced, and in part it was a direct response to the challenge of a renewed SPD. Even though the FRG economy had grown during the 1950s, wages still followed profits somewhat belatedly, and German social benefits were no longer substantially more generous than those elsewhere in Europe.

Alfred Müller-Armack (1982), a prominent Christian Democratic economist and policy maker, suggested that the focus of the social market economy should be redefined in several ways. In particular, he suggested an increase in spending for university and vocational education; more government support for smaller firms and the self-employed; renewed vigilance with regard to monetary stability (given the tightening labor market); more government spending for health and worker safety; an expanded environmental policy; and an industrial policy based on retraining to deal with a slump in the coal industry. Most of these measures were adopted by the CDU/CSU–FDP coalition government in the early and mid-1960s. In one light, these measures could be seen as stimuli to demand, especially given the higher spending they allocated to education, business subsidies, the environment, and vocational retraining. However, the Christian Democratic-led coalition never viewed them in that context. Rather, they saw these measures as infrastructural supply-side aids designed to enhance competitiveness. This was clearly not Keynesianism through the back door.

A more important and, to some degree deliberate, step toward Keynesianism was taken with the creation of a Council of Experts *Sachverständigenrat*, known colloquially as the Five Wise Men, in 1963. The Council was to provide an institutional means for canvassing the opinions of the country's leading economists, in part because recent changes in the German economy were seen as genuinely puzzling by the government and, in part, because the government felt increasing pressure to respond to the new interest that the left was showing in Keynesianism (Wallich, 1968). That pressure intensified in the 1960s as the annual growth rate slowed down to 4.1 percent and 3.5 percent during 1962 and 1963, only to rebound to 6.6 percent and 5.6 percent during 1964 and 1965 before falling off again to 2.9 percent in 1966 and −0.2 percent in 1967 (Hardach, 1980, 162).

Adenauer and Erhard turned to the academic economists – in Germany, a profession of considerable esteem – in the hope that their expert analyses would lead to policy recommendations that would bolster the position of the government and undercut the critiques of the left. The center-right government assumed correctly that most private economists would support the policies of the Social Market Economy. But surprisingly, the Council soon became a forum for the articulation of Keynesian ideas and a context, which lent a hitherto unattained institutional legitimacy to those ideas. Karl Schiller (1971) was the economist on the Council most critical of the Social Market Economy. He took advantage of his position there to offer explicit Keynesian proposals and had begun to press other members of the Council on the appropriateness of Keynesian policies. Schiller had been advising the SPD and the unions to add reflation to their traditional platform since the mid-1950s. By the mid-1960s, both he and they – the SPD and DGB – were well placed to push Keynesianism on the Federal Republic.

During the course of the 1966–67 recession, the first in the Federal Republic, the center-right coalition collapsed in stages, prompting the entry of the SPD into the "Grand Coalition" in 1966. This watershed finally allowed Keynesians some access to the policy arena, and, as Economics Minister, Schiller was finally able to secure passage of a Stability and Growth Law in 1967, which officially recognized the government's responsibility for employment and mandated macroeconomic measures to secure the goals of the "magic polygon" consisting of price stability, economic growth, full employment, and balanced trade (Riemer, 1982, 1983, 1985). However, the first and fourth goals outlined in this polygon received much more stress than did the second and third. Debate about this legislation began in 1965, and the lines of battle were quickly drawn. The Social Democrats and the trade unions sought additional macroeconomic measures to safeguard employment and growth. The business community, banks, and center-right parties felt that major new measures were superfluous, as the social market economy needed only fine-tuning. This alignment suggests that the Keynesian forces faced an uphill battle. Nevertheless, the law was passed.

However, legislation is usually only the beginning of policy. In this case, a number of factors continued to constrain the full implementation of Keynesianism in Germany. The two most important constraints on the Schiller-influenced Social Democratic Party were: first, its coalition partners, the CDU/CSU during the Grand Coalition and the FDP from 1969–82, since the Social Democrats *never* governed with an absolute majority, and the fiercely independent Bundesbank, which exercised great influence over monetary policy. In the face of these constraints, the most that the FRG was able to achieve on this front is what Riemer has called a "qualified Keynesian design." He notes several important constraints on the development of a more full-blown Keynesianism:

1. The Bundesbank placed strict monetary limits on deficit spending. It was able to do so because it never allowed the Finance Ministry and the Economics Ministry to be headed by Keynesians (or Schillerites). It also could claim a quantitative monopoly on economic wisdom since it employed over 1000 economists while the Economics Ministry employed only 200 (Katzenstein, 1987).
2. Influential conservative forces in the business community used Keynesian ideas to emphasize the need for an income policy and to resist reflation in the absence of one.
3. The proposals that were ultimately embodied in the Basic Law on Growth and Stability were actually formulated in 1965, prior to the 1966 recession as a compromise between left and right. Hence, they were always a political artifact based on a tenuous compromise rather than a part of received economic wisdom ready for automatic use in the face of recession (Riemer, 1983, 86).

Given these conditions, it is not surprising that even this "qualified Keynesian design" proved remarkably short-lived. Its high point was the 1969–72 period when Social Democrats controlled both the economics and finance ministries; Schiller was forced to give the Economics Ministry to the FDP as part of a political compromise in 1972. This was a period when:

> ... Schiller succeeded in installing global guidance – which was under suspicion of being a planned economy – simply by maintaining that state guidance was intended to affect only macro relations, while the freedom

and autonomy of those responsible for the allocation process would not be disturbed thereby. (cited in Riemer, 1983)

The government successfully survived the "wildcat" strikes for higher wages in 1969, and expanded the welfare state in the "reform euphoria" of the Willy Brandt-led government. It even smoothly handled the upward revaluation of the DM during the early 1970s in the face of a weakening dollar as the Bretton Woods system broke down. Yet, because Keynesianism was subject to the tight money policies of an independent Bundesbank, even in the mid-1960s, there was an upper limit to these experiments. After Schmidt replaced Schiller as the economic leader in the Brandt government, the SPD itself showed increased concern about inflation.

Schiller was the first widely influential "post Freiburg" economist on the left in Germany, and, as we have seen, his views did not achieve currency until the 1960s. Yet, with the rise in inflation in 1972, precipitating Schiller's departure from the Economics Ministry, the leading Keynesian theorist had lost some of his luster. The increased inflation opened the door for criticism of Keynesian ideas from descendants of the original Freiburg school (Tuchfeldt, 1973). How did these economists deal with the revival of Keynesianism in the late 1960s and early 1970s? They attacked both the practice and theory of the 1967 Stability and Growth Law. In general, they were less critical of demand stimulus *per se* than of the government's failure to apply the brakes when appropriate. Keynesianism was criticized for manipulating rather than diminishing the fluctuations of the business cycle. They argued that macroeconomic equilibrium was simply not attainable and the pretense of aiming at quantifiable targets a dangerous illusion. Finally, they argued that the instruments needed to secure stable outcomes, especially with regard to wages in light of the breakdown of the system of "concerted action" between union and management in the late 1960s, were absent.

When reflationary policies began to produce an average inflation rate of 5.5 percent in the early 1970s (Kloten *et al*, 1985, 360) the Bundesbank reined in the Keynesian experiment in order to keep wages in check. But the Bundesbank had always moved toward a more restrictive policy in such situations. What really sounded the death knell for Keynesianism in the FRG were the oil crisis-induced recession of 1974–75 and the replacement of Brandt by Helmut Schmidt as Chancellor in 1974. The oil crisis brought "stagflation," the combination of inflation and unemployment which brought Keynesian policies everywhere into question. Schmidt's rise in the SPD was important because he generally favored more fiscally conservative policies, which now seemed justified by the appearance of stagflation. Under his aegis, the Keynesian experiment of the late 1960s gradually gave way and – although the Schmidt government did not use the term – the social market economic paradigm was felt once again (Scharpf, 1984).

What happened to Keynesianism after Schiller? During the mid- and late 1970s, the primary proponents of Keynesianism were located in the trade unions' research institute, the WSI (Markovits and Allen, 1984). But by that time international economic constraints and domestic forces had relegated "Keynes Plus" to a position of diminished importance vis-a-vis the dominant paradigm. The 1980s did not see any significant resurgence of Keynesianism, although "Keynes Plus" remained a part of trade union economic thought for a short time. However, since the unions then began to stress such issues as work time reduction and "qualitative" collective bargaining, they departed from their brief flirtation with Keynesianism (Allen, 1987). Within the economics profession, the descendants of the Freiburg school – most notably Norbert Walter of the Deutsche Bank – have little competition.

Thus the period from the mid-1970s to unification produced no more innovative demand-stimulus experiments. When the unions pushed for increased spending to alleviate unemployment and President Carter asked the Germans to play the role of economic "locomotive" for the rest of the world in 1978, Chancellor Schmidt reluctantly proposed a modest DM 16 billion package of measures to stimulate demand, but this neither revived growth nor satisfied the Americans (Bayne and Putnam, 2000). When pressed by the party's rank-and-file to stimulate the economy further, Schmidt demurred, arguing that his fiscally conservative coalition partner, the FDP, would leave the coalition if he did so. In essence though, Schmidt had partially given in to the locomotive theory after 1978 since the stimulus package did coincide with the second oil crisis. This, of course, was perceived as a "mistake" by the FDP, thereby hardening the junior party's veto stance. As unemployment climbed toward 10 percent in 1982 – this time without a subsequent policy response from Schmidt – the FDP then could say "never again" rather than just "never" to demand stimulus policies. It then left the coalition anyway becoming the junior partner in a new center-right-coalition under Helmut Kohl. Unsympathetic to demand management, the Kohl government argued that Germany's economic problems were now structural not cyclical. In fact, this latter distinction is familiar territory. German economics – particularly at the influential Kiel Institüt für Weltwirtschaft – has always paid a lot of attention to this distinction and emphasized the structural dimension of the German economy, thereby institutionally establishing a policy bias against cyclical policies.

IV Germany, Europe and entrenched monetarism in the 1990s

Conventional wisdom during the 1990s suggested that the arrival of the EMU explained the dominance of monetarism – and the demise of Keynesianism – in most European states. In other words, even though national governments might have desired to stimulate their economies, external constraints limited the capacities of domestic actors to simulate their economies and increase aggregate demand (Dyson and Featherstone, 2000). While this explanation may hold for some countries, it does not apply to Germany for two reasons (Siegel, 2001). First, unlike countries such as France and Sweden that flirted with expansionary policies during the early 1980s, Germany had remained rooted to its ordo-liberal monetarist economic policy since the exhaustion of the short-lived Keynesianism of the 1970s. In other words, the prevailing position on economic policy remained firm in Germany because the EMU was deeply compatible with the kind of German monetarism practiced for much of the post-war period. Second, even if German policy-makers had desired to re-stimulate aggregate demand with aggressive Keynesian policies, they faced the daunting constraints of the costs of German unification.

This huge challenge to the German government actually produced a hasty departure from prevailing economic policy by then-Chancellor Helmut Kohl in the form of an understandable – but ultimately misguided – one-to one currency reform in 1990. Its purpose was to keep eastern Germans from migrating rapidly to the west. It was partially successful in that respect, but it was not enough to encourage sustained economic stimulus (Allen, 1997). Indeed, after that uncharacteristic – and unintentional – stimulatory economic policy, German monetary policy returned to its more traditional pattern of monetarism with an ordo-liberal accent. For the decade following unification, economic policy was framed almost exclusively in the language of the *supply* of infrastructural investment in eastern Germany rather than an explicit attempt to stimulate economic *demand*.

In some respects, this outcome was a foregone conclusion, as the Bundesbank wouldn't have had it any other way.[5] The major architects of EMU in 1988, Germany (Helmut Kohl and Hans Dietrich Genscher) France (Francois Mitterand) and the EU (Jacques Delors) understood that adhering to this path would require satisfying the stabilization concerns of the Bundesbank as a first priority. Essentially, as Carl Lankowski (1982) suggested, the Bundesbank always viewed as its major external obligation the necessity of making EEC, EC, and EU monetary policy compatible with its own. Lankowski's interpretation suggests that this was as true in the early 1970s as it was in the late 1980s. The Bundesbank and German industry had no fear that European monetary policy would depart from orthodoxy – notwithstanding the abrupt lurch from "Europhoria" by French and German political leaders in the late 1980s to the subsequent sobering realization by Helmut Kohl shortly thereafter that unification costs were woefully underestimated. Ultimately, the primary difference between the failure of EMU in the early 1970s and its success in the late 1980s was that Mitterand was forced to face the reality of the constraints that monetary policy could place on independent domestic economic policy (Hall, 1986). After bruising battles with both the PCF and the French right over such policies in the early and mid-1980s, he finally acceded to a monetary policy that was compatible with the prevailing European orthodoxy.

The 1990s saw this restrictive neo-liberal policy in Germany become more palatable, by default, to the social force most likely to object – the trade unions – for two reasons. One, the institutions of worker participation (*Mitbstimmung* and *Betriebsrte*) gave workers the perception that they had greater opportunity to shape changes in work, technology, organizational design, and perhaps even investment due to the institutional access that these organizations seemed to provide them. They hardly gave German workers the kind of workplace and boardroom power that they might have promised on paper, but they did give unions the perception that they had the opportunity to do so. A more cynical view would suggest that this institutional presence allowed the core of the German labor movement to more easily ignore the adverse labor market conditions in eastern Germany (Jacoby, 2000). In fact, the very institutional structures upon which the German labor market rested were either underdeveloped or badly atrophying in the east (Silvia, 1997).

Two, German unions' *Tarifautonomie*, independent collective bargaining, enabled German unions for the entire post-war period to overcome the absence of an FRG government incomes policy (Streeck, 1994). Specifically, unions had the ability to negotiate wage and benefit increases on a sector-by-sector basis that – at least in several core sectors – allowed them to align their bargaining closely with changes in inflation and productivity that proved beneficial for them until the 1990s. This pattern allowed considerable "wage drift," additional wage and fringe benefits in certain firms over and above industry-specific negotiated outcomes. What Streeck questions here, however, is whether this policy would be sustainable across the entire workforce. In fact, in a later work, he was much more critical of the ability of this German "model" to persist in a very different domestic and international environment (Streeck, 1997).

Politically, the Red-Green government elected in 1998 and headed by Social Democrat Gerhard Schröder faced daunting policy choices in the face of the 1990s neo-liberal monetary policy reality. Much of the Social Democrats' electoral rhetoric concerned an emphasis on the *neue Mitte* that would position the Social Democrats in an ideological orbit not far from Bill Clinton or Tony Blair. But Schröder was vague and imprecise about exactly what the *neue Mitte* meant for the core constituency of the SPD. Clearly there were forces inside the Social Democrats, particularly among the party's rank and file, who wished to see more traditional social democratic programs such as those that would overcome the country's structural unemployment that had persisted throughout the 1990s. The primary advocate who trumpeted these positions was the charismatic Oscar Lafontaine who used his position as the Minister President of the economically disadvantaged Saarland to try to pull the Schröder government more to the left of the "New Middle."

Yet the first six months of the government saw the resignation – whether forced or voluntary – of SPD party leader and finance minister, Oskar

Lafontaine. In the short run, the removal of the left-leaning Lafontaine assuaged the financial community and seemed to remove a growing point of contention between the two party rivals. Schröder wanted to take more moderate positions while Lafontaine wanted to seize the opportunity that a left wing coalition promised and develop progressive, expansionary economic policies (Lafontaine, 1999). The latter's removal from both his cabinet and party positions seemed to finally crystallize *die Neue Mitte* and a Clinton/Blair economic moderation that pre-election pundits had forecast. This was followed by a major retrenchment in the generous provisions of the German welfare state that provoked widespread protest among usually supportive SPD constituencies.

Cynics within the SPD, particularly within the party's left wing, saw the departure of Lafontaine as confirmation that the Schröder government's drift to the middle was complete. As finance minister in the initial stages of the Red-Green government, Lafontaine took positions to the left of both Schröder and of the European central bank. Rather than advocating the kind of fiscal prudence long associated with the Bundesbank – and now the European central bank – Lafontaine advocated the kind of left-Keynesianism long associated with social democracy elsewhere in Europe.

Lafontaine had achieved this influential cabinet position by virtue of his representing a significant constituency within the Social Democratic Party. Yet once in government, the ideological and institutional tensions within both party and government proved too difficult to maintain. Rather than seeing Lafontaine's departure as a heavy handed purge by Schröder and his more centrist allies, a less cynical interpretation grounded in the institutional realities of German domestic politics would suggest that Lafontaine realized that he would not win any further tests of will with Schröder. His exit option was to simply resign and hope to fight the battle on another day.

Yet, this view of Schröder gently easing out a leftist rival in order to find moderate positions and thereby make the new German government less threatening to international financial interests misses the forest for the trees. Just as the larger issues of globalization and the democratic deficit continued to fester both in Germany and throughout Europe, segments of the left – in the German case embodied by Lafontaine – were being marginalized (Kitschelt, 1999).

Despite the hegemonic position of ordo-liberal monetarism in both Germany and the EU, its durability was not assured. The smooth transfer of monetary authority from the Bundesbank to the ECB has produced a series of unintended consequences and appears to compromise the vision of the twenty-first-century European ordo-liberalism. One of the essential components of effective Bundesbank policy in Germany during the post-war period was its institutional integration with a number of public policy areas, one of the most important being wage-policy. Hall and Franzese (1998) point out that the EU's avoidance of developing a robust Social Charter limits the possibility of developing wage-coordinating institutions to support monetary policy. More seriously, they suggest that implementing such a policy in the face of wide disparities in labor market conditions would be difficult at best. Thus, the only tool that the ECB would have to moderate the inevitable wage pressure would be tighter monetary policy and the increased unemployment that would predictably follow.

> The larger point here is that creating a monetary union in Europe will generate a variety of new coordination problems that will not automatically be solved by the presence of a relatively independent central bank. Resolving such problems will depend on the development of a larger system of institutional arrangements. An independent central bank trying to impose its will on a reluctant government or recalcitrant workforce may be only a second-best solution to problems that could be tackled more effectively through a broader range of institutions. In this respect, creating an EMU is likely to be only the first step in a more extensive process of institution building, bearing on both the coordination of monetary and fiscal policy at the European level and the character of collective bargaining within its member-states. The success of the EMU will ultimately depend on this wider process. (Hall and Franzese, 1998, 530–1)

The irony, of course, is some observers believed at the onset of Maastricht over a decade ago that the model for the EU would be *Modell Deutschland*. They envisioned a EU that contained many of the more socially beneficial trappings of a modern mixed economy along with the legacy of some pre-second world war baggage (Markovits and Reich, 1991). Among the more beneficial outcomes were to be a generous welfare state that built on the 1970s social democratic expansion of the paternalistic Christian Democratic welfare state and the dissemination of the most progressive kinds of work reform and employee organization such as works councils and codetermination. Yet, to those who appreciate the difficulty of both building new institutions and diffusing old ones (Jacoby, 2000), the triumph of monetarism not only in Germany but also in the EU since Maastricht is hardly surprising. It is simply a lot easier to let markets loose than it is to mobilize the political capital to build and maintain institutions. Yet what Hall and Franzese suggest is that the triumph of monetarism is not that simple (Hall and Franzese, 1998). More importantly they imply that to even work as well as its adherents postulate, monetarism must function in tandem with existing institutional structures if it is going to replicate the kind of economic success that it did in the post-war FRG. In fact, their argument stands on its head the conventional wisdom assertion that markets trump politics. Instead, they suggest that the door may be open for European actors who wish to advance the case for placing political and institutional constraints on the hegemony of neo-liberal monetarist orthodoxy.

Conclusion

Keynesianism was not as influential in Germany as one might have expected for many reasons. Some of these have to do with reactions against the interwar experience. There is little doubt, for instance, that German economists took a more jaundiced view of reflation as a result of experiencing it first under the Third Reich. However, I have argued that the rejection of Keynesianism and its ultimate weakness in the FRG did not depend simply on the quality of reaction to the inter-war period. First, there was more than reaction involved. German policymakers were able to ignore Keynesianism because they had developed a viable alternative of their own. And, second, that alternative was built on an accumulation of historical experiences that stretch back many decades before the Third Reich. These nineteenth century-rooted policies were only reinforced by Freiburg school economic theories that developed in response to the wild experimentation and policy swings of the 1920s and 1930s (James, 1989).

The construction of a national conception of appropriate economic policy is a complex matter. Even in Britain, post-war policy did not flow full-blown from the head of Keynes. It develops in stages according to the ideas that reach fruition at each stage and the experiences a nation seems to have with them. In Germany, Social Market Economics was initially a rather artificial notion, devised in reaction to the disasters of Weimar and refined in light of the Third Reich. Its initial influence in the immediate post-war years owed a good deal to the talents and good fortune of Ludwig Erhard, but Social Market Economics became a powerful set of organizing principles and a political symbol largely because the economic experience of the 1950s, when it was being utilized, was so favorable. Few nations would reject a policy that brought them 8–9 percent annual rates of growth. In that respect, it mattered very little whether the policy was responsible for the growth rate. Just as a reaction against Weimar, Hitler and the Allied controls had given some initial impetus to social market concepts, the experience of the 1950s lent real ideological force to them. Within a few years, the concepts had such credibility that few were interested in what Keynesianism could add. Even today, despite the Stability and Growth Law of 1967, German policy-making is still founded on social market ideas rather than Keynesianism.

If another set of concepts had been important to policy-making during the boom of the 1950s, they might matter more in Germany today. However, the social market ideas also build upon long-standing, path-dependent German notions about how the economy functions. As I have indicated, the Social Market Economy is not a synonym for laissez-faire. On the one hand, it contains a rationale for the welfare state that Keynesianism appropriated in other nations. That was possible, in part, because the social market economists built upon nineteenth century notions of governmental responsibility. As Frederick Reuss (1963) has observed: "The German government uses incentives for the upper groups and paternalism for the lower." This has long been an important formula in German history. On the other hand, the conception of the private economy implicit in social market concepts is not quite that of the classical economists. As I have noted, it builds upon a long-standing conception of "organized capitalism" whose pedigree goes back to the German experience of late industrialization. Only when one realizes how many institutional mechanisms for coordination are an accepted part of the private economy in Germany can one dismiss some of Keynes' concerns about the fundamental instability of markets and the need for state intervention. As the Canadian official quoted at the beginning of this chapter implicitly observed, most Germans are working with a conception of the economy that is quite different from the one on which many Keynesians rely.

In sum, if German policy-makers were initially predisposed against Keynesian ideas, they were able to ignore those ideas for a long time only because they were constructing an alternative amalgam, whose credibility was firmly established early on in the post-war period. As time passed, the institutional structures for policy-making also took on forms that militated in favor of the reigning orthodoxy and against a break toward Keynesianism. In both respects, the development of a prevailing set of economic policies clearly depends a great deal on the accumulation of ideas and institutions and on the sequence in which particular options come to the fore.

Yet as effective as these policies were for post-Second World War years, the pressures of globalization, Europeanization, and the still considerable residual costs from unification have strained elements of the institutional model that hitherto so effectively underpinned macroeconomic policy. Beyond these three empirical conditions, however, lie two more fundamental factors that suggest that German economic policy in the early twenty-first century may see greater movement toward neo-liberalism and away from its half-century of "ordo-liberalism."

First, the hegemony of the latter concept is not immutable. Such sets of policies are dynamic forces which – at their best – are embodied by purposeful policy-makers and patterns of understood responses to a wide range of policy outcomes. But they are not spontaneously occurring phenomena. They need to be understood, reinforced, and continually tested against new challenges if they are to retain the capacity to produce suitable economic policies. But because the German model of ordo-liberalism has not been touted as an explicit ideology since the heyday of the Freiburg School, a half-century ago, contemporary German policy makers who have internalized this pattern of behavior – but rarely discussed it explicitly – may be less able to defend its merits when attacked by adherents of deregulation, *laissez faire*, and neo-liberalism. In other words, among policymakers patterns of responses are often more intuitively understood than explicitly discussed. In one sense, this might suggest a beneficial shared understanding of a range of suitable responses. However, it also might indicate an inability to actually understand how to use past, prevailing institutional patterns with contemporary problems (Allen, 1997).

Second, Mark Blyth (2002b) argues for "the importance of ideas as integral components of institutional construction and change by conceptualizing them as weapons, blueprints, and cognitive locks." In recent years, neo-liberalism has acted as a weapon against ordo-liberalism by advancing a blueprint for macroeconomic policy that has begun to erode the cognitive lock that ordo liberalism has had on German economic policy. In other words, neo-liberal thought has crept into German economic policy not only because it appears hegemonic across advanced industrialized states, but also because German ordo-liberalism has failed to adapt to the challenges that neo-liberalism has placed in its path. But can the rise of neo-liberal economic policy in both Germany and the EU address the formidable concerns of Hall and Franzese? This question must remain the subject of future study.

Acknowledgement

An earlier version of this piece appeared in Hall, 1989. Much appreciation goes to Bernard Moss for helpful suggestions and useful formulations for the period since the 1990s. Thanks to the members of the "Workshop on the Neo-liberal Turn in the European Union and its Member-States," which Bernard Moss organized at the University of Nottingham, UK, June 8, 2002, especially Tobias Abse, Dorothee Heisenberg, Andreas Bieler, Erik Jones, and Mette Jolly. I would also like to acknowledge the sage advice of Peter Hall, Peter Katzenstein, Jeremiah M. Riemer, and Margaret Weir for their support on the original project. I am grateful to Lichao He for her excellent research assistance, and to the Minda de Gunzburg Center for European Studies at Harvard University for providing research facilities for the Spring and Summer of 2002.

Notes

1. I have argued (Allen, 1983), extending Alexander Gershenkron's late industrialization thesis, that the modern German economy was of a "fragile strength" that required sound foundations in the post-war period.
2. Leading members of this school were Eucken, 1951, 1952, 1954; Röpke, 1947, 1960, 1963; Rüstow, 1968; also Müller-Armack, 1971; Erhard, 1958.
3. Ambrosius, 1977; Hardach, 1980; Balabkins, 1964; Botting, 1985.
4. For a critical view see Abosch, 1963.
5. Thanks to Bernard Moss for his helpful comments on this issue.

10
The Political Economy of the UK, 1979–2002

Jonathan Michie

The first Thatcher Government was elected in 1979 on the promise of squeezing inflation out of the system – permanently. How did she and her Government propose to do this, given the reluctance to use the structures and policies of the European Community, as it then was? The answer was monetarism: the control of the money supply. The theory – as espoused by Nobel Prize winning economist Professor Milton Friedman – was that since the stock of money multiplied by the number of times that stock circulates each year must by definition equal the quantity of goods and services bought during that period times their price, if you reduced (the growth of) the money supply, you must also thereby reduce (the growth of) prices.

However, the immediate effect of attempting to reduce the growth of the money supply was to increase interest rates, cause the currency to become overvalued, squeeze exports, and subject domestically produced goods to greater competition from imports made cheaper by the overvaluation of sterling, put off investment, bankrupt firms particularly in the traded goods sector, increase unemployment, choke off domestic consumer spending, and push the economy into recession. Instead of reducing the prices at which goods and services were sold, the above identity was preserved – as it must be – by reducing the quantity of goods and services being sold. In other words, economic growth slowed, turned negative, and national production and income actually declined.

Of course, such recessions do themselves have an anti-inflationary effect, as companies limit or postpone price rises in a desperate attempt to hold onto their shares of declining markets. And so inflation did at first decline. However, following the recovery from the first Thatcher recession of 1979–81, inflation began rising again from mid-1983; following a dip in 1986, inflation continued rising until the end of 1990. Thatcher's premiership ended with inflation at around the same level as she had inherited in 1979: the annual increase in the Retail Price Index stood at 10.3 percent when the first Thatcher government took office in May 1979, while when

Mrs Thatcher left office in November 1990 it was 9.7 percent. So much for inflation being eliminated for all time.

This chapter evaluates the government's anti-inflation policies since 1979, through to today. The first section reviews the theory and concludes that the belief that targeting the growth in the money supply would eliminate inflation, gave way to old-style policies of high interest rates and deflation combined with labor market policies to restrain wages. The impact of labor market policy on wage determination is then analyzed. The implications of all this for the inflation record in the 1980s, and for the legacy left by the three Thatcher governments, are then considered. The Major years are then reported, with the ill-fated attempt to use the Exchange Rate Mechanism (ERM) of the European Monetary System (EMS) to control inflation. Finally, the current Labor Government's policies are discussed.

I Inflation: theory and practice[1]

Monetary targets had been used prior to 1979; indeed, they were included in the 1976 loan conditions from the International Monetary Fund (IMF) to the Labor Government of the day. However, prior to 1979, in neither theoretical nor policy areas was the monetarist explanation generally accepted as being adequate on its own, and the Labor Government of Jim Callaghan continued to rely on incomes policies as their main anti-inflationary device. Full acceptance by the government of monetarist theory and policy prescriptions came only in 1979, although even then these were pursued by means of controlling the public sector borrowing requirement (PSBR – the fiscal deficit); Friedman himself disowned the use of fiscal policy as the leading method of controlling the money supply and argued before the House of Commons Treasury and Civil Services Committee that the market should be left to determine the interest rate.

Policy developments under the Thatcher governments began with strict monetary targets that required public expenditure cuts. Within a year of Thatcher taking office exchange controls had been abolished, direct controls on the growth of bank deposits ("the corset") scrapped, reserve asset ratios abolished and the minimum lending rate consigned to virtual oblivion. Ironically, the original aim of the Thatcher government to impose monetary control proved to be incompatible with the financial liberalization which freed the banking system's money-creating potential.

Monetary control also proved difficult as inflation accelerated, generated by the second oil shock and fed by the switch from direct to indirect taxation. The tight credit policy exacerbated the cash-flow problem of firms as costs rose sharply. The consequences were two-fold: a rapid increase in bankruptcies and plant closures as firms cut back their operations, and a sharp increase in lending as banks supported their clients (and their own previous loans to their clients) so that the money supply increased by much more than the policy targets. Nevertheless there was a tight monetary squeeze in both 1979 and 1980. Interest rates rose sharply and this, combined with the beneficial balance of payments effects of North Sea oil and the popularity of the Thatcher policies with the international financial community, caused the sterling exchange rate to rise by almost 20 percent above its 1978 level by 1980.

High interest rates, the growing competition from imports and reduced profitability of exports as the sterling exchange rate rose, reinforced the effect of the tight monetary squeeze on the level of activity and the overall level of employment fell by almost eight percent between 1979 and 1982. Unemployment, which was 1.3 million in 1979, reached almost 3 million in 1982 and crossed that threshold in 1983. In face of the deepening recession, monetary constraints were relaxed. The money supply increased by around 19 percent in 1981 and 1982 (respectively 7 percent and 10.5 percent in real terms), interest rates fell in nominal terms but rose in real terms and the rise in the exchange rate was first checked and then reversed. The pace of inflation accelerated in 1979 and 1980 but then declined with the downward pressure on domestic prices exercised by the high exchange rates and with the fall in commodity prices as the world recession intensified. Wage increases also moderated under the influence of sharply rising unemployment, direct government pressure in the public sector and the deceleration of the increase in retail prices, and this further contributed to a slowing of inflation.

However, bank lending to the private sector increased by 50 percent between 1981 and 1984 and by almost 200 percent from 1984 to 1988. In addition, the various forms of credit used to finance consumer expenditure increased two and a half times between 1981 and 1988. Consumer expenditures increased by almost 32 percent in real terms between 1981 and 1988, fueled by a 21 percent increase in real disposable income and a fall in the personal savings ratio from 12.8 percent to 4.4 percent. The rapid growth in demand for consumer goods and the slow growth in domestic production combined to weaken the balance of payments. The current balance, which benefited from the import-saving and export-creating effects of North Sea oil and gas, and which had registered a surplus of more than £6 billion in 1981, was in deficit by £14.6 billion in 1988 and £20 billion in 1989, before the growing recession eased the pressure.

The recovery from 1981 was based, then, on an increase in credit as monetary control was relaxed and a rise in disposable income as the pace of inflation slowed relative to the growth in money income. The depletion of the manufacturing base meant that the economy was increasingly supply-constrained and consequently unable to respond to the increase in home demand for consumer goods and for exports as, with rapidly growing productivity and the depreciation of sterling, the competitiveness of British manufacturing goods improved. This supply shortage was not confined to finished consumer goods; the production infrastructure of intermediary and capital goods had been particularly eroded so that the increase in output and investment as manufacturing industry responded to the new market opportunities itself sucked in imports.[2] The foreign exchange surplus that resulted from North Sea oil and gas shielded the economy from the balance of payments consequences of these developments until 1986 when declining oil prices and a fall in British oil production began to add to the growing balance of payments problem.

II Non-monetarist alternatives

The Phillip's curve apparently lost its explanatory value as, from the middle of the 1960s, unemployment and inflation appeared to be directly rather than inversely related. To explain this, monetarists broke the link between labor market conditions and nominal wages by hypothesising that money wage increases are determined by the rate of increase of the money supply. Real wages, they argued, are determined by supply and demand in the labor market so that unemployment is essentially voluntary. Neo-Keynesian analysis incorporated elements of monetarism, most notably the transformation of the Walrasian market-clearing concept of a "natural rate of unemployment" into the neo-Keynesian idea of there being a "non-accelerating inflation rate of unemployment" (NAIRU) which need not imply market clearing. The essence of the neo-Keynesian analysis is that whilst involuntary unemployment is a possibility, reducing it by increasing monetary demand depends on money wage pressure; the faster the increase in wages, the higher will be the level of unemployment associated with any increase in nominal income. This focused attention on the relationship between unemployment and money wage increases, a tendency reinforced by the apparent re-emergence of the Phillip's curve from the late 1970s.

One issue of major policy significance that arises from the non-monetarist debate on inflation is the theoretical perception of the process of wage determination. Keynesians have traditionally held to the view that the wage structure is institutionally determined and rigid so that a wage increase in any one sector is rapidly transmitted into the general level of wage inflation by the restoration of customary differentials. Neo-Keynesians identify monopoly power of trade unions as the determining factor that drives wages faster than increases in productivity and hence generates inflation. From this perspective, an increase in the monopoly power of trade unions in the 1970s explains "stagflation" – the coincidence of high unemployment and high inflation. Both Keynesian and neo-Keynesian approaches direct policy toward intervention in the wage determining process by such measures as incomes policy or the weakening of trade unions.

In their analysis of the inflationary process the Cambridge Economic Policy Group focused attention on the interaction of price and wage setting.

Firms mark up on costs to restore profitability whilst workers target real wage levels, which they attempt to establish and maintain in the face of erosion of living standards by inflation. Periods of accelerating inflation, both contemporary and historical, are identified as times when real disposable income from employment is eroded, whilst inflation tends to subside when real wages are rising; processes which are largely independent of the level of employment (Tarling, 1977, 1982).

This idea – that inflation is related to "real wage resistance" – stood up well to econometric testing by Henry and Ormerod (1978). Rowthorn provided a synthesis of real wage targeting, a Phillip's curve relationship between unemployment and nominal wages and an active role for money, and located it within a "conflict" model of inflation. He argued that both capital, in marking-up costs to form prices, and labor, in formulating wage claims, aspired to particular shares of the national income. When the shares demanded by labor and capital are greater than the income available for distribution, after allowing for the "burdens" of taxation and the terms of trade, a price spiral results. The aspiration gap could be closed and inflationary pressures controlled, Rowthorn argued, by monetary means. A reduction in the money supply would increase unemployment and activate the reserve army of labor mechanism to reduce wage pressure, whilst intensified competition in the product market would squeeze profit margins. Thus, the weakening of workers in the labor market and of capital in the product market serves to bring aspirations into line with income availability and reduces pressure on prices.

Outside monetarist circles, then, students of inflation have retained an attachment to conditions in the labor market as an important determination of inflation. Numerous explanations have been offered as to why this relationship should have changed, and therefore be difficult simply to read off from the historical record. These include changes in the degree of trade union monopoly power, hysteresis modifications to the Phillip's curve, the changing relations between out-of-work benefits and earnings, the effect of long periods of joblessness on the ability of the unemployed to compete in the labor market, and the effects of technical and other changes on the relative power of insiders relative to outsiders.

III The impact of labor market policy on relative earnings

There is little evidence that employers in manufacturing made much use of the new powers given to them by the Thatcher governments' anti-trade union legislation. Although there was an increase in flexibility in the use of labor, this was compensated for by increased wages (Brown, 1990; Blanchflower, 1991). Consequently, although earnings in manufacturing grew relatively slowly as employment fell sharply between 1979 and 1981, from 1981 to 1990 average earnings in manufacturing increased by 8.9 percent on average per year compared with 8.0 percent in the rest of the economy. Information on occupational earnings from the *New Earnings Survey* reveals that between 1979 and 1990 manual earnings in a wide range of manufacturing occupations increased at annual rates of between 9 and 9.5 percent whilst the increases for white-collar workers and foremen were in excess of 10 percent.

In banking, finance, insurance, and related services, the general trend was toward a higher degree of industrial concentration and this tended to increase the importance of the internal labor market in these sectors, resulting in higher pay, more organized promotion systems and greater job security. These changes, which originated in the 1970s, were accompanied by a switch in recruitment toward graduate entry for professional and managerial grades. Consequently, the status and pay of such jobs tended to increase, and the promotion paths of individuals recruited by traditional methods were undermined. The more extensive use of graduate recruitment also enhanced the status of accountant and related professions in the financial sector. This, and the market pressure from the rapid growth of financial and business services, substantially improved their relative pay. Earnings for the occupational category including accountants and professionals in insurance and finance, increased by 12 percent between 1979 and 1990.

The most dramatic changes in labor market organization, however, were to be found in the public sector. The government engineered major job reductions, changes in the terms and conditions of employment, and labor restructuring in the then nationalized industries including coal, steel, the railways, postal services, airlines, and automobile industries. Privatization continued this process. In other public sector areas, especially in local government, which was subjected to a tight financial squeeze, the job security for "core" professional and non-professional staff was reduced with the increasing use of fixed-term and temporary contracts, particularly in education. The government response to the opposition from school teachers' trade unions was to impose a legal settlement to a protracted dispute over terms and conditions of employment and to scrap long-established bargaining machinery. However, the government's success in implementing its policy even in the public sector was limited. In 1987 the Treasury concluded a long-term agreement with the Institute of Professional Civil Servants which provided for an annual pay review, regular pay comparability exercises, job evaluation, and a national pay scale – all of which government ministers had argued strongly against. Nurses, civil servants, soldiers, policemen, and judges also had pay review bodies, which produce pay increases at least in line with the wage movements of comparable grades in the private sector. For professional and related occupations in education, welfare, and health, earnings grew at an average annual rate of around 11 percent from 1979 to 1990.

The Thatcher governments were more successful in engineering a progressive erosion in the terms and conditions of employment of the low-paid in the public sector. The privatization of an increasing proportion of central government, Local Authority and National Health Service services (including cleaning, catering, and laundry), the scrapping of the Fair Wage Resolution, and new legislation outlawing the insertion of fair labor standard clauses in Local Authority contracts placed an increasing number of low-paid public sector workers outside the scope of collective bargaining. As a consequence there were reductions in pay, a shortening of the hours of part-time work and the elimination of holiday and sickness pay and other fringe benefits. Where services were not privatized, workers were obliged to accept an intensification of work and worsened terms and conditions of employment under the threat of privatization, or were obliged to impose similar cuts on themselves when formulating bids for their own jobs in competition with private sector contractors. The earnings increase of low-paid public sector workers and those most affected by policy-induced privatization averaged not much more than 8 percent per year between 1979 and 1990.

IV Implications for inflation

The Thatcher governments' labor market policies, rather than improve the operation of the labor market, tended to reinforce its rigidities, and the cost of adjustment fell on those least able to bear – and least able to resist – the imposition. As a consequence, inequalities of earnings and of job opportunities increased. What implications did these policies have for inflation? Such measures might affect the rate of inflation via a number of routes, but most directly by influencing the rate of (nominal) wage increases or the level (or rate of growth) of productivity. Either of these effects would impact on unit labor costs and hence, with a given mark-up, on prices.

On the first effect, to the extent that the power of trade unions was weakened, wage rises might be expected to be lower than otherwise. The actual effects reflect the differential impact of government policies. While groups such as those working for firms bidding for contract cleaning did in some instances have their wage levels reduced, others were able to continue to achieve substantial increases in both nominal and real wages. In certain sections of the economy, then, the Thatcher governments' labor market and other deregulatory measures (privatization and contracting out) reduced wage costs and hence, potentially, reduced the price of the relevant final consumer goods and services below what they would otherwise have been. However, the areas where this effect occurred were in many cases labor-intensive with significant opportunities for productivity growth based on new technology; the worsening of terms and conditions of employment, and intensification of work effort, reduced the pressures for such technical change, thus losing potential long-term reductions in unit costs.

In other sectors of the economy where labor productivity rose and/or where firms benefited from reductions in the cost of material inputs, pay increased so as to secure substantial real advances. Thus the two components to reducing unit labor costs tended to work against each other: where the government succeeded in reducing (increases in) pay, this was often at the expense of productivity; and where productivity was enhanced, this was generally taken out in profits and dividends[3] and to a lesser extent in wage earnings, rather than in lower prices.

By these means the economically powerful groups in society expropriated a more than proportionate share of the additional resources made available by the increase in productivity and the surplus from abroad. To this bounty were added the benefits of widening earning differentials and the regressive fiscal redistribution secured by cuts in the higher rates of tax, the switch from direct to indirect taxes and reductions in social benefits. Enough of this reverse Robin-Hoodism percolated down to appease the well-organized and economically powerful in society, and changes in labor and employment law combined with manipulation of the social security system served to suppress resistance from the less powerful. Under these multiple pressures, inflation subsided.

V The Major years[4]

The UK was a late entrant into the ERM of the EMS, joining in October 1990 when Margaret Thatcher was still Prime Minister, with John Major as Chancellor of the Exchequer. Britain joined at an over-valued rate for the pound sterling. Those of us who warned at the time that sterling would need to be devalued were dismissed out of hand. A number of arguments were advanced to suggest that sterling should remain fixed within the ERM. Some suggested that the exchange rate no longer mattered now that trade was predominantly within multinational corporations. Others asserted that were Britain to leave the ERM, interest rates, far from being allowed to fall, would have to rise. In an extraordinary move, the *Observer* newspaper advanced these arguments in opposition to a report from the Cambridge Economic Policy Group[5] that had urged the cutting of interest rates and the devaluation of the exchange rate – a report that the *Observer* had actually commissioned and published itself. Following sterling's exit from the ERM and subsequent economic recovery, no more was heard from the *Observer* on the matter.[6]

All three political parties fought the 1992 general election on a platform of maintaining sterling's membership of the ERM. In the event, of course, the Conservative Government admitted defeat and withdrew sterling. This was forced on them, as it was simply not regarded as credible that any Government could and would pursue the deflationary policies required. Leaving the ERM, cutting interest rates, and devaluing sterling allowed the economy to recover and helped sustain that recovery through the 1990s.

VI The Labor Governments from 1997[7]

The Labor Government elected in 1997 and re-elected in 2001 has, at the time of writing (January 2003) enjoyed a relatively easy ride on the economy. Not least, it inherited fast growth, which remained sufficient for employment to continue rising and unemployment falling.

The main macroeconomic questions hinge on two factors that the Chancellor of the Exchequer, Gordon Brown, may be able to influence, but to some extent are out of his hands – whether the world economy slides into recession, and whether the Prime Minister Tony Blair calls a referendum on Britain joining the Euro.

One economic factor that has remained – so far – firmly in the hands of the Chancellor, though, is taxation. In the first term of the Labor Government (1997–2001), the Treasury's task had been to deliver increased public spending, lower taxes, and reduced borrowing. They largely achieved this through a combination of good fortune and stealth. Although Labor had made various promises requiring public spending – and hence taxation – the commitment to stick to the Tories' spending plans let the Chancellor off this particular hook for the first two years. Alongside this, the economic growth inherited from Kenneth Clarke's low interest rate regime provided healthy tax revenues. And the combination of these, along with windfalls from higher oil prices and hence tax revenues plus the mobile phone auction, allowed budget surpluses to reduce the national debt.[8]

There were, though, a number of worrying developments on taxation. First there was a switch from progressive direct taxation to regressive indirect taxation. This switch contributed to increased inequality during the Labor Government's first term, with the proportion of income paid in tax falling for the richest 20 percent of households since 1997–98 but rising for the bottom 80 percent. Someone in the poorest fifth of households now pays on average 41 percent of their overall income on tax compared to 36 percent for the richest fifth.

Coupled with this, the expansion of means testing has resulted – ironically, given the low tax rhetoric – in extremely high marginal tax rates for the least well-off as benefits get withdrawn following any rise in earnings. This shift away from universal benefits also threatens to undermine the political and social support for the welfare state, changing it from being a collective enterprise to which all contribute and from which all benefit, to a large charity-giving exercise. This combination of moving to regressive indirect taxation and means-testing benefits has resulted in tax rates – both marginal and average – being higher for the least well-off than they are for the rich.

The Labor Government opened its first term by handing interest rate policy to the Bank of England's Monetary Policy Committee. The rationale was that this would avoid sterling being forced down by international currency markets suspicious of a Labor Government. The result has been that the currency has been overvalued instead, damaging the traded goods sector, most dramatically with BMW abandoning Rover and Corus closing steel plants.

Such problems would be considerably amplified if the UK were to join the Euro. The danger is that within the single currency, the economy would become tied to an inappropriate interest rate and/or exchange rate. Recent events have demonstrated that the European Central Bank makes interest rate decisions according to the economic needs of Germany rather than Ireland. If the Euro were to become over-valued against the dollar in the future, this would be less of a problem for other European economies than for the UK. In this situation, the danger would be that the European Central Bank might allow such a state of affairs to continue rather than cut interest rates.

Either of these possibilities – of the Euro resulting in either an inappropriate interest rate or exchange rate for the UK economy – could prove disastrous economically, socially, and politically. The key aim of the Labor Government – well before any consideration of whether or not to join the single currency is made – should therefore be to bring about change in the nature of European Monetary Union. In particular, it is vital to democratize the institutions and functioning of the single currency, and to challenge the orthodox, deflationary logic that has driven the single currency process to date. The so-called Stability and Growth Pact, under which the Irish Government was reprimanded in 2001 for planning tax cuts, despite having a large budget surplus, needs to be abandoned. Indeed, the same meeting of European Finance Ministers that reprimanded Ireland in 2001 also warned that Gordon Brown's taxation plans might fail their test.

Conclusion

We now, in 2004, face the mystifying prospect of a Labor government apparently cherishing the idea of repeating the most egregious mistakes of recent British economic history by joining the euro.

Governments of the European Union have been pursuing deflationary, low growth, high unemployment policies, first under the Maastricht convergence criteria and now under the auspices of the so-called Stability and Growth Pact. The resulting unemployment should come as no surprise. As I have described in detail elsewhere, similar policies were pursued in Britain under the Gold Standard of the 1920s, with parallel results in terms of deflationary government economic policies and the creation of mass unemployment (Kitson *et al*, 2000, ch. 6).

It seems that nothing has been learned. The world economy only managed to pull itself out of the Great Depression in the 1930s by abandoning fixed exchange rates, cutting interest rates and boosting growth. Yet when similar policies were advocated prior to September 16, 1992, when Britain left the ERM, such policies were denounced as "anti-European." But it did our European partners no favors having our economy in recession, any more than Britain is now being helped by our EU partners pursuing restrictive policies. As the economist Joan Robinson put it: "Of all bad-neighborly conduct among trading nations, the worst is to go into a slump."

Unless current European economic policy shifts toward the objective of full employment, embracing an active industrial and regional policy, rather than being stuck on the myopic concern with zero inflation, Europe will never tackle mass unemployment. The route forward must once again be based on independent national growth strategies, which would not only allow countries to help themselves, but by doing so would help each other. Competitive deflation – not competitive devaluation – was the real "beggar thy neighbour" policy of the 1990s.

Notes

1. Further details in Michie, 1992.
2. On UK under-investment see Kitson and Michie, 1996.
3. "Among appropriations, dividend payments rose by 17 percent in 1990, a lower growth rate than in the preceding two years (27 percent in 1989 and 33 percent in 1988), but one that was still surprisingly rapid. The dividend payout ratio, defined as the ratio of dividend payments to total income after deducting tax and interest payments, rose to 56 percent in the fourth quarter of 1990 and 64 percent in the first quarter of this year ... Such a level of dividend payments is not only high by historical standards but exceptional given the current downturn in company profitability," Bank of England, 1991, 364.
4. Further see Michie, 2002.
5. The Cambridge Economic Policy Group (CEPG) was led by Professor Wynne Godley who at the time of the CEPG's formation was also Director of the Department of Applied Economics at the University of Cambridge. Despite – or perhaps because of – being the only group to correctly forecast the rises in unemployment in the early 1980s, the CEPG had its funding withdrawn. The CEPG was reformed briefly in the 1990s by Wynne Godley, Ken Coutts, John Grieve Smith, Jonathan Michie, and Bob Rowthorn.
6. See CEPG,1992; Raphael,1992; and Coutts *et al*, 1992.
7. See Michie, 2001.
8. Public spending as a proportion of national income at the end of the fourth year of the Labor Government was the lowest for 27 years, at 38.7 percent compared to John Major's 41.4 percent and Margaret Thatcher's 43.0 percent.

11
The "Monetarist" Turn in Belgium and the Netherlands

Erik Jones

Belgium and the Netherlands (the Low Countries) were among the first West European countries to use their economic relationship with Germany in order to support domestic adjustment. At the start of the 1980s, the governments of both countries stabilized their exchange rates with the Deutschemark (DM), they began to cut spending and raise taxes, and they negotiated and enforced wage moderation on the part of the major trade union confederations. In the short term, the net effect of these policies was to slow down domestic price inflation, to redistribute income from labor to industry, and to raise the profitability of capital. In the medium term, both countries saw a rise in unemployment simultaneous to a rise in exports, investment, and corporate profitability. They also witnessed a shift in employment from manufacturing to services and a decline in trade union membership.

Over the longer term, inflation decreased further in both countries, unemployment receded, and real GDP (gross domestic product) growth recovered. However, the redistribution of income from labor to capital was not reversed, the share of government spending as a percentage of domestic product was lower, the movement away from manufacturing and toward service sector employment accelerated, and the popularity of the trade unions declined – particularly in the Netherlands. Across the whole of the period, therefore, the adjustment policies of Belgium and the Netherlands coincided with a hardening of the DM exchange rate, a weakening of organized labor, and a retreat of the welfare state (Table 11.1, Jones, 1999).

But was this experience of Belgium and the Netherlands during the 1980s really an ideological turn in the sense that terms like "monetarism" or "neo-liberalism" would imply? It is doubtful (cf. Kurzer, 1993). To begin with, the process of adjustment was incremental and extends across a 15-year period from 1972 to 1987. Second, although a major part of the adjustment process in both countries took place under the auspices of center-right coalitions, these coalitions emerged in the 1981–82 period out of the failure of center-left governments to implement similar reforms and not as a result of some ideological conversion. Third, the pattern of adjustment in both countries

Table 11.1 A statistical overview of "neo-liberal" adjustment

Period averages		**1972–77**	**1977–82**	**1982–87**	**1987–92**
Price inflation (average annual percentage change)	*Belgium*	*8.4*	*6.3*	*4.9*	*2.5*
	Netherlands	8.1	5.6	2.2	1.8
Adjusted wage share (percentage GDP at factor cost)	*Belgium*	*74.0*	*77.1*	*74.5*	*71.5*
	Netherlands	73.4	72.6	67.0	65.6
Profitability of capital (index 1995 = 100)	*Belgium*	*87.5*	*71.5*	*82.0*	*99.5*
	Netherlands	80.2	71.2	82.1	87.1
Current account balance (percentage GDP)	*Belgium*	*0.9*	*−2.6*	*−0.3*	*1.3*
	Netherlands	2.8	0.5	3.3	2.6
Net fixed capital Formation (percentage GDP)	*Belgium*	*11.8*	*9.8*	*5.1*	*7.3*
	Netherlands	11.7	8.6	6.2	6.9
Unemployment (percentage labor force)	*Belgium*	*3.8*	*8.0*	*10.4*	*7.7*
	Netherlands	4.1	7.4	8.9	6.3
Total government expenditure (percentage GDP)	*Belgium*	*47.5*	*56.4*	*59.5*	*54.3*
	Netherlands	46.1	53.9	57.4	54.4
Real GDP growth (average annual percentage change)	*Belgium*	*3.3*	*1.7*	*1.6*	*2.9*
	Netherlands	3.2	1.1	1.8	2.9

Source: European Commission.

can be explained in terms that are pragmatic (if not opportunistic) rather than orthodox. What matters is that the governments of both countries relied on pre-existing economic institutions – both domestic and international – rather than that they had any particular conception of the role of the state in the market. Finally, the focus for political competition post-1982 lay within the ruling coalitions as much as between government and opposition (or between right and left).

None of this is to deny that income was redistributed from labor to capital or that the state was withdrawn from the market. Rather my point is to underscore the conditions necessary for a particular pattern of adjustment to come about. Belgium and the Netherlands may again face a choice between strategies for adjustment, and next time the choice might be different. By the same token, the two countries may have no alternative but to choose differently – if only because the mechanisms that underwrote the adjustments of the 1980s are no longer available.

This argument is made in four sections. The first looks at the emergence of hard currency policies during the early- to mid-1970s. The second analyzes reform efforts on the center-left and the center-right in the late 1970s and early 1980s. The third examines the structure of political competition during the 1980s. The fourth section considers whether the pattern of adjustment witnessed in Belgium and the Netherlands was ideological, whether it was necessary, and whether it could be repeated.

I From dollars to DMs

Belgium and the Netherlands have relied on fixed exchange rates throughout the post-Second World War period. During the Bretton Woods era (1948–71), the central anchor for the Belgian frank and the Dutch florin (or guilder) was the US dollar. Between the cessation of dollar convertibility into gold in 1971 and the floating of the dollar in 1973, Belgian and Dutch monetary authorities followed a cluster of targets including the dollar, the DM, and each other. From1973, the DM became an increasingly central (or exclusive) point of reference. After 1982, the stability of bilateral exchange rates with Germany operated as a cornerstone for macroeconomic policy-making in Belgium and the Netherlands.

This progression from the dollar to the DM was gradual, incremental, experimental, and (at times) reluctant. It was underwritten by a consistent set of preferences for price stability, export competitiveness, and macroeconomic autonomy. It was stimulated by periods of profound instability in international currency markets. And, it was supported by the construction of bi- and multi-lateral arrangements including the European "snake" and the European Monetary System (EMS).

Seen this way, it is difficult to interpret Belgian and Dutch participation in the greater DM zone as an expression of sudden ideological conversion at the beginning of the 1980s. Rather it is a response to the failure of alternatives. Had the Bretton Woods system never collapsed, the Belgians and the Dutch would not have needed to turn to the DM. Had some other multilateral arrangement succeeded in stabilizing exchange rates – like the European monetary union proposed in 1970, the snake arrangement implemented in 1972, or the EMS adopted in 1979 – then the question of DM dominance would never have arisen. However, these things did not happen. By implication, Belgium and the Netherlands resorted to DM exchange rate targets as if by a process of elimination.

The one alternative that was not pursued by monetary policy-makers in Belgium and the Netherlands was floating exchange rates – whether in the pure sense of unencumbered market forces or the "dirty" sense of government-sponsored managed floats or crawling pegs. The exchange-rate preference in both countries centers on strong government intervention to fix the price of the domestic currency in world markets. This preference extends across the political spectrum and is held by labor as well as industry, sheltered sectors as well as those exposed to world markets (Jones, 1998a, b). Such apparent consensus exists for three reasons. First, stable exchange rates are viewed as an essential bulwark for export-led growth given the large share of capital goods and inputs to production which are imported. Second, considering the widespread consumption of imports by households, floating (or depreciating) exchange rates are viewed as having an inequitable and even unpredictable impact on the distribution of income. Third, and belatedly, fixed exchange rates make it easier for governments to borrow from abroad.

This exchange-rate preference implies costs as well as benefits. For exports to remain price competitive across a stable exchange rate, monetary policy-makers must ensure that domestic prices do not rise faster than those abroad. Failure in this regard would raise the relative cost of manufacturing for export. For governments to retain some effectiveness in the area of fiscal policy, they must ensure that households do not become excessively dependent upon the consumption of imports. Alternatively, efforts at fiscal stimulus will threaten the balance of payments. Finally, foreign borrowing cannot be allowed to give rise to substantial outflows of debt service payments that must be financed with ever-increasing volumes of exports. By implication, no strategy is invulnerable to poor application or to the perils of its own success.

Belgium and the Netherlands were not unique in their preference for fixed exchange rates. West Germany held similar preferences and so experienced similar challenges (Kreile, 1977). Where Belgium and the Netherlands were unique, however, was in the extent of their exposure to world markets. By the late 1960s, the ratio of exports or imports to domestic production was more than twice as high in Belgium and the Netherlands as it was in Germany (see Table 11.2). As a result, the challenge of responding to the costs implied by the fixed exchange-rate preference was much greater.

Table 11.2 Trade exposure to world markets

1969 (percentage GDP)	Exports	Imports
Belgium	50	49
Netherlands	41	42
West Germany	22	19

Source: European Commission.

The Belgians and the Dutch relied on price-incomes policy to help ease the tension between their preference for exchange rate stability and their extreme exposure to world markets (cf. Katzenstein, 1985). Price controls provided the basis for export competitiveness while income moderation helped to hold down the consumption of imports. Importantly, however, the discipline of the Bretton Woods system was not extravagant. Domestic prices could not be allowed to rise above those abroad, but the "abroad" that mattered was the US, and price inflation there was relatively high. Indeed, where the Netherlands ran into difficulty (with Germany) was in its failure to generate sufficient inflation to avoid over-stimulating its export manufacturers by (effectively) under-pricing their wares abroad. Belgium was never so successful in the application of price-incomes policy and so almost always generated sufficient inflation to take the pressure out of export demand and yet sufficient stability to ensure a positive balance of payments.

Toward the late 1960s, the strategy for maintaining stable exchange rates and extreme openness to world markets began to come undone. As the US ran ever-higher levels of domestic inflation, the threat of overheating in the Low Countries increased. Meanwhile, both imported goods and export earnings began to contribute to domestic inflation both directly and indirectly. The direct effect worked through aggregate price levels, where any increase in import prices has an immediate impact on the consumer price index. The indirect effect took the form of more aggressive wage claims on the part of trade unions, which feared that higher consumer prices would erode real incomes.

It would be a mistake, however, to attribute all of the strain in the Belgian and Dutch economies at the end of the 1960s to developments taking place outside the country. Even without the contribution of external factors, the discipline required for the management of price incomes policy had eroded, and government efforts to maintain control over prices and wages only served to incite further discontent. On the side of industry, this discontent showed up as defections from national wage agreements with employers seeking to attract more productive workers with the promise of higher wages. It also emerged through subtle changes in the pattern of investment toward ever-increasing capital intensity and therefore ever-decreasing requirements for labor inputs to production. Both such developments were encouraged by the actions of the trade unions. Not only did the workers want to receive higher wages, but also – by making higher wage claims – they made it more attractive for employers to switch their investment patterns toward capital and away from labor.

With the sudden devaluation of the notional dollar–gold exchange rate and the end of dollar convertibility into gold in 1971, the Belgians and the Dutch lost the denominator for their exchange-rate preference. Although they remained interested in stabilizing exchange rates, the first question they had to consider was "exchange rates with whom?" Between December 1971 and March 1972, the governments of both countries decided to stabilize exchange rates with each other and with West Germany. From a trading perspective, this choice was advantageous given the high volume of goods that circulate within the Low Countries and across Northern Europe. Looking at the cost side of the preference for fixed exchange rates, however, the advantages of the choice were less obvious. All three countries – Belgium, the Netherlands, and West Germany – hoped to achieve export-led growth and all three were used to controlling domestic prices and wages in the interests of maintaining cost competitiveness. Hence instead of facing the relatively lax discipline implied by shadowing the US economy, the Belgians and the Dutch faced the much harsher discipline of shadowing West Germany.

The collapse of domestic institutions for ensuring price wage restraint meant that the challenge of shadowing West Germany was all the more difficult to meet. Almost immediately, the Belgians and the Dutch looked to dilute this challenge by building other currencies into their designs for exchange rate stability. In part, the solution lay in shifting from an emphasis on bilateral exchange rates to multilateral commitments – such as the 1972 European snake mechanism. To a much greater extent, however, the solution lay in finding multilateral arrangements that offered both stability and flexibility at the same time. Here the currency snake was a disappointment. Although ostensibly a multilateral arrangement, the snake included intervention requirements, which fell asymmetrically on weaker currencies. By implication, the DM not only emerged as the strongest currency in the system, but also many of the other larger countries – such as France and Italy – simply fell out of the system. As the snake broke apart in the mid-1970s, Belgium and the Netherlands were left increasingly isolated in their attempts to shadow West Germany (Thygesen, 1979). The formal dissolution of the dollar-exchange standard in 1976 made this isolation virtually absolute.

The 1979 EMS was intended to rectify such asymmetries and thereby to build a more inclusive arrangement – at least from the perspective of the Belgians and the Dutch (Ludlow, P. 1982). In their contributions to the negotiations leading up to the EMS, the representatives of both countries emphasized the importance of erecting flanking institutions that would make it easier for weaker currencies to be supported in their parity with the DM. The Belgians and the Dutch also advocated using a weighted basket currency as the denominator for the monetary system, so that domestic price competitiveness would be relative to aggregate – and not German – levels of inflation. The EMS was to be easier to maintain and more flexible to live within.

The domestic situation in both countries deteriorated throughout this period of international institutional experimentation. Although price inflation remained in check, labor costs continued to rise leading to unemployment, government deficits, and a deterioration of export performance. In turn such developments only exacerbated the domestic political situation. Conflict between labor and capital increased, elections became more volatile, and governing coalitions became more unstable than before. If there had ever been any illusion that the problems besetting Belgium and the Netherlands were primarily international in origin, it was soon dispelled by the crisis in domestic politics.

By the beginning of the 1980s, it became clear that Belgian and Dutch policy-makers could not resolve the tension between economic stability and the need for adjustment solely through the construction of multilateral arrangements at the European level. Indeed, the most pressing action required lay in the area of domestic reform. Without sacrificing their exchange rate preference, Belgium and the Netherlands had to find a new formula for maintaining competitiveness through relative price restraint. Part of the solution lay in changing the fiscal structures linking taxation to benefits – using a reduction in payroll taxes to lower relative labor costs. Part lay in improving the institutions for restraining the growth of prices and wages – in effect, recreating the discipline of the 1950s and 1960s. But efforts in these two areas could not succeed on their own. In addition, the governments of Belgium and the Netherlands had to find some way to shift resources from labor to industry, to encourage industry to engage in productive (and therefore revenue-raising) investment, and to stimulate the creation of jobs as a means of removing workers from already burgeoning unemployment rolls. The necessary agenda for political and economic adjustment was exceedingly complicated. However, the broad outline was known well in advance. The problem was finding the capacity for implementation.

II Implementing the obvious

The features initially lacking in Belgium and the Netherlands during the late 1970s and early 1980s were political determination and economic self-discipline. Politicians wavered in adopting difficult reform measures and both voters and trade unions refused to accept painful adjustments. In part this was due to the progressive weakening of ideology as a force for political mobilization. For much of the twentieth century, the two countries were "pillarized" into rigidly demarcated subnational political cultures with strong ideological identities – Catholicism, Protestantism, Socialism, or Liberalism. Within these ideological pillars, politicians benefited from a high degree of voter loyalty and even control. Until the 1960s, the political representatives of the main ideological pillars dominated the electorate, and together accounted for more than 90 percent of the votes cast at polling time. Such control extended beyond the electorate and deep into organized labor, which was ideologically pillarized along with the rest of society. As a result, politicians could take difficult decisions in the confidence that their policies would be followed without effective dissent or defection. Indeed it was the pillarization of Belgium and the Netherlands which made possible the successful price-incomes policies of the 1950s and 1960s (Steiner and Ertman, 2002). This is true both where labor adhered to the Christian democratic preference for collaboration across social classes and where former advocates of class conflict – as among the Socialists – admitted to the necessity of consensus (even in economic matters) for the survival of the political system as a whole.

However, deference to elite authority was much diminished by the 1970s as was the voter loyalty, which it engendered. Politicians could no longer rely on a strong ideological attachment within the electorate and instead had to depend upon the construction of more pluralistic coalitions of support. Broad evidence for this point can be found in the collapse of aggregate support for the traditional political parties of the pillarized system, which dropped to just over 70 percent of the votes cast in national elections. However it can also be seen in the tactical maneuvering of different political groups – all of which splintered in Belgium to reflect the emerging political significance of that country's linguistic cleavages, and some of which fused in the Netherlands in line with the more general decline in religious devotion. Along the way, politicians in both countries faltered in their commitment to reforms because of the risk that adjustment will translate into unpopularity or dissent. Voters and workers turned against reform measures because they entailed too much personal sacrifice. And, at the juxtaposition of these two sets of forces, both Belgium and the Netherlands (Andeweg and Galen, 2002) experienced prolonged periods of social unrest and government instability.

The change came in Belgium in the closing months of 1981. After a series of efforts to forge a stable reform coalition on the center-left, the party leadership of the centrist Christian Democrats accepted the inevitability of looking for support on the right. Wilfried Martens, who had led four unsuccessful coalitions in almost as many years, was allowed to negotiate a coalition with the right-wing Liberal parties. In those negotiations, Martens conceded some of the principal economic portfolios to his Liberal coalition partners. But he insisted that his coalition be allowed to govern the process of economic adjustment by decree and without consulting parliament on specific policy measures. As a result, Martens secured the passage of broad enabling legislation within weeks of his taking office.

Armed with decree powers, Martens could rule over the economy without consulting Parliament – but also without paying too much attention to his

Liberal coalition partners. So far as the broad strategy for adjustment was concerned, this capacity was unimportant. The Liberals agreed with the Christian Democrats (and indeed virtually all Belgian political elites) that wage growth had to be moderated, that expenditures had to be reined in, that taxes had to be reformed – particularly as a means of strengthening corporate balances – and that the exchange rate between the Belgian frank and DM had to be defended. The points of disagreement were tactical and not strategic. They related to concessions that the government had to make in order to ensure that the complex package of reforms actually came about. Hence Martens exercised his autonomy in negotiating a trade-off between wage moderation and fiscal reforms with the Christian Democratic trade unions. Martens also determined the scale and timing of realignments in the DM exchange rate with his counterparts in the EMS. On such matters, the Liberal coalition partners were either ignorant of what Martens was doing (as in his dealings with the trade unions) or they were ignored.

The 1982 realignment of the Belgian frank within the EMS illustrates the extent of Martens' autonomy. Although Belgium had been running consistent current account deficits for five years, the Liberals resisted any change in the exchange rate between the DM and the frank – arguing that such a move would raise the cost of inputs to production while at the same time undermining business confidence. The opposition Socialists also resisted devaluation because they were concerned that this would effectively lower real wages. Nevertheless Martens and his economic advisors concluded that some change was necessary. Martens first consulted with representatives of the International Monetary Fund (IMF), who agreed with his assessment of the need for realignment. Only then did he tell his coalition partners and his counterparts within the EMS. The Liberals changed their position and claimed that if a revision is truly necessary, then it should also be substantial something on the order of 14 percent. The other participants in the EMS, and particularly Germany, argued against a large devaluation out of concern that this would have a disruptive effect on the system as a whole. Martens pitted the two forces off against each other and emerged from his negotiations within the coalition and within the EMS with a compromise figure that differed only slightly from the devaluation recommended by his own economic advisors in the first place (Jones, 1995b, 176).

The autonomy that Martens displayed in his relations with the trade unions relied less on his negotiating prowess than it did on the fact that almost no one knew that such a relationship existed. The meetings between Martens and the Christian Democratic trade union leader, Jef Houthuys, took place in secret and involved only two close economic advisors. In these meetings, Martens and Houthuys traded off wage moderation against fiscal consolidation – setting targets for how much restraint the unions could be expected to deliver and how much expenditure reduction they could be expected to tolerate. One result of these meetings was to focus attention on the introduction of subsidies from general coffers for social welfare outlays that traditionally received their financing through payroll taxes. In this way, Martens could use fiscal outlays to reduce labor costs and so compensate for any shortfall in wage moderation.

The success of Martens' relationship with Houthuys lay in their shared experience as Christian Democrats and in the institutional linkages between the Christian Democratic Party and the Christian labor movement. The pillarization of Belgian society had weakened greatly by the early 1980s. Nevertheless, most Belgian elites – Martens and Houthuys included – had strong memories of being socialized in a more disciplined and orderly political environment. They also shared a common formation within a Christian Democratic ideology that stressed the importance of consensus-building and cooperation across class groups. Houthuys in particular believed that the trade unions should reassert their self-discipline in the interests of the whole of the economy. In this sense, the collusion between Martens and Houthuys was conservative rather than radical. By meeting in secret, they hoped to recreate the ordered outcomes of pillarized Belgium in the more competitive and fluid context of the early 1980s.

The situation in the Netherlands was significantly less favorable to a Christian Democratic revival (Jong and Pijnenburg, 1986). To begin with, the Dutch do not have a long tradition of "Christian Democracy." On the contrary, they have a history of conflict between Catholics and Protestants that dates back to the origins of the United Provinces in their rebellion against the Habsburgs. As a result, Protestants and Catholics formed separate pillars in the Netherlands, leaving the Socialists and the Liberals together in a somewhat less rigorously institutionalized "non-confessional" group. This organization of Dutch political life only lasted so long as ideology or religion provided the principal means for political mobilization. With the decline in ideological conviction and church attendance, the divisions between pillars began to weaken – to be replaced by less well-defined cleavages around income distribution and quality of life issues. Electoral volatility increased and competition between political groups intensified. Hence, the formation of the non-denominational Christian Democratic Appeal (CDA) in the late 1970s was not a sign that the divisions between Catholics and Protestants had ended but rather an admission that competition between the confessional parties and their secular counterparts had become more important.

For the major trade unions – and particularly the Catholics – the strategy for survival was different. Rather than joining with other confessional groups, the Catholic trade union federation chose to merge with the Socialists in an ecumenical but left-leaning Federation of Dutch Unions (FNV). The cost of forming this combined union lay in weakening the links between trade unions and political parties. The political party most closely affiliated with the FNV is the Party of Labor (PvdA) and not the CDA. By implication, the scope for secret collusion between the leadership of the FNV and a CDA prime minister was limited. Nevertheless, the experience of socialization within the trade unions and within the political parties was similar – particularly for those elites who came of age in the waning years of the pillarized system. Hence both FNV leader Wim Kok and CDA minister president (prime minister) Ruud Lubbers aspired to create a system for concerted wage restraint. The difficulty lay in finding the means to bring it about.

The solution lay in the threat of direct state intervention. Upon the formation of his center-right cabinet in 1982, Lubbers made it clear that any failure of the trade unions to exercise restraint in wage bargaining would result in government sponsored wage controls. Kok responded by initiating discussions with the leader of the Union of Dutch Employers (VNO), Chris Van Veen. Together, Kok and Van Veen hammered out a general agreement between labor and employers to moderate wage claims in exchange for the promise of job creation. At the time, this agreement was not widely regarded as a breakthrough. Organized labor had little choice but to accept wage restraint or face rising unemployment. Meanwhile the commitment on the employers' side was difficult if not impossible to enforce (or even to monitor). Nevertheless, the Wassenaar Accord – as the agreement between Kok and Van Veen came to be known – was sufficient to forestall government intervention and to usher in a prolonged period of moderated wage claims.

In his relations with the social partners, Lubbers offered carrots as well as sticks. His cabinet agreed to moderate fiscal austerity in compensation for wage restraint and to extend business subsidies – both direct and indirect – in return for the promise of productive investment. Lubbers remained committed to welfare state reform and to fiscal consolidation. However, he preferred to moderate the timing of his policies rather than to engender or exacerbate unnecessary conflict. This tactic was evident in the conflict between Lubbers and the trade unions over the reduction of public sector wages. The government's initial proposal was to cut wages by 3.5 percent with effect from 1984. After a series of strikes on the part of the unions, however, Lubbers agreed to lessen the cuts to 3 percent and to defer implementation until 1986 (Visser and Hemerijck, 1997, 100–1).

Not all of Lubbers' actions were so effective at forestalling conflict or improving economic conditions. During the 1983 currency realignment within the EMS, Lubbers' Finance Minister, Onno Rudding, refused to allow the guilder to revalue in line with the DM. His concern was that such a revaluation would hamper Dutch competitiveness and so neutralize the benefits of wage moderation. The new President of the Dutch National Bank, Wim Duisenberg, disagreed. Duisenberg acknowledged that the revaluation would hurt cost competitiveness and yet insisted that a failure to revalue would have an even greater impact on the ability of Dutch borrowers to access international capital markets. At the time, the Dutch Finance Minister had the power to overrule the central bank and so Rudding prevailed. Yet with hindsight Duisenberg was the more correct. The subsequent revaluation of the DM relative to the guilder sparked an immediate widening of the interest rate differentials between the Netherlands and Germany, which more than offset any advantages of the relative depreciation in Dutch exchange rates (Jones, 1998b, 153–4).

The experience of the 1983 realignment had a lasting impact on Dutch economic strategy – consolidating perceptions of the necessity of linking wage moderation with a hard currency policy. However, in the Netherlands – as in Belgium – such perceptions are more practical than ideological. Perceptions of the link between wage moderation and hard currency are also underwritten by the successes of the EMS. Where the snake system failed to hold together, the EMS succeeded in preventing countries such as France or even Italy from devaluing their currencies in order to offset the competitive advantages achieved by the Belgians and the Dutch. After 1983, EMS realignments became much less frequent than they had been during the first years of the system. After 1987, realignments virtually ceased. And in the hardening of the EMS, the Belgian and Dutch strategy for using wage moderation to gain export competitiveness was assured of success.

III Paying the price

Saying that their adjustment strategies were successful is not the same as saying that they were easy to implement or to accept. Neither secrecy and soft-pedaling at home nor strong institutions abroad could mitigate the impact that the adjustments of the early 1980s had on household incomes in Belgium and the Netherlands. By the same token, neither Wilfried Martens nor Ruud Lubbers lived under the illusion that fiscal austerity and wage moderation would be rewarded at the ballot box. Both leaders were practical in their politics as well as in their economics.

The challenge faced by Martens and Lubbers was to deflect popular discontent either away from the governing coalition or, where that was not possible, away from their own Christian Democratic parties. The fact that both governed from the center-right made this much easier than if they had governed from the center-left – for three reasons. First, because they could distance themselves from the actions of the trade unions in enforcing wage moderation. Second, because they could appeal to the economic self-interest of their core constituencies in the business sector. And third, because they could make their Liberal coalition partners responsible for any perceived "excesses" in the implementation of austerity measures.

Creating distance from the actions of the trade unions was clearly easier for Lubbers than for Martens. As already mentioned, the Dutch CDA does not have a direct trade union affiliation in the way that the Belgian Christian Democratic parties do. This explains why Martens was so eager to keep secret his meetings with the trade union leader, Jef Houthuys. However, the point to note is that the Christian labor movement in Belgium organizes only a fraction of the workforce. The remainder is organized by the socialist General Federation of Belgian Labor. These socialist unions initially resisted the implementation of wage restraint. However, lacking support from the Christian Democratic labor movement, the socialists recognized that they could not overturn government policy and that they risked being tarred with the responsibility for continuing economic failure. Hence the leadership of the socialist unions ended up providing tacit support for Martens' policy of wage moderation – and thereby accepting responsibility for their less aggressive behavior in wage bargaining.

The trade unions were not long in discovering their vulnerability. This explains why the Dutch unions were so eager to resist Lubbers' attempts to cut back on public sector pay in 1984. It also explains why the Belgian unions formed a common front – Christian Democrat and Socialist – to propose alternative measures for fiscal austerity in 1985 (Lecher and Neumann, 1994, 8). Such efforts were only palliative and not curative. The trade unions were responsible for moderating wage claims and their members were aware of this responsibility. As a result, Dutch trade union density dropped precipitously during the 1980s as workers saw little utility in paying their membership dues. The Belgian trade unions were more organizationally robust if only because they provided more services. Not only are the unions responsible for dispersing unemployment benefits, but they also provide representation on health and safety councils and on works councils within firms. In addition, the Belgian unions benefited in that they were not so publicly identified with government policy, as were the Dutch unions via the Wassenaar accord. Yet when the full complicity of the Belgian Christian Democratic unions was revealed in the 1991 publication of a deathbed interview with Jef Houthuys, the effect was a minor political crisis and a prolonged period of labor unrest (Jones, 1995b).

While organized labor bore some of the burden of implementing wage restraint, business interests clearly benefited from the reduction in real labor costs. These benefits were not restricted to manufacturing for export and indeed spread through the business sector and into non-traded services. If anything, the service sector benefited disproportionately. Not only did the service industries gain from the reduction in labor costs (which count for a much greater percentage of production costs in services than in manufacturing) but they also benefited from the lower cost of imports implied by the hard currency policy. As a result, profitability and employment recovered more quickly in the service sector than in manufacturing. Moreover, much of this service sector is constituted by small firms, which traditionally have tended to support the Christian Democrats in both countries. The argument here is not that the Christian Democrats were able to gain constituents through this combination of influences. Rather it is that they were able to contain the losses that they otherwise might expect to face given the depth of the austerity that they implemented.

The illustration of this claim can be found in the electoral contests that were fought in 1985 in Belgium and 1986 in the Netherlands. These elections also reveal the extent to which the Christian Democrats succeeded in displacing opposition to their adjustment programs onto their Liberal coalition partners. The pattern of events is much the same in both countries. Although there were clear tensions within the center-right coalitions, the Christian Democrats and the Liberals made the unusual choice to declare their intention to form a government before the election took place. This commitment was more important for the Liberals than for the Christian Democrats – without whom it would be nearly impossible to form a government. Hence the commitment signaled that the process of adjustment would continue in any event. The only question facing the voters, then, was who would map the strategy. In both cases, the polling outcome displayed a shift in support from the Liberals to the Christian Democrats. The Belgian Christian Democrats picked up six seats from their Liberal coalition partners, primarily in the Flemish speaking north of the country. Meanwhile, the Dutch CDA took nine seats from the Liberals.

The continuation of center-right coalitions into the latter part of the 1980s resulted in a deepening of austerity measures in both countries. However, the formula for deflecting popular discontent away from the government and away from the Christian Democrats soon ran its course. Unhappy with their decline in electoral support – particularly in relation to their coalition partners – the Liberals in both countries became much less willing either to be ignored or to shoulder the blame for government policy. Meanwhile, the left-wing opposition began to campaign for a change in the adjustment strategy, which would build upon the achievements made while at the same time moderating the impact of policy on household incomes. The governing coalitions moved to the right and the opposition moved to the center (Smits, 1986; Wolinetz, 1990).

This phase of the adjustment process closes toward the end of the 1980s as Martens and Lubbers form coalitions on the center-left. In both cases, their center-right coalitions collapsed early as a result of conflict between the Christian Democrats and the Liberals. For Martens, this shift occurs in 1987 and coincides with a loss of support for the Christian Democrats (at least in Flanders). For Lubbers, the shift to the center-left takes place in 1989 and results in modest gains for the CDA. A majority on the center-right was nevertheless possible in both countries and the desire to proceed with austerity measures remained apparent. What had changed was the need to engineer the process of adjustment from the center-right. By the end of the 1980s, commitment to the adjustment process was as much a part of the economic consensus as was commitment to fixed exchange rates. As a result, Martens and Lubbers could continue on the center-left with policies that less than a decade earlier could only be initiated on the center-right.

IV Ideology, necessity, and repetition

By the 1990s, the adjustment strategies pursued by Martens and Lubbers had become something of a way of life in Belgium and the Netherlands. Indeed, the Dutch version became celebrated as a "model" for economic success. The point to note, however, is that these strategies became embedded in the Low Countries not as an expression of ideology but rather because of their lack of precise ideological content. The shift to the center-left at the end of the 1980s signaled a rejection of "liberalism" but an acceptance of the strategies giving rise to neo-liberal outcomes – such as a shift in the distribution of income from labor to capital and a retreat of the state from the market.

The neo-liberal outcomes were accepted not because they were neo-liberal but because they were necessary. Returning to the data provided in Table 11.1, neither Belgium nor the Netherlands could have survived a continuation of those trends in income distribution, corporate profitability, and unemployment that were initiated in the 1970s. They also could not have survived the inexorable expansion of the public sector and the uncontrollable escalation of public debts that these trends implied. Some change was necessary and few strategies were available.

The choice of strategy was institutionally determined. The hegemonic position of the Christian Democratic Parties in both countries set the agency. The encompassing nature of the trade unions provided the instrument. And the EMS provided the context. The question now is whether these institutions remain available. Since the 1980s, the Christian Democrats have fallen out of power in both countries. Whether or not they return to power – as they did during the May 2002 elections in the Netherlands (Jones, 2002) – their hegemonic position is now clearly in doubt. This means that the Christian Democrats are going to be less likely to take risks in the future on the scale that leaders such as Martens and Lubbers were willing to countenance in the past. The trade unions have also changed their position both in terms of who they represent and how they choose to work with government. The desire for cooperation remains but the capacity to do so effectively has been weakened.

Finally, the broader economic context has changed in Europe. The EMS has evolved into an economic and monetary union (EMU) with ambiguous implications. On the one hand Belgium and the Netherlands need no longer concern themselves with a strong currency policy. On the other hand, both countries must now consider more carefully the effects of their own strategies on their European partners. They must also consider how the behavior of other European countries will affect monetary conditions across EMU as a whole. The contrast between economic and fiscal performance in the Low Countries – which have abided by the European Union's Stability and Growth Pact – and in Germany – which has not – suggests a new raft of challenges to be faced in the future. Given these changes in both capacity and context, it is unlikely that any similar pattern of adjustment can be repeated in the near future (Jones, 1995a).

Acknowledgement

This chapter is based on Jones *Small States*. I would like to thank Bernie Moss for encouraging me to participate in this project. I would also like to thank the University Association for Contemporary European Studies and the Centre for the Study of European Governance at the University of Nottingham for supporting a seminar at which an earlier version of this chapter was discussed. The usual disclaimer applies.

12
Italy's Long Road to Austerity and the Paradoxes of Communism

Tobias Abse

The story of Italy's evolution toward neo-liberalism is a long and complex one; there is no neat linear narrative comparable to the British one in which 1976 was clearly the turning point, even if the monetarist crusade gathered pace under Thatcher after 1979. Whilst the Italian turn toward neo-liberalism was bound up with the process of European integration, particularly after 1992, the external constraint was by no means the only factor pushing in the direction of monetarism or austerity. The beginnings of a turn to neo-liberalism can be traced back to the mid-1970s and have to be seen in the context of the domestic class struggle, even if external pressures, particularly from West Germany, played their part. Nonetheless, even if the 1980s were a decade full of defeats for the Italian labor movement, the full implementation of a neo-liberal program, including the relatively rapid privatization of the bulk of the vast array of enterprises associated with the massive state holding company IRI, created by Mussolini in 1933 and only officially dissolved in 2000, was only possible after the collapse of the Christian Democratic regime in 1992–93. This collapse, which was in part precipitated by Maastricht, but which also has to be linked at the international level with the end of the Cold War, and which cannot be divorced from domestic factors such as North/South divisions, discredited the whole political elite and decisively shifted the balance of forces in favor of the neo-liberal project, to the extent that two of the prime ministers of the last decade have been bankers by profession – Ciampi and Dini – and another two technocratic professors – Amato and Prodi.

It could be argued that the purely intellectual climate in Italy always favored neo-liberalism; the massive obstacles to it had arisen for essentially practical and pragmatic reasons. Whilst policies that could, in broad terms, be categorized as Keynesian were adopted in Italy during the long post-war boom, Keynesianism was never hegemonic intellectually. Italy had a tradition of doctrinaire economic liberalism – *liberismo* as the Italians called it – that preceded the establishment of the European Economic Community. This tradition, which became dominant at the Bank of Italy after 1945, could stress its anti-fascist credentials in the post-war world, which meant that it was not automatically seen as a discredited remnant of the pre-war order in the way monetarism was in some other European countries before the mid-1970s.

The first phase of monetarist austerity came during the 1944–47 era of national unity governments, when hostility toward the statist and interventionist heritage of fascism – a regime which during the inter-war period had created, through IRI, the largest state sector outside the Soviet Union – gave hard-line monetarists like Einaudi a chance to push their deflationary recipes in the years before Christian Democracy had really consolidated itself. Whilst Catholic social teaching, from Leo XIII's *Rerum Novarum* encyclical onwards, had always had reservations about economic liberalism, it is worth pointing out that the Christian Democrat leader who seemed most enthusiastic about state intervention and least concerned with keeping on good terms with the giants of private industry was the former fascist intellectual Amintore Fanfani.

It also needs to be stressed that the PCI itself, as distinct from the CGIL trade union confederation in which it had influence, only really turned to Keynesianism in 1986, when the implosion of the Euro-communist project and the subsequent desire to find a new reference point in the Western European left led it to gravitate toward ideas current in the SPD, theorized in Peter Glotz's *Manifesto for a New European Left*; throughout most of the post-war period, the PCI oscillated between catastrophic predictions of capitalism's imminent collapse and the enthusiastic endorsement of gruesome monetarist policies in the name of an allegedly supra-class national interest as in 1944–47 and 1976–79. This miserable heritage may explain the speed of the abject capitulation to neo-liberalism of the PDS/DS over the last decade, a capitulation to which the man who started off as a self-styled traditionalist – D'Alema – proved no more immune than the self-conscious emulator of Blair, Veltroni.

I think it is simplistic to assume that the bankers, the industrialists, and the politicians linked to these economic categories had a consistent and unified strategy over the last quarter of a century, which, whether, intentionally or not, is the impression given to us by Leila Simona Talani's (2000) work about Italy and European monetary integration. In the Italian case it is even more difficult than usual to give purely economic explanations for economic policy. The whole edifice of Christian Democratic power that dominated Italy between 1948 and 1992/93 was fundamentally incompatible with a rigorous neo-liberalism, and even the neo-liberal rhetoric of Ciriaco De Mita, who presented himself as the advocate of a new course for the party after 1983, should be taken with far more than just a pinch of salt; he was a politician whose brother was at the heart of a scandal over the misappropriation of Campanian earthquake money. Christian Democracy, in so far as it was more than just political Catholicism that defended the Church's stance over issues like divorce and abortion, was based on anti-communism, not monetarism. Christian democracy aimed to create a social bloc strong enough to resist the advance of a Communist-dominated left which had been seen as a very serious threat in both Rome and Washington in April 1948. The two parties which espoused monetarism and, at different times, had the closest links with the industrialists, the Liberals and the Republicans, were never able to create such a social bloc.

Christian Democracy's mass base, particularly in the South of Italy, was created in large part by the clientelistic and frequently corrupt use of state resources, so the party tended to favor state spending, even if that spending was not always well-directed and some of it ended up as a subsidy to organized crime in regions such as Sicily, Campania, and Calabria. Christian Democrat clientelism meant that the Giolittian and Fascist tradition of a bloated and inefficient state bureaucracy, largely staffed by political appointees, was perpetuated into the post-war era. Moreover, self-employed groups ranging from artisans and shopkeepers to lawyers and dentists formed a central part of Christian Democracy's electorate, so the party was prone to indulgence toward their outrageous tax evasion.[1] Whilst periodic attempts were made to balance Italy's budgets by increasing the tax burden on the working class and the public sector middle class, [2] the Christian Democrats were far too shrewd as politicians to push this strategy to the limit and risk losing any support they had amongst wage and salary earners, so an increasing gap between revenue and expenditure was, in practice, inherent in the system on which this "catch-all" populist party depended for its own survival.

If the basic mechanisms of Christian Democrat consensus militated against rigorous neo-liberalism, the astonishing upsurge in class struggle in the late 1960s could only be bought off by further concessions. The Italian upheavals of 1967–69, first among students and then, more importantly, among workers, had a far deeper and longer-term impact on Italy than comparable militancy elsewhere in Europe; FIAT only regained full control over its factories in Turin in 1979–80. Whilst the initial revolt was outside the control of the trade union leaders and often directed against them as well as against the bosses, the union leaders demonstrated considerable flexibility in absorbing this discontent within modified union structures based on factory councils that incorporated many of the militants of the Hot Autumn of 1969 and provided the impetus behind the establishment of the *Federazione Unitaria* CGIL-CISL-UIL, in 1972, a halfway house toward full unity between the labor confederations, a goal that seemed possible until the splits of the 1980s.

The unions then used their newfound power to bargain with the state and the employers, and increased their relative autonomy from the political parties, which had treated the three rival confederations – CGIL, CISL, and UIL – as transmission belts during the Cold War. Suffice it to say that the *Statuto dei Lavoratori* of 1970 was the most pro-trade union industrial relations act to be passed anywhere in Europe and that the *scala mobile* – a system of wage indexation linked to inflation and first introduced in 1945–46 – was enormously strengthened in 1975, protecting the value of real wages to an extent unparalleled in any advanced capitalist country. The appeal of collective action spread far beyond the big northern factories that had been the storm centers of the Hot Autumn; union density rates peaked at 49 percent in 1978, 18.2 percent up on 1969.

The late 1970s saw the beginnings of a turn to neo-liberalism and a gradual decline in the power of what had been the strongest labor movement in Western Europe. Rather paradoxically, the decline began when the electoral strength of the Communists was at its highest point. Despite their rather ambivalent attitude toward the upheavals of the late 1960s and early 1970s, the PCI, rather than the far-left groups like *Avanguardia Operaia, Il Manifesto* or *Lotta Continua*, had been the main electoral beneficiary of the changes in Italian society. The regional elections of 1975 – the first in which 18–21-year-olds could vote – had seen the PCI reach 32.4 percent, 5 percent more than in the 1972 general election, allowing them to add Piedmont and Liguria to their strongholds in the traditionally red regions of Emilia-Romagna, Tuscany, and Umbria. The general election of June 1976 saw a further jump in the PCI vote, to 34.4 percent, which seemed to bring the party to the threshold of power, even if the Communists, contrary to some predictions, failed to overtake the DC, which remained the first party at 38.7 percent.

The PCI leader Enrico Berlinguer, far from seeking to build a left majority with the Socialists and minor left groups, which was an arithmetical possibility, was totally committed to an Historic Compromise with Christian Democracy, a strategy that he had first elaborated in 1973, allegedly in response to the Chilean Coup. In reality this strategy drew on the conception of a "new majority" first put forward by Togliatti in the years immediately before his death in 1964, and was a logical development of the earlier national unity line that Togliatti had advocated in 1944–47 and, in broad terms, of the pre-war Popular Front strategy first developed by Stalin, Togliatti and Dimitrov in 1934–35, all of which had sought to avoid an outright counter-position between the representatives of labor and the representatives of capital. The PCI hungered after cabinet office in a broad-based government involving the DC, the Socialists, and others.

The DC was all too aware that a parliamentary majority could not be constructed against, and without, the PCI, because the DC's traditional allies among the minor parties of the Center and Center-Right (Liberals, Republicans, Social Democrats), squeezed by the political polarization of 1975–76, no longer had sufficient numbers in parliament to form a viable coalition, whilst the Socialist Party was not prepared to back the DC in introducing unpopular austerity measures if the price to be paid for such a partnership was further inroads into their vote by a PCI enjoying the luxury of opposition, as it had done during the first Center Left government of

1964–68. The DC, faced with vociferous American objections to Communist participation in the Italian government, probably never envisaged more than an arrangement allowing the PCI to give external support to a DC government, although some claim that, at the time of his kidnapping by the Red Brigades in 1978, Moro was seriously considering making an offer of ministerial posts to the PCI as a means of absorbing them into the system in exactly the same way as he had absorbed the Socialists in 1964. In any event, the whole period of National Solidarity between 1976 and 1979, during which the Communists gave parliamentary backing to a Christian Democrat government, was characterized by unremitting austerity.

It needs to be underlined that this austerity was not imposed by a frontal assault on organized labor, which would have been a very risky course at this stage, but came about with the consent of the leaders of the labor movement. As Berlinguer himself put it on January 30, 1977, "The old ruling classes and the old political personnel know that by now they are no longer able to *impose* sacrifices on the working class and Italian workers; today *they must ask*, and *they do ask*, for sacrifices" (cited in Golden, 1988, 69). Large sections of the Communist rank and file, especially in industrial cities like Turin, where the party's social composition was predominantly proletarian had no enthusiasm for austerity and doubts about the Historic Compromise, but opposition to Berlinguer had been marginalized at the national leadership level. Ingrao, the leader of the party's left wing, who had been more open to the new social movements than Berlinguer or Amendola, had already been defeated at two party congresses in January 1966 and January 1969 before being further weakened by the expulsion of his best-known followers in November 1969 over their involvement in the dissident journal *Il Manifesto*. The PCI as a party and Luciano Lama, the PCI leader of the largest trade union confederation, the CGIL, played an indispensable role in the erosion of the working class gains of the previous decade; indeed in 1977 Lama, ideologically convinced of the merits of the Historic Compromise strategy, was much less responsive to working class discontent with austerity than his more pragmatic and opportunist rivals in the non-Communist CISL and UIL.

The DC lost little time in exploiting the indirect support from the PCI they had obtained from August 1976, introducing a package of classic deflationary measures in October 1976. The interest rate was pushed up by 3.4 percent to discourage borrowing, and a large number of government controlled prices – petrol, heating, oil, gas, tobacco, postal charges, and rail fares – were raised, hitting the poorest groups hardest. In 1977 the three trade union confederations signed an important cost-of-labor agreement with the employers' federation *Confindustria* in which the unions agreed to a revision of seniority bonuses and severance pay, the abolition of seven paid holidays, factory-level bargaining over the annual calendar, greater flexibility of shift work, more use of overtime, more flexibility of labor within plants and firms and greater control of absenteeism.

This was the first time the unions had made concessions on any of these issues since the Hot Autumn. The confederations, faced with a deteriorating economic situation and intense political pressure, declared their "willingness to coordinate factory and sectoral bargaining activities, in order to guarantee full coherence with the primary objectives of the fight against inflation and the defense of the lira, through the containment of the global cost of labor dynamic and the increase of productivity, the growth of employment and a gradual policy of productive re-conversion." In case there was any doubt about their commitment to some degree of wage restraint, they added "generalised demands for wage increases though articulated bargaining are not proposed" (cited in *id.*, 1988, 72).

In 1979, the OECD retrospectively acknowledged that this agreement led to "an appreciable slowdown in wage costs" and "remarkable improvements" in the Italian economy in 1978, including a reversal of the balance of payments crisis, a temporary halving of the inflation rate, an expansion of the GDP, and a recovery of investments. However, the unions had not signed the agreement with any enthusiasm – their offer "to coordinate factory and category bargaining" was a defensive reaction to a government threat to freeze factory bargaining altogether, which was originally a precondition of the IMF loan being negotiated at the time, and some of the other concessions were designed to avoid any outright attack on the 1975 wage indexation agreement. Whilst most trade union leaders realized that they had little alternative in the short term to curbing wage demands, quite a number, especially in the *Federazione Lavoratori Metalmeccanici* (FLM), did not want to permanently abandon the principle of using plant-level bargaining as a supplement to any national agreement.

The formalization of the neo-corporatist strategy implicit in the 1977 agreement would have been impossible without Lama's enthusiastic cooperation. In his notorious interview with the bourgeois daily *La Repubblica* on January 24, 1978, Lama's views were set out with much greater clarity than would have been possible in any Communist or trade union publication; "The improvement of conditions for the employed workforce must take second place ... since 1969, the union has placed its bets on the rigidity of the labour force ... [but] we have now realised that an economic system cannot tolerate independent variables ... [T]he workers and their unions have maintained that wages were an independent variable ... [But] this was nonsense, because in an open economy all variables are dependent on each other" (cited in *id.*, 1988, 95). It has to be underlined that this was no personal outburst by a maverick; Lama was putting the official PCI line.

This became apparent in March when a leading figure on the PCI's right wing, Giorgio Napolitano, announced that "We cannot ignore the weight that the related increase of wages and pensions has assumed, and the effect that a containment of the wage dynamic can have for increasing the margin of investment" (cited in *id.*, 1988, 69–70). Whilst the EUR line of austerity was passed by an enormous majority with only 12 dissident votes[3] and 103 abstentions, the final declaration was more ambiguous than Lama would have liked because of the internal opposition of the FLM, Italy's most powerful industrial union, which prevented the kind of explicit endorsement of incomes policy for which Lama was pressing. Nonetheless, this period had seen the trade union leadership being seduced into tripartite negotiations with the employers and the state, being granted the illusion of an important role in determining government policy on employment and investment in return for material concessions at their members' expense.

By 1979, it was plain that the workers had gained very little beyond some decrease in the rate of inflation; contrary to the politicians' promises, unemployment did not diminish and little was done for the South. As Ginsborg points out, the much-heralded law on industrial re-conversion of August 1977 proved to be a fiasco (Ginsborg, 1990, 389). The trade unionists' approval of the EUR document had been premised on the mistaken assumption that the PCI was about to be given cabinet posts, which would have enabled it to fight for union objectives inside the government, and some union leaders later privately regretted their willingness to go along with it (Golden, 1988, 78).

Golden's claim that the opposition of "Communist union dissidents" to austerity "probably cost their party the chance to obtain power" (Golden, 1988, 244) is unconvincing. The world view of a clerical politician like Andreotti bore no resemblance to that of the professional economist Harold Wilson, or the renegade former trade union official James Callaghan, even if the contemporary British situation had ample resonance for the militant trade unionists of the FLM who forced Lama to reject the notion of a "social contract" (Golden, 1988, 94) and the acceptance of a formal incomes policy was not central to DC decision-making in this period. The PCI and the trade unions had by late 1978 fulfilled the DC's basic requirements of imposing a measure of austerity on the working class; the DC discarded the PCI like the proverbial squeezed lemon because it had carried out its allotted task and was now superfluous, not because the terms of the EUR agreement were insufficiently watertight – Golden seems to forget that for the DC ambiguous verbal formulations were second nature.

Whilst Italy's entry into the Exchange Rate Mechanism (ERM) in 1979 was another tactic to weaken organized labor, Talani probably overemphasizes its importance in shifting the balance of class forces, given the ample repertoire of more domestic expedients that had been used to roll back workers' gains in 1977–78. Nonetheless, since Italy's immediate participation in the EMS made little economic sense when domestic inflation was at 20 percent, it seems more likely that, as Simonazzi and Vianello (2002, 109) argue, the Christian Democrats were using it against the Communists, who felt obliged to protest at its likely consequences for organized labor, hastening the end of the National Solidarity government with which the Christian Democrats had become increasingly weary. Talani is right to underline that the leading Italian industrialists De Benedetti (of Olivetti), Agnelli, and Pirelli were the most active supporters of Italian entry. Agnelli's statement to the British Foreign Trade Convention in London in mid-November 1978 that the weaker nations were "to accept fewer jobs for their workers and less popularity for their governments, as the price for entering a more stable world" (cited in Talani, 2000) gives a clear indication of the motives behind his support.

Although by January 1979 Andreotti may have been anxious to provoke a split with the PCI on an issue where he could present himself as the defender of a wider national interest against a narrow sectional one, it is equally probable, in view of his subsequent record on European affairs in the early 1990s, that his initial enthusiasm for Italy's entry owed at least as much to considerations of national prestige. In February 1973, Italy had no choice but to leave the European currency "snake" and Ginsborg argues that by 1975 Italy's high inflation and considerable debts with the IMF and West Germany had left her "on the outer edge of Europe" (Ginsborg, 2001, 243). The Bank of Italy played a leading role in the negotiations, which led to the establishment of a two-band system for the new EMS. The first of these bands permitted currencies a very limited degree of fluctuation, whilst the second one, into which the lira was inserted, would allow much more leeway. Given the way Agnelli had vigorously rejected such flexibility and delighted in the harsh conditions to which he assumed Italy would be subjected, Talani's thesis about the total agreement between Italian bankers and Italian industrialists over Italy's entry into the ERM seem a bit hyperbolic, however close the relationship between the government and the central bank may have been.

Autumn 1979 saw further indications of Agnelli's eagerness to inflict a blow against his workers. Sixty one carefully selected militants were sacked from the Turin FIAT plants, allegedly because of links with terrorism. One of the actions to which the company objected was the blocking of factory gates during the 1979 contract dispute. This was neither more nor less illegal than anything done in the FIAT plants during the industrial disputes since 1969. The PCI did nothing to defend the 61 against what was clearly political victimization, and the elderly leader of the PCI's right wing, Amendola, wrote an article declaring that the party and the unions had to take a much clearer and more vigorous stand against all forms of violent struggle, as well as advocating the limitation of the *scala mobile* and a reduction in absenteeism.

However, this episode was just a preliminary skirmish. The epoch that had begun with the Hot Autumn of 1969 really ended in the autumn of 1980. In September, FIAT announced that it was going to sack 14,000 workers. The metalworkers' union FLM responded by calling an indefinite stoppage which in fact lasted for 35 days. This was the longest strike in a major Italian industry since Liberation. The struggle began well. The PCI declared its sympathy and Berlinguer went to the factory gates, even offering to support an occupation.[4] Workers from other cities joined the picket lines and money poured into the strike fund. Secondary industrial action, albeit of a symbolic kind, was mounted with a one-day general strike in Piedmont and a one-day national strike of the FLM. Then on October 14, 1980, thirty to forty thousand FIAT supervisors, guards, technicians, and office workers marched through the center of Turin claiming that the FLM did not represent them. A few hundred production workers, mainly Piedmontese, joined in. That night the union surrendered to FIAT, signing an agreement which allowed the company to lay off 23,000 workers rather than the original 14,000. FIAT used its victory with complete ruthlessness. The 23,000 people expelled from the plants were not picked at random; among them were a disproportionate number of political militants, women, young people, and disabled workers, all categories held to be in some way deviant. For the survivors, the atmosphere in the plants changed radically, FIAT lost only one million work-hours in 1981, compared with 13.5 million the previous year. Absenteeism, which had ranged between 14 percent and 18 percent before the strike, fell to between 3 percent and 5 percent, well below the average Japanese rate of about 8 percent.

The next milestone in Italy's long march toward neo-liberalism was the renewed attack on the *scala mobile*. In June 1982, Confindustria announced that it was unilaterally canceling the *scala mobile* as of January 1983. Prolonged negotiations followed, culminating in a cost-of-labor accord signed by the unions, employers and government which cut protection against inflation and allowed firms to increase labor flexibility – two major victories for the employers' association. Nonetheless, the unions tied these concessions to government promises of tax reform and family allowances, which were designed to compensate the workers for drops in real wages. The leaders of the confederations would have settled for less, but the more militant FLM put a brake on the tripartite bargaining, which it would have liked to prevent altogether, and only grudgingly accepted because of Confindustria's absolute refusal to negotiate on national labor contracts in individual industries until a general settlement had been reached (Golden, 1988, 97–8).

The harsh economic climate had some impact on the June 1983 general election result, triggering a decline in the DC vote and a rise in the PSI vote, which paved the way for Craxi to assume the premiership. Craxi then launched the most sustained attack on working-class organization and living standards that Italy had seen for 20 years. The new government gave absolute priority to the battle against inflation. Together Craxi and Confindustria demanded a second and deeper round of cuts in the *scala mobile*. The trade union confederations could not agree on a negotiating position, each going its own way. Craxi rapidly issued a government decree slashing indexation by 38 percent. The UIL, CISL and Socialists in the CGIL accepted it; only the Communists and the far left in the CGIL were opposed to it. But widespread resistance surged up from below. Weeks of strikes, mass demonstrations, and workers' assemblies culminated in a rally of 700,000 people in Rome in March 1984.

The PCI, fearful of *Democrazia Proletaria* (DP), which had played a considerable role in transforming popular anger into organized resistance and seemed to be making inroads into the factory councils at the PCI's expense, was forced to back the mass movement and to join DP in talking out Craxi's first *scala mobile* decree in parliament. However, the PCI was at least equally responsive to pressure from its right. Lama was anxious to avoid a split with his Socialist colleagues in the CGIL, so the party allowed Craxi's second decree cutting the *scala mobile* to pass in parliament, claiming that to have blocked it for months was already a great victory for the workers and the time had come to reach a deal. Unimpressed by the PCI's retreat, DP proceeded to collect signatures for a referendum on the *scala mobile*. The PCI would have liked to avoid this referendum, but rank and file pressure made a compromise with Craxi impossible and in June 1985 the referendum was duly held. This bid to protect wage indexation was lost, albeit relatively narrowly, by 54.4 percent to 45.6 percent. Never again was the PCI to show even this degree of determination in defense of organized labor.

The mid-1980s saw a new kind of consumer boom in Italy as GDP rose by over 2.5 percent a year between 1983 and 1987, compared with virtual stagnation between 1979 and 1983. Treasury minister Goria even claimed Italy had overtaken Britain in 1987 (Ginsborg, 1990, 408). This boom was associated with a liberalization of the Milan stock exchange and a growth in financial speculation. The new-found prosperity of the *ceti rampanti* (yuppies) centered on services rather than industry with the growth of private television, advertising, and public relations. This was the period in which Berlusconi, described by Ginsborg as "an intimate friend of Bettino Craxi" (Ginsborg, 2001, 155), established his near monopoly over commercial television. Craxi defended Berlusconi against the magistrates, who blacked out his television stations in some regions on the grounds that the constitutional court in 1976 had permitted local but not national commercial broadcasts. Craxi's concern about his friend reached its culmination when on a Saturday, October 20, 1984, he issued what subsequently proved to be an unconstitutional decree law allowing Berlusconi to continue broadcasting. Whilst the Craxi years saw inflation fall from 10.8 percent to 4.7 percent, in other respects this administration was not noted for monetarist virtue. The annual government-spending deficit remained very high, only declining from 14.3 percent to 11.6 percent, and public debt spiraled right out of control, leaping from an already high 72 percent of GDP to an astonishing 93 percent (Ginsborg, 2001, 153).

Craxi was arguably more consistently willing to promote neo-liberal ideas at a European than at a national level. He can be held partly responsible for the Single European Act because of the role he played as President of the Council of Europe in Milan in June 1985. Craxi overrode Mrs Thatcher by putting Chancellor Kohl's proposal for an intergovernmental conference to revise the founding treaty of the community to a majority vote. The conference led to the drafting of the Single European Act, which took effect on July 1, 1987, hastening Europe's integration on neo-liberal lines.

The widespread popular interpretation of the 1989–92 period as one in which the CAF (Craxi-Andreotti-Forlani), having ousted the self-proclaimed reformer Ciriaco de Mita, presided over an immobile *ancien regime*, needs some qualification. Alongside the profligate expenditure and corruption usually associated with the era, the neo-liberal offensive continued in some spheres and made a considerable contribution to the system's self-destruction via Maastricht. Italy's promotion of neo-liberalism in Europe did not come to an end with the Socialist premiership (Ginsborg, 2001, 246–8). In January 1990, Andreotti decided to move the lira into the narrow band of currencies in the European Monetary System. This was a major gamble; Andreotti must have been aware of the poor state of Italian public finances and the possible danger to Italian exports posed by a less favorable rate of exchange. In May 1990, Italy introduced free short-term movement of capital, in line with the agreement on the completion of the single market. Italy was one of the last of the EC countries to adopt this standard neo-liberal position, even if previous Italian capital controls had never prevented large-scale illegal movement out of Italy, which was a marked feature of the crises of the mid-1970s. This removal of controls on capital intensified the risk involved in moving the lira into the narrow band of the EMS. However, such measures gave Italy more credibility with the Community and this enabled her to play a larger role on the international stage, which appealed to both Andreotti and his flamboyant foreign minister De Michelis.

The Italian Presidency in the latter half of 1990 coincided with a crucial phase in the history of European integration. Despite British opposition, Andreotti persuaded the European Council that Stage 2 of Economic and Monetary Union could start in January 1994. Andreotti built on this success, playing an important part in the process that led to the agreement at Maastricht on December 9–10, 1991 and the subsequent signing of the Maastricht Treaty on February 7, 1992. The Maastricht Treaty proved a trap for Italy, setting requirements that appeared so severe that Italy was unlikely to meet them. One has to assume that Italian negotiators placed all their hopes in a modification of the wording of the final draft which stated that an annual public deficit of more than 3 percent of GDP and a debt to GDP rate of more than 60 percent might not be judged "excessive" if they were seen to be declining sufficiently fast toward the required level (Ginsborg, 2001, 248). It is worth underlining that in 1992 Italy's debt reached 109 percent of GDP and comprised a third of the total government debt owed within the entire European Community, whilst the annual public deficit reached 10 percent of GDP.

The neo-liberal initiatives in relation to Europe were mirrored at home. A number of neo-liberal measures were introduced during the period between 1989 and 1992 when Carli, an ardent neo-liberal who had been a long-serving

Governor of the Bank of Italy in the 1960s and 1970s, was minister for the Treasury (Ginsborg, 2001, 165). These included the Amato Law (July 30, 1990), which allowed public sector banks to change their legal status into joint stock companies, the anti-trust law of 1990, and a law on insider trading. Moreover, a 1991 law granted the Bank of Italy full autonomy from the Treasury to fix interest rates, thus depriving the Italian government of control over a major part of macroeconomic policy. Nonetheless, the career politicians set certain limits to the project of the neo-liberal ideologues determined to roll back the frontiers of the state, precisely because their own clientelistic and corrupt use of the public sector made them dependent on the existence of a public sector, albeit an inefficient and flawed one. Carli might have dreamt of widespread privatizations and neo-liberal reforms of health and pensions, seeing privatization as "the key to everything," but Andreotti knew this would erode the consensus on which the DC had depended since 1948 (Ginsborg, 2001, 69, 223).

The year 1992 was crucial in Italy's turn toward neo-liberalism. The general election of April 1992 saw the DC fall below 30 percent for the first time – 29.7 percent to be exact – and gave 8.7 percent of the vote to the Northern League, whose economic policy was rabidly neo-liberal, favoring tax cuts, reductions in welfare spending and privatization of state-owned firms. Before embarking on a discussion of the impact of Italy's enforced exit from the EMS in September, reference will be made to the final liquidation of the *scala mobile* in July. Amato, the new prime minister, who had devised plans to reduce the deficit by 3000 billion lire – through cutting spending and reducing taxation – within a week of taking office, rapidly discovered that even this was not enough to ease the pressure on the lira in the wake of the Maastricht Treaty, and therefore decided to increase pressure on the trade unions to consent to the abolition of wage indexation in order to save the lira (Ginsborg, 2001, 265).

Whether or not Talani (2000, esp. 174) is right that by this stage the bankers and industrialists had decided in favor of devaluation in order to increase the competitiveness of Italy's industries and counteract the dramatic fall in profits that had hit that sector between 1988 and 1992, and only sought to postpone it until they had tricked the trade unions into accepting the destruction of the one guarantee that would have safeguarded their members' wages against the inflationary effects of devaluation, it is quite clear that organized labor gained nothing from these tripartite negotiations, which gave leading bureaucrats apparent prestige at the expense of their members' living standards. The decision of Trentin, the CGIL leader, to accept the liquidation of the *scala mobile* through the agreement of July 31, 1992 cannot be regarded as anything other than selling the pass without a fight, as many of his rank and file felt at the time.

September 1992 was a disastrous month for the lira. On Friday September 11, the Bundesbank refused to continue to defend the lira against speculation, having bought 24 billion DM worth of lire since Monday September 7, and told the Italians to devalue. The initial 7 percent devaluation proved insufficient and, when the pound collapsed on September 16, 1992, the lira fell alongside it and Italy was forced to exit from the European Monetary System along with Britain. On September 11, Amato had tried, albeit unsuccessfully, to suggest a joint strategy to British Prime Minister John Major, hoping to devalue but stay within the EMS, and all the evidence suggests that he left the EMS because he felt he had no alternative – the Germans, who had already agreed a new fixed parity with Italy on September 11, were unlikely to give Italy a second chance. Indeed, after September 1992 the Germans began to theorize a two-tier Europe in which Italy would be the only founder member of the EU to be excluded from the EMU, at least initially, an outcome that not only Amato but Italian politicians in general perceived as humiliating (Ginsborg, 2001, 270–1). Amato's comment to Ciampi on September 16, 1992 that "As you can see, my dear Governor, in Italy it is only possible to take remedial measures once the roof over our heads has already fallen in," adds weight to the view that the Italian exit from the EMS was not a voluntary or conscious choice pursued because of some overlap between the views of exporters and politicians.

Eventually the lira's value settled at about 15 percent below the rate on September 11. Amato resorted to a drastic austerity budget, slashing state spending on health and social insurance as well as introducing new taxes on house ownership and imposing a minimum tax on the self-employed. Whilst the last tax represented a measure of social justice – even if it only curbed rather than ended the outrageous tax dodging of large sections of the Italian middle class so central to the DC's consensus, the bulk of the 93 billion lire package was an attack on wage-earners and the poor. The simultaneous abolition of the special intervention in the South, which had already diminished after the winding-up by Craxi in 1984 of the *Cassa per il Mezzogiorno*, which had coordinated such aid over decades, meant that growing inequality between the classes was compounded by an increase in regional inequality. Amato's austerity politics, implemented in a conjuncture in which nearly all Italy's neighbors were taking similar action, led Italy into recession. Consumption fell for the first time since the war, by 2.5 percent, whilst GDP declined by 1.2 percent, worsening the public debt (Ginsborg, 2001, 272).

Unsurprisingly, this period also saw a rise in working-class militancy under the leadership of *Rifondazione Comunista*, the left-wing minority that had rejected the old PCI's transformation into the PDS in February 1991. Rifondazione had no hesitation in challenging the trade union bureaucrats who were complicit in austerity, as well as the Amato government that had introduced it.

In April 1993, Amato – a politician who, for all his technocratic pretensions, could not shake off his links with the increasingly discredited

Craxi – resigned in the wake of the referendum abolishing proportional representation in parliament, a regressive shift packaged as a blow against old corruption and supported by the major industrialists and the daily newspapers owned by them (*La Repubblica, La Stampa, Il Corriere della Sera)* and intended to marginalize the voice of those like *Rifondazione Comunista* who opposed the neo-liberal consensus. This consensus included the PDS, the main successor of the old PCI, who acted as the industrialists' foot soldiers in the referendum campaign from which the totally disorientated bourgeois parties were virtually absent. The next prime minister was Ciampi, the Governor of the Bank of Italy since 1979. This 73-year-old embodiment of the spirit of neo-liberal austerity duly forced through another budget on the lines of his predecessor's one.

The trade union leaders accepted another agreement on the cost of labor on July 3, 1993, introducing a new incomes policy and regular tripartite discussions. Whilst the tripartite model of industrial relations favored by both Amato and Ciampi would not be endorsed by hard-line Thatcherite neo-liberals, any realistic evaluation has to accept that it was a good way, perhaps the only way, to achieve neo-liberal objectives in slow motion in a country with a strong tradition of union militancy, by getting trade union bureaucrats to make concession after concession in return for the delusion of influence over government policy.

The willingness of the mainstream left, in the form of the PDS, to endorse both Ciampi and his line of austerity assisted in the triumph of Berlusconi and his newly founded *Forza Italia* in the general elections of 1994. Whilst Berlusconi was probably ideologically even more of a neo-liberal than Ciampi, his upbeat populist demagogy about "one million new jobs" accompanied by the promise of tax cuts sounded more attractive to floating voters, particularly young ones, than the ceaseless austerity of Amato and Ciampi which the PDS effectively endorsed.

In reality, Berlusconi's first government made little concrete progress toward neo-liberal objectives. This was partly the result of the fractious nature of his coalition, which included both the neo-liberal regionalist Northern League and the self-styled post-fascists of *Alleanza Nazionale*, who remained rather attached to the authority of the central state in both politics and economics. In addition, there were acute divisions on Europe within the Berlusconi cabinet. On the one hand, Lamberto Dini, the minister of the treasury, a technocrat who had been a leading figure in the Bank of Italy, was a staunch supporter of European integration. On the other hand, Antonio Martino, Berlusconi's foreign minister and *Forza Italia*'s principal economist, was a member of the Europhobe Bruges Group associated with Mrs Thatcher, and opposed EMU on principle, rather than having reservations about whether Italy should join in the first wave. Fini, in keeping with the ultra-nationalist traditions of the old MSI, was also rather skeptical about further European integration.

The Berlusconi government was less rigorous about balancing the budget than the administrations of Amato and Ciampi had been, and this was one of the factors behind the currency crisis of July 1994, although Fini's notorious remark praising Mussolini as "the greatest statesman of the century" and the anti-Semitic tirades of ex-Christian Democrat labour minister Mastella played their role in generating unease in both the EU and, eventually, the US. Border disputes with Slovenia and Croatia stirred up by *Alleanza Nazionale* further irritated European partners, particularly the Germans, who had been the principal sponsors of those seceding from Yugoslavia. Berlusconi's attempts to undermine the authority of the Bank of Italy angered ideological neo-liberals both at home and abroad. Such privatization as occurred under Berlusconi was carried through in an almost Russian oligarchic manner rather than on strict Anglo-Saxon free market lines. Berlusconi's confrontation with the unions over pensions ended in disaster when he was forced to back-track by a million-strong demonstration on November 12, 1994, and a subsequent fall of the Lira against the Mark. By the time Berlusconi lost his majority in parliament, as a result of the Northern League's defection in December, it is probable that the economic establishment, both domestic and foreign, was glad to see him go.

The technocratic government of Lamberto Dini, which succeeded Berlusconi, carried through a number of neo-liberal measures with the backing of the mainstream parliamentary left, whose prime concern was to avoid an election in circumstances that favored Berlusconi. By reverting to tripartite negotiations rather than all out confrontation, Dini succeeded in persuading the trade union leaders to accept a pension reform that was only slightly milder than the Berlusconi proposals which had brought the country to a halt. Whilst Dini undoubtedly saw pension reform as an indispensable prerequisite for any Italian re-entry into the EMS, let alone EMU, some claim his attitude toward the budget deficit became a little reckless as the election finally approached in 1996 (Simonazzi and Vianello, 2002, 109).

When Prodi became Prime Minister in 1996, Italy was further away from meeting the Maastricht criteria than she had been in 1992. In 1996 the budget deficit was 6.7 percent of GDP and the public debt had risen to 123.8 percent of GDP (Ginsborg, 2001, 304). In 1996–97 it was by no means clear that Italy would be able to enter the Euro, at least in the first wave. Prodi and his close associates within the government, treasury minister Ciampi and foreign minister Dini, had to cope with a certain amount of hostility from the Germans and, initially, the French, as well as an unexpected desire on the part of the Spaniards to enter in the first wave without relaxing any of the Maastricht criteria. It was Prodi's administration that ensured, first Italy's re-entry into the EMS on November 24, 1996, and then her inclusion in the April 30, 1998 list of eleven countries approved by the European parliament as participants in the single European currency, on the recommendation of the European Commission that judged them to have satisfied the Maastricht criteria. Prodi's strategy of deficit reduction in order to re-enter the EMS and join the EMU attempted to combine austerity and equity – most notably in his special Tax for Europe, which was levied on a progressive rather than a flat-rate basis – and he refused to carry out many of the drastic cuts in pensions and social spending which the more extreme neo-liberals claimed to be essential. The former Christian Democrat was more willing to compromise with *Rifondazione Comunista* than his nominally more left-wing successors D'Alema and Amato.

It could be argued that it was only after Prodi's downfall in October 1998 that the Ulivo government drifted in an irrevocably neo-liberal direction, that *Rifondazione*'s withdrawal of parliamentary support actually provoked the very trend it claimed to fear. D'Alema's latter-day conversion to neo-liberalism, particularly in relation to labor-market flexibility (Abse, 2001, 61–74), undoubtedly played its part in the Ulivo's defeat at the May 2001 general election, as a section of the Center-Left's electorate felt betrayed by its abandonment of traditional left-wing values and, in the case of low-paid or unemployed workers in the South, saw more potential benefits in Berlusconi's renewed demagogy about extensive public works, most notably the projected bridge over the Straits of Messina which, if it is ever completed, will be the longest suspension bridge in the world, and new jobs.

The first three years of Berlusconi's second government suggest that he has adopted a more consistent neo-liberal approach and forged more organic links with FIAT and *Confindustria,* which rallied to the media magnate in the face of the attack by the foreign economic establishment, represented by *The Economist,* on his fitness to govern. Nonetheless, there is some element of continuity with his first administration; the budget deficit seems to be increasing, with the EU criticizing Italy for failing to keep to the criteria laid out in the Stability Pact (*id.*, 2002, 18–23) and some have argued that once again Berlusconi has paid far more attention to his private war against the judiciary than to running the Italian economy. Whilst his attempt to scrap Article 18 of the 1970 *Statuto dei Lavoratori,* and thus undermine job security, seems to have been defeated by a wave of renewed trade union militancy which forced the CGIL to break with the tripartite consensus, Berlusconi succeeded in enacting a further neo-liberal reduction in pension provisions in July 2004. *Forza Italia's* disappointing result in the June 2004 European elections enabled the more statist post-fascist and ex-Christian Democrat elements in Berlusconi's coalition to force the resignation of his influential Economics minister Tremonti, a close political ally of the neo-liberal Northern League, but the effect of this on the government's economic policy, as opposed to its political equilibrium, remains uncertain. The virtual bankruptcy of Alitalia has led to demands for the rapid privatisation of the national airline from an EU Commission which firmly opposed any suggestions of long-term state aid coming from *Alleanza Nazionale.* On the other hand, widespread public sector pay disputes seem likely to restrict the scope for a neo-liberal offensive by an increasingly unpopular premier more concerned with his own re-election than with any consistent economic strategy. In short, the erratic economic record of the second Berlusconi government, which has oscillated between reckless creative accountancy in fiscal matters and deflationary austerity over wages means that it is too soon to say whether Italy's neo-liberal turn is speeding up or slowing down.

Notes

1. Shop-owners and artisans very often declared incomes that were the same or lower than those of their employees. In 1993, owners of electrical goods shops declared an average income of 16.2 million lire against the 20.2 million of their shop assistants; jewellers declared 22.5 million against the 19.8 million of their employees, and owners of *autosaloni* declared 13.4 million against the 27.2 million of car salesmen (Ginsborg, 2001, 50).
2. Those with modest incomes of between 15 and 30 million lire per year contributed 62 percent of total tax in 1989 (*id.*, 2001, 26).
3. All the "no" votes seem to have come from members and supporters of *Democrazia Proletaria*, whose adherents were instructed to vote against the document. Dissident PCI members were under severe pressure to vote for the motion and other trade union militants preferred abstention to outright opposition (Golden, 1988, 148).
4. Golden, 1988, 80, describes this as "the party's ambivalent return to the core industrial working class" and points out that the PCI was secretly trying to negotiate a compromise solution at the very moment of Berlinguer's visit.

13

Globalization, the Rise of Neo-liberalism, and the Demise of the Swedish Model: An Analysis of Class Struggle

Andreas Bieler

Introduction

Throughout the post-war era, Sweden was praised for its progressive economic-political model successfully combining international economic competitiveness with generous compensatory mechanisms at the national level to soften the impact of constant structural adjustment (Katzenstein, 1985). It was based on a corporatist policy-making system ensuring the close involvement of trade unions and employers' associations in economic and social policy decision-making with the main goal of full employment (Heclo, 1987). The core feature was a sophisticated economic model, developed by the trade union theorists Gösta Rehn and Rudolf Meidner at the beginning of the 1950s, which allowed the combination of full employment with low inflation. Based on an equal, solidaristic wage across all industrial sectors, it forced the constant shift of resources, investment, and labor from declining to expanding sectors (Ryner, 1994, 400–1).

The state supported this through an active manpower policy (Esping-Andersen, 1985, 229–31). Full employment, especially in the 1970s, was further sustained through an expansion of the public sector, absorbing workers, who could not be re-employed in the private sector (Heclo, 1987, 165–6), and frequent devaluations to engender export-led growth (Moses, 1995, 418). In the 1970s, when the model was further pushed into areas of industrial democracy via an active industrial policy by the state, the stronger involvement of workers in decision-making at the workplace, and workers' control over investment via the so-called Employee Investment Funds (EIFs) initiative (Pontusson, 1995a, 28; Wilks, 1996, 96), people started to speak about the gradual transformation of Swedish capitalism into socialism.

However, by the late 1980s and early 1990s, the Swedish model had been abandoned. The Confederation of Swedish Employers (SAF) left the tripartite decision-making bodies, they abandoned multi-sector collective bargaining, and the Social Democratic government dropped full employment as most important policy goal and replaced it with an emphasis on price stability and low inflation. Application to the EU was made in June 1991 and accession itself followed in January 1995. This was not so much the cause of the abandonment of the Swedish Model than the logical result of it. European integration since the mid-1980s driven by the Internal Market and plans for Economic and Monetary Union revolved around the neo-liberal restructuring of social relations and further cemented the changes already under way in Sweden since the early 1990s (Bieler, 2000).

This chapter has the task to explain the abandonment of the Swedish Model. It is argued that this has to be understood against the background of globalization and the transnational restructuring of social relations. Most importantly, globalization is characterized by the transnationalization of production, expressed in the rise of transnational corporations (TNCs), and the transnationalization of finance, embodied in the emergence of a globally integrated financial market. Additionally, a shift from Keynesian economic policy to neo-liberal economics can be observed at the ideological level as well as the actual level of state policies (Cox, 1993, 259–60, 266–7).

The definition of globalization is widely contested. While so-called internationalists argue that only the levels of exchange between states has intensified leaving states as most important actors in international relations (e.g. Weiss, 1998; Hirst, 1996), liberals identify a fundamental structural change characterized by the transnationalization of production and finance and sometimes the emergence of a global civil society (e.g. Strange, 1996; Held, 2000; Scholte, 2000). Although the analysis of change differs drastically, the neo-Gramscian perspective employed in this chapter follows the liberal conceptualization of globalization (Bieler, 2000, 18–27).

The next section will discuss the conceptualization of globalization and its impact on national economic-political models. Then, the transnational restructuring of the Swedish social relations of production will be outlined. The fourth section will look at the demise of the Swedish Model and the reasons behind it, before the conclusion assesses the future of the Swedish form of state.

I Globalization and class struggle

Comparative political economy approaches regard the production sector as an important explanatory variable (e.g. Gourevitch, 1986, 54–68; Frieden, 1991, 438). The response of trade unions and employers' associations to opening up the economy to international competition depends very much on the nature of the sector. Unions and employers' associations in export sectors tend to favor open borders, while unions and employers' associations in domestic production sectors generally prefer closed borders and state protectionism. Fioretos, for example, states that Swedish EU membership was the result of increasing levels of international economic interdependence, which changed the balance between government and business resulting in new domestic coalitions dominated by export-oriented companies. In other words, accession to the neo-liberal EU was the result of a politics from below, in which economic interest groups constrained and pushed the Swedish government toward further integration (Fioretos, 1997, 295–7; also Ingebritsen, 1998). This echoes the general argument that the Swedish Model's demise was due to a change in capital's strategy. "What undermined the model was the rejection of the 50-year old historical compromise by Swedish business" (Wilks, 1996, 94). In sum, the abandonment of the Swedish Model exemplified in, and cemented by, accession to the EU is explained as the result of pressure by export-oriented TNCs. Global structural change is incorporated in this analysis through an emphasis on export-oriented sectors, gaining predominance at the national level against the background of increasing international economic interdependence.

There are, however, two main problems with these political economy analyses. First, despite acknowledging the increasing levels of TNCs' structural power resulting from the possibility to move production units from one country to another, they are still treated as domestic actors. Nevertheless, globalization as a new phenomenon is first and foremost characterized by the transnationalization of production, affecting different countries in different sectors to a different extent, not merely by increasing levels of economic interdependence. TNCs are transnational actors, not domestic actors, and therefore clearly differ from export-oriented companies, the production facilities of which are still located at the national level. Second, phrasing their analysis in terms of governments being constrained by business, political economy approaches fall into the trap of taking the separation of states and markets, historically specific of the capitalist mode of production, as their ahistoric starting-point of analysis. As a result, the inner connection between the political and the economic cannot be problematized by these approaches. State and market are fetishized as externally related "things" (Burnham, 1995).

By contrast, Open Marxism, a separate group of approaches within International Political Economy, suggests taking the social relations of production as starting-point. Instead of separating state and market, both are treated as different forms of the very same social relations of production. Thus, the apparent separation of state and market is understood as the result of the way the social relations of production are organized in capitalism. Based on the institution of private property, society is split in the bourgeoisie, that is, those who own the means of production, and labor, that is, those who only have their labor power to sell. Thus, economic exploitation is not politically enforced, but the result of the "free" sale and purchase of labor power (Holloway, 1977, 79). Furthermore, "open Marxism" avoids economic deterministic explanations through a focus on class struggle. "Struggle by definition is uncertain and outcomes remain open" (Burnham, 1994, 225).

Nevertheless, Open Marxism's ability to account for structural change is limited. While the character of the accumulation of capital and, thus, class struggle is considered to be global in substance (Holloway, 1994, 30), the conditions of exploitation are standardized at the national political level. The form of class struggle at the global level is the interaction of states, which "are interlocked internationally into a hierarchy of price systems" (Burnham, 1995, 148). In other words, class struggle is only in substance but not in form understood as taking place at the global level. This state-centric focus is also apparent in Jonathan Moran's account of the demise of the Swedish Model. Class struggle at the national level is assumed to determine globalization. "The continuing importance of national social formations has not been diminished, indeed it has been accentuated by globalization" (Moran, 1998, 54). Hence, TNCs, being far less global than assumed, are considered to concentrate on class politics at home.

In the case of Sweden, then, the demise of the Swedish Model is not the result of globalization and the transnationalization of Swedish capital, but the outcome of class struggle around capital's response to labor's EIFs initiative in the mid-1970s (Moran, 1998, 71–2). While this captures some of the dynamics underlying the Swedish restructuring processes, it underestimates the importance of Swedish capital's structural power as a result of the increasing transnationalization of production. Without the possibility to transfer production units abroad, the abandonment of the Swedish Model would have been much more difficult. This became especially apparent in the struggle for EU membership, when Swedish capital did not have to mount a political strategy in contrast to Austrian capital, the production of which is predominantly organized at the national level (Bieler, 2000, 85–7). Moreover, this focus on national class struggle further overlooks the split between national and transnational labor, facilitating restructuring, as well as the significance of core social democratic policy-makers within state institutions adopting neo-liberal economic policies. In short, neither the transnational dimension of class struggle, nor the importance of a shift toward neo-liberal economics at the ideological level, both part of globalization, is fully acknowledged.

Another set of different, yet related, neo-Gramscian perspectives in International Political Economy emerged in the early 1980s (Morton, 2001). Drawing on the work of the Italian Communist Antonio Gramsci (1971) as interpreted by Robert Cox (1981, 1983), these perspectives include the most important features of Open Marxism. First, the social relations of production are considered to engender social forces as the most important actors and are, therefore, the starting-point of analysis. This allows us to perceive entities such as "state" and "market" as different forms of the very same social relations of production. Second, a neo-Gramscian analysis is open-ended through an emphasis on class struggle. It "rejects the notion of objective laws of history and focuses upon class struggle [be they intra-class or inter-class] as the heuristic model for the understanding of structural change" (Cox with Sinclair, 1996, 57–8).

Class can be identified by relating social forces to their place in the production process. This makes structural changes such as globalization accessible. The capitalist mode of production is organized around wage, labor, and private property. This leads to the opposition between the bourgeoisie, the owner of the means of production, on the one hand, and workers, who can only sell their labor power, on the other. The partial transnationalization of national production systems due to globalization, however, implies that there is not only class struggle between labor and capital at the national level, but also between national capital and labor and transnational forces of capital and labor. The former can further be subdivided in nationally oriented social forces, engendered by production processes organized at the national level producing predominantly for national consumption, and internationally oriented social forces, stemming from national production, which is geared toward export markets. Hence, in contrast to Open Marxism, it is acknowledged that class struggle potentially takes place in form not only at the national, but also at the international level, and in contrast to political economy approaches, the partial transnationalization of national production systems is realized. As a result, globalization has not only strengthened social forces of export-oriented sectors. It has also engendered new, transnational social forces.

The focus on social forces and the sphere of production, however, does not imply that the state is overlooked. Neo-Gramscian perspectives distinguish several forms of states and the national interest, the "raison d'état", cannot be separated from society, as it depends on the configuration of social forces at the state level. Importantly, for Gramsci (1971, 257–63, 271) the form of state consists of "political society," that is, the coercive apparatus of the state more narrowly understood including ministries and other state institutions, and "civil society," made up of political parties, unions, employers' associations, churches, etc. In other words, the form of state is regarded as a structure within which and through which social forces operate. Hence, explanations are not phrased in the form of states responding to pressure by employers' associations or trade unions that treat state and market as externally related. Instead, it has to be analyzed how transnational social forces and their neo-liberal project, representing the interests of capital, have become internalized in the Swedish form of state, which led to the collapse of the Swedish Model. "In this sense the state forms the political framework within which internationally operating concepts of control can be synthesized with particular national political cultures, attitudes, constitutional arrangements and so on, or, conversely, the very medium through which hegemonic concepts of control can transcend national frontiers" (Holman, 2001, 169).

II Globalization and the transnational restructuring of Swedish social relations

Following the definition of globalization in the introduction, in order to assess the impact of globalization on Sweden, it has to be investigated to what extent Swedish production and finance have become transnationalized and economic policy has moved from Keynesianism to neo-liberalism in theory and practice.

The transnationalization of Swedish production

Swedish production has always been characterized by TNCs. Through a wave of mergers since the end of the 1960s and a trend toward cross-ownership since the late 1970s the central importance of TNCs for the Swedish economy has further increased. Four main ownership groups emerged in a dominant position in the Swedish production structure by the mid-1980s, the Wallenberg empire, the closely linked Volvo and Skanska spheres, and Industrivarden-Svenska Handelsbank (Olsen, 1991, 117–19).

The degree of transnationalization increased dramatically in the second half of the 1980s, when there was a drastic upturn in outward FDI. While inward FDI had only risen from US$ 396 m in 1985 to US$ 2328 m in 1990, outward FDI increased from US$ 1783 m to US$ 14136 m during the same period (Luif, 1996, 208). This is even more dramatic, if one takes into account that "in 1989 for the first time ever, Sweden invested more abroad than at home" (Kurzer, 1993, 133). The transnationalization of Swedish production is also expressed in the change in the Swedish and foreign share of TNCs' employees and production. In 1965, TNCs employed 33.9 percent of their employees abroad, where they achieved 25.9 percent of their turnover. By 1990, the situation had drastically changed. Of the workforce 60.6 percent was employed in the production abroad, accounting for 51.4 percent of the turnover (Braunerhjelm, 1996, 10).

In sum, Sweden has experienced a high increase in the degree of the transnationalization of its production structure since the late 1960s. In accordance with the neo-Gramscian identification of social forces through an analysis of the production structure, it can be concluded that the main line of division in Sweden is likely to be between national and transnational forces of capital and labor.

The transnationalization of Swedish finance

The Swedish post-war financial system was dominated by banks. They provided the long-term loans to industry, with which they maintained close links (Olsen, 1991, 125). This did not, however, imply that banking capital led overall. At the outbreak of the Second World War, foreign exchange controls and other forms of capital market regulations had been introduced, only to be strengthened during the 1950s. These regulations, including lending ceilings, liquidity ratios, cash ratios, investment ratios, bond issue control, and interest rate regulations, were administered by the Riksbank, the Swedish Central Bank (Jonung, 1986, 109–11; Kurzer, 1993, 176). The Riksbank is directly responsible to the Swedish parliament. Six of its seven directors are elected by parliament, the seventh director and chairman is appointed by the government.

This institutional structure guaranteed the governing party, and by implication the Swedish Social Democratic Party (SAP), which was in power for most of the post-war era, a controlling influence over the bank and, in extension, the financial markets. In fact, "the Riksbank functioned as an agency affiliated with the Ministry of Finance" (Kurzer, 1993, 175). Together with the pension funds, established in 1960, which gave the SAP some degree of credit steering and investment control capacity, the party's control over the Riksbank and the financial market regulations was a cornerstone of its full-employment policy. The control of the financial markets separated the domestic from the international financial markets and provided the necessary economic autonomy for the counter-cyclical Keynesian economic policy.

From 1974 onwards, but especially after the SAP had returned to power in 1982, the financial market regulations were removed step by step. Amongst others, the liquidity ratio requirements for banks were abolished in 1983 and the ceiling on lending by banks removed in 1985 (Jonung, 1986, 111). There are several reasons for the eventual deregulation of the financial markets. Firstly, against the background of the severe economic crisis, government had run up a budget deficit of 13 per cent and a current account deficit of 3.7 per cent by 1982. In order to service these debts, they had to devise new forms of finance, often via finance houses outside the regulated markets. Additionally, "the Swedish government was forced to start borrowing from abroad which contributed to a reduction in Sweden's financial isolation" (Jonung, 1986, 113). The government's influence over monetary, credit, and exchange-rate policies started declining.

Second, the regulations themselves had been an incentive to the formation of finance houses. They grew rapidly in numbers in the 1970s and 1980s. "Almost half of them were subsidiaries created by the large commercial banks in order to evade the restrictions imposed by the Riksbank" (Olsen, 1991, 128). From the early 1980s onwards, attempts were made to regulate these finance houses, but new ways of financing were developed with every new regulation, while the de facto control of Swedish banks was disturbed. Eventually, the government opted for deregulation (Notermans, 1993, 145–6). In 1986, foreign banks were allowed to open branches in Sweden and, three years later, the SAP government made the final step and abolished foreign exchange controls.

Overall, the deregulation of the financial markets deprived the SAP government to a large extent of its monetary and economic policy autonomy. Swedish financial markets have become integrated into the world financial market. Nevertheless, although this was predominantly a response to outside pressure (Jonung, 1986, 116; Olsen, 1991, 128), there was also a voluntary element to it. As outlined below, in 1982, the SAP adopted a hard currency policy. The liberalization of the financial markets increased the costs of pursuing a flexible exchange rate and, thereby, gave more credibility to the policy of stable exchange rates and a hard currency.

Changing economic policy

In 1976, when the SAP went into opposition for the first time in the post-war era, it could not overlook the rising budget deficits and general economic crisis in the late 1970s and early 1980s. While in opposition, it formulated a crisis program in 1981, which became its guideline for economic policy, when it was back in government in 1982. As a "third way" between traditional Keynesianism and neo-liberalism, the program included both traditional policies and departures (Sainsbury, 1993, 56). "The immediate aim of the 'third way' was to reverse the trend of industrial decline through a dramatic increase in net exports, profitability and fixed investments" (Ryner, 1994, 392). A 16 percent devaluation of the SKr was to ensure export-led growth and the recovery of the Swedish economy.

This time, however, the devaluation was the start of a new monetary policy, not the continuation of the past, and "the Big Bang's yield was to be insured with a new commitment to a fixed exchange rate regime" (Moses, 1995, 313). The SAP's crisis program of 1981 had spelled out the need for a restrictive fiscal and monetary policy and called for a new hard currency policy with the goal of getting inflation under control. Credibility for this new policy was not achieved by linking the SKr to the DM, but by the Riksbank's action in the market place. In 1985 and 1990, it did not float the currency to relieve the pressure building up on the Swedish reserves. "Instead, both times, it preferred to hike its overnight interest rates rather than devalue" (*id.*, 1995, 318). The liberalization of the financial markets gave further credibility to the hard currency policy, since it made a flexible exchange-rate policy more expensive.

Two tax reforms lowering the marginal rates of income tax implied "an acceptance that high marginal taxation reduces incentives to save and work" (Stephens, 1996, 44). First, in 1981, the SAP still in opposition participated in a compromise on tax reforms together with the government, which lowered the marginal rates of national income tax in general and for the highest rates from 85 percent to 50 percent. Then, in another drastic reform, national income tax was abolished for around 85 percent of the taxpayers in 1990/91. These reforms, the cuts of which were higher for the well-off than for the poorly paid groups, "imply a departure from earlier SAP tax policies, which emphasized income taxation as a key instrument of redistribution" (Sainsbury, 1991, 37). Nonetheless, this did hardly result in an overall tax decline, since other taxes were increased to finance these cuts.

A similar "third way" strategy was adopted toward the public sector. "To defend the basic accomplishments of the 'Swedish model' against the specter of radical privatization it was deemed necessary to adopt a two-pronged strategy: to halt the growth of the public sector and to decentralize its organisation and management" (Premfors, 1991, 91). One way of reducing the budget deficit was to control the payroll cost in the public sector. The government attempted to stop the linkage between pay rises in the public with pay rises in the private sector. In 1983, the Metal Workers' Union, affiliated to the LO, had accepted a separate deal with the engineering employers. They received salary increases above average but had to renounce their automatic pay drift compensation clause. The engineering employers wanted to pay higher salaries in order to attract more highly qualified workers, important for the maintenance of international competitiveness. The compensation clause guaranteed workers in one industrial sector automatic adjustment to higher pay raises obtained in other sectors. Instead of opposing this breach of the centralized solidaristic wage negotiations, the government supported this move with the result, that all unions had lost their compensation clauses by 1986. The way was open for increasing pay differentiation between the private and the public sector (Swenson, 1991, 383–7).

The reform of the public sector further led to the political and administrative decentralization from the state sector to local government. "Decentralization-cum-efficiency" replaced the "decentralization-cum-participation" principle from the 1970s (Premfors, 1991, 92). State and local government companies had to adhere to newly introduced profitability criteria derived from the private sector. Overall, the SAP succeeded in stopping the growth of the public sector relative to the economy as a whole.

The original success of the "third way" strategy was impressive. Sweden, at less than 2 percent, maintained one of the lowest unemployment rates of the OECD countries and a 13 percent budget deficit was transformed into a 1 percent surplus. At the beginning of the 1990s, however, the economy faced the same problems as at the beginning of the 1980s. "The growth rate was sluggish, wage increases outstripped those of international competitors, the current-account deficit began to grow again, and inflation was on the rise" (Sainsbury, 1991, 39). As it turned out, while the macroeconomic balance had been restored, the structural problems of the Swedish economy had not been solved. Consequently, "productivity growth increased only slightly between 1982 and 1990 to an average annual increase of 1 percent" (Ryner, 1994, 396). Moreover, while unemployment had successfully been checked, inflation had not been brought under control by the one-sided adoption of a hard currency regime. At an average of 8.6 percent, it was significantly higher than the German rate of 3 percent (Notermans, 1993,139; also Glyn, 1995a, 51–3). The abolition of foreign exchange controls in 1989 was one way of importing price stability from the outside.

Nonetheless, even further measures were necessary in order to achieve wage moderation and, thereby, avoid inflation. "In February 1990, the government put forward a drastic action programme which among other things included a statutory pay freeze and a ban on strikes" (Bergström, 1991, 15). This was defeated in parliament due to an outcry by the rank and file of trade unions. After a new currency crisis in October 1990, the government, this time successfully, put forward another emergency package, including a partial privatization of the Swedish state sector (e.g. the telecommunications system and the electricity network) and a cut in the level of sickness benefits (Luif, 1996, 215). It was further concluded that a general expansive fiscal policy in order to counter rising unemployment was no longer possible. "Social Democrats eventually saw no other way than to abandon their central policy goal ... [of full employment] ... and institute a policy regime which consciously created unemployment in order to restore price stability" (Notermans, 1993, 148). This was further highlighted through the declaration that the government intended to apply to the EU for membership, announced as a part of the economic crisis package (Bieler, 2000, 81–4). The Swedish Model had come to an end.

III Causes of the demise of the Swedish model

It is frequently argued that the demise of the Swedish Model is due to the rejection of it by Swedish capital (e.g. Wilks, 1996, 94). And correctly, from the mid-1970s onwards, Swedish capital started to oppose the various features of the Swedish Model. It was especially the EIFs component of the labor reform offensive in the 1970s that ran into fierce opposition from employers. From the SAP's and trade unions' point of view, the EIFs were an attempt to re-establish wage restraint in the dynamic sectors in exchange for collective control over investment (Swenson, 1988, 163). Moreover, the EIFs were also perceived as a progressive step toward "transforming the traditional welfare state into an economic democracy" (Heclo, 1987, 253). Especially the original plan, developed by Meidner in 1975, focused on the question of social power and workers' control over investment. When a slightly changed version was put before the SAP for adoption in 1978, "it was estimated that with average profits of 15 percent it would take 25 years for labour to achieve over 50 percent of the voting rights in a company" (Wilde, 1992, 10). This objective, however, did not only threaten particular capitalist interests, it threatened capitalism and its prerogative over investment and management decisions as such. Unsurprisingly, the EIFs "deeply antagonized employers in SAF, mobilizing and unifying the economic and political right to a degree highly unusual in Sweden" (Swenson, 1988, 176).

The export-oriented capital fraction dominated over the home-market-oriented fraction in the mid-1970s and its members took over key leadership positions in the employers' associations (Olsen, 1991, 131). When Curt Nicolin became the SAF's new chairman in 1976, the association did not only change its policies toward neo-liberalism but also the nature of its activities. The SAF attempted "to assume leadership in defining the terms of political discourse, not only at the level of policy, but also at the level of popular culture" (Ryner, 1996, 20). In other words, the SAF started transforming itself from a wage-bargaining institution into an ideologically motivated think tank, which offered the platform for "organic intellectuals" to spread their neo-liberal message. It "expanded into the political arena, where it ventured into 'the marketing of capitalism' by establishing a range of publishing houses and by organizing campaigns aimed at selected target groups to promote pro-capitalist ideology, particularly amongst the young" (Whyman, 1993, 607). In 1982, the SAF spent almost as much on anti-EIF propaganda than all five political parties together during this general election year. The Swedish public as a whole was influenced by this offensive, and some of the largest demonstrations in modern Swedish history took place in Stockholm (Burkitt, 1994, 25). Overall, the issue of the EIFs led to an increased class conflict and started the process toward the eventual break-up of the Swedish Model.

The SAP's loss of power in 1976 prevented the establishment of EIFs. After their return to power in 1982, the fund system was implemented, but only in a watered-down version and with little reference to workers' control over capital and decision-making (Heclo and Madsen, 1987, 282). None of the five regional funds was allowed to own above 8 percent (6 percent in 1988) of the total stock in any public company. They received finance only until 1990, of which two-thirds stemmed from the payroll, not from a profit tax. Theoretically, together these funds could have acquired as much as 50 percent of the votes in corporations, but there was little coordination in practice toward this goal (Pontusson, 1992, 210).

The SAF's efforts were at first directed against the EIFs. Then, the attack went against the solidaristic wage policy, corporatism, and the welfare state (Olsen, 1991, 131–6). Central wage negotiations could temporarily be restored in the years after the separate deal between the engineering employers and the Metal Workers' Union in 1983, but eventually SAF as a whole left the system:

> Under pressure from engineering firms and other foes of centralized bargaining, the SAF simply closed down its negotiations and statistics departments in the spring of 1990. The following winter, it withdrew from the system of corporatist representation on government bodies (Pontusson, 1995a, 39).

Since 1993, negotiations have been carried out at the sectoral level between the SAF's member associations and individual trade unions (The Swedish

Institute, 1994, 2). The success of the SAF strategy has to be understood against the background of the increasing transnationalization of production outlined above. Without the related increase in structural power, it would have been much more difficult for Swedish capital to carry out its strategy against trade unions and the SAP government.

Nevertheless, the offensive by capital is only one part of the story. The SAP also contributed to it. It is in the Swedish "third way," where it can be identified how neo-liberal ideas representing the interests of transnational capital have become internalized in the Swedish form of state. The "third way" never really represented a viable alternative to Keynesian and neo-liberal economic policies. By accepting some principles of neo-liberalism, the seeds were sown for the demise of the Swedish Model. First, "combined, the fixed exchange rate strategies and liberalized capital markets undermined what little monetary autonomy might have remained in the hands of ... [Swedish] ... policy-makers" (Moses, 1995, 342). When the economic crisis in 1989/90 hit Sweden, it had to adapt to the global economy, concentrating on price stability via austerity measures in order to avoid the flight of capital. By opening itself up to international capital through the deregulation of foreign exchange controls, the pursuit of a full employment policy was foreclosed. For the same reason, capital flight by Swedish TNCs could not be controlled.

Second, the SAP government actively supported export-oriented employers and unions in their quest for different inter-sectoral wage levels. "In 1986 the government successfully fought to eliminate earning guarantee clauses from public-sector agreements" (Mahon, 1999, 136). However, as a result, the eventual collapse of the total system of multi-sector centralized wage bargaining had been prepared. Finally, by introducing efficiency as the main principle in the public sector, this sector's original role of achieving full employment and the democratization of society had been abandoned. In short, "at the beginning of the 1980s, the Swedish state possessed the institutional requisites for a national economic policy. A good part of the story of the Third Road is the story of how these controls were dismantled, increasing the country's vulnerability to continental and global developments. Such vulnerability, in turn, became the standard rationale for unpopular decisions in the 1990s" (Mahon, 1999, 139).

The "third way" with its neo-liberal ingredients was not the only option available to the SAP after its return to power in 1982. To adopt the "third way" and to reject the alternative of EIFs was a conscious political decision. Moreover, as Glyn outlines, the substitution of price stability for the full employment policy at the beginning of the 1990s was not a necessity. The expansion of employment was still possible despite the structural changes since the early 1970s, provided the entailed costs are "explicitly counted and willingly shouldered by the mass of wage and salary earners" (Glyn, 1995b, 55). The actual decisions taken by the SAP in both instances were partly a response to structural changes associated with globalization, including the establishment of neo-liberalism as a part of the structure in the form of intersubjective meanings, and to the SAF's neo-liberal offensive, which gained in strength and conviction within the neo-liberal structure.

These decisions were, however, also partly due to the SAP-internal ideological changes (Olsen, 1996, 10). From 1976 onwards, the SAP leadership had only half-heartedly supported the LO-initiative of EIFs. Additionally, after its electoral defeat of the same year, it had formed its own research unit under Kjell Olof Feldt, the later Finance Minister. The team around Feldt consisted of young people shaped by the experience of the recession in the 1970s. Especially the OECD was a crucial influence on how to cope with it. Gunnar Lund, Michael Sohlman, and Leif Pagarotzky, all people close to Feldt, had been working there in the early 1980s and been put into contact with neo-liberal ideas. "Feldt and his advisors were determined to give priority to private-sector growth, profits, and market forces" (Pontusson, 1995a, 35). It was this group, which formulated the "third way" strategy and put it into practice after 1982. The LO, on the other hand, was significantly weakened. "Intellectual authority had passed from its researchers to the policy unit of the party" (Pontusson, 1995a, 28). Hence, neo-liberal economics had become internalized within core state institutions such as the Finance Ministry. Unsurprisingly, it was the Finance Ministry together with the Prime Minister's Office, which had been the driving force within the SAP government in 1990 behind the decision to apply to the EU. Application was the attempt to refer a "sound" economic policy to supranational restrictions and to have a scapegoat for harsh domestic policy measures. It was a way of regaining economic credibility and stability, budgetary discipline and a structural reform of the economy. Thus, application was regarded as a way of introducing greater discipline (Bieler, 2000, 83).

Finally, another reason for the demise of the Swedish Model was the division within the labor movement between national and transnational labor resulting from globalization. For example, the separate wage agreement between the LO affiliate the Metal Workers' Union and the Engineering Employers' Association in 1983 had not only resulted in a conflict between SAP and LO, but also in an LO-internal conflict between the Municipal Workers' Union, representing workers in the domestic public sector, and the Metal Workers' Union, organizing workers in transnational manufacturing, undermining labor unity (Sainsbury, 1991, 41). This split became further visible in the debates around the referendum on EU membership in 1994. Transnational sector unions supported membership arguing that Sweden had to follow the de facto move to the EU by the TNCs via their FDI activities. National production sector unions, on the other hand, were concerned about the impact of the neo-liberal economic-political model of the EU on the Swedish Model and here especially on the extensive public sector spending in Sweden. Consequently, they argued for a "no" in the referendum (Bieler, 2000, 102–7).

Conclusion

In conclusion, the demise of the Swedish Model cannot solely be explained by the pressure of capital on the state, as political economy approaches tend to do. Nor was it due to a purely domestic class struggle between capital and labor, as Open Marxists would argue. Rather, the demise of the Swedish model is the result of a combination of a political strategy by Swedish transnational capital, supported by an intensification of the transnationalization of production, in tandem with the internalization of neo-liberalism in the SAP government's "third way" strategy in the 1980s and a rift within the labor movement between national and transnational labor, the latter frequently supporting the projects of transnational capital. In short, the transnational restructuring of the Swedish social relations of production due to globalization is at the heart of the explanation and it is the understanding of this transnational class formation, which makes a neo-Gramscian perspective valuable here.

Since the end of the Swedish Model, Sweden has clearly moved toward a neo-liberal, Anglo-American model of capitalism. When the social democrats returned to power in 1994 "the SAP's actions [were] much more severely circumscribed in a neo-liberal environment dominated by TNCs and business organisations, and the convergence rules of the European Union's Maastricht Treaty ..." (Olsen, 1996, 16; also Mahon, 1999, 140). This, together with the SAP's own conversion on neo-liberal policies, ensures that a return to the Swedish Model within Sweden is currently unlikely. In August 1998, LO and SAF negotiated on a partial re-centralization of wage bargaining in exchange for union acceptance of EMU and concessions in the area of labor law legislation and taxes. The initiative failed, however, due to disagreements within the labor movement and continued skepticism by employers about a strengthened political role for LO (Stephens, 2000, 11–12). Especially the Engineering Employers' Association would prefer even further decentralization of wage bargaining toward cross-collar agreements at the firm or divisional level (Mahon, 1999, 134).

Nevertheless, there are always possibilities for alternative developments. Two possible scenarios are indicated here. First, although Swedish transnational sector unions supported transnational capital in the drive toward EU membership, they did this for a different rationale. While transnational capital saw enlargement as a way of ensuring that Sweden would not return to the Swedish model, transnational unions argued that because labor had lost control over capital at the national level, EU membership would be a way of regaining some of this control at a higher level. In other words, it was hoped that a further development of the EU Social Dimension would lead to a re-regulation of capital at the European level. Hence, in this scenario the struggle over the future Swedish model of capitalism has been postponed and transferred to the European level (Bieler, 2000, 116–17, 120–1).

Alternatively, recent developments indicate that a re-nationalization of industrial relations at the sectoral level may occur in Sweden. Resistance within SAF and even the Engineering Employers' Association itself, as well as a higher collective agreement in the paper and pulp industry in 1995, forcing the metal working sector into a similar agreement, led to a renewed commitment by transnational capital to collective bargaining, this time however at the sectoral level. Transnational sector unions, evaluating low inflation more positively from 1997 onwards, experiencing that low inflation implied an increase in real wages despite lower nominal wage increases, also committed themselves to sectoral wage bargaining in Sweden. Hence, it was the transnational sector unions and capital, which signed an Industrial Agreement in 1997, formulating common positions as well as laying out procedures to ensure that wage bargaining could be conducted at the sectoral level without industrial action (Industrial Agreement, 1999). This was soon followed by similar agreements in other sectors as well as the establishment of a Mediation Authority by the Swedish government in 2000 to cover those sectors, which had not formulated their own agreement (Eironline, 2001).

Clearly, sectoral collective bargaining at the national level is not necessarily a contradiction to cooperation at the European level (Crouch, 2002, 302). Nevertheless, it is questionable whether an emphasis on the national level as outlined in the second possible future development can be combined with a serious development of industrial relations at the European level, envisaged in the first potential development. Additionally, the fact that Swedish unions have accepted a main policy focus on low inflation – which has not been a problem in the second half of the 1990s, characterized by economic growth – also questions to what extent they are prepared to challenge neo-liberalism at the European level.

Acknowledgments

I am indebted to Bernie Moss and the participants of the workshop "The Neo-liberal Turn in the European Union and its Member-States," held at Nottingham University on June 8, 2002, for comments on earlier drafts.

Bibliography

(Unless otherwise indicated French books are published in Paris, British in London and American in New York.)

Abosch, H. (1963) *The Menace of the Miracle: Germany from Hitler to Adenauer* (Monthly Review Press).

Abse, T. (2001) "From PCI to DS: How European Integration Accelerated the 'Social Democratization' of the Italian Left," *Journal of Southern Europe and the Balkans*, 3.

—— (2002) "Berlusconi and Europe," *What Next?*, 21.

Adams, W. and Stoffaes, C. (eds) (1986) *French Industrial Policy: its Practice and Applications* (Washington, DC: Brookings Institution).

Aeschimann, E. and Riché, P. (1996) *La Guerre de sept ans: histoire secrète du franc fort, 1989–1996* (Calmann-Lévy).

Aglietta, M. (1995) *Macroéconomie financière* (La Découverte).

Aglietta, M. and Baulant, C. (1993) "Le Franc de l'instrument de croissance à la recherche de l'ancrage nominal," in Lévy-Leboyer, M. *et al* (eds), *Du Franc Poincaré à l'Ecu* (Ministère de l'économie).

Ahlén, K. (1989) "Swedish Collective Bargaining Under Pressure: Inter-union Rivalry and Income Policies," *British Journal of Industrial Relations*, 27, pp. 330–46.

Albert, M. (1991) *Capitalisme contre Capitalisme* (Le Seuil).

Alesina, A. (1989) "Politics and Business Cycles in Industrial Democracies," *Economic Policy*, 8, pp. 55–98.

Alexander, K. (2003) "European Securities Regulation and Financial Markets," London Metropolitan University, Global Finance and Social Europe.

Allen, C. (1983) "Structural and Technological Change in West Germany: Employer and Trade Union Response in the Chemical and Automobile Industries" (PhD, Brandeis University).

—— (1987) "Worker Participation and the West German Trade Unions: An Unfulfilled Dream?," in Sirianni, C. (ed.), *Worker Participation: The Politics of Reform* (Philadelphia: Temple University Press).

—— (1989) "The Underdevelopment of Keynesianism in the Federal Republic of Germany," in Hall, P. (ed.), *The Political Power of Economic Ideas: Keynesianism across Nations* (Princeton, N.J.: Princeton University Press).

—— (1997) "Institutions Challenged: German Unification, Policy Errors, and the 'Siren Song' of Deregulation," in Turner, L. (ed.), *Negotiating the New Germany: Can Social Partnership Survive*? (Ithaca, N.Y.: Cornell University Press).

——, Gasiorek, M. and Smith, A. (1998) "The Competition Effects of the Single Market in Europe," *Economic Policy*, vol. 13, pp. 439–86.

Allen, D. (1996) "Cohesion and Structural Adjustment," in Wallace, W. and Wallace, H. (eds), *Policy-Making in the European Union*, 3rd edn (Oxford University Press).

Alter, K. and Meunier-Aitsahalia, S. (1994) "Judicial Politics in the European Community: European Integration and the Pathbreaking *Cassis de Dijon* Decision," *Comparative Political Studies*, 26, pp. 535–61.

Althusser, L. (1979) *For Marx* (Verso).

Ambrosius, G. (1977) *Die Durchsetzung der Sozialen Markwirtschaft in Westdeutschland 1945–49* (Stuttgart: Deutsche Verlags-Anstalt).

Andersen, T. *et al* (2000) "Labor Market Implications of EU Product Market Integration," *Economic Policy*, 30, pp. 105–34.
Andeweg, R. and Galen, I. (2002) *Governance and Politics of the Netherlands* (Palgrave).
Andrews, D. and Willett, T. (1997) "Financial Interdependence and the State: International Monetary Relations at Century's End," *International Organization*, 51, pp. 479–511.
Apple, N. (1983) "The Historical Foundations of Class Struggle in Late Capitalist Liberal Democracy" in Clegg, S., Dow, G. and Boreham, P. (eds), *The State, Class and the Recession* (Croom Helm).
Arestis, P. (2003) "Macroeconomic Policies of the Economic and Monetary Union: Theoretical Underpinnings and Challenges," Bard College, Working Paper, no. 385.
—— and Sawyer, M. (2003) "Reforming the Euro's Institutional Framework," *Levy Economics Institute Policy Note 2003/2* (Annandale-on-Hudson, NY).
—— Brown, A. and Sawyer, M. (2003) *The Euro: Evolution and Prospects* (Cheltenham, UK: Edward Elgar).
Armstrong, P., Glyn, A. and Harrison, J. (1991) *Capitalism since 1945* (Basil Blackwell).
Aron, R. *et al* (1957) *L'Unification économique en Europe* (Neuchâtel).
Artis, M. and Cobham, D. (eds) (1991) *Labour's Economic Policies, 1974–79* (Manchester University Press).
Aspinwall, M. (2002) "Preferring Europe: Ideology and National Preferences on European Integration," *European Union Politics*, 3.
Attali, J. (1992) *Verbatim*, 3 vols (Seuil).
Bahu-Leyser, D. (1981) *De Gaulle, les Français et l'Europe* (Presses Universitaires de France).
Bairoch, P. (1996) "Globalization Myths and Realities: One Century of External Trade and Foreign Investment," in Boyer, R. and Drach, D. (eds), *States against Markets: The Limits of Globalization* (Routledge).
Baker, D., Epstein, G. and Pollin, R. (1990) *Globalization and Progressive Economic Policy* (Cambridge: Cambridge University Press).
Bakker, A. (1996) *The Liberalization of Capital Movements in Europe: The Monetary Committee and Financial Integration, 1958–1994* (Kluwer).
Balabkins, N. (1964) *Germany under Direct Controls* (New Brunswick: Rutgers University Press).
Balleix-Banerjee, C. (1999) *La France et la banque centrale européenne* (Presses Universitaires de France).
Bank of England (1991) *Quarterly Bulletin*, August.
Banuri, T. and Shor, J. (1992) *Financial Openness and National Autonomy: Opportunities and Constraints* (Oxford: Clarendon).
Barkin, S. (ed.) (1983) *Worker Militancy and its Consequences: The Changing Climate of Western Industrial Relations*, 2nd edn (Praeger).
Barreau, A. (1976) *Histoire inachevé de la convention collective nationale de la métallurgie* (Fédération des Travailleurs de la Métallurgie).
Barreau, J. (1990) *L'Etat entrepreneur: nationalisations, gestions du secteur public concurrentiel, construction européenne, 1982–1993* (L'Harmattan).
Barro, R. (1997) *Determinants of Economic Growth: A Cross-Country Empirical Study* (Cambridge, MA: M.I.T. Press).
Bates, R.H., *et al* (1998) *Analytic Narratives* (Princeton, N.J.: Princeton University Press).
Bauchard, P. (1986) *La Guerre des deux roses: du rêve à la réalité, 1981–85* (Grasset).
Baumol, W. *et al* (1992) *Productivity and American Leadership: The Long View* (Cambridge, MA.: Harvard University Press).

Bayne, N. and Putnam, R. (2000) *Hanging Together: The G7 and G8 Summit in Maturity and Renewal* (Hants, England: Aldershot).

Bayoumi, T. and Eichengreen, B. (1993) "Shocking Aspects of European Monetary Union," in Torres, F. and Giavazzi, F. (eds), *Adjustment and Growth in the European Monetary Union* (Cambridge: Cambridge University Press).

—— (1999) "Operationalising the Theory of Optimum Currency Areas," in Baldwin, R.E. *et al* (eds), *Market Integration, Regionalism and the Global Economy* (Cambridge: Cambridge University Press).

Bean, C. (1992) "Economic and Monetary Union in Europe," *Journal of Economic Perspectives*, 6, pp. 31–52.

Beard, C. (1913) *An Economic Interpretation of the Constitution of the US* (Macmillan).

Beaud, M. (1985) *La Politique économique de la gauche*, 2 vols (Syros).

Belassa, B. (1975) "Trade Creation and Trade Diversion in the European Common Market: An Appraisal of the Evidence," in Belassa, B. (ed.), *European Economic Integration* (Amsterdam: Elsevier).

—— (1986) "Intra-Industry Trade among Exporters of Manufactured Goods," in Greenaway, D. and Tharakan, P. (eds), *Imperfect Competition and International Trade: The Policy Aspects of Intra-Industry Trade* (Brighton: Wheatsheaf).

—— (1988) "The Determinants of Intra-European Trade in Manufactured Goods," *European Economic Review*, 19.

Bempt, P. van der (1999) "The Political Aspects of Economic and Monetary Union: A View from Brussels," in Minkkinen, P. and Patomāki, H. (eds), *The Politics of Economic and Monetary Union* (Boston: Kluwer).

Berger, S. (2002) "French Democracy without Borders?," *French Politics, Culture and Society*, 20, pp. 1–12.

Berghahn, V. (1986) *The Americanisation of West German Industry, 1945–73* (Cambridge: Cambridge University Press).

Bergström, H. (1991) "Sweden's Politics and Party System at the Crossroads," *West European Politics*, 14, pp. 8–30.

Berstein, S., Mayeur, J-M. and Milza, P. (eds) (1993) *MRP et la construction européenne* (Ed. Complexe).

Bertaud, J.P. *et al* (1978–81) *L'Histoire de la France contemporaine*, 8 vols (Messidor).

Bieler, A. (2000) *Globalization and Enlargement of the European Union: Austrian and Swedish Social Forces in the Struggle over Membership* (Routledge).

—— and Morton, A.D. (2001a) "Globalization, the State and Resistance: A 'Critical Economy' Response to Open Marxism," British International Studies Association conference.

—— (2001b) *Social Forces in the Making of the New Europe: The Restructuring of European Social Relations in the Global Political Economy* (Palgrave).

Bjöl, E. (1966) *La France devant l'Europe: la politique européenne de la IVe République* (Copenhagen: Thesis).

Blackbourn, D. and Eley, G. (1984) *The Peculiarities of German History* (Oxford University Press).

Blanchard, O. and Katz, L. (1992) "Regional Evolutions," *Brookings Papers on Economic Activity*, no. 1, pp. 1–75.

Blanchard, O. and Muet, P.-A. (1993) "Competitiveness through Disinflation: An Assessment of French Economic Strategy," *Economic Policy*, 16, pp. 11–58.

Blanchflower, D.G. (1991) "Fear, Unemployment and Pay Flexibility," *Economic Journal*, 101, pp. 483–96.

Blank, S. (1973) *Industry and Government in Britain: The Federation of British Industries in Politics, 1945–65* (Westmead, Hants: DC Heath).
Block, F. (1977) *The Origins of International Economic Disorder: A Study of United States Monetary Policy from WW II to the Present* (Berkeley: University of California Press).
—— (2000) "The Case of Control over Cross Border Capital Flows," in Polanyi-Levitt, K. and McRobbie, K. (eds), *Karl Polanyi in Vienna: The Contemporary Significance of the Great Transformation* (Black Rose Books).
Blum, R. (1969) *Soziale Marktwirtschaft: Wirtschaftspolitik zwischen Neoliberalismus und Ordoliberalismus* (Tübingen: Mohr).
Blyth, M. (2002a) "The Transformation of the Swedish Model: Economic Ideas, Distributional Conflict, and Institutional Change," *World Politics*, 54, pp. 1–26.
—— (2002b) Great Transformations: Economic Ideas and Institutional Change in the Twentieth Century (Cambridge: Cambridge University Press).
Boarman, P. (1964) *Germany's Economic Dilemma* (New Haven: Yale University Press).
Boddy, R. and Crotty, J. (1975) "Class Conflict and Macro-Policy: The Political Business Cycle," *Review of Radical Political Economy*, 7, pp. 1–19.
Böhm, F. (1982) "Left Wing and Right Wing Approaches to the Market Economy," in Wünche, F. (ed.), *Standard Texts on the Social Market Economy* (Gustav Fischer).
Boisseau, C. de and Pisani-Ferry, J. (1998) "The Political Economy of French Economic Policy in the Perspective of EMU," in Eichengreen, B. and Frieden, J. (eds), *Forging an Integrated Europe* (Ann Arbor: University of Michigan Press).
Boltho, A. (ed.) (1982) *The European Economy: Growth and Crisis* (Cambridge University Press).
Bonefeld, W. (ed.) (2001) *The Politics of European Integration: Monetary Union and Class* (Macmillan).
Bonin, H. (1987) *Histoire économique de la IVe République* (Economica).
Borrel, M. (1996) *Conflits du travail, changement social et politique en France depuis 1950* (L'Harmattan).
Bossuat, G. (1995) "The French Administrative Elite and the Unification of Western Europe, 1947–58," in Deighton, A. (ed.), *Building Post-War Europe: National Decision-Makers and European Institutions* (Macmillan).
—— (1996) *L'Europe des Français, 1943–1959* (Publications de la Sorbonne).
Botting, D. (1985) *From the Ruins of the Reich: Germany 1945–1949* (Crown).
Bourgeois, J. and Demeret, P. (1995) "The Working of EC Policies in Competition, Industry and Trade," in Buiges, P., Jacquemin, A. and Sapir, A. (eds), *Policies on Competition, Trade and Industry* (Aldershot: Edward Elgar).
Bourry, C. (1993) "Existe-t-il une industrie européenne?," *Etudes et recherches, ISERES*, no. 131.
Bouvier, J. *et al* (1982) "*L'Ere industrielle et la société d'aujourd'hui, 1880–1980,*" vol. 4, Braudel, F. and Labrousse, E. (eds), *Histoire économique et sociale de la France* (Presses universitaires de France).
Boy, D. and Mayer, N. (1997) *L'Electeur a ses raisons* (Presses de Sciences Pô).
Boyer, R. (1989) *The Regulation School: A Critical Introduction* (Columbia University Press).
—— (1996) "State and Market: A New Engagement for the Twenty-First Century?," in Boyer, R. and Drache, D. (eds), *States against Markets* (London: Routledge).
Braudel, F. (1972) *The Mediterranean and the Mediterranean World in the Age of Philip II* (Collins).
Braun, D. (1987) "Political Immobilism and Labor Market Performance: The Dutch Road to Mass Unemployment," *Journal of Public Policy*, 7, pp. 307–36.
Braun, N. (1969) "Le Patronat français et l'intervention européenne," *Projet*, 121.

Braunerhjelm, P. *et al* (1996) "Swedish Multinational Corporations: Recent Trends in Foreign Activities," *The Industrial Institute for Economic and Social Research*, Working Paper 462.
Braunthal, G. (1965) *The Federation of German Industry in Politics* (Ithaca, NY: Cornell University Press).
Brenner, R. (1998) "The Economics of Global Turbulence," in *New Left Review*, no. 229.
—— (2002) *The Boom and the Bubble: The US in the World Economy* (Verso).
Brenner, R. and Glick, M. (1991) "The Regulation Approach: Theory and History," *New Left Review*, no. 188, pp. 45–120.
Brown, W. and Wadhwani, S. (1990) "The Economic Effects of Industrial Relations Legislation since 1979," *National Institute Economic Review*, no. 131, pp. 57–70.
Brunet, J.P. (1987) "La Politique économique et sociale du gouvernement G. Mollet," in Ménager, B. *et al* (eds), *Guy Mollet: un camarade en République* (Presses universitaires de Lille).
Brusse, W. (1997) *Tariffs, Trade and European Integration, 1947–1957* (Macmillan).
Bührer, W. (1995) "German Industry and European Integration in the 1950s," in Wurm, C. (ed.), *Western Europe and Germany: The Beginning of European Integration, 1945–60* (Oxford: Berg).
Bulmers, S. and Paterson, W. (1987) *The Federal Republic of Germany and the European Community* (Allen & Unwin).
Burgess, M. (1989) *Federalism and the European Union: Political Ideas, Influence and Strategies in the European Community, 1972–1987* (London: Routledge).
Burkitt, Brian and Whyman, Philip (1994) "Employee Investment Funds in Sweden: Their Past, Present and Future," *European Business Review*, 94.
Burnham, Peter (1994) "Open Marxism and Vulgar International Political Economy," *Review of International Political Economy*, 1.
—— (1995) "State and Market in International Political Economy: Towards a Marxist Alternative," *Studies in Marxism*, 2.
Burley, A.M. and Mattli, W. (1993) "Europe before the Court: A Political Theory of Legal Integration," *International Organization*, 47, pp. 41–76.
Busch, A. (1993) "The Politics of Price Stability: Why the German-Speaking Nations are Different," in Castles, F. (ed.), *Families of Nations: Patterns of Public Policy in Western Democracies* (Aldershot: Dartmouth).
Cadiot, J-M. (1994) *Mitterrand et les Communistes, 1943–94* (Ed. Ramsay).
Callaghan, J. (2000) *The Retreat of Social Democracy* (Manchester: Manchester University Press).
Callinicos, A. (1989) *Against Post-Modernism: A Marxist Critique* (Cambridge: Polity).
—— (1995) *Theories and Narratives: Reflections on the Philosophy of History* (Cambridge: Polity).
Cambridge Economic Policy Group (CEPG) (1992) "Hands-off Economics Equals Stagnation," *The Observer*, 19 April.
Cameron, D. (1984) "Social Democracy and Labor Quiescence: The Representation of Economic Interests in Advanced Capitalist Societies," in Goldthorpe, J. (ed.), *Order and Conflict in Contemporary Capitalism* (Oxford: Oxford University Press).
—— (1995a) "From Barre to Balladur: Economic Policy in the Era of the EMS," in Flynn, G. (ed.), *Remaking the Hexagon: The New France in the New Europe* (Boulder, Col.: Westview).
—— (1995b) "Transnational Relations and the Development of European Economic and Monetary Union," in Risse-Kappen, T. (ed.), *Bringing Transnational Relations back in* (Cambridge: Cambridge University Press).

—— (1996) "National Interest, the Dilemmas of European Integration and Malaise," in Keeler, J. and Schain, M. (eds), *Chirac's Challenge: Liberalization, Europeanization and Malaise in France* (St. Martin's Press).

Capdevielle, J., *et al* (eds) (1981) *France de gauche, vote à droite* (Presses de la Fondation national des Sciences politiques).

CME (1971) *Le Capitalisme monopoliste de l'Etat. Traité marxiste d'économie politique* (Editions sociales).

Caporaso, J. (1995) "The European Union and Regional Integration Theory," in Rhodes, C. and Mazey, S. (eds), *The State of the EU: Building of a European Polity?* (Boulder, Col.: Lynn Riemer).

—— (1996) "The European Community and Forms of State: Westphalian, Regulatory or Post-Modern?," *Journal of Common Market Studies*, 34, pp. 29–52.

—— (1998) "Regional Integration Theory: Understanding Our Past and Anticipating our Future," in Sandholtz, W. and Stone Sweet, A. (eds), *European Integration and Supranational Governance* (Oxford University Press).

Carpenter, M. and Jefferys, S. (2000) *Management, Work and Welfare in Western Europe: A Historical and Contemporary Analysis* (Cheltenham: Edward Elgar).

Carr, E.H. (1961)*What is History?* (Macmillan).

Carré, J.-J., Dubois, P. and Malinvaud, E. (1972) *La Croissance française: un essai d'analyse économique causale de l'après-guerre* (Seuil).

Caron, F. (1981) *Histoire économique de la France* (A. Colin).

Cartelier, L. *et al* (eds) (1996) *Critique de la Raison communautaire* (Economica).

Cecchini, P. (1988) *The European Challenge, 1992: The Benefits of a Single Market* (Aldershot: Gower).

Centre d'étude des revenus et des coûts (1989) *Les Français et leurs revenus: le tournant des années 80* (La Découverte).

Cerny, P. (1997) "International Finance and the Erosion of Capitalist Diversity," in Crouch, C. and Streeck, W. (eds), *Political Economy of Modern Capitalism: Mapping Convergence and Diversity* (Sage).

Chang, H.-J. (2002) *Kicking Away the Ladder–Development Strategy in Historical Perspective* (Anthem Press).

Chevallier, F.-X. (2001) *Greenspan's Taming of the Wave: New Storms Challenging the New Economy* (Kogan Page).

Christiansen, N.F. (1994) "Denmark: End of an Idyll," in Andersen, P. and Camiller, P. (eds), *Mapping the West European Left* (Verso).

Christofferson, T. (1991) *The Socialists in Power, 1981–1986: From Autogestion to Cohabitation* (Associated University Press).

Clayton, R. and Pontusson, J. (1998) "The New Politics of the Welfare State Revisited: Welfare Reforms, Public Sector Restructuring and Inegalitarian Trends in Advanced Capitalist Societies," *European Union Institute*, 98/26.

Clegg, H. (1976) *Trade Unionism Under Collective Bargaining: A Theory Based on Comparisons of Six Countries* (Oxford University Press).

Coates, K. and Santer, J. (1996) *Dear Commissioner, Will Unemployment Break Europe?* (Nottingham: Spokesman).

Cohen, D. and Wyplosz, C. (1989) "The European Monetary System: An Agnostic Evaluation," in Bryant, R. *et al* (eds), *Macroeconomic Policies in an Interdependent World* (Washington, DC: Brookings Institution).

Cohen, E. (1992) *Le Colbertisme 'high tech': Economie des Telecoms et du Grand Projet* (Hachette).

—— (1995) "National Champions in Search of a Mission," in Hayward, J. (ed.), *Industrial Enterprise and European Integration: From National to International Champions* (Oxford University Press).

—— (1997) "The Interplay of Corporate, National and European Interest," in Wallace, H. and Young, A. (eds), *Participation in Policy-Making in the European Union* (Oxford: Clarendon).

Cohen, S. (1993) *When Strikes Make Sense–and Why: Lessons from the Third Republic French Coal Miners* (Plenum Press).

Collier, V. (ed.) (1998) *De-Regulation in the European Union: Environmental Perspectives* (Routledge).

Collignon, S. (2003) "Europe's Going Far Enough? Reflections on the Stability and Growth Pact, the Lisbon Strategy and the EU's Economic Governance," UACES Conference, Building EU Economic Government: Revising the Rules?

—— and Schwartzen, D. (2003) *Private Sector Involvement in the Euro: The Power of Ideas* (Routledge).

Combe, M. (1969) *L'Alibi: vingt ans d'un comité central d'entreprise* (Gallimard).

Commission Memorandum (1962) *Action Program of the Community for the Second Stage,* 24 October.

—— (1970) *Memorandum to the Council on the Preparation of a Plan for the Phased Establishment of an Economic and Monetary Union.*

Concialdi, P. (2001) "Pauvreté et politique sociale: la lente dérive vers le libéralisme," in Fondation Copernic (eds), *Un Social-Libéralisme à la française? Regards critiques sur la politique économique et sociale de Lionel Jospin* (La Découverte).

Corcoran, J. (1998) "The Economic Limits of European Integration," in Moss, B. and Michie, J. (eds), *The Single Currency in National Perspective: A Community in Crisis?* (Macmillan).

Cotta, A. (1991) *La France en panne* (Fayard).

Cotta, A. *et al* (1977) *Le Redeploiement industriel* (Ministère de l'industrie).

Cours-Salies, P. (1988) *La CFDT: un passé porteur d'avenir* (La Brèche).

Coutts, K. *et al* (1992) "Devaluation of Sterling is no 'Quick Fix' ", *The Observer*, 3 May.

Couve de Murville, M. (1971) *Une Politique étrangère, 1958–69* (Plon).

Cowles, M. (1995) "Setting the Agenda for a New Europe," *Journal of Common Market Studies,* 33.

—— (1997) "Organising Industrial Coalitions: A Challenge for the Future?," in Wallace, H. and Young, A. (eds) *Participation in Policy-Making.*

—— Caporaso, J. and Risse, T. (eds) (2001) *Transforming Europe: Europeanization and Domestic Change* (Ithaca, N.Y.: Cornell University Press).

Cox, R.W. (1981) "Social Forces, States and World Orders: Beyond International Relations Theory," *Millennium: Journal of International Studies,* 10.

—— (1983) "Gramsci, Hegemony and International Relations: An Essay on Method," *Millennium: Journal of International Studies,* 12.

—— (1987) *Production, Power and World Order* (Columbia University Press).

—— (1993) "Structural Issues of Global Governance: Implications for Europe," in Gill, S. (ed.), *Gramsci, Historical Materialism and International Relations* (Cambridge: Cambridge University Press).

—— and Sinclair, T. (1996) *Approaches to World Order* (Cambridge: Cambridge University Press).

Craig, G. (1965) *The Politics of the Prussian Army* (Oxford University Press).

Crouch, C. (1979) (ed.), *State and Economy in Contemporary Capitalism* (Croom Helm).

Crouch, C. (2002) "The Euro and Labour Market and Wage Policies," in Dyson, K. (ed.), *European States and the Euro: Europeanization, Variation, and Convergence* (Oxford University Press).

—— and Pizzorno, A. (1978) *The Resurgence of Class Conflict in Western Europe Since 1968*, 2 vols (Macmillan).

Crowley, P. (2003a) "Stupid or Sensible? The Future of the Stability and Growth Pact," *EUSA Review*, 16.

—— (2003b): UACES Conference, Building EU Economic Government. "Do We Need a Stability and Growth Pact for Europe?," *Revising the Rules?*

Cutler, T. *et al* (1989) *1992: The Struggle for Europe: A Critical Evaluation of the EC* (Oxford: Berg).

Dahl, R. (1998) *On Democracy* (New Haven: Yale University Press).

Dahrendorf, R. (1968) *Society and Democracy in Germany* (Vintage).

Daley, M. (1997) "Welfare States under Pressure: Cash Benefits in European States Over the Last Ten Years," *Journal of European Social Policy*, 7.

Dankert, P. and Kooyman, A. (eds) (1989) *Europe sans frontières: les Socialistes et l'avenir de la CEE* (Anvers: EPO).

Dang-Nguyen, G. *et al* (1993) "Networks in European Policy Making: Europeification of Telecommunications Policy," in Andersen, S. and Eliassen, K. (eds), *Making Policy in Europe: The Europeification of National Policy-Making* (Sage).

Davis, J. (1989) "Socialism and the Working Classes in Italy before 1914," in Geary, D. (ed.), *Labour and Socialist Movements in Europe before 1914* (Oxford: Berg).

DDF (1989) *Documents diplomatiques français, 1956* (Imprimerie nationale).

Deeg, R. (1998) *Finance Capital Unveiled: Banks and Economic Adjustment in Germany* (Ann Arbor: University of Michigan Press).

Dehousse, R. (1998) *The European Court of Justice: The Politics of Judicial Integration* (Basingstoke: Macmillan).

Delorme, R. and André, C. (1983) *L'Etat et l'économie: un essai d'explication de l'évolution des dépenses sociales en France (1870–1980)* (Le Seuil).

Delors Report (1989) "Committee for the Study of Economic and Monetary Union in Europe," *Report on Economic and Monetary Union in the European Community* (Official Publications of the EC).

Denison, E. (1967) *Why Growth Rates Differ* (Washington, DC: Brookings Institution).

Denton, G. (1969) "Planning and Integration: Medium-Term Policy as an Instrument of Integration," in Denton, G. (ed.), *Economic Integration in Europe* (Weidenfeld and Nicolson).

Deutsch, K. (1957) *Political Community and the North Atlantic Area: International Organization in the Light of Historical Experience* (Princeton, N.J.: Princeton University Press).

De Vos, T. (1989) *Multinational Corporations in Democratic Host Countries: US Multinationals and the Vredeling Proposal* (Aldershot: Dartmouth).

De Winter, L. (1993) "Socialistes belges entre région et l'Europe," in Telo, M. (ed.), *De la Nation à l'Europe: paradoxes et dilemmes de la social-démocratie* (Brussels: Bruyand).

Dickhaus, M. (1996) "Facing the Common Market: The German Central Bank and the Establishing of the EEC, 1955–58," *Journal of European Integration History*, 2.

Dierickx, G. (1994) "Christian Democracy and its Ideological Rivals: An Empirical Comparison in the Low Countries," in Hanley, D. (ed.), *Christian Democracy in Europe: A Comparative Perspective* (Pinter).

Dignon, T. (1996) "Regional Disparities and Regional Policy in the EU," *Oxford Review of Economic Policy*, 11.

Dillard, D. (1989) "The Influence of Keynesian Thought on German Economic Policy," in Hall, P.A. (ed.), *The Political Power of Economic Ideas: Keynesianism across Nations* (Princeton, N.J.: Princeton University Press).

Dinan, D. (1994) *Ever Closer Union? An Introduction to the European Community* (Macmillan).

Dobb, M. (1963) *Studies in the Development of Capitalism* (Routledge and Kegan Paul).

Dobbin, F. (1993) "What Do Markets Have in Common? Toward a Fast Train Policy for the EC," in Andersen, S. and Eliassen, K. (eds), *Making Policy in Europe.*

Doremus, P. *et al* (1998) *The Myth of the Global Corporation* (Princeton, N.J.: Princeton University Press).

Drake, H. (2000) *Jacques Delors: Perspectives on a European Leader* (Routledge).

Dreyfus, F.-G. (1993) *France and EC Membership Evaluated* (St. Martins Press).

Duchêne, F. (1991) *Jean Monnet: The First Statesman of Interdependence* (Norton & Co.)

Dumenil G. and Lévy D. (2000) *Crise et sortie de crise: ordre et désordres néoliberaux* (Presses universitaires de France).

Durand, C. (1974) *La Mort de l'état patron* (Editions ouvrières).

Duverger, M. (1955) "SFIO: Mort ou Transformation?," *Temps modernes*, nos. 112–13, pp. 1863–85.

Dyson, K. (1994) *Elusive Union: The Process of Economic and Monetary Union in Europe* (Longman).

—— (ed.) (2002) *European States and the Euro.*

—— and Featherstone, K. (1999) *Road to Maastricht: Negotiating Economic and Monetary Union* (Oxford University Press).

Ebbinghaus, B. and Visser, J. (1994) "Barriers and Pathways to 'Borderless' Solidarity: Organized Labour and European Integration," unpublished paper.

—— (1999) "European Labor and Transnational Solidarity: Challenges, Pathways and Barriers," in Klausen, J. and Tilly, L. (eds), *European Integration in Social and Historical Perspective* (Rowman).

Edelman, M. and Fleming, R.W. (1965) *The Politics of Wage Price Decisions: A Four Country Analysis* (Chicago: University of Illinois Press).

Eichener, V. (1992) "Social Dumping or Innovative Regulation? Processes and Outcomes of European Decision-Making in the Sector of Health and Safety at Work Harmonisation," European Union Institute Working Paper 92/28.

Eichengreen, B. (1992) "Is Europe an Optimum Currency Area?" in Borner, S. and Gruld, A. (eds), *The European Community after 1992* (IIFC).

—— and Frieden J. (1994) "The Political Economy of European Monetary Unification: An Analytical Introduction," in Eichengreen, B. and Frieden, J. *The Political Economy of European Monetary Unification* (Boulder, Col.: Westview).

Eironline (2001) "Mediation authority seeks to improve wage-formation process," (28/05/2001), *http://www.eiro.eurofound.ie*, 17/06/2002.

Eley, G. (1980) *Reshaping the German Right: Radical Change and Political Change after Bismarck* (New Haven: Yale University Press).

Elgey, G. (1972) *La République des Tourmentes, 1954–59* (Fayard).

Elgie, R. (1998) "Democratic Accountability and Central Bank Independence: Historical and Continental, National and European Perspectives," *West European Politics*, 21, pp. 53–76.

Emerson, M. *et al* (1988) *The Economics of 1992: The EC Commission's Assessment of the Economic Effects of Completing the Internal Market* (Oxford University Press).

Emerson, M. (1990) *One Market, One Money: An Evaluation of the Potential Benefits and Costs of Forming an Economic and Monetary Union* (Oxford University Press).
Epstein, G. and Schor, J. (1989) "Divorce of the Bank of Italy and the Treasury," in Lang, P. and Regini, M. (eds), *State, Market and Social Regulation: New Perspectives on Italy* (Cambridge: Cambridge University Press).
—— (1990) "Macropolicy in the Rise and Fall of the Golden Age," in Marglin, S. and Schor, J. (eds), *The Golden Age of Capitalism: Reinterpreting the Post-War Experience* (Oxford: Clarendon).
—— (1996) "International Capital Mobility and the Scope for National Economic Management," in Boyer, R. and Drache, D. (eds), *States versus Markets.*
—— and Gintis, H. (1995), *Macroeconomic Policy after the Conservative Era* (Cambridge: Cambridge University Press).
Erhard, L. (1958) *Prosperity Through Competition* (Praeger).
—— (1962) *Deutsche Wirtschaftspolitik: der Weg der sozialen Marktwirtschaft* (Düsseldorf: Econ).
Esping-Andersen, G. (1980) *Social Class, Social Democracy and State Building* (Copenhagen).
—— (1985) *Politics Against Markets: The Social Democratic Road to Power* (Princeton, N.J.: Princeton University Press).
—— (1990) *The Three Worlds of Welfare Capitalism* (Princeton, N.J.: Princeton University Press).
Essex, M. (2003) "German Woes Set to Continue," *The European Journal*, 10.
Eucken, W. (1950) *The Foundations of Economics: History and Theory* (Hodge).
—— (1951) *The Foundations of Economics* (Chicago: University of Chicago Press).
—— (1952) *This Unsuccessful Age; or the Pain of Economic Progress* (Oxford University Press).
—— (1954) *Kapitaltheoretische Untersuchungen* (Tübingen: Mohr).
European Commission (1990) *European Economy: Social Europe* (Brussels).
—— (1994) "One Market, One Money," *European Economy*, 58.
Evans, A. and Martin, S. (1991) "Socially Acceptable Distortion of Competition: Community Policy on State Aid," *European Law Review*, 16.
Fagenberg, J. and Verspagen, B. (1996) "Heading for Divergence? Regional Growth in Europe Reconsidered," *Journal of Common Market Studies*, 34, pp. 431–38.
Faini, R. (1999) "European Migrants: An Endangered Species?" in Baldwin, R.E. *et al* (eds), *Market Integration.*
Farnetti, R. and Warde, I. (1997) *Le Modèle anglo-saxon en question* (Economica).
Favier, P. and Martin-Rolland, M. (1990) *La Décennie Mitterrand: les ruptures (1981–1984)* (Seuil).
Featherstone, K. (1988) *Socialist Parties and European Integration: A Comparative History* (Manchester: Manchester University Press).
—— (2002) "The Political Dynamics of External Empowerment: The Emergence of EMU and the Challenge to the European Social Model," ECSA Conference.
Federal Trust (2003–04a) Workshops: From the Convention to the IGC, 10 July, What Union after the IGC?, 16 December.
—— *(2003–04b) EU Constitution Project Newletter.*
Feenstra, R. (1998) "Integration of Trade and Disintegration of Production in the Global Economy," *Journal of Economic Perspectives*, 12, pp. 31–52.
Feldstein, M. (1997) "The Political Economy of the European Economic and Monetary Union: Political Sources of an Economic Liability," *Journal of Economic Perspectives*, 11, pp. 23–42.

Fioretos, K.-O. (1997) "The Anatomy of Autonomy: Interdependence, Domestic Balances of Power, and European Integration," *Review of International Studies*, 23, pp. 293–320.
Flam, H. (1992) "Product Markets and 1992: Full Integration, Large Gains?," *Journal of Economic Perspectives*, 6, pp. 7–30.
Flanagan, R. (1993) "European Wage Equalization since the Treaty of Rome," in Ulman, L., Eichengreen, B. and Dickens, W.T. (eds), *Labor in Integrated Europe* (Washington, DC: The Brookings Institution).
Fligstein, N. and Brantley, P. (1995) "The 1992 Single Market Program and the Interests of Business," in Eichengreen, B., Frieden, J. and von Hagen, J. (eds), *Politics and Institutions in an Integrated Europe* (Springer).
Fontagné, L. *et al* (1997) "Trade Patterns Inside the Single Market," *Document du travail*, no. 97–07 CEPII.
Fondation Copernic (2001) *Social-libéralisme à la française.*
Fonteneau, A. and Muet, P.-A. (1985) *La Gauche face à la crise* (Presses de la Fondation nationale des sciences politiques).
Forsyth, D. and Notermans, T. (eds) (1997) *Macroeconomic Policy Regimes and Financial Regulation in Europe, 1931–1994* (Oxford: Berghahn).
Fouskas, V. (1998) *Italy, Europe, the Left: The Transformation of Italian Communism and the European Imperative* (Aldershot: Ashgate).
Frank, R. (1995) "Pompidou, le franc et l'Europe," in Association Georges Pompidou (ed.), *Georges Pompidou et l'Europe* (Brussels: Editions Complexe).
Franzese, Jr., R. (1999) "Partially Independent Central Banks, Politically Responsive Governments, and Inflation," *American Journal of Political Science*, 43, pp. 687–706.
—— (2000) "Electoral and Partisan Cycles in Economic Policies and Outcomes," unpublished paper and personal communication.
—— (2002) "Electoral and Partisan Cycles in Economic Policies and Outcomes," *Annual Review of Political Science*, 5.
—— and Hall, P. (2000) "Institutional Dimensions of Coordinated Wage Bargaining and Monetary Policy," in Iversen, T. (ed.), *Unions, Employers and Central Banks* (Cambridge: Cambridge University Press).
Freeman, R. (1994) "On the Divergences of Unionism among Developed Countries," in Brunetta, R. and Dell'Aringa, C. (eds), *Labor Relations and Market Performance* (Macmillan).
Frieden, J. (1991) "Invested Interests: The Politics of National Economic Policies in a World of Global Finance," *International Organization*, 45, pp. 425–52.
—— (1996) "The Impact of Goods and Capital Market Integration on European Monetary Politics," *Comparative Political Studies*, 29, pp. 197–222.
—— (1998) "Making Political Commitments: France and Italy in the EMS, 1979–1985," in Eichengreen, B. and Frieden, J. (eds), *Forging an Integrated Europe* (Ann Arbor: University of Michigan Press).
Friedman, G. (1998) *State-Making and Labor Movements: France and the US, 1875–1914* (Ithaca, N.Y.: Cornell University Press).
—— (2003) "Has the Forward March of Labor Halted? Union Growth and Decline in Comparative and Historical Perspective," unpublished paper.
Friot, B. (2003) "The French Social Wage and Welfare," French Labour Seminar.
Frost, R. (1991) *Alternating Currents: Nationalized Power in France* (Ithaca, N.Y.: Cornell University Press).
Fukuyama, F. (1992) *The End of History and the Last Man* (Hamish Hamilton).
Furlong, P. (1982) "Political Underdevelopment and the Economic Recession in Italy," in Cox, A. (ed.), *Politics, Policy and the European Recession* (Macmillan).

Gabel, M. (1998) *Interests and Integration: Market Liberalization, Public Opinion and the European Union* (Ann Arbor: University of Michigan Press).
Galbraith, K. (1956) *American Capitalism: The Concept of Countervailing Power* (Boston: Houghton Mifflin).
Garrett, G. (1998) *Partisan Politics in the Global Economy* (Cambridge: Cambridge University Press).
Gauron, A. (1983) *Histoire économique et sociale de la Cinquième République* (La Découverte).
Gelber, H. (1997) *Sovereignty through Interdependence* (Cambridge, Mass.: Kluwer).
Gélédan, A. (ed.) (1993) *Le Bilan économique des années Mitterrand, 1981–1994* (Le Monde-Editions).
Gerbet, P. (1983) *La Construction de l'Europe* (Imprimerie nationale).
Giddens, A. (1998) *The Third Way: The Renewal of Social Democracy* (Cambridge: Cambridge University Press).
Giersch, H. *et al* (1992) *The Fading Miracle: Four Decades of the Market Economy in Germany* (Cambridge: Cambridge University Press).
Giesbert, F.O. (1990) *Le Président* (Seuil).
Gill, S. (ed.) (1993) *Gramsci, Historical Materialism and International Relations* (Cambridge: Cambridge University Press).
Gillingham, J. (1991) *Coal, Steel and the Rebirth of Europe: The Germans and French from Ruhr Conflict to the Economic Community* (Cambridge: Cambridge University Press).
—— (2003) *European Integration, 1950–2003: Superstate or New Market Economy?* (Cambridge: Cambridge University Press).
Ginsberg, R. (2003) "European Security and Defense Policy: The State of Play," *EUSA Review*, 16.
Ginsborg, P. (1990) *A History of Contemporary Italy: Society and Politics, 1943–1988* (Harmondsworth: Penguin).
—— (2001) *Italy and its Discontents: Family, Civil Society, State, 1980–2001* (Harmondsworth: Penguin).
Giscard d'Estaing, V. (1976) *La Démocratie française* (V. Giscard d'Estaing.)
Glyn, A. (1990) "Productivity and the Crisis of Fordism," *International Review of Applied Economics*, 4, pp. 28–44.
—— (1995a) "Stability, Inegalitarianism and Stagnation: An Overview of the Advanced Capitalist Countries in the 1980s," in Epstein, G.A. and Gintis, H.M. (eds), *Macroeconomic Policy after the Conservative Era: Studies in Investment, Saving and Finance* (Cambridge: Cambridge University Press).
—— (1995b) "Social Democracy and Full Employment," *New Left Review*, no. 211, pp. 33–55.
Golden, M. (1988) *Labor Divided: Austerity and Working Class Politics in Contemporary Italy* (Ithaca, N.Y.: Cornell University Press).
—— and Pontusson, J. (eds) (1992) *Bargaining for Change: Union Politics in North America and Europe* (Ithaca, N.Y.: Cornell University Press).
Golub, J. (ed.) (1998) *New Instruments for Environmental Policy in the EU* (Routledge).
Goodman, J. (1992) *Monetary Sovereignty: The Politics of Central Banking in Western Europe* (Ithaca, N.Y.: Cornell University Press).
Gordon, D.R., Edwards, R. and Reich, M. (1982) *Segmented Work, Divided Workers: The Transformation of Labor in American History* (Cambridge: Cambridge University Press).
Gough, I. (1979) *The Political Economy of the Welfare State* (Macmillan).

Gourevitch, P. (1986) *Politics in Hard Times: Comparative Responses to International Economic Crises* (Ithaca, N.Y.: Cornell University Press).
Graf, W. (1976) *The German Left Since 1945* (Cambridge: Cambridge: The Oleander Press).
Gramsci, A. (1971) *Selections from the Prison Notebooks* (Lawrence and Wishart).
Grande, E. (1988) "West Germany: From Reform Policy to Crisis Management," in Damgaard, E., Gerlich, P. and Richardson, J.J. (eds), *Politics of Economic Crisis: Lesssons from Western Europe* (Aldershot: Avebury).
—— (1987) "Neoconservatism and Conservative-Liberal Economic Policy in West Germany," *European Journal of Political Research*, 15, pp. 281–97.
Grant, C. (1994) *Delors: Inside the House that Jacques Built* (Brealey).
—— (1996) "The Theory and Practice of Delorism," in Bond, M., Smith, J. and Wallace, W. (eds), *Eminent Europeans: Personalities Who Shaped Contemporary Europe* (The Gregcourt Press).
Grant, W., Duncan, M. and Newell, P. (2000) *The Effectiveness of EU Environmental Policy* (Macmillan).
Grauwe, P. de (2002) "The Euro at Stake? The Monetary Union in an Enlarged Europe," *CES Forum*, 15, pp. 31–33.
Green, D. (1999) "Who are the Europeans?," ECSC conference.
Greenwood, J. (1997) *Representing Interests in the European Union* (Macmillan).
Grieco, J. (1995) "The Maastricht Treaty Economies, Monetary Union and the New Realist Research Program," *Review of International Studies*, 21, pp. 21–40.
Griffiths, R. (ed.) (1993) *Socialist Parties and the Question of Europe in the 1950s* (E.J. Brill).
—— (ed.) (1997a) "The Common Market," in *The Economic Development of the E.E.C.* (Cheltenham, UK: E. Elgar).
—— (ed.) (1997b) *The Netherlands and the Integration of Europe, 1945–1957* (Amsterdam: NEHA).
Griffuelhes, V. (1910) "L'Inferiorité des capitalistes française," *Mouvement socialiste*, 226, pp. 321–28.
Groeben, H. von der (1987) *The European Community–The Formative Years: The Struggle to Establish the Common Market and the Political Union (1958–66)* (Brussels: Official Publications of the European Communities).
Gros, D. and Thygesen, N. (1998) *European Monetary Integration*, 2nd edn (Longman).
Grossman, G. (1990) "The Economics of 1992: The EC Commission's Assessment of the Economic Effects of Completing the Internal Market," *Journal of International Economics*, 28, pp. 385–88.
Guibert, B. (1975) *La Mutation industrielle de la France* (INSEE).
Guillen, P. (1980) "Frankreich und der Europaïsche Wiederaufschnung," *Vierteljahrshefte für Zeitgeschichte*, 28, pp. 1–19.
—— (1988) "L'Europe remède à l'impuissance française: le gouvernement G. Mollet et la négotiation du traité de Rome," *Revue d'histoire diplomatique*, 102, pp. 319–35.
Haas, E. (1958) *The Uniting of Europe: Political, Economic and Social Forces, 1950–57* (Stevens & Sons).
—— (1964) *Beyond the Nation State: Functionalism and International Organization* (Stanford: Stanford University Press).
—— (1975) *The Obsolescence of Regional Integration Theory* (Berkeley: Institute of International Studies).
Halimi, S., Michie, J. and Milne, S. (1994) "The Mitterrand Experience," in Michie, J. and Smith, J.G. (eds), *Unemployment in Europe* (Academic Press).

Hall, M. (1992) "Behind the European Work Council Directive: The European Commission's Legislative Strategy," *British Journal of Industrial Relations*, 30, pp. 547–66.

Hall, P. (1986) *Governing the Economy: The Politics of State Intervention in Britain and France* (Oxford University Press).

—— (ed.) (1989) *The Political Power of Economic Ideas: Keynesianism Across Nations* (Princeton, N.J.: Princeton University Press).

—— and Franzese, R. (1998) "Mixed Signals: Central Bank Independence, Coordinated Wage Bargaining, and European Monetary Union," *International Organization*, 52, pp. 505–35.

Hall, M. and Gold, M. (1994) "Statutory European Works Councils: The Final Countdown?," *Industrial Relations Journal*, 25, pp. 177–98.

Hall, P. and Soskice, D. (eds) (2001) *Varieties of Capitalism: The Institutional Foundations of Comparative Advantage* (Oxford University Press).

Hallstein, W. (1962) *United Europe: Challenge and Opportunity* (Cambridge, Mass.: Harvard University Press).

—— (1972) *Europe in the Making* (George Allen & Unwin).

Hamon, H. and Rotman, P. (1982) *La Deuxième gauche: histoire intellectuelle et politique de la CFDT* (Ed. Ramsey).

Hancké, B. (2002) *Large Firms and Institutional Change: Industrial Renewal and Economic Restructuring in France* (Oxford University Press).

Hanley, D. (ed.) (1994) *Christian Democracy*.

Hanson, B. (1998) "What Happened to Fortress Europe? External Trade Policy Liberalization in the European Union," *International Organization*, 52, pp. 55–85.

Hardach, K. (1980) *The Political Economy of Germany in the Twentieth Century* (Berkeley: University of California Press).

Harrison, R. (1974) *Europe in Question: Theories of Regional International Integration* (Allen and Unwin).

Harryvan, A.J. *et al* (1993) "Dutch Attitudes Toward European Military, Political and Economic Integration (1951–54)," in Trausch, G. (ed.), *European Integration from the Schuman Plan to the Treaties of Rome* (LGDJ).

Hartley, T. (1994) *The Foundations of European Community Law*, 3rd edn (Oxford: Clarendon).

Hartwell, R.M. (1995) *A History of the Mont Pelerin Society* (Indianapolis: Liberty Fund).

Hassel, A. and Ebbinghaus, B. (2000) "Concerted Reforms: Linking Wage Formation and Social Policy in Europe," International Conference of Europeanists.

Hay, C. (1999a) "Contemporary Capitalism, Globalisation, Regionalisation and the Resistance of National Variation," *Review of International Studies*, 26, pp. 509–32.

—— (1999b) *The Political Economy of New Labour: Labouring under False Pretences?* (Manchester: Manchester University Press).

Hayek, F. (1944) *The Road to Serfdom* (Routledge and Kegan Paul).

—— (1949) "The Economic Conditions of Inter-State Federalism," in his *Individualism and Economic Order* (Routledge and Kegan Paul).

—— (1972) *A Tiger by the Tail* (Institute of Economic Affairs).

—— (1976) *Denationalisation of Money: An Analysis of the Theory and Practice of Concurrent Currencies* (Institute of Economic Affairs).

—— (1982) *Law, Legislation and the Liberty: A New Statement of the Liberal Principles of Justice and Political Economy*, 3 vols (Routledge and Kegan Paul).

—— (1991) *Economic Freedom* (Basil Blackwell).

Hayward, J. (1995) "Europe's Industrial Champions," in Hayward, J. (ed.), *Industrial Enterprise and European Integration: From National to International Champions in Western Europe* (Oxford University Press).

Heclo, H. and Madsen, H. (1987) *Policy and Politics in Sweden: Principled Pragmatism* (Philadelphia: Temple University Press).
Heffernan, R. and Marqusee, M. (1992) *Defeat from the Jaws of Victory: Inside Kinnock's Labour Party* (Verso).
Heisenberg, D. (1999) *The Mark of the Bundesbank: Germany's Role in European Monetary Cooperation* (Boulder, Col.: Lynne Rienner).
—— and Richmond, A. (1999) "Supranational Institution-Building in the European Union," EUSA conference.
Held, D. *et al* (eds) (2000) *The Global Transformations: Politics, Economics and Culture* (Stanford: Stanford University Press).
Held, M. (1982) *Sozialdemokratie und Keynesianismus* (Frankfurt: Campus).
Helleiner, E. (1994) *States and the Re-Emergence of Global Finance from Bretton Woods to the 1990s* (Ithaca, N.Y.: Cornell University Press).
Hellman, J. (1981) *Emmanuel Mounier and the New Catholic Left, 1930–50* (Toronto: University of Toronto Press).
Helpman, E. and Krugman, P. (1985) *Market Structure and Foreign Trade: Increasing Returns, Imperfect Competition, and the International Economy* (Cambridge, MA.: Harvard University Press).
Henry, S. and Ormerod, P. (1978) "Incomes Policy and Wage Inflation: Empirical Evidence for the UK, 1961–77," *National Institute Economic Review*, 85.
Herr, H. (1997) "The International Monetary System and Domestic Economic Policy," in Forsyth, D.J. and Notermans, T. (eds), *Regime Changes: Macroeconomic Policy and Financial Regulation in Europe from the 1930s to the 1990s* (Providence, R.I.: Berghahn).
Heylen, F. and Poech, H. von (1995) "National Labor Market Institutions and the European Economic Integration Process," *Journal of Common Market Studies*, 33, pp. 573–96.
Hibbs, D. (1985) "Inflation, Political Support and Macroeconomic Policy," in Lindberg, L. and Maier, C. (eds), *The Politics of Inflation and Economic Stagnation* (Washington, DC: The Brookings Institution).
—— (1987) *The Political Economy of Industrial Democracies* (Cambridge, Mass.: Harvard University Press).
Hilferding, R. (1981) *Finance Capital* (Routledge and Keegan Paul).
Hine, C. (1985) *The Political Economy of European Trade: An Introduction to the Trade Policies of the EEC* (Harvester).
Hirst, P. and Thompson, G. (1996) *Globalization in Question: The International Economy and the Possibilities of Governance* (Polity).
Hitchcock, W. (2002) "Crisis and Modernization in the Fourth Republic: From Suez to Rome," in Mouré, K. and Alexander, M. (eds), *Crisis and Renewal in France – 1918–1962* (Oxford: Berghahn)
Hix, S. (1999) *The European Union as a Political System* (Macmillan).
—— (2004) "The Prospect of 'United Centre-Right Government' in the EU", *European Union Studies Association,* 17 (3), pp. 6–7.
—— and Lord, C. (1997) *Political Parties in the European Union* (Macmillan).
Hobsbawm, E. (1978) *The Forward March of Labour Halted.* (Verso).
—— (1998) "Introduction," in Marx, K. and Engels, F., *The Communist Manifesto: A Modern Edition* (Verso).
Hodges, M. (1977) "Industrial Policy: A Directorate in Search of a Role," in Wallace, H. Wallace, W. and Webb, C. (eds) *Policy-Making in the EC* (Wiley).
Hodges, M. and Wallace, W. (eds) (1981) *Economic Divergence in the European Community* (Allen & Unwin).

Hodson, D. and Maher, I. (2003): "Hard, Soft and Open Methods of Policy Co-ordination and Reform of the SGP," *Revising the Rules?*
Hofnung, T. (2001) *Georges Marchais: l'inconnu du Parti communiste français* (L'Archipel).
Holden, R. (1999) "Labour's Transformation: Searching for the Point of Origin – The European Dynamic," *Politics*, 19.
Holland, S. (1980) *The Uncommon Market* (Macmillan).
Holloway, J. (1994) "Global Capital and the National State," *Capital and Class*, no. 52, pp. 23–50.
—— and Picciotto, S. (1977) "Capital, Crisis and the State," *Capital and Class*, no. 29, pp. 76–101.
Holman, O. (2001) "The Enlargement of the European Union towards Central and Eastern Europe: The Role of Supranational and Transnational Actors," in Bieler, A. and Morton, A.D. (eds), *Social Forces in the Making of the New Europe: The Restructuring of European Social Relations in the Global Political Economy* (Palgrave).
—— and Pijl, K. van der (1996) "The Capitalist Class in the European Union," in Kourvitaris, G.A. (ed.), *The Impact of European Integration: Political, Sociological and Economic Change* (Praeger).
Hooghe, L. and Marks, G. (1999) "The Making of a Polity: The Struggle over European Integration," in Kitschelt, H. *et al* (eds), *Continuity and Change in Contemporary Capitalism* (Cambridge: Cambridge University Press).
Hopkins, T. and Wallerstein, I. (eds) (1980) *Processes of the World-System* (Sage).
Hoskyns, C. (1996) *Integrating Gender: Women, Law and Politics in the EU* (Verso).
Howarth, D. (2001) *The French Road to European Monetary Union* (Palgrave).
Huang-Ngoc, I. (2001) "Politique de l'emploi: baisse du coût du travail et réforme du financement français," in Fondation Copernic (ed.), *Social-Libéralisme à la française*.
Huber, E. and Stephens, J.D. (2001) *Development and Crisis of the Welfare State: Parties and Policies in Global Markets* (Chicago: The University of Chicago Press).
Huelshoff, M. (1997) "German Business and the 1992 Project," in Lankowski, K. (ed.), *Germany and the EC: Beyond Hegemony and Containment* (Macmillan).
Huemer, G. *et al* (eds) (1999) *The Role of Employer Associations and Labour Unions in the EMU: Institutional Requirements for European Economic Policies* (Aldershot: Ashgate).
Husson, M. (1996) *Misère du capital: une critique du néolibéralisme* (Syros).
—— (2001a) "Paradoxes et l'incertitude de l'euro," in Fondation Copernic (ed.), *Social-Libéralisme à la française*.
—— (2001b) "Minimum Wage and Real Income Outcomes in France, 1950–present," French Labour Seminar.
Hutton, W. (1995) *The State We're In* (Jonathan Cape).
Hyman, R. (1996) "Union Identities and Ideologies in Europe," in Pasture, P. *et al* (eds) *The Lost Perspective? Trade Unions between Ideology and Social Action in the New Europe: Significance of Ideology in European Trade Unionism*, vol. 2 (Aldershot: Avebury).
Industrial Agreement (1999) *Agreement on Industrial Development and Wage Formation*, Stockholm.
Ingebritsen, C. (1998) *The Nordic States and European Unity* (Ithaca, N.Y.: Cornell University Press).
Ingham, G. (1984) *Capitalism Divided? The City and Industry in British Social Development* (Macmillan).
Inglehart, R. (1977) *The Silent Revolution: Changing Values and Political Styles among Western Publics* (Princeton, N.J.: Princeton University Press).

—— *et al* (1987) "The Evolution of Public Attitudes towards European Integration, 1970–86," *Journal of European Integration*, 10.

International Monetary Fund (1952–99) *Annual Report* (Washington, DC).

Italiener, A. (1993) "Monetary Maastricht: EMU Issues and How They Were Settled," in Gretschmann, K. (ed.), *Economic and Monetary Union: Implications for National Policy-Makers* (Dordrecht: Martin Nijhoff).

Irving, W. (1973) *Christian Democracy in France* (George Allen & Unwin).

Iversen, T., Pontusson, J. and Soskice, D. (eds) (2000) *Unions, Employers and Central Banks: Macro-economic Coordination and Institutional Change in Social Market Economies* (Cambridge: Cambridge University Press).

Jacoby, W. (2000) *Imitation and Politics: Redesigning Germany* (Ithaca, N.Y.: Cornell University Press).

Jacquemin, A. and Jong, H. de (1977) *European Industrial Organization* (Macmillan).

Jacobi, O. (1986) "Economic Development and Trade Union Collective Bargaining Policy since the mid-1970s," in Jacobi, O. *et al* (eds), *The Economic Crisis, Trade Unions and the State* (Croom Helm).

Jacobs, F., Corbett, R. and Shackleton, M. (1995) *The European Parliament*, 3rd edn (Stockton).

James, H. (1989) "What is Keynesian About Deficit Financing? The Case of Interwar Germany," in Hall, P.A. (ed.), *The Political Power of Economic Ideas: Keynesianism across Nations* (Princeton, N.J.: Princeton University Press).

Jaumont, B., Lenègre, D. and Rocard, M. (1973) *Le Marché commun contre l'Europe* (Seuil).

Jeanneney, S. (1991) "L'Alternance entre dririgisme et libéralisme monétaire," in Lévy-Leboyer M. and Casanova, J.C. (eds), *L'Etat et le marché: l'économie française des années 1880 à nos jours* (Gallimard).

Jefferys, S. (2002) "The French Minimum Wage, Incomes Policies and Inequality, 1950–1981," French Labour Seminar.

—— (2003a) *Liberté, égalité et fraternité at Work: Changing French Employment Relations and Management* (Palgrave).

—— and Contrepoids, S. (2003b) "French State Pay Intervention and Incomes Policy Before 1981," unpublished paper.

Jobert, B. (ed.) *Le Tournant Néo-libéral en Europe* (L'Harmattan).

Johnson, P. (1998) *The Government of Money: Monetarism in Germany and the US* (Ithaca, N.Y.: Cornell University Press).

Jones, E. (1995a) "Economic Adjustment and the Political Formula: States and Change in Belgium and the Netherlands" (PhD: Johns Hopkins University).

—— (1995b) "Monetary Integration and Small Country Adjustment: A Necessary Trade-off?," *ECU*, 30, January.

—— (1995c) "The Transformation of the Belgian State," in McCarthy, P. and Jones, E. (eds), *Disintegration or Transformation? The Crisis of the State in Advanced Industrial Societies* (St. Martin's Press).

—— (1998a) "Belgium: Keeping up with the Pack?" in Jones, E. *et al* (eds), *Joining Europe's Monetary Club: The Challenge for Smaller Member-States* (St. Martin's Press).

—— (1998b) "The Netherlands: Top of the Class," in Jones, E. *et al* (eds), *Joining Europe's Monetary Club: The Challenge for Smaller Member-States* (St. Martin's Press).

—— (1999) "Is Competitive Corporatism an Adequate Response to Globalization? Evidence from the Low Countries," *West European Politics*, 22, pp. 159–81.

—— (2002) "Politics Beyond Accommodation? The May 2002 Dutch Parliamentary Elections," *Dutch Crossing*, 26.

Jones, E. (forthcoming) "Economic Adjustment and Political Transformation in Small States" (Lanham, MD: Rowman and Littlefield).
Jong, H. de (1988) *The Structure of European Industry* (Boston: Kluwer).
—— (1993) "Market Structures in the EEC," in Jong, H. de (ed.), *The Structure of European Industry* (Dordrecht: Kluwer).
Jong, J. de and Pijnenburg, B. (1986) "The Dutch Christian Democratic Party and Coalitional Behavior in the Netherlands: A Pivotal Party in the Face of Depillarization," in Pridham, G. (ed.), *Coalitional Behavior in Theory and Practice* (Cambridge: Cambridge University Press).
Jonung, L. (1986) "Financial deregulation in Sweden," *Skandinaviska Enskilda Banken: Quarterly Review*, 4.
July, S. (1986) *Les Années Mitterrand* (Bernard Grasset).
Junne, G. and Tulder, R. von (1988) *European Multinationals in Core Technologies* (John Wiley).
Kaldor, N. (1964) *Causes of the Slow Rate of Economic Growth of the UK* (Cambridge: Cambridge University Press).
Kaltefleiter, W. (1968) *Wirtschaft und Politik in Deutschland*, 2nd edn (Cologne: Westdeutscher Verlag).
Kalthenthaler, K. (1998) *Germany and the Politics of Europe's Money* (Chapel Hill, NC: Duke University Press).
Kapteyn, P.J.G. and van Themaat, P.V. (1989) *Introduction to the Law of the European Communities after the Coming into Force of the Single European Act* (Boston: Kluwer).
Kassim, H. *et al* (2000) *The National Coordination of EU Policy: The Domestic Level* (Oxford University Press).
Katzenstein, P. (1985) *Small States in World Markets: Industrial Policy in Europe* (Ithaca, N.Y.: Cornell University Press).
—— (1987) *Politics and Policy in West Germany: The Growth of a Semi-Sovereign State* (Philadelphia: Temple University Press).
Kaye, H. (1984) *British Marxist Historians: An Introductory Analysis* (Cambridge: Polity).
Kelly, J. (1996) *Re-thinking Industrial Relations: Mobilization, Collectivism and Long Waves* (Routledge).
Keohane, T. (1985) "The International Politics of Inflation," in Lindberg L.N. and Maier, C.S. (eds), *Politics of Inflation and Economic Stagnation: Theoretical Approaches and International Case Studies* (Washington, DC: Brookings Institution).
Kersbergen, K. van (1994) "The Distinctiveness of Christian Democracy," in Hanley, D. (ed.), *Christian Democracy in Europe: A Comparative Perspective* (Pinter).
—— (1995) *Social Capitalism: A Study of Christian Democracy and the Welfare State* (Routledge).
Khaffa, P. (2001) "Services publics: un déperissement progressif?," in Fondation Copernic (ed.), *Social-Libéralisme à lá française.*
Kindleberger, C. (1967) *Europe's Post-War Growth: The Role of Labor Supply* (Cambridge, Mass.: Harvard University Press).
Kilborn, P. (1987) "Kohl's Seizure of Key Economic Role," *New York Times*, 11 June.
King, D. and Wood, S. (1999) "The Political Economy of Neoliberalism in Britain and the US in the 1980s," in Kitschelt, H. *et al* (eds), *Continuity and Change in Contemporary Capitalism* (Cambridge: Cambridge University Press).
Kitschelt, H. (1999) "European Social Democracy Between Political Economy and Electoral Competition," in Kitschelt, H. *et al* (ed.), *Continuity and Change in Contemporary Capitalism.*

Kitson, M. and Michie, J. (1996) "Britain's Industrial Performance since 1960: Underinvestment and Relative Decline," *Economic Journal*, 106.
—— (2000) *The Political Economy of Competitiveness: Essays on Employment, Public Policy and Corporate Performance* (Routledge).
Kitson M., Martin, R. and Wilkinson, F. (2000) "Labor Markets, Social Justice and Economic Efficacy," *Cambridge Journal of Economics*, 24: 631–41.
Kloten, N. (1981) *Die Deutsche Mark als internationale Anlage-und Reservewährung: Folgen für den Kapitalmarkt* (Frankfurt: Knapp).
—— *et al* (1985) "West Germany's Stabilization Performance," in Lindberg, L.N. and Maier, C.S. (eds), *Politics of Inflation and Economic Stagnation*.
Kocher, E. (1989) "Le Rôle de la France dans les Négotiations des Traités de Rome" (Mémoire, University of Paris I).
Kohler-Koch, B. (1997) "Organized Interests in European Integration: The Evolution of a Type of Governance?," in Wallace, H. and Young, A. (eds), *Participation and Decision-Making in the European Union*.
—— (1999) "The Evolution and Transformation of European Governance," in Kohler-Koch and Eising, R. (eds), *The Transformation of Governance in the European Union* (Routledge).
Korpi, W. and Shalev, M. (1980) "Strikes, Power and Politics in the Western Nations, 1900–1976," in Zeitlin, M. (ed.), *Political Power and Theory* (JAI).
Kotz, D., McDonough, T. and Reich, M. (eds) (1994) *Social Structures of Accumulation* (Cambridge: Cambridge University Press).
Kreile, M. (1977) "West Germany: The Dynamics of Expansion," *International Organization*, 31, pp. 77–808.
—— (1978) "West Germany: The Dynamics of Expansion," in Katzenstein, P. (ed.), *Between Power and Plenty* (Madison: University of Wisconsin Press).
Krisler, S., *et al* (eds) (1986) "The Political Organs and Decision-Making Process in the US and European Community," in Weiler, J. *et al* (eds), *Integration through Law* (Berlin: Walter de Gryter).
Krugman, P. (1993) "Lessons of Massachusetts for EMU," in Torres, F. and Giavazzi, F. (eds), *Adjustment and Growth in the European Monetary Union* (Cambridge: Cambridge University Press).
Kruse, D. (1980) *Monetary Integration: EMU, EMS and Beyond* (Routledge).
Kuisel, R. (1981) *Capitalism and the State in Modern France: Renovation and Economic Management in the Twentieth Century* (Cambridge: Cambridge University Press).
Kurzer, P. (1988) "The Politics of Central Banks: Austerity and Unemployment in Europe," *Journal of Public Policy*, 8, pp. 21–48.
—— (1993) *Business and Banking: Political Change and Economic Integration in Western Europe* (Ithaca, N.Y.: Cornell University Press).
—— and Allen, C. (1993) "United Europe and Social Democracy: The EC, West Germany and its Three Small Neighbors," in Lankowski, C.F. (ed.), *Germany and the EC: Beyond Hegemony and Containment* (St. Martin's Press).
Küsters, H. (1982) *Die Grundung der Europaïschen Wirtschaftsgemeinshaft* (Baden-Baden).
—— (1989) "The Origins of the EEC Treaty," in Serra, E. (ed.), *Il rilancio dell'Europa e i trattati di Roma* (LGDJ).
Labrousse, E. (1947) *La Crise de l'économie française à la fin de l'ancien régime et au début de la Révolution* (Presses universitaires de France).
Lacroix-Riz, A. (1983) *La CGT de la libération à la scission de 1944–1947* (Editions sociales).

Lacroix-Riz, A. (1999) *Industriels et banquiers français sous l'Occupation: la collaboration économique avec le Reich et Vichy* (A. Colin).
—— (2001) "Origins of the Minimum Wage, 1936–1947," French Labor Seminar.
Ladrech, R. (1996) "Political Parties in the European Parliament," in Gaffney, J. (ed.), *Political Parties and the European Union* (Routledge).
Lafay, G. (1997) *L'Euro contre l'Europe* (Arléa).
—— and Unal-Kesenci, D. (1990) *L'Intégration européenne: bilan et perspectives* (Economica).
Lafontaine, Oskar (1999) "A Global Era Requires Modernizing Social Democracy," *NPQ: New Perspectives Quarterly*, 34.
Lakatos, I. (1970) "Falsification and the Methodology of Scientific Research Programmes," in Lakato, I. and Musgrave, A. (eds) *Criticism and the Growth of Knowledge* (Cambridge: Cambridge University Press).
Lancelot, A. (ed.) (1986) *1981: les élections de l'alternance* (Presses de la Fondation nationale des Sciences politiques).
Landes, D. (1949) "French Entrepreneurship and Industrial Growth in the Nineteenth Century," *Journal of Economic History*, 9, pp. 45–61.
Lange, P. and Vannicelli, M. (1982) "Strategy under Stress: The Italian Union Movement and the Italian Crisis in Development Perspective," in Lange, P., Ross, P.G. and Vannicelli, M. (eds), *Unions, Change and Crisis in French and Italian Union Strategy and the Political Economy, 1945–1980.* (George Allen & Unwin).
Lankowski, C. (1982) "Germany and the EC: Anatomy of a Hegemonial Relation" (PhD, Columbia University).
—— (ed.) (1994) *Germany and the European Community: Beyond Hegemony and Containment?* (Macmillan).
Lash, S. and Urry, J. (1987) *The End of Organised Capitalism* (Cambridge: Polity).
Laurent, P.H. (1994) "Reappraising the Origins of European Integration," in Michelmann, H. and Soldatos, P. (eds), *European Integration: Theories and Approaches: Theories and Approaches* (Lanham, MD: University Press of America).
Layard, R., Nickell, S. and Jackman, R. (1991) *Unemployment: Macroeconomic Performance and the Labor Market* (Oxford University Press).
Leander, A. and Guzzini, S. (1997) "European Economic and Monetary Union and the Crisis of European Social Contracts," in Minkkinen, P. and Patomaki, H. (eds), *The Politics of Economic and Monetary Union* (Boston: Kluwer).
Lecher, W. and Naumann, R. (1994) "The Current State of Trade Unions in the EU Member States," in Lecher, W. (ed.), *Trade Unions in the European Union: A Handbook* (Lawrence and Wishart).
Lecointe, F. *et al* (1989) "Salaires, prix et répartition," in Jeanneney, J-M. (ed.), *L'Economie française depuis 1967: la traversée des turbulences mondiales* (Seuil).
Lee, S. (1995) "German Decision-Making Elites and European Integration, 1948–1958," in Deighton, A. (ed.), *Building Post-War Europe: National Decision-Making and European Institutions, 1948–1958* (Macmillan).
Lemaire-Prosche, G. (1990) *Le PS et l'Europe* (Ed. Universitaires).
Lembcke, J. (1991) "Why 50 Years? Working-Class Formation and Long Economic Cycles," *Science and Society*, 55, pp. 417–45.
Lemke, C. and Marks, G. (1992) "From Decline to Demise? The Future of Socialism in Europe," in Lemke and Marks, (eds), *The Crisis of Socialism in Europe* (Chapel Hill, N.C.: Duke University Press).
Lévy-Leboyer, M. and Casanova, J-C. (eds) (1991) *Entre l'état et le marché* (Gallimard).
Leyser, D. (1981) *De Gaulle, les Français et l'Europe* (Presses universitaires de France).

Lidtke, V. (1966) *The Outlawed Party: Social Democracy in Germany, 1878–1890* (Princeton, N.J.: Princeton University Press).
Lillo, F (2003) "L'impossible citoyenneté européenne," European Counter-Forum, La Sorbonne, 14 November.
Lindberg, L. (1963) *The Political Dynamics of European Economic Integration* (Stanford: Stanford University Press).
—— and Scheinberg, S. (1970) *Europe's Would-Be Polity* (Englewood Cliffs, N.J.: Prentice Hall).
Linsenmon, I. (2003) "Fiscal Policy-Making under the Stability and Growth Pact: The SGP's Impact on Domestic Institutions," VACES Conference, Building EU Economic Government, *Revising the Rules?*
Lord, C. (1994) *The European Union: Creating the Single Market* (Wiley Chancery).
Lordon, F. (2001) "Financer les retraites ou finir écraser la société?," in Fondation Copernic (ed.), *Social-Libéralisme à la francaise.*
Loriaux, M. (1991) *France after Hegemony: International Change and Financial Reform* (Ithaca, NY : Cornell University Press).
Lorwin, V. (1958) "Working-Class Politics and Economic Development in Western Europe," *American History Review*, 63, pp. 338–51.
Ludlow, P. (1982) "The Making of the European Monetary System: A Case Study in the Politics of the EC" (Butterworth Scientific).
Luif, P. (1996) *On the Road to Brussels. The Political Dimension of Austria's and Finland's Accession to the European Union* (Vienna: Braumüller).
Lustig, R. (1982) *Corporate Liberalism: The Origins of Modern American Political Theory, 1890–1920* (Berkeley: University of California Press).
Lynch, F. (1997) *France and the International Economy: From Vichy to the Treaty of Rome* (Routledge).
MacEwan, A. (1999) *Neoliberalism or Democracy? Economic Strategy, Markets, and Alternatives for the 21st Century* (Zed).
Machlup, F. (ed.), (1976) *Economic Integration: Worldwide, Regional, Sectoral* (Macmillan).
—— (1977) *A History of Thought on Economic Integration* (Columbia University Press).
Maddison, A. (1964) *Economic Growth in the West in Comparative Perspective in Europe and North America* (Allen & Unwin).
—— (1991) *Dynamic Forces in Capitalist Development: A Long-Run Comparative View* (Oxford University Press).
Madrick, J. (1997) "In the Shadows of Prosperity," *New York Review of Books*, 14 August.
Maes, I. (2002) *Economic Thought and the Making of European Monetary Union* (Cheltenham: Edward Edgar).
Mahant, E. (1969) " 'French and German Attitudes to the Negotiations about the EEC 1956–7" (PhD, London University).
Mahon, R. (1999) " 'Yesterday's Modern Times Are No Longer Modern': Swedish Unions Confront the Double Shift," in Martin, A. and Ross, G. (eds), *The Brave New World of European Labour: European Trade Unions at the Millennium* (Berghahn).
Maier, C. (1978) *The Origins of the Cold War and Contemporary Europe* (New Viewpoint).
Maier, C. (1981) "The Two Post-War Eras and the Conditions of Stability in Twentieth-Century Europe," *American Historical Review*, 86, pp. 327–52.
—— (ed.) (1991) *The Cold War in Europe: Era of a Divided Continent* (M. Wiener).
Majone, G. (1993) "The EC between Social Policy and Social Regulation," *Journal of Common Market Studies*, 31, pp. 153–70.
—— (ed) (1996) *Regulating Europe* (Routledge).
Mandel, E. (1970) *Europe versus Amerika?: The Contradictions of Imperialism* (New Left Books).

Mandel, E. (1975) *Late Capitalism* (New Left Books).
Mamou, Y. (1988) *Une Machine de pouvoir: la direction du Trésor* (La Découverte).
Marchand, O. and Thélot, C. (1991) "Montée du chomage," in Lévy-Leboyer, M. and Casanova, J-C. (eds), *Entre l'Etat et marché.*
Marcussen, M. (1997) "The Role of 'Ideas' in Dutch, Danish and Swedish Economic Policy in the 1980s and the Beginning of the 1990s," in Minkkinen, P. and Patomāki, H. (eds), *The Politics of Economic and Monetary Union* (Boston: Kluwer).
—— (1998) *Central Bankers, the Ideational Life-Cycle and the Social Construction of EMU,* European University Institute, No. 98/33.
—— (2000) *Ideas and Elites: The Social Construction of Economic and Monetary Union* (Aolborg University Press).
—— and Zolner, M. (2001) "Monetarism and the Masses: The Danish Case."
Margairez, M. (1991) "L'Etat, les finances et l'économie: histoire d'une conversion, 1932–52," 2 vols (Comité pour l'histoire économique et financière de la France).
—— (1987) "Direction du Trésor: de l'orthodoxie à la réforme (1930–50)," in Friedenson, P. and Strauss, A. (eds), *Le Capitalisme français, XIXe-XXe siècles: blocages et dynamisme d'une croissance* (Fayard).
—— (ed.) (1988) *Pierre-Mendès France et l'économie* (Odile Jacob).
Marglin, S. and Schor, J. (eds) (1990) *The Golden Age of Capitalism: Reinterpreting the Post-War Experience* (Oxford: Clarendon).
Marjolin, R. (1986) *Architect of European Unity* (Weidenfeld and Nicolson).
Markovits, A. and Allen, C. (1981) "Trade Union Response to the Centemporary Economic Problems in Western Europe: The Context of Current Debates and Policies in the Federal Republic of Germany," *Economic and Industrial Democracy,* 2, pp. 49–86.
—— (1984) "The Trade Unions and the Economic Crisis: The West German Case," in Gourevitch, P. (ed.), *Unions and Economic Crisis, Britain, West Germany and Sweden* (Allen and Unwin).
—— and Reich, S. (1991) "Modell Deutschland and the New Europe," *Telos,* 89, pp. 45–64.
—— and Otto, A. (1993) "West German Labor and Europe '92'," in Lankowski, C.F. (ed.), *Germany and the European Community: Beyond Hegemony and Containment?* (St. Martin's Press).
Marks, G. (1993) "Structural Policy and Multi-level Governance," in Cafuny, A. and Rosenthal, G. (eds), *The State of the European Community,* vol. 2, *The Maastricht Debates and Beyond* (Boulder, Col.: L. Rienner).
—— *et al* (1996) "European Integration from the 1980s: State Centric v. Multi-Level Governance," *Journal of Common Market Studies,* 34, pp. 341–78.
—— (1997) "A Third Lens: Comparing European Integration and State Building," in Goldsmith, M.J.F. and Klausen, K.K. (eds), *European Integration and Local Government* (Edward Elgar).
—— (2000) "The Past in the Present: A Theory of Party Response to European Integration," *British Journal of Political Science,* 38.
—— and Wilson, C. (1999) "National Parties and the Contestation of Europe," in Banchoff, T. and Smith, M. (eds), *Legitimacy and the European Union* (Routledge).
Martin, A. (1979) "The Dynamics of Change in a Keynesian Political Economy: The Swedish Case and its Implications," in Crouch, C. (ed.), *State and Economy.*
—— (1984) "Trade Unions in Sweden" in Gourevitch, P. (ed.), *Unions and Economic Crisis: Britain, West Germany and Sweden* (Allen & Unwin).
—— (1986) "Wages, Profits and Investment in Sweden," in Lindberg, L.N. and Maier, C.S. (eds), *Politics of Inflation and Economic Stagnation.*

Martin, J. (1996) *EC Public Procurement Rules: A Critical Analysis* (Oxford: Clarendon).
—— and Stehmann, O. (1991) "Product Market Integration versus Regional Cohesion," *European Law Review*, 16.
Martin, P. (2003) "L'Election présidentielle et les élections légisatives françaises," *French Politics, Culture and Society*, 21, pp. 1–19.
Marx, K. (1967) *Capital: A Critique of Political Economy*, vol. I (International Publishers).
Mayes, D. and Viren, M. (2003) "The Pressures on the Stability and Growth Pact from Asssymetry in Policy?," Revising the Rules?
Mayer, N. and Perrineau, P. (1989) *Le Front national à découvert* (Presses de la Fondation nationale de Sciences politiques).
Mazier, J., Baslé, M. and Vidal, J-F. (1984) *Quand les crises durent* (Economica).
—— translated by Rosen, M. (1999) *When Economic Crises Endure* (M.E. Sharpe).
McNamara, K. (1998) *The Currency of Ideas: Monetary Politics in the European Union* (Ithaca, N.Y.: Cornell University Press).
—— (2001) "Globalization, Institutions and Convergence: Fiscal Adjustment on the Way to EMU," in Kahler, M. and Lake, D. (eds), *Globalizing Authority: Economic Integration and Governance* (Berkeley, Cal: Institute on Global Conflict and Co-operation).
—— and Jones, E. (1996) "The Clash of Institutions: Germany in European Monetary Affairs," *German Politics and Society*, 14, pp. 31–53.
Megan, N. (1987) *The Kondratieff Wave* (Praeger).
Menon, A. and Wright, V. (eds) (2002) *From the Nation State to Europe? Essays in Honour of Jack Hayward* (Oxford University Press).
Mény Y., Muller, P. and Quermonne, J-L. (1996) *Adjusting to Europe: The Impact of the European Union on National Institutions and Policies* (Routledge).
Mertens de Wilmar, J. (1993) "The Case Law of the Court of Justice in Relation to the Review of the Legality of Economic Policy in Mixed Economy Systems," in Snyder, F. (ed.), *European Community Law*, 2 vols (Aldershot: Dartmouth).
Messerlin, P. and Stephane, B. (1986) "Intra-Industry Trade in the Long Run: The French Case, 1850–1913," in Greenaway, D. and Tharakan, P. (eds), *Imperfect Competition and International Trade: The Policy Aspects of Intra-Industry Trade* (Brighton: Wheatsheaf).
Michelat, G. amd Simon, M. (1985) "Déterminismes socio-économiques, organisations symboliques et comportement électoral," *Revue française de sociologie*, 26.
Michelmann, H. and Soldatos, P. (eds) (1994) *European Integration: Theories and Approaches* (Lanham, Md: University Press of America).
Michie, J. (ed.) (1992) *Economic Legacy, 1979–1992* (Academic Press).
—— (1999) "Globalization, governance and public policy", Inaugural lecture, Birkbeck College, July 9.
—— (2001) "Economy," in Harvey, A. (ed.), *Transforming Britain: Labour's Second Term* (The Fabian Society).
—— (2002) *Public Services Yes. Euro No* (New Europe).
—— and Wilkinson, F. (1992) "Inflation Policy and the Restructuring of Labour Markets," in *Economic Legacy*.
Middlemass, K. (1994) "The Party, Industry and the City," in Seldon, A. and Bell, S. (eds), *Conservative Country: The Conservative Party since 1900* (Oxford University Press).
Milner, H. (1988) *Resisting Protectionism: Global Industries and the Politics of International Trade* (Princeton, N.J.: Princeton University Press).
Milner, S. (2000) "Introduction: A Healthy Skepticism?" and "Euroscepticism in France and Changing State-Society Relations," *Journal of European Integration*, 22.
—— (2003) "EU Employment Policy," French Labour Seminar.

Milner, S. (2004) "For an Alternative Europe: Euroskepticism and the French Left Since the Maastricht Treaty," in Harmsen, R. and Spierung, M. (eds), *Euroscepticism, Party Politics, National Identity and European Integration* (Rodopi B.V.).
Milward, A. (1984) *The Reconstruction of Western Europe, 1945–51* (Berkeley: University of California Press).
—— (1992) *European Rescue of the Nation State* (Routledge).
Mioche, P. (1987) *Le Plan Monnet: genèse et élaborations, 1945–47* (Sorbonne, 1987).
—— (1993) "Le Patronat français et les projets d'intégration économique européenne dans les années cinquante," in Trausch, G. (ed.), *European Integration from the Schuman Plan to the Treaties of Rome* (LGDJ).
Mitrany, D. (1943) *A Working Peace System: An Argument for the Functional Development of International Organization* (Royal Institute of International Affairs).
Molle, W. (1994) *The Economics of European Integration: Theory, Practice, Policy* (Brookfield, Vt.: Dartmouth Publishers).
Monbiot, G. (2003) *The Age of Consent: A Manifesto for a New World Order* (Flamingo).
Moneckonberg, U. (1986) "Labor Law and Industrial Relations," in Jacobi, O. (ed.), *Economic Crisis, Trade Unions and the State* (Croom Helm).
Monetary Committee (1986) *Compendium of Committee Monetary Texts* (Luxembourg: Office for Official Publications).
Monti, M. (1996) *The Single Market and Tomorrow's Europe: A Progress Report from the European Commission* (Luxembourg: EU Publications).
Moore Jr., B. (1966) *Social Origins of Dictatorship and Democracy* (Boston: Beacon).
Moran, J. (1998) "The Dynamics of Class Politics and National Economies in Globalisation: The Marginalisation of the Unacceptable," *Capital and Class*, no. 66, pp. 53–84.
Moravcsik, A. (1991) "Negotiating the Single European Act: National Interests and Conventional Statecraft in the European Community," *International Organization*, 45, pp. 19–56.
—— (1998a) *The Choice for Europe: Social Purpose and State Power from Messina to Maastricht* (Ithaca, N.Y.: Cornell University Press).
—— (ed.) (1998b) *Centralization or Fragmentation? Europe Facing the Challenges of Deepening, Diversity and Democracy* (Council on Foreign Relations).
—— (2003) "Reassessing the Fundamentals," in Weiler, J.H.H., Begg, I. and Peterson, J. (ed.), *Integration in an Expanding European Union: Reassessing the Fundamentals* (Blackwell).
Morel, C. (1981) *La Grève froide: stratégies syndicales et pouvoir patronal* (Editions d'organisation).
Morton, A. (2001) "The Sociology of Theorising and Neo-Gramscian Perspectives: The Problems of 'School' Formation in IPE," in Bieler, A. and Morton, A.D. (eds), *Social Forces in Making of the New Europe.*
Moses, J.W. (1995) "Devalued Priorities: The Politics of Nordic Exchange Rate Regimes Compared" (PhD, University of California at Los Angeles).
Moss, B. (1984) "Ideology and Industrial Practice: CGT, FO, CFDT," in Kesselman, M. (ed.), *The French Workers' Movement: Economic Crisis and Political Change* (George Allen & Unwin).
—— (1988) "After the Auroux Laws: Employers, Industrial Relations and the Right in France," *West European Politics*, 11, pp. 68–80.
—— (1990) "Workers and the Common Program (1968–1978): The Failure of French Communism," *Science & Society*, 54, pp. 42–66.
—— (1993a) "Labour and Economic Growth under the Fourth French Republic" (Birmingham: Aston University Papers).

Moss, B. (1993b) "Republican Socialism and the Making of the Working Class in Britain, France and the United States: A Critique of Thompsonian Culturalism," *Comparative Studies in Society and History*, 35, pp. 399–413.

—— (1998) "Economic and Monetary Union and the Social Divide in France," *Contemporary European History*, 7, pp. 227–47.

—— (1999) "Socialism and the Republic in France: A Long View," *Socialist History*, 18, 170–89.

—— (2000) "The European Community as Monetarist Construction: A Critique of Moravcsik," *The Journal of European Area Studies*, 8, pp. 247–65.

—— (2001a) "Marxist Theories of Integration: The EU as Neoliberal Construction."

—— (2001b) "The EC's Free Market Agenda: The Myth of Social Europe," in Bonefeld, W. (ed.), *Politics of Union: Monetary Union and Class* (Palgrave).

—— (2003a) "The *Eighteenth Brumaire* as Disengagement from History: A Parody of the Old Mole," *Studies in Marxism*, 9.

—— (2003b) "The Hidden Marxism in The Making of the English Working Class," *What Next?*, 26.

—— and Michie, J. (eds) (1998) *The Single European Currency in National Perspective. A Community in Crisis?* (Macmillan).

Müller-Armack, A. (1957) "Fragen des Europaïschen Integration," in Beckerath, E. von, (ed.), *Wirtschaftsfragen der Freien Welt* (Frankfurt: F. Knapp).

—— (1971) *Auf den Weg nach Europa* (Tübingen).

—— (1982) "The Second Phase of the Social Market Economy: An Additional Concept of a Humane Economy," in Wünche, H.F. (ed.), *Standard Texts on the Social Market Economy: Two Centuries of Discussion* (Stuttgart).

Mundell, R. (1961) "A Theory of Optimum Currency Areas," *American Economic Review*, 51, pp. 657–66.

Nay, C. (1984) *Le Noir et le rouge ou l'histoire d'ambition* (Grasset).

Neumann, M. (1999) "Monetary Stability, Threat Power and Response," in Baltensperger, E. and Deutsche Bundesbank (eds), *Fifty Years of the Deutsche Mark: Central Bank and Currency in Germany since 1948* (Oxford University Press).

Neunreither, K. (1994) "The Democratic Deficit of the European Union: Toward Closer Cooperation Between the European Parliament and National Parliaments," *Government and Opposition*, 29, pp. 299–314.

Newman, R. (1983) *Socialism and European Unity: The Dilemma of the Left in Britain and France* (Junction Books).

Nichols, A. (1994) *Freedom with Responsbility: The Social Market Economy in Germany, 1948–1963* (Oxford: Clarendon).

Niedemayer, O. and Sinnoth, R. (1995) *Public Opinion and International Governance* (Oxford University Press).

Niethammer, L. (1991) "Structural Reform and a Compact for Growth: Conditions of a United Labor Movement in Western Europe after the Collapse of Fascism," in Maier, C. (ed.), *The Cold War in Europe: Era of a Divided Continent* (Markus Wiener).

Notermans, T. (1993) "The Abdication of National Political Policy Autonomy: Why the Macroeconomic Policy Regime has been so Unfavourable to Labour," *Politics and Society*, 21, pp. 133–68.

Oatley, T. (1997) *Monetary Politics: Exchange Rate Cooperation in the European Union* (Ann Arbor: The University of Michigan Press).

O'Conner, J. (1979) *The Fiscal Crisis of the State* (St. Martin's Press).

Olsen, G. (1991) "Labour Mobilization and the Strength of Capital: The Rise and Fall of Economic Democracy in Sweden," *Studies in Political Economy*, 34, pp. 109–46.

Olsen, G. (1996) "Re-Modeling Sweden: The Rise and Demise of the Compromise in Global Economy," *Social Problem*, 43, pp. 1–20.
Olson, M. (1971) *The Logic of Collective Action: Public Goods and the Theory of Groups* (Cambridge, Mass.: Harvard University Press).
Organization for Economic Cooperation and Development (1999) *OECD Economic Outlook*, December *1998*.
Otto, E. (1957) *Die Deutsche Industrie in Gemeinsamen Markt* (Bonn: Verlag August Lutzeyer).
Owen, N. (1983) *Economies of Scale, Competitiveness and Trade Patterns within the European Commuity* (Oxford: Clarendon Press).
Padoa-Schioppa, T. (1987) *Efficiency, Stability and Equity: A Strategy for the Evolution of the Economic System of the European Community* (Oxford University Press).
Page, E. (2001) "The European Union and the Bureaucratic Mode of Production," in Menon, A. and Wright, W. (eds), *From Nation State to Europe: Essays in Honour of Jack Hayward* (Oxford University Press).
Panitch, L. (1976) *Social Democracy and Industrial Mlitancy: The Labour Party, the Trade Unions and Incomes Policy*, 1945–1974 (Cambridge: Cambridge University Press).
Peacock, H. and Willgeracht, H. (1989) *Germany's Social Market Economy: Origin and Evolution* (Macmillan).
Pearce, J. and Sutton, J. (1985) *Protection and Industrial Policy in Europe* (Routledge and Kegan Paul).
Pekkarinen, J. (1989) "Keynesianism and the Scandinavian Models of Economic Policy," in Hall, P.A. (ed.), *The Political Power of Economic Ideas: Keynesianism across Nations* (Princeton, N.J.: Princeton University Press).
Pentland, C. (1973) *International Theory and European Integration* (Faber and Faber).
Percheron, A. (1991) "Les Français et l'Europe: acquiescement de façade ou adhésion véritable," *Revue francaise de science politique*, 41.
Peridon, C. van (1996) "European Economic Integration: Did it Matter in the Past? Will it Matter in the Future?" in Tilly, C. and P. Wolfens, P. (eds), *European Economic Integration as a Challenge to Industry and Government* (Springer).
Pernin, A. (1996) "Des Dysfonctionnements de la raison communautaire," in Cartelier, L., *et al* (eds), *Critique de la raison communautaire*.
Perraton, A. *et al* (1997) "The Globalization of Economic Activity," *New Political Economy*, 2.
Perrineau, P. (1995) "Dynamique du vote Le Pen: le poids du 'gaucho-lepenisme,'" in Perrineau, P. and Ysmal, C. (eds), *Vote sanction: les législatives des 21 et 28 mars 1993* (Presses de la Fondation nationale des Sciences politiques).
—— and Ysmal, C. (eds) (2003) *Le Vote de tous les refus: les élections présidentielles et législatives 2002* (Presses Sciences – Pô).
—— (1994) *Le Vote des douze: les élections européennes de juin 1994* (Presses de la Fondation nationale de Sciences politiques).
Peters, B.G. (1994) "Agenda Setting in the EC," *Journal of European Public Policy*, 1.
Petit, P. (1989) "Expansionary Policies in a Restrictive World: The Case of France," in Guerrieri, P. and Padoan, P. (eds), *The Political Economy of European Integration* (Harvester).
Peyrefitte, A. (1997) *C'était de Gaulle*, 2 vols (Fayard).
PEW Research Center (2003) "View of a Changed World after the Iraqi War," 3 June, Public Opinion Institute.
Phelps, N.A. (1997) *Multinationals and European Integration: Trade, Investment and Regional Development* (Jessica Kingsley).

Philip, A. (1957) "Social Aspects of European Economic Cooperation," *International Labour Review*, no. 76, pp. 244–56.

Pierson, P. (1996) "The Path to European Integration: A Historical Institutional Analysis," *Comparative Political Studies* 29, pp. 123–63.

Piketty, T.C. (2001) *Les Hauts Revenus en France au XXe siècle: inégalités et redistributions,* 1901–1998 (Bernard Grasset).

Pijl, K. van der (1984) *The Making of an Atlantic Ruling Class* (Verso).

Pijnenburg, B. (1988) "Belgium in Crisis: Politics and Policy Responses, 1981–5," in Damgaard, E., Gerlich, P. and Richardson, J.J. (Brookfield: Avebury) (eds), *The Politics of Economic Crisis* (Aldershot: Aveling).

Pinder, J. (1969) "Problems of European Integration," in Denton, G.R. (ed.), *Economic Integration in Europe* (Weidenfeld and Nicholson).

Pineau, C. and Rimbaud, C. (1991) *Le Grand Pari: l'aventure du traité de Rome* (Fayard).

Pinto Lyra, R. (1978) *La Gauche en France et la construction européenne* (L.G.D.J).

Piore, M. and Sabel, C. (1984) *The Second Industrial Divide: Possibilities for Prosperity* (Basic Books).

Pipe, A. (2003) "European Securities Regulation and Financial Markets," Global Finance and Social Cohesion.

Pittman, P. (1993) "Le Retour de la convertibilité monétaire en Europe occidentale et le redressement financier français," in Lévy-Leboyer *et al* (eds), *Franc Poincaré.*

Pivetti, M. (1998) "Monetary versus Political Unification in Europe," *Review of Political Economy*, 10.

Pollack, M. (1994) "Creeping Competence: The Expanding Agenda of the European Community," *Journal of Public Policy*, 14, pp. 95–145.

—— (1998) "The Engines of Integration? Supranational Autonomy and Influence in the EU," in Sandholtz, W. and Stone Sweet, A. (eds), *European Integration and Supranational Governance.*

Polanyi, K. (1956) *The Great Transformation: The Political and Economic Origins of our Time* (Boston: Beacon Press).

Polanyi-Levitt, K. and McRobbie, K. (eds) *Karl Polanyi in Vienna: The Contemporary Significance of The Great Transformation.* (Montreal: Black Rose Books).

Pontusson, J. (1987) "Radicalization and Retreat in Swedish Social Democracy," *New Left Review*, 165, pp. 5–33.

—— (1992) *The Limits of Social Democracy: Investment Politics in Sweden* (Ithaca, N.Y.: Cornell University Press).

—— (1995a) "Sweden: After the Golden Age," in Andersen, P. and Camiller, P. (eds), *Mapping the West European Left* (Verso).

—— (1995b) "Explaining the Decline of European Social Democracy: The Role of Structural Change," *World Politics*, 47, pp. 495–533.

Popper, K. (1945) *The Open Society and its Enemies* (Routledge).

Portelli, H. (1980) *Le Socialisme français tel qu'il est* (Presses universitaires de France).

Prate, A. (1995) *France en Europe* (Economica).

Premfors, R. (1991) "The 'Swedish Model' and Public Sector Reform," *West European Politics*, 14, pp. 83–95.

Projet sur l'union monétaire et financière (1991) *Petits bleus*, 21 January.

Puetter, U. (2003) "Governing Informally: The Central Role of the Eurogroup within EMU and the Stability and Growth Pact," *Revising the Rules?*

Quenouelle-Carre, L. (2000) *La Direction du trésor, 1947–1967: l'état banquier et la croissance* (Comité pour l'histoire économique et financière de la France).

Quilliot, R. (1972) *La SFIO et l'exercise du pouvoir, 1944–58* (Fayard).

Rader, M. and Ulman, L. (1993) "Unionism and Unification," in Ulman, L., Eichengreen, B. and Dickens, W.T. (eds), *Labor and an Integrated Europe* (Washington, D.C.: Brookings Institution).

Rand Smith, W. (1990) "Nationalization for What? Capitalist Power and Public Enterprise in Mitterrand's France," *Politics and Society*, 18, pp. 75–100.

Rasmussen, H. (1986) *On Law and Policy in the European Court of Justice: A Comparative Study in Judicial Policymaking* (Boston: Kluwer).

Reichlin, L. and Salvati, M. (1990) "Industrial Employment in Italy: The Consequences of Shifts in Union Power," in Brunetta, R. and Dell'Aringa, C. (eds), *Labour Relations and Economic Performance* (Macmillan).

Reuss, F. (1963) *Fiscal Policy for Growth Without Inflation* (Baltimore: Johns Hopkins Press).

Rhodes, M. (2002) "Why EMU Is – Or May Be – Good for European Welfare States?," in Dyson, K. (ed.), *European States and the Euro.*

Riemer, J. (1982) "Alterations in the Design of Modell Germany," in Markovits, A.S. (ed.), *The Political Economy of West Germany: Modell Deutschland* (Praeger).

—— (1983) "Crisis and Intervention in the West German Economy: A Political Analysis of Changes in the Policy Making Machinery during the 1960s and 1970s," (PhD, Cornell University).

—— (1985) "West German Crisis Management: Stability and Change in the Post-Keynesian Age," in Vig, N. and Schier, S. (eds) *The Political Economy of Advanced Industrial Societies* (Holmes and Maier).

Rioux, J.-P. (1983) L'Expansion et l'impuissance, 1952–58, vol. 2 *L'Histoire de la IVe République* (Seuil).

Risse-Kappen, T. (1996) "Exploring the Nature of the Beast: International Relations Theory and Comparative Policy Analysis Meet the EU," *Journal of Common Market Studies*, 34, pp. 53–80.

—— (1997) "Identity Politics in the European Union: The Case of Economic and Monetary Union," in Minkkinen, P. and Patomäki, H. (eds), *Politics of Economic and Monetary Union.*

Robinson, A. (1998a) "Why Employability Won't Make EMU Work," in Moss, B.H. and Michie, J. (eds), *Single Currency in National Perspective.*

Robinson, W. and Harris, J. (2000) "Towards a Global Ruling Class: Globalization and the Transnational Capitalist Class," *Science & Society*, 64, pp. 11–54.

Rodrik, D. (1999) "Globalisation and Labour, or, if Globalisation is a Bowl of Cherries, Why are so many Glum Faces around the Table?," in Baldwin, R. and Cohen, D. (eds), *Market Integration.*

Romero, F. (1996) "US Attitudes toward Integration and Interdependence in the 1950s," in Heller, F. and Gillingham, J. (eds), *The United States and the Integration of Europe: Legacies of the Post-War Era* (St. Martin's Press).

Ronge, V. (1979) *Bankpolitik im Spätkapitalismus: Politische Selbstverwaltung des Kapitals?* Starnberger Studien, 3 (Frankfurt: Suhrkamp).

Röpke, W. (1947) *The Solution of the German Problem* (G.P. Putnam and Sons).

—— (1960) *A Humane Economy* (Chicago: Henry Regnery Company).

—— (1963) *Economics of the Free Society* (Chicago: Henry Regnery Company).

—— (1982) "The Guiding Principles of the Liberal Programme," in Wünche, H.F. (ed.) *Standard Texts.*

Rosanvallon, P. (1989) "The Development of Keynesianism in France," in Hall, P.A. (ed.), *The Political Power of Economic Ideas: Keynesianism Across Nations* (Princeton, N.J.: Princeton University Press).

Rosenthal, G. (1975) *The Men Behind the Decisions* (Lexington Books).
Ross, G. (1993) "Social Policy in the New Europe," *Studies in Political Economy*, 40, pp. 41–72.
—— (1995) *Delors and European Integration* (Oxford: Polity).
Rousso, H. (ed.) (1987) *De Monnet à Massé: enjeux politiques et objectifs économiques dans le cadre des quatre premiers Plans (1946–1965)* (Editions du CNRS).
Raphael, A. (1992), "Beware the Siren Devaluers who Lure us to Ruin,' *The Observer*, 26 April.
Rowthorn, R. (1980) *Capitalism, Conflict and Inflation: Essays in Political Economy* (Lawrence and Wishart).
—— (1995) "Capital Formation and Unemployment," *Oxford Review of Economic Policy*, 11, pp. 26–39.
Rozès, S. (2003) "The Alienation of Public Opinion from Jospin," French Labour Seminar.
Ruggie, J. (1982) "International Regimes, Transactions and Change: Embedded Liberalism in the Postwar Economic Order," *International Organization*, 36, pp. 379–416.
Rüstow, A. (1968) *Zwischen Politik und Ethik* (Cologne: Westdeutscher Verlag).
Ryner, M. (1994) "Assessing SAP's Economic Policy in the 1980s: The 'Third Way', the Swedish Model and the Transition from Fordism to Post-Fordism," *Economic and Industrial Democracy*, 15, pp. 385–428.
—— (1996) "The Politics of Transition: The Swedish Case," *RIES: Occasional Paper*, no. 4.
Sabel, C. and Zeitlin, J. (1985) "Historical Alternatives to Mass Production," *Past and Present*, 108, pp. 133–76.
Sachs, J. and Sala-I-Marin, X. (1992) "Fiscal Federalism and Optimum Currency Areas: Evidence for Europe and from the United States," in Canzoneri, M., Grilli, V. and Masson, P.R. (eds), *Establishing a Central Bank: Issues in Europe and Lessons from the United States* (Cambridge: Cambridge University Press).
Sainsbury, D. (1991) "Swedish Social Democracy in Transition: The Party's Record in the 1980s and the Challenge of the 1990s," *West European Politics*, 14, pp. 31–57.
—— (1993) "The Swedish Social Democrats and the Legacy of Continuous Reform: Asset or Dilemma?," *West European Politics*, 16.
Saint-Martin, O. (1996) "L' Anti-Politique industrielle de la C.E." in Cartelier, L. *et al* (eds), *Critique de la raison communautaire*.
Salesse, Y. (1997) *Propositions pour une autre Europe: construire Babel* (Arléa).
Salvati, M. (1986) "The Italian Inflation," in Lindberg, L.N. and Maier, C.S. (eds), *The Politics of Inflation and Economic Stagnation*.
Sandholtz, W. (1992) *High-Tech Europe: The Politics of International Cooperation* (Berkeley: University of California Press).
—— and Stone Sweet, A. (1998) "The Emergence of a Supranational Telecommunications Regime," in Sandholtz, W. and Stone Sweet (eds), *European Integration*.
Scharpf, F. (1971) "Gesprach," in Brawand, L. (ed.), *Wohin steuert die deutsche Wirtschaft?* (Munich: Verlag Kurt Desch).
—— (1984) "Economic and Institutional Constraints of Full Employment Strategies: Sweden, Austria, and Western Germany, 1973–82," in Goldthorpe, J.H. (ed.), *Order and Conflict in Contemporary Capitalism*.
—— (1991) *Crisis and Choice in European Social Democracy* (Ithaca, NY: Cornell University Press).
—— (1996) "Negative and Positive Integration in the Political Economy of European Welfare States," in Marks, G. *et al* (eds), *Governance in the European Union* (Sage).

Schiller, K. (1964) *Die Ökonomie und die Gesellschaft* (Stuttgart: Fischer).
Schmidt, M. (1978) "The Politics of Domestic Reform in the Federal Republic of Germany," *Politics and Society*, 8.
—— (1982) "The Role of Parties in Shaping Macroeconomic Policy," in Castles, F. (ed.), *The Impact of Parties: Politics and Policies in Capitalist States* (Sage).
Schmidt, V. (1996) *From State to Market? The Transformation of French Business and Government* (Cambridge: Cambridge University Press).
Schmitt, H. and Thomassen, J. (1999) *Political Representation and Legitimacy in the European Union* (Oxford University Press).
Schmitter, P. (1989) "Corporatism is Dead 'Long Live Corporatism'," *Government and Opposition*, 24, pp. 54–73.
—— (2000) *How to Democratize the EU and Why Bother?* (Lanham, MD: Rowman & Littlefield).
Scholte, J. (2000) *Globalization: A Critical Introduction* (Macmillan).
Schor, J. (1985) "Wage Flexbility, Social Welfare Expenditures and Monetary Restrictiveness," in Jarsulic, M. (ed.), *Money and Macro Policy* (Boston: Kluwer).
Schwarzmantel, J. (1991) *Socialism and the Idea of the Nation* (Harvester).
Scott, R. (2002) "The UK and the Information and Consultation Directive: Transposition or Transformation?" (unpublished paper).
Screpanti, E. (1984) "Long Economic Cycles and Recurring Labor Insurgencies," *Review*, 7.
—— (1989) "Long Cycles and Demographics," in Goodwin, R.M., Malteo, M.D. and Vercelli, A. (eds), *Technological and Social Factors in Long-Term Fluctuations* (Springer).
Serra, E. (ed.) (1989) *Il rilancio dell'Europa e i trattati di Roma* (L.G.D.J.).
Sharp, M. (1993) "The Community and New Technologies," in Lodge, J. (ed.), *European Community and the Challenge of the Future* (Pinter).
Shaw, J. (1994) "Twin-Track Social Europe-The Inside Track?," in O'Keefe, D. and Twomey, P. (eds), *Legal Issues of Maastricht* (Wiley).
Shonfield, A. (1965) *Modern Capitalism: The Changing Balance of Public and Private Power* (Royal Institute of International Affairs).
Shorter, E. and Tilly, C. (1974) *Strikes in France, 1830–1968* (Cambridge: Cambridge University Press).
Siegel, N. (2001) "German Welfare Capitalism and European Monetary Integration," EMU/EMSO Project, EMU and the European Model of Society.
Silvia, S. (1991) "The Social Charter of the European Community: Defeat for European Labour," *Industrial and Labour Relations Review*, 44, pp. 626–43.
—— (1997) "German Unification and Emerging Divisions within German Employers' Associations," *Comparative Politics*, 29.
Simonazzi, A. and Vianello, F. (2002) "Italy Towards European Monetary Union (and Domestic Disunion)," in Moss, B.H. and Michie, J. (eds), *The Single Currency in National Perspective*.
Simonian, H. (1985) *The Privileged Partnership: Franco-German Relations in the European Community, 1969–1984* (Oxford: Clarendon).
Sklar, H. (1980) *Trilateralism: The Trilateral Commission and Elite Planning for World Management* (Montreal: Black Rose Books).
Skidelsky, R. (1992) *John Maynard Keynes*, vol. 2. *The Economist as Saviour, 1920–37* (Macmillan).
—— (2000) *"John Maynard Keynes," vol. 3. Fighting for Britain, 1937–1946* (Macmillan).
Smith, A. (1976) [originally published in 1776] *An Enquiry into the Nature and Causes of the Wealth of Nations* 2 vols (Oxford: Clarendon).

Smith, M. (1998) "Rules, Transgovernmentalism, and the Expansion of European Political Cooperation" in Sandholtz, W. and Stone Sweet, A. (eds), *European Integration*.

Smits, J. (1986). "Belgian Politics in 1985: 'No Turning Back'," *Res Publica*, 28, pp. 441–74.

Snyder, F. (ed.) (1996) *Constitutional Dimensions of European Economic Integration* (The Hague: Kluwer).

Solomou, S. (1987) *Phases of Economic Growth, 1880–1913: Kondratieff Waves and Kutznets Swings* (Cambridge: Cambridge University Press).

Soskice, D. (1990) "Wage Determination: The Changing Role of Institutions in Advanced Industrialized Countries," *Oxford Review of Economic Policy*, 6, pp. 36–61.

—— (2000) "Macroanalysis and the Political Economy of Unemployment," in Iversen, T., Pontusson, J. and Soskice, D. (eds), *Unions, Employers and Central Banks: Macroeconomic Co ordination and Institutional Change in Social Market Economics* (Cambridge: Cambridge University Press).

Soutou, G.-H. (1990) "Le Général de Gaulle et le plan Fouchet," in Institut Charles de Gaulle (ed.), *De Gaulle en son siècle*, vol. V. *Europe* (Institut Charles de Gaulle).

Spaak Report (1956) "Comité intergouvernmental crée par la Conférence de Messine," *Rapport des chefs de délégation aux ministres des affaires étrangères* (Brussels: Secrétariat).

Spahn, H.-P. (1979) *Die Stabilitätspolitik des Sachverständigenrats* (Frankfurt: Campus Verlag).

Spierung, M. (2004) "British Euroscepticism," in Harmsen, R. and Spierung, M. (eds), *Euroscepticism*.

Stein, E. (1991) "Lawyers, Judges and the Making of a Transnational Constitution," *American Journal of International Law*, 75, pp. 1–27.

Steiner, J. and Ertman, T. (eds) (2002) "Consociationalism and Corporatism in Western Europe: Still the Politics of Accommodation?," *Acta Politica*, 37.

Steinhouse, A. (2001) *Workers' Participation in Post-Liberation France* (Lexington Books).

Stephens, J. D. (1980) *The Transition from Capitalism to Socialism* (Chicago: University of Illinois Press).

—— (1996) "The Scandinavian Welfare States: Achievements, Crisis, and Prospects," in Esping-Andersen, G. (ed.), *Welfare States in Transition: National Adaptations in Global Economies* (Sage).

—— (2000) "Is Swedish Corporatism Dead? Thoughts on its Supposed Demise in the Light of the Abortive 'Alliance for Growth' in 1998," International Conference of Europeanists.

Stephens, P. (1996) *Politics and the Pound: The Conservative's Struggle with Sterling* (Macmillan).

Sterdyniak, H. (2001) "Une Stratégie macroéconomique timide" in Fondation Copernic (ed.), *Social-libéralisme à la française*.

Stoffaes, C. (1991) "La Reconstruction industrielle, 1945–90," in Lévy-Leboyer, M. and Casanova, J.-C. (eds), *Entre l'etat et le marché* (Gallimard).

Strange, G. (1997) "The British Labour Movement and Economic and Monetary Union in Europe," *Capital and Class*, 63, pp. 13–24.

Strange, S. (1996) *The Retreat of the State: The Diffusion of Power in the World Economy* (Cambridge: Cambridge University Press).

Streeck, W. (1994) "Pay Restraint without Incomes Policy: Institutional Monetarism and Industrial Unionism in Germany," in Dore, R. *et al* (eds), *The Return to Incomes Policies* (Pinter).

—— (1995) "From Market Making to State Building? Reflections on the Political Economy of European Social Policy," in Liebfried, S. and Pierson, P. (eds), *European*

Social Policy: Between Fragmentation and Integration (Washington, DC: The Brookings Institution).
—— (1996) "Public Power Beyond the Nation State: The Law of the European Community" in Boyer, R. and Drache, D. (eds), *States against Markets*.
—— (1997) "German Capitalism: Does It Exist? Can It Survive?," in Crouch, C. and Streeck, W. (eds), *Political Economy of Modern Capitalism: Mapping Convergence and Diversity* (Sage).
—— and Schmitter, P. (1991) "From National Corporatism to Transnational Pluralism: Organized Interests in the Single European Market," *Politics and Society*, 19, pp. 133–65.
Stone Sweet, A. and Caporaso, J. (1998) "From Free Trade to Supranational Polity: The European Court and Integration," in Sandholtz, W. and Stone Sweet, A. (eds), *European Integration and Supranational Governance*.
Stuart, G. (2003) *The Making of Europe's Constitution* (Fabian Society/609).
Suleiman, E. (1974) *Politics, Power and Bureaucracy in France: The Administrative Elite* (Princeton, N.J.: Princeton University Press).
Sutcliffe, B. and Glyn, A. (1999) "Still Underwhelmed: Indicators of Globalization and their Misrepresentation," *Review of Political Economy*, 31.
Swedish Institute (1994) *Labour Relations in Sweden. Fact Sheets on Sweden* (Stockholm: The Swedish Institute).
Sweezy, P. (1978) *The Transition from Feudalism to Capitalism* (Verso).
Swenson, P. (1988) *Fair Shares: Unions, Pay and Politics in Sweden and West Germany* (Adamantine).
—— (1991) "Labor and the Limits of the Welfare State: The Politics of Intraclass Conflict and Cross-Class Alliances in Sweden and West Germany," *Comparative Politics*, 23, pp. 379–99.
Szokoloczy-Syllaba, J. (1965) *Les Organisations professionnelles françaises et le marché commun* (Armand Colin).
Szyszczak, E. (1994) "Happy Tale or Remaking the Fairy Tale?" in O'Keefe, D. and Twomey, P. (eds), *Legal Issues of Maastricht* (Wiley).
Talani, L. (2000) *Betting For and against EMU: Who Wins and Who Loses in Italy and the UK in the Process of European Monetary Integration* (Aldershot: Ashgate).
Tarling, R. and Wilkinson, F. (1977) "The Social Contract: Post-War Incomes Policies and their Inflationary Impact," *Cambridge Journal of Economics*, 1, 631–41.
—— (1982) "The Movement of Real Wages and the Development of Collective Bargaining in the Period 1855 to 1920," *Contributions to Political Economy*, 1.
Taylor, C. (1995) *EMU 2000: Prospects for European Monetary Union* (Royal Institute of International Affairs).
Taylor, P. (1980) *The Limits of Integration* (Croom Helm).
Taxler, F. (1999) "Wage Setting Institutions and European Monetary Union," in Huemor, G. *et al* (eds), *Employers' Associations and Labour*.
Temin, P. (1990) *Lessons from the Great Depression* (Cambridge, Mass.: MIT Press).
Thelen, K. (1999) "Historical Institutionalism in Comparative Perspective," *Annual Review of Political Science*, 2.
Thompson, E.P. (1965) *The Making of the English Working Class* (Vintage Books).
Thompson, H. (1996) *The British Conservative Government and the European Exchange Rate Mechanism, 1979–1994* (Polity).
Thygesen, N. (1979) "Exchange-rate Experiences and Policies of Small Countries: Some European Examples of the 1970s," *Essays in International Finance, 137* (Princeton: Department of Economics, Princeton University).

Tilly, C. (1978) *From Mobilization to Revolution* (McGraw-Hill, 1978).
Tinbergen, J. (1965) *International Economic Integration* (Amsterdam: Elsevier).
Todd, E. (1995) "Aux Origines du malaise politique français: les classes sociales et leurs repésentations," *Le Débat*, nos 83–5, pp. 98–120.
—— (1998) *L'Illusion économique: essai sur la stagnation des sociétés développées* (Gallimard).
Tomlinson, J. (1998) *Hayek and the Market* (Pluto Press).
Tranholm Mikkelsen, J. (1991) "New Functionalism: Obstinate or Obsolete: A Re-Appraisal in the Light of the New Dynamic of the EC," *Millennium: Journal of International Studies*, 21, pp. 1–22.
Trausch, G. (ed.) (1993) *European Integration from the Schuman Plan to the Treaties of Rome* (LGDJ).
Tsoukalis, L. (1977) *The Politics and Economics of European Monetary Integration* (Allen & Unwin).
Tuchfeldt, E. (1973) "Soziale Marktwirtschaft und Globalsteurung," in Tuchfeldt, E. (ed.), *Soziale Marktwirtschaft im Wandel* (Breisgau: Rombach).
Turner, L. (1991) *Democracy at Work: Changing World Markets and the Future of Labor Unions* (Ithaca, N.Y.: Cornell University Press).
Tyson, L. (1992) *Who's Bashing Whom? Trade Conflict in High Tech Industries* (Washington, D.C.: I.I.E.).
United Nations (2000) *Statistical Yearbook: Forty-fourth Issue* (New York: United Nations).
—— (1998) *World Trade Statistics* (New York: United Nations).
—— (1958–99) *Yearbook of International Trade Statistics* (New York: United Nations).
Uri, P. (1989) *Penser pour l'action: fondateur de l'Europe* (Odile Jacob).
Vaisse, M. (1998) *La Grandeur: politique étrangère du Général de Gaulle, 1958–1969* (Fayard).
Verdier, D. and Breen, R. (2001) "Europeanization and Globalization: Politics against Markets in the European Union," *Comparative Political Studies*, 34, pp. 227–62.
Verdun, A. (1996) "An 'Asymmetrical' Economic and Monetary Union in the EU: Perceptions of Monetary Authorities and Social Partners," *Journal of European Integration/Revue d'intégration européenne*, 20.
—— (2000) *European Responses to Globalization and Financial Market Integration: Perceptions of Economic and Monetary Union in France and Germany* (Macmillan).
Verloren van Thematt, P. (1996) "Propositions on the Legal Analysis of Economic and Monetary Union," in Snyder, F. (ed.), *Constitutional Dimensions of European Economic Integration* (Cambridge, Mass. Kluwer Law International).
Virard, M.-P. (1993) *Comment Mitterrand a découvert l'économie* (Albin Michel).
Visser, J. and Hemerijck, A. (1997) *"A Dutch Miracle": Job Growth, Welfare Reform, and Corporatism in the Netherlands* (Amsterdam: Amsterdam University Press).
Vogel, D. (1995) *Trading Up: Consumer and Environmental Regulation in a Global Economy* (Cambridge, Mass.: Harvard University Press).
Vogel-Polsky, E. and Vogel, J. (1991) *L'Europe sociale 1993: illusion, alibi ou réalité?* (Geneva: Institut d'études européennes).
Wade, R. (1996) "Globalization and its Limits: Reports of the Death of the National Economy are Greatly Exaggerated," in Berger, S. and Dore, R. (eds), *National Diversity and Global Capitalism* (Ithaca, N.Y.: Cornell University Press).
Walker, J.G. (2000) "The Labour Market and Rising Living Standards in the 1950s Western Europe: The Case of the Netherlands" (PhD, London School of Economics).
Walker, P. (ed.) (1978) *Between Labor and Capital* (Montreal: Black Rose Books).
Wallace, W. (1994) "Rescue or Retreat? The Nation State in Western Europe, 1945–93," *Political Studies*, 42.

Wallace, W. and Wallace, H. (1977) (1983) (1996) (eds) *Policy-Making in the European Community* (Wiley).
Wallace, H. and Young, A. (eds) (1997) *Participation and Policy-making in the EU.*
Wallerstein, M. (1998) "The Impact of Economic Integration on European Wage-Setting Institutions," in Eichengreen, B. and Frieden, J. (eds), *Forging an Integrated Europe* (Ann Arbor: University of Michigan Press).
Wallich, H. (1955) *Mainsprings of the German Revival* (New Haven: Yale University Press).
—— (1968) "The American Council of Economic Advisors and the German Sachverständigenrat: A Study in the Economics of Advice," *The Quarterly Journal of Economics*, 82, pp. 349–79.
Walsh, J. (1994) "Politics and Exchange Rates: Britain, France, Italy and the Negotiation of the European Monetary System," *Journal of Public Policy*, 14, pp. 345–69.
—— (2001) *European Monetary Integration and Domestic Politics: Britain, France and Italy* (Boulder, Col.: Lynn Rienner).
Wattel, H. (ed.) (1985) *The Policy Consequences of John Maynard Keynes* (Armonck, NY: M.E. Sharpe).
Weber, H. (1991) *Le Parti des patrons: le CNPF,* 1946–1986 (Seuil).
Weber, M. and Rigby, D. (1996) *The Golden Age Illusion: Rethinking Post-war Capitalism* (The Guildford Press).
Weiler, J. (1981) "The Community System: The Dual Character of Supranationalism," *Yearbook of European Law*, 1.
—— (ed.) (1986) *Integration through Law.*
—— *et al* (2003) *Integration in Expanding European Union.*
—— (1991) "The Transformation of Europe," *Yale Law Journal*, 100, pp. 2405–83.
—— (1993) "The Community System: The Dual Character of Supranationalism," in Snyder, F. (ed.), *European Community Law.*
—— (1999) *The Constitution of Europe* (Cambridge: Cambridge University Press).
Weiss, L. (1998) *The Myth of the Powerless State: Governing the Economy in a Global Era* (Cambridge: Polity).
Weisskopf, T. (1979) "Marxism in Crisis Theory and the Role of Profit in the Post-War US Economy," *Cambridge Journal of Economics*, 3.
Welteke, E. (2002) "The Monetary Union in an Enlarged Europe," *CES Forum*, 15, pp. 34–7.
Werner Report (1970) *Report to the Council and the Commission on the Realization By Stages of the Economic and Monetary Union in the Community* (Luxembourg: Office of Official Publications).
Wessels, W. (1997) "An Ever Closer Fusion? A Dynamic Macropolitical View on Integration Processes" *Journal of Common Market Studies*, 35, pp. 267–99.
Western, B. (1997) *Between Class and Market: Postwar Unionization in the Capitalist Democracies* (Princeton, N.J.: Princeton University Press).
Whiteley, P. (1986) *Political Control of the Macroeconomy: The Political Economy of Public Policy Making, 1970–83* (Macmillan).
Whyman, P. and Burkitt, B. (1993) "The Role of the Swedish Employers in Restructuring Pay Bargaining and the Labour Process," *Work, Employment and Society*, 7, pp. 603–14.
Wickham-Jones, M. (1996) *Economic Strategy and the Labour Party: Politicians and Policy-Making, 1970–83* (Macmillan).
Wiebe, S. (2003) "How We Defeated the Euro," *Socialist Campaign Group News*, November.
Wilde, L. (1992) "The Politics of Transition: The Swedish Case," *Capital and Class*, 47, pp. 7–18.

Wilkinson, F. (1988), "Real Wages, Effective Demand and Economic Development," *Cambridge Journal of Economics*, 12.

Wilks, S. (1996) "Class Compromise and the International Economy: The Rise and Fall of Swedish Social Democracy," *Capital and Class*, 58, pp. 89–112.

Willis, R. (1968) *France, Germany and the New Europe, 1945–1967* (Oxford University Press).

Wilson, G.K. (1982) "Why is There No Corporatism in the United States?" in Lehmbruch, G. and Schmitter, P.C. (eds), *Patterns of Corporatist Policy-Making* (London: Sage).

Winicott, D. (1995) "Institutional Interaction and European Integration: Towards an Everyday Critique of Liberal Intergovernmentalism," *Journal of Common Market Studies*, 33, pp. 597–610.

Wolinetz, S. (1990) "The Dutch Election of 1989: Return to the Centre-Left," *West European Politics*, 13, pp. 184–202.

Wyplosz, C. (1997) "EMU: Why and How It Might Happen," *Journal of Economic Perspectives*, 11, pp. 3–21.

Zeitlin, J. (1985) "Industrial Structure, Employer Strategy and the Diffusion of Job Control in Britain, 1880–1920," in Mommsen, W. and Husung, H.-G. (eds), *The Development of Trade Unionism in Great Britain and Germany, 1880–1914* (Allen & Unwin).

Zinsou, L. (1985) *La Fer de lance sur les nationalisations* (Olivier Urban).

Index

academics, adoption of Europhilia, 88
acquis communautaire, 43
Adenauer, Konrad, 37, 81, 199, 208, 210
Agenda 2010, 161
allocative efficiency, 174–82
Alternative Economic Strategy, 14, 118, 119
Amato, Giuliano, 261–2
American Exceptionalism, 192–3
Amsterdam Summit 1997, 141, 161
Amsterdam Treaty, 141, 146
AMUE (Association of the Monetary Union of Europe), 154, 157
Andreotti, Giulio, 259–60
Attali, Jacques, 155
Austrian banks, 117
automatic stabilizer, 165

Balladur, Edouard, 140, 154
Bangemann, Martin, 44, 65
banks
  independence, 115–17
  and industry, 81–4, 115–17
  see also individual countries
Barcelona Summit 2002, 142
Barre Plan, 129, 131
Barre, Raymond, 16, 131
Barroso, José Manuel, 48
Bayoumi, Tamim, 190
BDI (Union of German Industry)
  and banks, 81
  monetarism of, 37
  support for EC, 37
Belassa, Bella, 182
Belgium, 233–48
  banks, 81
  Christian Democrats, 240–1
  Competitiveness Act, 59
  exchange rates, 236
  federalism, 166
  Liberals, 241
  loss of productivity, 151
  monetarist turn, 17, 151–2
  neo-liberalism, 234
  per capita income, 184
  trade, 237
  unemployment, 191
Benelux countries, 37, 166
Bérégovoy, Pierre, 136, 155, 158
Berlin Wall, 209, 210
Berlinguer, Enrico, 252
Berlusconi, Silvio, 258, 262–3
Beyen Plan, 29
Bismarck, Otto von, 201, 202
Blair, Tony, 21, 47, 149
  Amsterdam Summit 1997, 141, 161
  'third way', 6
Blyth, Mark, 221
Brandt, Willy, 56, 108, 129, 199, 201, 213
Bretton Woods, 7–8, 23, 84, 86, 99, 103, 146, 235
Britain, 222–32
  anti-federalism of, 43, 47–8
  CBI (Confederation of British Industry), 82–3, 157–8
  and City, 82–4, 157–8
  Conservative Government, 6, 13, 14–15, 63, 116, 149, 154, 222
  contracting out, 228
  electoral abstentionism in, 163
  ERM, 157–8
  Euroskeptics, 3
  fine-tuning, 33
  inflation, 223–5, 228–9
  labor market policy, 226–8
  labor shortages, 32
  Labour Government, 119, 189, 194, 223, 230–1
  Lawson boom, 83, 149, 157
  monetarist turn, 149
  privatization, 227, 228
  support for single market, 149
  unemployment disguise, 152
Brown, Gordon, 149, 166
Bundesbank, *see* Germany
Bush, George, 166

Callaghan, James, 189, 194, 223
Cambridge Economic Policy Group, 225–6, 229
Camdessus, Michel, 135, 136
CAP, *see* Common Agricultural Policy
Capitalists
  advantage in EC, 69–70, 81–2
  advantage in wage restraint, 146
  corporate tax, 18, 61
  social divide, 139–44
  support for EC, 10, 14–15, 20, 24, 29, 30, 34, 37, 38, 72–3, 95
    for EMU, 157
    for ERM, 151
Carter, Jimmy, 8, 14, 17, 116
Castle, Barbara, 6
Catholics, attachment to property, 35–6
  see Christian Democrats
CBI, *see* Confederation of British Industry
CDU (Christian Democratic Party), 108, 208
Cecchini Report, 54
central banks, independence, 115–17
CERES (French Socialist Left), *see also* Chevenement
CFDT (French New Left Labour Central), 16, 84, 114, 129–30, 140
CGIL (Majority Italian Labour Central), 251
CGT (Majority French Labour Central), 114, 125–30
Chaban-Delmas, Jacques, 56, 129–30
Charter of Fundamental Rights, 48
Chevènement, Jean-Pierre, 134
Chirac, Jacques, 82, 86–92, 139, 140, 142–4, 157
Christian Democrats, 5, 167
  monetarist turn, 17, 21
  property-orientation, 21, 35–6
  ruling-party, 10, 32
  social dimension, 45, 56, 59
  support for EC, 10, 30
  see also European People's Party; and individual countries
Ciampi, Carlo Azeglio, 262
CISL (Catholic Italian Labor Central), 251
Clarke, Kenneth, 230
class struggle, 95–120, 144–8, 267–71
CNPF (Confederation of French Employers), 10, 38, 122–3, 127–8, 157
Cockcroft, Lord Arthur, 43–4
Colbertism, 124
Cold War, 207
Colonna Report, 62
comitology, 67
commercialization of public sector, 24, 63–5, 149, 163
Commission (European Commission), 2, 37, 39, 67–8, 80, 136, 167, 177, 180
  committees, 40, 147
  concessions to member-states, 41
  green paper on telecommunications, 44–63
  Medium-Term Committee, 31, 147
  neo-liberal, 48
  retreat from activism, 46
  second action paper, 11, 147
    see also agricultural policies; Barroso; Delors; employment policies; Hallstein; industrial policies; Santer; social policies
  Werner Report, 16
  White Paper on Employment and Competitiveness, 161
Common Agricultural Policy (CAP), 11, 78, 177
Common Market, 39, 65, 147, 209
Common Program of the French Left, 39, 65, 147
Commons, John, 102
Communism, 3–4, 9, 32, 84
  see also individual countries
Community Charter of Fundamental Social Rights, 58
comparative advantage, 175–6
comparative disadvantage, 177
Confederation of British Industry (CBI), 82–3, 157–8
Conservatives, 6, 154
Constitution, 4, 48–9
convention, 2, 8, 47
conventional view of EC, 1, 2, 30
corporatism, 104–5
  Netherlands, 110

Council of Ministers, 2
Craxi, Bertino, 17, 257–9
CSU (Christian Social Union in Bavaria), 108, 210
currency controls, 137, 153–4
currency speculation, 86

Davignon, Vicomte Etienne, 15, 62–4, 90
De Gaulle, General Charles, 8–72, 40, 127–8
Delors, Jacques, 17, 18, 21, 44–6, 57–8, 61–2, 65, 129–30, 132, 134, 149, 158, 161, 215
Delors Report on EMU, 154, 156, 157, 159, 161
Denmark
  environmental protection, 66
  monetarist turn, 150
  opposition to Maastricht, 45
  per capita income, 184
  unemployment, 191
Deutsch, Karl, 76
Deutsche Mark (D-M), 11, 206
devaluations, 29, 39, 135, 136, 147, 151–3
Dini, Lamberto, 263
dollar convertibility, 235, 238
Duisenberg, Wim, 159, 243
Duverger, Maurice, 35

ECB, *see* European Central Bank
ECOFIN (Council of Finance Ministers), 40, 147, 158, 167
economic integration, 175
Economic and Monetary Union, 24, 145
  capitalist support for, 157
  see also single currency
economic policy, 173–4
  see also individual countries
economic policy model, 201
ECU (European Currency Unit), 150, 154
EDF (Eléctricité de France), 142, 143, 144
Eichengreen, Barry, 190
Emerson, Michael, 15, 90
Emerson report, 156–7
employment policy, 5, 6, 59–60
EMS, *see* European Monetary System
enhanced cooperation, 3
enlargement to East, 3, 46
enmeshment of national officials, 78
Environmental Agency, 67
environmental policy, 22, 52, 65–7
Erhard, Ludwig, 13, 34, 199, 207, 208, 210, 219
ERM, *see* Exchange Rate Mechanism
ERT (European Round Table), 24, 70, 89
Esprit, 62–3, 90
ETUC (European Trade Union Confederation), 45, 60, 70, 88
Eucken, Walter, 205
Eureka, 64
euro, *see* single currency
Euro line, 112, 113
Euro-group (also Euro-x), 2, 71, 159
European Central Bank (ECB), 6–81, 146, 166
European Coal and Steel Community (ECSC), 9, 31, 34, 74, 76–8
European Commission, *see* Commission
European Council, 2, 48, 49, 158, 166–7
European Court of Justice (ECJ), 11, 30, 39, 41–3, 49, 61, 63
European elections, 21, 48, 68–9, 73
European Monetary System (EMS), 187, 188, 194, 235, 238–9
European Parliament (EP), 2, 48, 67–70
  see also European elections, 21, 48, 73
European People's Party (EPP), 69
European Regional Development Fund, 61
European Round Table, 64, 161
European snake mechanism, *see* snake in tunnel
European Social Forum, 164
European social model, 163
Europhilia, 1–2, 88, 154
Euroskeptics, 4, 154
Exchange Rate Mechanism (ERM), 3, 17, 18, 19–20, 23, 82–4, 86, 118, 146–55, 223
  capitalist support for, 151
exchange rates, 236
exports, 177–8, 186
  see also individual countries

Fabius, Laurent, 135–7, 144
Fanfani, Amintore, 249
FDP, *see* Germany

Fed (Federal Reserve Bank), 8, 116, 146, 166
Federation
  capitalist interest, 12–13, 37
  subsidiarity, 36, 42, 45
Fifth Directive, 58
financialization, 83, 138, 146
Fischer, Joschka, 66
Five Wise Men (*Sachverständigenrat*), 211
flexible specialization, 181
Foot, Michael, 119
foreign direct investment, 83, 85–6
Fouchet Plan, 40
France, 121
  CFDT, 10, 84, 114, 129–30, 140
  CGT, 84, 114, 125–30
  class politics, 121–44
  CNPF, 84, 114, 125–30
  Common Program of the Left, 119
  ECU, 154
  EDF (Eléctricité de France), 142, 143, 144
  ERM, 153
  exports, 177–8
  Gaullists, 16, 125, 128, 129, 147, 148, 149, 157
  and Germany, 38–9, 51, 72, 135–6, 148, 168
  growth, 124–5, 137–9
  industrial policy, 63, 89, 124–7, 134–7
  May-June 1968, 14, 56, 118
  Mitterrand, 7, 18-20, 23, 45-6, 64, 82, 131-9, 154, 155–?
  monetarist turn, 12, 18–19, 137–8
  PCF (French Communist Party), 114, 125–39, 142, 144, 154
  per capita income, 184
  plan, 33, 125–8
  public opinion on EC, 139–40
  revolutionary challenge, 112, 114–15, 122, 125
  social divide, 20–1, 24
  Socialist Party, 124, 130–44, 158
  soft money, 8, 19
  state capitalism, 123
  telecommunications, 89–90
  unemployment, 191
  view of EC, 37–8, 55, 84
  wages, 14
free trade, 180
Freiburg school, 204–6, 214
Friedman, Milton, 13, 109, 222

gains from membership, 182–6
General Agreement on Tariffs and Trade (GATT), 37, 107
Genscher, Hans-Dietrich, 20, 137, 155, 215
Germany
  Basic Law on Growth and Stability, 211
  BDI (Union of German Industry), 37, 81
  Betriebsräte, 209, 216
  Bundesbank, 9, 16, 17–34, 83, 106–7, 109, 154, 155–7, 204, 211, 213
  Bundesverband der Deutschen Industrie, *see* BDI
  capitalists, 83–4
  CDU (Christian Democratic Party), 108, 208
  Constitution, 106
  Constitutional Court, 3
  CSU (Christian Social Union in Bavaria), 108, 210
  DGB (trade union confederation), 208, 210
  economic policy, 199–221
  environmental protection, 66
  ERM, 148–54
  Five Wise Men (*Sachverständigenrat*), 211
  Grand Coalition, 210
  growth, 32
  industrialization, 201–2
  Keynesianism, 209–14
  Mitbestimmung, 209, 216
  monetarist turn, 15–17, 19, 22, 23, 30, 45, 55, 86, 108–9, 138
  neo-corporatism, 33, 105–8
    crisis of, 138, 160–1
  neo-liberalism, 206
  neue Mitte, 216
  ordo-liberalism, 8, 33–4, 147, 201–9
  per capita income, 184
  reunification, 81
  Second Reich, 201, 203
  single currency, 20, 155–60
  social market economy (Sozialemarktwirtschaft), *see* BDI

Germany – *continued*
SPD (Social Democratic Party of Germany), 33, 101–10, 208, 210
support for EC, 30, 36–7, 38, 39
Tarifautonomie, 216
Third Reich, 201, 203
trade, 8, 23–4, 33
trade deficit, 17
unemployment, 191
wages, 14–16, 107–10
Weimar Republic, 201
Giscard d'Estaing
monetary policies of, 130–1
globalization, 22, 70–2, 85–90, 94, 117, 145–6, 267–71
and intellectuals, 88–90
Glotz, Peter, 249
Gorbachev, Michel, 159
Gramsci, Antonio, 269–70
Grauwe, Paul de, 191
Greens, 66, 67, 69, 118
Greenspan, Alan, 115–16
Groeben, Hans von der, 35
gross domestic product, 183
growth, 15, 18, 22, 23, 32, 41, 52–6, 93, 115, 124–5, 137–8, 141, 143, 145, 184
see also individual countries

Haas, Ernst, 76–7
Hallstein Commission, 77
Hallstein, Walter, 11, 147
Hayek, Friedrich, 6, 12–13, 14, 19, 40
Hobsbawn, Eric, 85
Holland, Stuart, 119
'hot Autumn', 7
Houthuys, Jef, 241–2, 244, 245

IMF, *see* International Monetary Fund
impossible trilogy principle, 187
industrial and technological policy, 5, 11, 21, 29, 62–5, 89–90
inflation, 18, 101–2, 194, 223–5, 228–9
Inter-Governmental Conferences, 47, 159
inter-governmental liberalism, 79–85
interest rates, 193
International Monetary Fund (IMF), 8, 149, 223, 241
investment, intra-EC, 22

Italy, 249–65
Activists, 32
Alleanza Nazionale, 262, 263
Amato Law, 260
Bank of Italy, 146, 152
CGIL, 251
DC (Christian Democratic Party), 113, 251, 252
devaluation, 113
disinflation, 152–3
ERM, 84, 255
Federazione Lavoratori Metalmeccanici (FLM), 254, 257
Federazione Unitaria (CGIL-CISL-UIL), 251
FIAT, 256–7
Forza Italia, 262, 264
inflation, 32
labor reserves, 32
liberismo, 249
mixed polity, 166
monetarist turn, 17, 148, 152–3
PCI (Italian Communist Party), 17, 112, 113, 152–3, 250, 252
per capita income, 184
scala mobili, 256, 257
Socialist Party
unemployment, 191
wage-price spiral, 14, 16–17
worker mobilization, 113

James, Harold, 200
Jenkins, Roy, 119
Joseph, Keith, 14
Jospin, Lionel, 141–2, 143, 159
Juppé, Alain, 60, 140

Keynes, John Maynard, 8, 202
Keynes Plus, 209, 214
Keynesianism, 32, 33, 93, 118, 199–221
Kinnock, Neil, 119
Kohl, Helmut, 20, 81, 137, 140, 155–6, 159, 200, 215
Kok, Wim, 243
Kondratieff, Nicholas, 97
Kroes-Smit, Nechie, 48

labor ideology, 93, 100–6
Lafontaine, Oscar, 46, 108, 142, 160, 199, 216–17

laissez faire, 200, 203, 205
Lama, Luciano, 253, 254
Lankowski, Carl, 215
Larosière, Jacques de, 155–6, 189
late capitalism, *see* welfare state
Lawson, Nigel, 116, 149, 157
Le Pen, Jean-Marie, 142
Liberal Charter, 128
liberal pluralism, 2–3, 36, 74–87
Lindberg, Leon, 78–9
Lisbon summit and strategy, 2, 21, 48, 60, 162–3
lobbyists in EC, 68–70
long economic cycles, 96–100, 146
Lubbers, Ruud, 243, 244, 246
Lund, Gunnar, 278

Maastricht Treaty, 4, 6, 45–6, 49, 64–5, 66, 143, 155–60
  Danish rejection of, 140
  referendum on, 139–40
McCracken Report (OECD), 15
Macmillan, Harold, 6
Maddison, Angus, 178, 181
Madison, James, 13
Major, John, 223, 229, 261
Maldague Commission, 104
Malfatti, Franco, 129
Mandelson, Peter, 48–9
Marchais, Georges, 133
Marjolin, Robert, 31
Marshall Plan, 6, 74, 206, 207
Martens, Wilfried, 151–2, 240–2, 244, 246
Marx, Karl, 13, 85, 87, 88
Mauroy, Pierre, 18, 132
May-June 1968, 7, 14, 78
Medium-term Committee, 31
Mendès-France, Pierre, 34, 121, 127
Mer, Francis, 166
Merger Regulation (1989), 43
Messina Resolution, 10, 34–5
minimum efficient technical size (METS), 179, 180–1
Mita, Ciriaco De, 249
Mitrany, David, 76
Mitterand, François, 7, 18–20, 23, 43, 45, 61, 64, 82, 131–9, 154, 155–6, 194, 215
Mollet, Guy, 40, 127
monetarism, 6–7, 214–18
Monetary Committee, 135, 136, 150, 156
monetary restriction, 14–15
Monnet, Jean, 2, 9, 31, 76
Mont Pelerin Society, 12, 13
Moravcsik, Andrew, 79–82
Moro, Aldo, 113, 253
Mousnier, Emmanuel, 35
Müller-Armack, Alfred, 13, 37, 210
multi-level governance, 3, 61–2, 189–90
multinationals, 64, 70, 82–3, 85–6
  see also AMUE; ERT
Mundell law of incompatibilities, 154
Mundell, Robert, 187
mutual recognition, 43
Mutual Security Pact, 6

NAIRU, 6
Napolitano, Giorgio, 254
nation state
  inroads on, 41–3
  labor, 12
  loyalty, 7, 71–3
  mercantilism, 34
  regulation, 11, 12, 13, 41, 71–2
  sovereignty, 71–2
  see also renationalization
neo-corporatism, 106–12
neo-functionalists, 2, 39, 74–8, 90
neo-liberalism, 206, 234
Netherlands, 233–48
  banks, 81, 117
  Christian Democratic Appeal, 242
  corporatist system, 110
  Dutch National Bank, 243
  environmental protection, 66
  exchange rates, 236
  federalism, 166
  Federation of Dutch Unions (FNV), 242
  Germany, 110, 151
  labor reserves, 32
  loss of productivity, 151
  monetarist turn, 17, 116–17, 151–2
  neo-corporatism, 110
  neo-liberalism, 234
  Party of Labor (PvdA), 242
  per capita income, 184
  trade, 237

Netherlands – *continued*
  trade unions, 241–2, 244
  unemployment, 191
  Union of Dutch Employers (VNO), 243
  wage share, 16, 17
  Wassenaar Agreement, 152
New Left, 18, 118, 133, 152
  see also Second Left
Nice Treaty, 46–7, 48
Nicolin, Curt, 276
non-accelerating inflation rate of unemployment (NAIRU), 225
non-corporatism, 106–12
non-governmental organizations (NGOs), 87
non-quantitative barriers, 29

OECD (Organization for European Cooperation and Development), 15, 117, 120, 161
Olson, Mancour, 91
Open Marxism, 268–70
ordo-liberalism, 107, 199–221
organized capitalism, 209, 220

Padoa-Schioppa, Tomasso, 15, 90, 155
Pagarotzky, Leif, 278
Palme, Olaf, 5
Paris Summit, 1972, 56, 66
PCF (French Communist Party), 122–39, 142, 144
Pekkarinen, Jukka, 201
per capita income, 184, 185
  regressions, 186
PES (Party of European Socialists), 69
Philip, André, 31
Phillips curve, 102–3, 225, 226
Pinay, Antoine, 126, 127
political business cycle, 103
Pompidou, Georges, 16, 129
positive integration
  failure of, 10–11, 37–9, 56–67
  function of, 5
  limited success, 51, 56–7, 65–7
  undermining of, 5
privatization, 15, 24, 63–5, 136, 141, 149, 153, 163, 227, 228
Prodi, Romano, 166, 263–4
productive specialization, 176
productivity gains, 183
public opinion on EC, 20–1, 24, 45–6, 48, 52, 71–3, 139–40, 143
  and globalization, 163–4
public procurement, 5, 21, 29, 30, 44
public services, 41, 60–1, 63–5

qualified majority voting, 48

RACE, 63–4
Raffarin, Jean-Pierre, 142–3, 167
re-nationalization, 3, 43, 45–6, 47–9, 87–8, 166, 168–9
regional policy, 5, 21, 22, 52, 57, 61–2
Reichsmark, 206
Reuss, Frederick, 219
revolutionary unionism, 84, 104–5, 112–15, 125–30
Ricardo, David, 53, 175
Rocard, Michel, 137
Rome Treaty, 10, 29, 31, 37–40, 56, 67–8, 80–1, 136–40, 147
  judicial committee, 41, 147
Röpke, Wilhelm, 205
Rudding, Otto, 243
Rueff, Jacques, 13, 127

Saltjabaden Pact, 111
Sandholtz, Wayne, 89–90
Santer, Jacques, 46, 161
SAP (Swedish Social Democratic Party) *see* Sweden
Schiller, Karl, 109, 201, 210, 212–13
Schmidt, Helmut, 16, 199, 213
Schröder, Gerhard, 21, 41, 46, 160–3, 199, 216–17
SEA (Single European Act), 44, 66–7
'Second Left', 18, 132–3, 134
Second World War, 200, 205
Séguin, Philippe, 20, 140
Shonfield, Andrew, 32–3
single currency (euro), 24, 145–69
  drawbacks, 163–9
  first EMU, 16–17, 147–9
  labor, 24
  Mitterand's role in, 20, 155–6, 159
  theory of, 11, 12, 31, 84, 147, 154
Single European Act, 44
single European market, 11, 19, 29, 34, 39, 41, 43–4, 153, 168
  see also Single European Act

Smith, Adam, 9, 34
'snake in tunnel', 16–17, 148–51, 235, 238
Social Charter, 21–2, 58
Social democracy, *see* Socialists
Social divide, 20–1, 24, 72–3, 139–44, 163–4
social market economy, 200, 201, 202, 203–9, 219
social policy, 11, 21–2, 29, 31, 35, 38, 44, 46, 47, 51, 52, 55–61, 78
  benefit cuts, 59–61, 163
  introduction of, 5
Socialists, 2, 10, 17, 21, 23, 35–6, 56, 69, 117, 120
  see also individual countries
soft law, 2
Sohlman, Michael, 278
Spaak Report, 10, 29, 34–5, 39, 79, 147
Spain, 46, 47, 61, 62, 73, 139–40, 165, 166, 169
SPD (Social Democratic Party of Germany), 33, 101–10, 208, 210
spillover, 75–9
Spinelli, Altieri, 63
Stability and Growth Pact, 2, 49, 59, 141, 143–5, 159–60, 165–9
stagflation, 213, 225
state aid, 41, 44, 81, 134
state capitalism, 123–8
  see also welfare state
Stoiber, Edouard, 160
Strauss-Kahn, Dominique, 141
structural explanations, 92–5
Suez crisis, 10, 39
supranationalism, 21, 48
Sweden
  banks, 117
  Confederation of Swedish Employers (SAF), 267, 276–7
  neo-corporatism, 110–12
  economic policy, 273–5
  Employee Investment Funds (EIFs), 266, 275–6
  employment policy, 266
  neo-corporatism, 111–12
  Riksbank, 272, 273
  Social Democratic Party (SAP), 111, 273, 276–8
  trade unions, 84, 278
  transnationalization of finance, 271–2
  transnationalization of production, 271
Swedish Model, 266–80
  demise of, 275–8

tariffs, 11, 78
Thatcher, Margaret, 6, 13, 14–15, 63, 116, 149, 154, 222
TINA, 155
Tocqueville, Alexis de
trade, 39, 44, 168, 174–82
  intra-EC, 3, 22, 39–40, 54–5, 78
  intra-sectoral, 56
  managed, 34
  see also individual countries
trade balance, 188
trade union power, 12, 23, 30, 40, 55, 59–60, 69–70, 88, 94, 97, 116, 120, 124–7, 136–7, 146, 157, 160–1
  centralization of, 101–2
  wage bargaining, 103–4
  see also CFDT; CGIL; CGT; CISL; UIL; and individual countries
transnational corporations, 267, 268
transnationalization, 271–2
Treaty of Rome, 9, 29–30
Trichet, Bernard, 159
Trilateral Commission, 15, 117
Trotsky, Leon, 88
TUC (Trade Union Congress), 149

UIL (Italian Union of Labor)
UMP (French Union of the Parliamentary Majority), 141
unemployment, 15, 18, 20–1, 22, 23, 45–6, 95, 109, 185, 191, 194
  regressions, 192
UNICE (European Employers' Confederation), 14, 20, 24, 45, 69, 157
United Kingdom, *see* Britain
United States, 8, 15, 23, 30, 53, 74, 86, 146, 164–5, 166
  restrictive policies, 192–3

Van Veen, Chris, 243
Vogel-Polsky, Eliane, 57
Volker jolt, 138
Volker, Paul, 6, 8, 14, 17, 116

wage labor, exploitation of, 10, 32–5, 92–120, 124–7, 130, 136–8
wage restraint, 103–6
wage share, 14, 18, 30, 32, 33, 55, 60–1, 95, 96, 101–3, 109, 111, 113, 137–8, 151–2, 160–1, 162
Walter, Norbert, 214
Wassenar Accord, 243
welfare state, 32–3, 38
Welteke, Ernst, 187
Werner Report, 16, 31, 129
White Paper on Employment and Competitiveness, 59, 161
women's policy, 22, 52, 57
worker consultation, 57–9
working class, 70, 87, 92–120, 124

x-efficiency, 183